IN HER PLACE

A Documentary History of Prejudice against Women

IN HER PLACE

Edited by

S.T. JOSHI

 **Prometheus Books**

59 John Glenn Drive
Amherst, New York 14228–2197

Published 2006 by Prometheus Books

Inquiries should be addressed to
Prometheus Books
59 John Glenn Drive
Amherst, New York 14228–2197
VOICE: 716–691–0133, ext. 207
FAX: 716–564–2711
WWW.PROMETHEUSBOOKS.COM

10 09 08 07 06   5 4 3 2 1

Library of Congress Cataloging-in-Publication Data

In her place : a documentary history of prejudice against women / edited by S.T. Joshi.
    p. cm.
Includes bibliographical references and index.
ISBN 1–59102–380–7 (alk. paper)
    1. Sexism—History—Sources. 2. Sex role—History—Sources. 3. Prejudices—
History—Sources. I. Joshi, S. T., 1958–

HQ1075.I52 2006
305.4209181'1—dc22

2005032639

CONTENTS

5

PART 2: WOMAN'S "PLACE"

PART 3: SCIENTISTS ON WOMEN

PART 4: WOMEN AND INTELLECT

PART 8: WOMEN AND MARRIAGE

PART 9: WOMEN AND RELIGION

PART 10: WOMEN AND SUFFRAGE

PART 11: WOMEN HATING WOMEN

PART 12: BACKLASH—MEN FIGHT BACK

ACKNOWLEDGMENTS

*I*t is the belief of the editor and publisher that most of the contents of this book are in the public domain. For those items still under copyright, we are grateful to the following authors and publishers for permission to reprint:

Steven Goldberg, *The Inevitability of Patriarchy,* copyright © 1973 by Steven Goldberg. Reprinted by permission of the author.

Sigmund Freud, "Female Sexuality," in *Collected Papers,* Volume 5, copyright © 1950 by the Hogarth Press. Reprinted by permission of Random House UK and Perseus Book Group.

George Gilder, *Men and Marriage,* copyright © 1986 by George Gilder. Reprinted by permission of Pelican Publishing Company.

Roy U. Schenk, "So Why Do Rapes Occur?" *Humanist*, March–April 1979, copyright © 1979 by the *Humanist*. Reprinted by permission of the author.

INTRODUCTION

*I*n the space of this introduction it would be impossible to provide anything approaching a comprehensive account of the progress of women's rights, or of the prejudice that compelled women at long last to throw off the political, economic, intellectual, and social shackles that had bound them. Even within the limited range of American history, the progress of women's struggle for equality is immensely complex and tortuous; for the attitudes supporting their subjugation had developed not over a few decades, centuries, or even millennia, but had its foundations at the very beginning of civilized history.

The present anthology seeks to show that prejudice against women has extended to virtually every aspect of human life—sex, marriage, education, the workplace, the arts and sciences, and, preeminently, political engagement as symbolized in the vote—and, more dismayingly, that that prejudice was justified by transparently specious and fallacious arguments. The focus here is on American writers and thinkers, although some Europeans who influenced American thought have been included. It need hardly be added that the present selection represents only a tiny fraction of all that has been written on the subject, and a diligent search will uncover a dozen repetitions of any single idea set forth in these pages. It may, then, be advisable to approach these writings not historically but analytically: by studying the philosophical, scientific, and other errors embodied in them, we may be able to understand the extent to which unthinking prejudice has masqueraded as reasoned argument.

The chief error made by so many of those who have sought to restrict women's freedom of thought and action is a version of the philosophical fallacy known as *essentialism*. In this context, this fallacy assumes that women are "naturally" endowed with certain intrinsic characteristics that debar them from broader participation in society, so that their chief or only "proper" functions are their roles as mothers and housekeepers. Perhaps the greatest exemplar of this fallacy was the Scottish scientist Alexander Walker, who, in *Woman: Physiologically Considered* (1843), attributed to women traits of character (modesty, coquetry, etc.) that, as we now see, were manifestly the traits common only to a specific class of women for a limited period in the history of Western Europe. Ultimately, this fallacy rests upon a single actual fact—the brute fact that women are the childbearers of the species. What should now be evident is that this inescapable physiological necessity in no way entails the vast complex of social, intellectual, economic, and political restrictions that men have inflicted upon women for tens of thousands of years.

For millennia, religion was used to bolster the suppression of women's rights. As Eleanor Flexner wrote long ago, "Next to common law, the most potent force in maintaining woman's subordinate position was religion."[1] Since the major scriptures of the world were written at a time when women's inferiority on many levels was assumed without question, it is no surprise that nearly every sacred text embodies restrictions upon women's sphere of action that now seem preposterous and absurd. Christianity, in this regard, is no better than Judaism or Islam; as the atheist Elizabeth Cady Stanton wrote more than a century ago, "the [Christian] Church has done more to degrade woman than all other adverse influences put together."[2] It is predictable that such writers as Jonathan Stearns, in *Female Influence, and the True Christian Mode of Its Exercise* (1837), would assert that these restrictions were "designed, not to *degrade*, but to *elevate* her character,—not to cramp, but to afford a *salutary* freedom, and give a useful direction to the energies of the feminine mind."

This passage exhibits another favorite weapon of those opposed to women's rights—what might be called the golden chains argument. Women's relegation to homemaking and child-rearing was portrayed by its advocates as designed for their own benefit and protection: after all, were they not queens of their respective households? (That this argument applied only to well-to-do wives and mothers, taking no account of lower-class women who were frequently brutalized by their mates, was conveniently forgotten.) Charles W. Eliot, president of Harvard University, presented a clever twist to this argument when, in 1908, he maintained that the "normal" American woman could find abundant opportunities for the exercise of her intellect in running the home. But if the task was so intellectually stimulating, what was pre- . venting men from taking part in it?

In the course of the nineteenth century, the assumption that scripture was an authoritative guide to human conduct began to be challenged, and a new arbiter of truth, science, gradually took its place. Those who sought to keep women in their "proper" place turned to anatomy, physiology, and other sciences to establish that women were still not capable of competing on a level field with men. George J. Romanes, a leading Anglo-Canadian biologist of the later nineteenth century, asserted that a woman's brain size was, on average, five ounces smaller than a man's. This argument—so similar to that of other craniologists of the period who felt they had demonstrated that the brain size of African Americans and other minorities was smaller than that of Caucasians—is now seen to be untenably crude: further research in brain function repudiates any simple correlation between brain size or weight and mental acuity.[3] Already by the early twentieth century it was becoming increasingly implausible to maintain the *intrinsic* intellectual or creative inferiority of women, so such thinkers as the psychologist James H. Leuba were forced to appeal only to women's supposed deficiency of "energy" to account for their presumed inability to compete with men. We continue to see the tendentious use of science in such recent works as Steven Goldberg's *The Inevitability of Patriarchy* (1973) and George Gilder's *Men and Marriage* (1986), where highly debatable sociological doctrines serve as the basis for a radical suppression of women's influence.

It was concerns about women's physiological capacity for mental activity that led to efforts by men to restrict their education, or prohibit it altogether. John Todd, whose compact pamphlet *Woman's Rights* (1867) presents a comprehensive argument justifying prejudice against women, bluntly asserted that "the great danger of our day is forcing the intellect of woman beyond what her physical organization will possibly bear." It did not occur to him that the coddling of (upperclass) women in the nineteenth century had had a deleterious effect upon their "physical organization"; nor did it dawn upon him that similar arguments were used to justify the denial of education to African American slaves. Female pioneers of the early nineteenth century such as Frances Wright and Catherine Beecher were correct in believing that enhanced educational opportunities for women were vital in securing their ultimate equality with men, and the first "women's movement" in the United States focused on this issue. In the later nineteenth century, the movement toward coeducation elicited a furious backlash on the part of conservatives: Edward H. Clarke, whose *Sex in Education* (1873) was an influential best seller, argued that women's reproductive organs were endangered by too much education—a point followed up by A. Lapthorn Smith, who in 1905 actually asserted that overly educated women would bring about "race suicide" for Anglo-Saxons by being unable or unwilling to bear children. It is not surprising that John M. McBryde Jr., a professor at Tulane University, would seek to restrict female education to the "domestic" arts in order that they could fulfill their "natural" destiny of being fit wives and mothers for Southern gentlemen.

McBryde's 1915 article points to another favorite weapon used by prejudiced male writers—an appeal to sentiment rather than argument.

It is amusing to note that, for all their assertions that women are the more emotional and irrational members of the species, it is men who seek to make their case by appeals such as this: "Among our young women of to-day we miss that exquisite grace, that refinement, rare tact, wonderful directing power, calm dignity, and absolute self-possession which characterized the women of the Old South." What this passage also betrays is that much of the hostility toward women's rights is a hostility directed not solely at women but more broadly at the onrushing advance of society as a whole. This attitude is embodied in Hugh McMenamin's article of 1927: "Look about you. The theatre, the magazine, the current fiction, the ball room, the night clubs and the joy-rides—all give evidence of an ever-increasing disregard for even the rudiments of decency in dress, deportment, conventions and conduct. Little by little the bars have been lowered, leaving out the few influences that held society in restraint." The understated assumption in this passage, as in so many others like it in this volume, is that sexual liberation, both of men and of women, presents some kind of apocalyptic danger to society. It is this assumption that is behind the quest of so many opponents of women's rights to justify the "double standard" of conduct—the standard that permitted men to engage in sexual dalliance with only minimal moral and societal condemnation but brought down the full wrath of outraged society upon a woman's similar dalliance. The root cause behind the maintenance of the double standard was, of course, physiology; as Edward Sandford Martin stated with rare candor in 1913: "The dual standard, which cannot be admired ethically, is based on the very practical consideration that it is the girl [*sic*], not the man, who has the baby."[4] And behind this, of course, lies men's ever-present uncertainty that the child their wives produce is actually their own. It now becomes clear why birth control—specifically, the development of the Pill in 1960—was the necessary prelude to the women's liberation movement of the 1970s: it was only when women gained control of their own reproductive functions that they could legitimately assert their independence from, and concomitant equality with, men.

Many people of today find it inconceivable that women's lives, for the great majority of human history, were so circumscribed. All women, until very recent times, were barred from voting or sitting on juries, but married women in particular suffered under still further restrictions: among other things, they were not entitled to their own earnings (if any), could not own property apart from their husbands, could not sue in court, and could not make a will without the approval of their husbands. These legal disabilities were, in the United States, a product of the application of the British common law, as embodied in Sir William Blackstone's *Commentaries on the Laws of England* (1765–1769). Married women, in effect, disappeared as independent legal entities; as Blackstone blandly terms it, "By marriage, the husband and wife are one person in law: that is, the very being or legal existence of the woman is suspended during the marriage, or at least is incorporated and consolidated into that of the husband." (Blackstone is, of course, only enunciating the common law, not necessarily lending his stamp of approval to it.) Extensive and sustained lobbying by advocates of women's rights was required to remove these disabilities, but by the end of the nineteenth century many of them had been eliminated or modified in most American states. The one barrier that remained seemingly immovable was the suffrage.

The quest for women's right to vote is as spectacularly convoluted and, in some of its aspects, as seriocomically bizarre as any sociopolitical movement in American history. The question plainly did not trouble the Founding Fathers, who assumed axiomatically that only property-owning white males should be allowed to vote. In the landmark women's rights convention at Seneca Falls, New York, on July 19–20, 1848, organized by Elizabeth Cady Stanton and Lucretia Mott, woman suffrage was only one of several issues clamoring for attention. The first suffrage movement gained momentum after the Civil War: with women having expanded their economic roles when men went to battle, it was assumed that woman suffrage might come to fruition after the conflict was over; but, although women had been central figures in the abolitionist movement and in the nascent Republican party that dominated American politics for a generation after the Civil War, the focus remained on suffrage rights for the *male* African American. Two competing, and at times conflicting, groups—the National Woman Suffrage Association and the American Woman Suffrage Association—were both founded in 1869, the same year that Wyoming (then still a territory) granted women full suffrage rights. But this victory was only slowly and sporadically followed up in other states and territories; federal woman suffrage amendments were repeatedly sponsored in Congress from 1868 to 1896, but voted down every time.

Opponents of woman suffrage unleashed their wildest and most unrestrained attacks during the later nineteenth century. All the arguments that had been used to restrict women's activity in other areas were resurrected in this newest and, in the eyes of many, most apocalyptic struggle: women could trust their menfolk to cast votes for them (an argument unwittingly refuted by the parallel argument that granting women the vote would sow discord in the home if husband and wife were not of the same political persuasion); women needed to be protected from the rough-and-tumble of corrupt politics (an argument countered by suffragists with the naively optimistic hope that women's inclusion in politics would lead to cleaner elections); women were not sufficiently educated, politically, to cast intelligent votes (but were men any better educated in this regard?); most women did not want the vote (but what of those who did? and did all men want it or use it?); and so on.

One of the most curious arguments made in support of male suffrage was that women, being physically weaker than men, could never back up their votes with force. This argument—embodied in Rossiter Johnson's *The Blank-Cartridge Ballot* (1896)—was surprisingly prevalent, and its obvious fallacies were inexplicably overlooked by its advocates. First, the idea that, on any given political issue, women would predominantly vote on one side and men on the other, creating a problem of enforcing the outcome, is ludicrously improbable, and in fact has never occurred. Second, the elimination of physical force and its replacement by constitutional political process is surely one of the hallmarks of a civilized society, so that even if women were to vote on one side of an issue and men on the other, the latter would be obliged to acquiesce in it unless they wished to bring about the downfall of the nation. And third, the logical extension of this argument is that only the armed forces—the only body of individuals who could "enforce" their political decisions if it came to a conflict—should be allowed to vote, with the result that the United States would be transformed from a constitutional democracy to a military dictatorship.

By the turn of the twentieth century both the suffragists and their opponents had turned increasingly militant. Inspired by the violence and civil disobedience of their British counterparts (notably the Pankhursts, a mother and her two daughters who were frequently jailed for their activism for woman suffrage in England), American suffragists took to the streets, marching in parades, picketing the White House, and pressuring a reluctant President Wilson to adopt a woman suffrage plank in the Democratic party's platform. But if the advocates of woman suffrage were becoming increasingly impatient, their opponents were (dare we say it?) well-nigh hysterical. Probably sensing the ultimate defeat of their cause, they lashed out wildly in such treatises as James Monroe Buckley's *The Wrong and Peril of Woman Suffrage* (1909) and William Parker's *The Fundamental Error of Woman Suffrage* (1915). Perhaps the most breathtakingly misogynist tract was Harold Owen's *Woman Adrift: The Menace of Suffragism* (1912). This British polemicist blandly asserted that women were in no way essential to the state except in their function as child-producers, and should therefore have no say in the political governance of the nation. What Owen, in his pathological fury, fails to understand is that, even granting his argument (rendered highly dubious only a few years later, when women took over many vital functions in the British economy with the onset of World War I), a society in which women were abruptly thrust out of the job force, the arts, the sciences, and all other facets of the body politic is not a society that any civilized person would wish to live in. Here again the fear of modernism came into play: we find, in such a treatise as Benjamin Vestal Hubbard's *Socialism, Feminism, and Suffragism: The Terrible Triplets* (1915) and Parker's *The Fundamental Error of Woman Suffrage,* baleful warnings that woman suffrage would lead to socialism, the downfall of Christianity, and other supposed evils.

It now seems incredible that men (and some women) could be so petrified at the prospect of a female going to the polls and so fearful of cataclysmic effects upon the nation. To be sure, the millennium of clean, fair, uncorrupt elections and of altruistic, selfless politicians envisioned by the suffragists has not come to pass: at best, women voters and women politicians have shown themselves only marginally less susceptible to self-interest and chicanery than their male counterparts. But the apocalypse of social and political chaos so luridly predicted by antisuffragists has similarly failed to materialize: women and men have not, in general, lined up on opposite sides of political issues, and those families in which a husband and a wife have supported competing candidates have managed to weather the domestic strains; women have shown themselves no more, or less, intelligent than men in voting; and, in general, the nation's political life has been carried on pretty much as usual.

At this point it may seem merely an academic exercise to examine what were the real motives behind opposition to woman suffrage, but a study of the issue reveals that they were far different from the implausible arguments set down by political and social commentators. The opposition was widely variable in different parts of the country: in the South, white males feared that granting women the vote would ultimately lead to the overthrow of the Jim Crow principle that had effectively disenfranchised African Americans since Reconstruction; in the Midwest, opposition was fueled by brewing interests, since the leaders of the liquor industry were (rightfully) fearful that women's votes would lead to Prohibition; in the East, industry and business were fearful of reform-minded women voters, while such political machines as Tammany Hall in New York were uncertain of their ability to control a vast array of new voters whose stated aims included the elimination of dirty politics. But there was no revolution when the

Nineteenth Amendment was finally ratified on October 26, 1920: in the ensuing presidential election, women largely supported the Republican, Warren G. Harding, failing to reward Wilson for his support of woman suffrage by electing his chosen successor, James M. Cox.

One of the greatest evils of prejudice against women is the degree to which many women have internalized men's views of their inferiority. Perhaps the most astonishing example of this is Molly Elliot Seawell's "On the Absence of the Creative Faculty in Women" (1891), an article that created a sensation for its unrelenting, and seemingly gleeful, assertions of women's incapacity in any aspect of the creative arts. In this social brainwashing, the "women's" magazines and treatises of the nineteenth and twentieth centuries took a leading role, whether we look to such an archaic work as George W. Burnap's widely reprinted *Lectures on the Sphere and Duties of Woman* (1841) or something so relatively recent as Patricia Coffin's "Memo to the American Woman" (*Look*, January 11, 1966). Many of the women's magazines of the day were actually run by men, who either anonymously or under female guises (an amusing reversal of the scenario whereby such female writers as the Brontë sisters and George Eliot were obliged to take on male pseudonyms in order to get a hearing for their work) sought to restrain women's thirst for independence by emphasizing the difficulty of capturing a man while also competing for his job. That an otherwise so accomplished a woman as Ida M. Tarbell—the muckraker whose exposé of the Standard Oil Company effected an economic revolution—could write so reactionary a treatise as *The Business of Being a Woman* (1912) makes one realize that progressivism in one intellectual arena does not necessarily engender progressivism in others. Emily Green Balch won the Nobel Peace Prize in 1946, but in 1910 she asserted that women should stay out of industry altogether "because it is disastrous to the family for them to go in wholly and unreservedly, because their subsidized competition is likely to be injurious, and finally because the conditions of work are apt to be ruinous to their health."

It should not be assumed that the articles in this volume are merely historical curiosities that now merit only a scornful laugh. If it establishes nothing else, this book demonstrates that there has been not only a single women's rights movement but a succession of them—and, more disturbingly, that opposition to women's striving for equality has been repeatedly expressed in much the same terms from generation to generation, and continues to be expressed in muted and covert ways today. Consider Agnes E. Meyer's essay "Women Aren't Men" (1950), a perfect example of essentialism in its bland statement that "[w]omen have many careers but only one vocation—motherhood." Meyer later claims that she is "not trying to drive all women back into the home,"[5] but the overall thrust of her essay belies the assertion. That some of us haven't advanced very far from this view is demonstrated by Rush Limbaugh's comment, made as recently as 1992, that "[w]e just accept the fact [*sic*] that women have it in their nature to nurture children."[6] Limbaugh is only the latest instance of a succession of backlashes against women's rights, beginning no later than the turn of the twentieth century. Few, however, have been quite so blunt in their repudiation of female equality as Harry Thurston Peck, a noted professor and literary critic whose essay "For Maids and Mothers" (1899) is so filled with impotent rage that it enters the realm of pathology. Peck yearns for a "touch of masculine roughness" to suppress the hydra's head of feminism bursting about all around him, and in his wishful thinking he looks forward to the time when men will utter "a short, sharp word—and that will be the end of it." No one would express his misogyny quite in these terms today, but it was only a few decades ago that the journalist George Frazier could write an article titled "The Entrenchment of the American Witch" (one suspects that he would like to have used a different consonant in that last word).

The women's movement of the 1970s—the latest incarnation of feminism that reaches back at least a century and a half in this country—is perhaps to be criticized for being so focused on the need for women to slough off their legal and economic disabilities that they paid insufficient attention to the need for men to change their own minds, hearts, and behavior at the same time that women were changing theirs. For the transformation of society toward greater equality, whether in the realm of economics or of politics or of social relations, cannot occur until both men and women decide that it is in their own best interest, and in the interest of society as a whole, to adopt a modicum of those qualities that have, by purely factitious causes, been seen to be the prerogative of one sex alone. We have, by this time, been convinced that women can compete on a level of equality with men in science, literature, sports, the workplace, and many other facets of life; but the time has perhaps not yet come when we are in agreement that the nurturing of children, the tending of a home, and other features traditionally the province of women can be performed as well by a man as by a woman.

I hope I may end on a personal note. As a man, I might not be thought the ideal person to assemble a volume of this sort: on the one side, feminists might assert that only a woman could be fully attuned to the long history of prejudice against her sex, while on the other side some unregenerate males might feel that this book is a kind of betrayal to my own gender. But the overcoming of prejudice against women is not a male or a female function; it is a human function. This volume, a kind of intellectual companion to my *Documents of American Prejudice* (1999), which sought to display the long history of race prejudice in the United States, seeks not only to show where we have been, intellectually and culturally, as a nation, but also where we might go from here. There can be no denying that we have come a long way in two centuries; but we should not deceive ourselves into thinking that the sloughing off of prejudice, whether of gender or of race or of religion, has been an inevitable concomitant to the advance of civilization. It has taken the hard, laborious, and often thankless work of thousands of crusaders who endured scorn and hostility for a goal they felt to be morally sound and in consonance with the values upon which this nation and all other civilized nations were founded. It was by no means a foregone conclusion. The relations between the sexes cannot be said, at the present time, to be ideal, but, in spite of the naive sentimentalizing of many of the writers represented here, it would be difficult to find a time in our history, or in the history of the civilized world, when they could be said to have been ideal. The best we can do is struggle along with the tide of an evolving society, striving to apply to others those standards of fairness and equity that we would each wish applied to ourselves.

—S. T. JOSHI

A NOTE ON THE TEXTS

I have striven to reprint the essays in this volume as faithfully as possible; no attempt has been made to enforce uniformity of style. Editorial omissions are indicated by ellipses enclosed in brackets: [. . .]. Full bibliographical information on the works included is found at the bottom of the first page of each selection. I have supplied headnotes giving basic biographical information on the authors and providing some contextualizing background on the selection. I have also added explanatory endnotes, elucidating now obscure historical, political, and other references; no attempt has been made to correct factual or other errors made by the authors. Footnotes that appeared in the original text are enclosed in brackets in the endnotes section at the end of each chapter.

NOTES

1. Eleanor Flexner, *Century of Struggle: The Women's Rights Movement in the United States* (Cambridge, MA: Harvard University Press, 1959), p. 8.

2. Elizabeth Cady Stanton, *Bible and Church Degrade Woman* (1896); repr. in *Atheism: A Reader,* ed. S. T. Joshi (Amherst, NY: Prometheus Books, 2000), p. 315.

3. See, in general, Doreen Kimura, *Sex and Cognition* (Cambridge, MA: MIT Press, 1999).

4. Edward Sandford Martin, *The Unrest of Women* (New York: D. Appleton, 1913), pp. 119–20.

5. Agnes E. Meyer, "Women Aren't Men," *Atlantic Monthly* 186, no. 2 (August 1950): 32–36.

6. Rush Limbaugh, *The Way Things Ought to Be* (New York: Pocket Books, 1992), p. 198.

Part 1
SOME OVERVIEWS

1.

WOMAN'S RIGHTS

(1867)

John Todd

John Todd (1800–1873) graduated from Yale University and studied theology at Andover College, becoming a Congregational minister. He preached at churches in Groton, Connecticut; Northampton, Massachusetts; Philadelphia, Pennsylvania; and Pittsfield, Massachusetts. Adhering to the strict Calvinism of Jonathan Edwards, Todd was frequently criticized for his narrow and doctrinaire opinions. He wrote prolifically on religion and other subjects; his *Lectures to Children* (first series 1834; second series 1858) was a best seller, as was his treatise on education, *The Student's Manual* (1835). He addresses the subject of women's education in *The Daughter at School* (1854). In the pamphlet *Woman's Rights* (1867), Todd broaches many of the standard objections to the extension of civil and polit-

Source: John Todd, *Woman's Rights* (Boston: Lee & Shepard, 1867), pp. 7–27.

ical rights to women: women are intellectually and aesthetically inferior to men, women's sphere is and should be restricted to home and family, women who work are preventing men from securing gainful employment, women cannot endure the rigors of higher education, and, finally, that "God never designed" that women should be independent and self-supporting. The pamphlet was immediately rebutted by Mary Abigail Dodge in the substantial treatise *Woman's Wrongs: A Counter-Irritant* (1868).

EQUALITY OF THE SEXES

On this question I shall waste no words. Nobody pretends that the sexes are equal in weight, in height, or in bodily strength. The bodies of the two sexes seem to have been planned for different ends. As to the *mind*, I have no difficulty in admitting that the mind of woman is equal to ours,—nay, if you please, superior. It is quicker, more flexible, more elastic. I certainly have never seen boys learn languages or mathematics, up to a certain point, as fast or as easy as some girls. Woman's intuitions also are far better than ours. She reads character quicker, comes to conclusions quicker, and if I must make a decision on the moment, I had much rather have the woman's decision than man's. She has intuitions given her for her own protection which we have not. She has a delicacy of taste to which we can lay no claim. "Why, then," my lady reader will say, "*why can't we be independent of man?*" for this is the gist of the whole subject. I reply, you can't, for two reasons; first, God never designed you should, and secondly, your own deep instincts are in the way. God never designed that woman should occupy the same sphere as man, because he has given her *a physical organization* so refined and delicate that it can never bear the strain which comes upon the rougher, coarser nature of man. He has hedged her in by laws which no desires or efforts can alter. We, sons of dust, move slower; we creep, where you bound to the head of the stairs at a single leap. And now bear with me, and keep good-natured, while I show you, what you, dear ladies, cannot do, and God don't ask you to do.

1. You cannot invent. There are all manner of inventions in our age, steam, railroads, telegraphing, machinery of all kinds, often five hundred and fifty weekly applications for patents at the Patent Office, but among them all no female applicants. You have sewing machines almost numberless, knitting machines, washing, ironing, and churning machines—but I never heard of one that was the emanation of the female mind. Did you? Why sew, or wash, or card off your fingers, rather than to invent, if this was your gift? The old spinning-wheel and the old carding apparatus have gone by, but not by woman's invention. I suppose this power was denied you, lest it should take you out of your most important sphere—as I shall show.

2. You cannot compete with men in a long course of mental labor. Your delicate organization never has and never can bear the study by which you can become Newtons, La Places, or Bowditches in mathematics or astronomy.[1] The world never has seen, and never expects to see, woman excelling in architecture. Neither in ancient or modern times has she one monument of this kind, showing mastership. You do not find them in ancient Corinth, old Athens, great Rome, or in any city of the old or new world.

So of painting and sculpture. You need not tell us what you are hereafter to do; but you have never yet shown a Phidias, a Raphael, a Michael Angelo, or a Canova. You cannot point to a woman who can pretend to stand by the side of Homer, Virgil, Shakspeare, or Milton. The world has never seen a female historian who came near the first rank. And even in cooking and in millinery, as is well known, men must and do stand at the head of these occupations.

But, you will perhaps say, "we have never had a fair chance—a fair fight in the field. We have been held down by prejudice, and tyranny, and public opinion against us, and all that." Suppose it be so, fair one, there is *one* field you have had to yourself, and nobody has lifted against you one finger. I mean that, for the last half century, we, cruel men, have invented, manufactured, and bought, and brought home, the *piano*, and you have had it all to yourselves. What is the result? It is, that the master performers, and teachers, and musicians, are men,—is it not? Nay, have you never seen the girl thumping and drumming her piano for years, under the best teachers, and yet her brother come along and take it up, and without any teaching, soon go in advance of the sister? I have seen it often. In none of these departments can woman compete with man. Not because her immortal mind is inferior,—far from it,—but because her bodily organization cannot endure the pressure of continued and long labor as we can. We may deny this, and declare it is not so; but the history of our race, and the state of the world now, show that it is so. I don't say that here and there a woman can't endure much and long; but they are rare exceptions. Did you ever know a woman who could endure being a teacher till seventy-five, as men often do? The fact that in medical colleges, in medical books, in medical practice, woman is recognized as having a peculiar organization, requiring the most careful and gentle treatment, and the consent of the world, all go to show that her bodily powers are not able to endure like those of the other sex. The wheels and workmanship are too delicate to be driven with the mainspring of the old-fashioned bull's-eye. If what I have said seems to want gallantry, I reply, it is not gallantry that I am now after, but facts—truth—the true sphere and power and glory of woman. Be patient. I have some nice and pretty things to say, some garlands to weave, after I have led you to see the great facts of your being. As to "women's rights," I hold that they have great, inalienable, and precious rights, and which I will point out and defend. But he is a poor dog that barks up the wrong tree, however loud or earnest he may bark.

WOMAN'S SPHERE

The design of God in creating woman was to complete man—a one-sided being without her. Together they make a complete, perfect unit. She has a mission—no higher one could begiven her—to be the mother, and *the former of all the character of the human race*. For the first, most important earthly period of life, the race is committed to her, for about twelve years, almost entirely. The human family is what she makes them. She is the queen of the home, its centre, its light and glory. The home, the home is the fountain of all that is good on earth. If she desires a higher, loftier, nobler trust than this, I know not where she can find it. Mother, wife, daughter, sister, are the tenderest, most endearing words in language. Our mothers train us, and we owe everything to them. Our wives perfect all that is good in us, and no man is ashamed to say he is indebted to his wife for his happiness, his influence, and his character, if there is anything noble about him. Woman is the highest, holiest, most precious gift to man. Her mission and throne is the family, and if anything is withheld that would make her more efficient, useful, or happy in that sphere, she is wronged, and has not her "rights."

WHAT HER "RIGHTS" ARE

If woman steps out of her sphere, and demands to be and to do what men do, to enter political life, to enter the professions, to wrestle with us for office and employments and gains, she must understand that she will have to take the low places as well as the high places of life. She will not be allowed to be a man and be treated with the tenderness due to women. If she goes to Congress, she must also go to the heavy drudgery of earth.

I claim then for her, that it is her "right" to be treated with the utmost love, respect, honor, and consideration in her sphere. I claim that it is her "right" to have every possible aid and advantage to fulfil her mission. I claim that she has a "right" to be let alone there, and not be teased, or flattered, or wheedled out of her place, and made to believe what can never be.

She has a "right" then to be exempted from certain things which men must endure. It is her privilege and her right. She ought to be exempted from the hard drudgery of earth. She ought not to be made a sailor, to hang on the yard-arms,—to chase and kill and try up whales,—to be a surgeon, to pull teeth, cut off legs, or cut out tumors,—to go into the mines, and dig ore and coal,—to burn over the smelting-furnace. She ought not to be compelled to be a barber, a boot-black, to carry hods of brick and mortar up the ladder,—to be a soap boiler, to groom horses, dig canals, dig out peat, tan leather, and stir the tan vats,—to make coffins and dig graves,—to go to the Arctic Ocean for seals, or to spend the long winter in the forest cutting down timber, and in the snow-water of spring to drive logs for hundreds of miles to get these logs out of their native forests. She ought not to be made to butcher, bleed calves, knock down oxen, stick swine, and slaughter cattle. Now she must go in for all this if she leaves her sphere and tries to be a man. I claim that she has a "right" to be exempted. But you may ask, Has she not a *natural* right to enter any and all employments as well as men? Suppose we allow it, and admit that she has a *natural* right to wear jack-boots and spurs, horse-pistols and a sword, and be a complete soldier, and a "natural" right to sing bass and beat a bass-drum, and that *men* have a "natural" right to wear petti-coats, dress with low necks, short sleeves, wear pink slippers with paper soles,—but, would it be wise to do so? Dear sisters, you *can't* be good wives, mothers, and crowns of your families, and go into these things—can you?

DRESS

Some have tried to become semi-men by putting on the Bloomer dress.[2] Let me tell you in a word why it can never be done. It is this:

woman, robed and folded in her long dress, is beautiful. She walks gracefully. The very waving of her robes makes the walk graceful. If she attempts to run, the charm is gone. Even Venus never tried to run. *Et vera incessu patuit Dea.*[3] So long as she is thus clothed, there is just enough of mystery about woman to challenge admiration, and almost reverence. Take off the robes, and put on pants and show the limbs, and grace and mystery are all gone. And yet, to be like a man, you must doff your own dress and put on ours. In doing it, you lose more than I can tell. No! Ladies want our respect, and admiration, and reverence too much ever to lay aside their appropriate dress. Their very instincts make them safe here.

VOTING

A great hue and cry is set up about the right of women to vote, and the cruelty of denying them this right. Plainly this is merely a civil and not a natural right. Minors, foreigners, and idiots are denied it. The property of the world, for the most part, is, and ever has been, and must be, earned by men. It is useful only to support and educate families—our own, or those of others. It would seem best, then, for those who, at any hazard or labor, earn the property, to select the rulers, and have this responsibility. The wealth of the age is expended by woman—earned by the man—for the most part. He wants rulers in reference to the industry and business of his age. Let him select them. Moreover, there is something so unseemly in having woman wading in the dirty waters of politics, draggling and wrangling around the ballot-boxes, *e.g.*, mingling with the mobs and rowdies in New York city, that I wonder she ever thinks of it. But "she is a widow, and has property, and pays taxes,—why not vote?" Being a widow, or fatherless, is a misfortune. But the husband or father earned the property, and voted as long as he lived. It may be a misfortune that the property does not now vote, but not so great a misfortune to the world as to have the sex go out of their sphere and enter into political life. Indeed, it is allowed that voting is only the stepping-stone to civil office. But it is stepping out of her sphere, and the moment you do that, you put a few of the sex into office, but depress and degrade at least a thousand where you elevate one. If a few go up, the many go down.

WAGES

There is great complaint made because justice is not done in compensating labor. It is a hard problem to solve to do this. I know a most excellent pastor, with a noble head and heart, second to few in this commonwealth, who receives only four hundred dollars salary—less than he would have to pay a raw Irish laborer who boarded himself. I know of many receiving five or six hundred dollars. We can't have justice in these matters. But bear in mind that God has put the labor and the duty on men to support the families—wives and children. The man is recreant and guilty if he does not do that; and to do it, and bear the responsibility, he must receive wages accordingly. Is it then so very unjust that woman, who has no such responsibility, does not receive so high wages? You blame employers, and demand that they give females more—a vain demand so long as there are thousands ready to underbid them and do the work cheaper. The demand will pay in proportion to the supply, and no legislation or human power can alter this. Woman can't endure such heavy toil; she can't toil as many hours year after year; she expects to continue the employment but a short time; and the result is, she has to take for her labor the market price for that commodity. But there is a wonderful reason for this great supply, at our day, to which I will allude.

ABNORMITY OF THE COUNTRY

It must be plain to the thinker that our country and generation are abnormal. That when there are over seventy thousand more females in

Massachusetts than there are males,—and probably twice this number in the State of New York,—it is an unnatural condition of things. At the West, through most of the states, the number of men greatly preponderates. Our young men go off early in life, leaving homes, mothers, and sisters behind them. The prospect for these sisters to marry, then, is lessened by every such emigration. Now the question comes, What shall be done in behalf of these thousands of virtuous, educated, and noble girls? The cry is, "Make them into clerks, book-keepers, bankers, and give them all the employments of men. Open all the avenues to employment."

Let us think it over a moment. We are sorry for this state of things, and wish we could remedy it. It is the result of the state of our country, our immense territory, and of our enterprise. But suppose now we make these girls into clerks in stores, in the counting-room, in the insurance office, in the bank,—say ten thousand in Massachusetts and twenty thousand in New York,—don't we displace just so many young men; drive them off to the West; prevent so many new families from being established here; take away thirty thousand chances of marriage from these females, and enhance the evil we are trying to remedy? Is it a blessing to women to lessen her opportunities for marriage? This state of things will eventually right itself, but it bears hard upon women now; but to displace men, to increase the evil, to plan for a present exigency by upturning all the arrangements of Providence, is not wise. We must look at the grand total of results. It is *not* that we wish to keep women from enjoying anything and everything that is for the best good of her sex. I speak of displacing men, and forcing them away. I might add, that from the very instincts of the human heart every public employment diminishes woman's chance of marriage, and in proportion to its publicity.

WOMAN'S EDUCATION

I lately took up a religious paper, in which no less than *six* "Female Colleges" were advertised and puffed. And we are getting our legislatures to charter new "Female Colleges," and we are boasting how we are about to introduce all the studies and the curriculum of the colleges for men, and we are to put our daughters through them, and educate just as we do men. The thing can never be done. For forty years I have been connected with female seminaries, and have carefully watched their training and results. I say deliberately, that the female has mind enough, talent enough, to go through a complete college course, but her physical organization, as a general thing, will never admit of it. I think the great danger of our day is forcing the intellect of woman beyond what her physical organization will possibly bear. We want to put our daughters at school at six, and have their education completed at eighteen. A girl would feel mortified not to be through schooling by the time she reaches that age. In these years the poor thing has her brain crowded with history, grammar, arithmetic, geography, natural history, chemistry, physiology, botany, astronomy, rhetoric, natural and moral philosophy, metaphysics, French, often German, Latin, perhaps Greek, reading, spelling, committing poetry, writing compositions, drawing, painting, &c., *ad infinitum.* Then out of school hours, from three to six hours of severe toil at the piano. She must be on the strain all the school hours, study in the evening, till her eyes ache, her brain whirls, her spine yields and gives way, and she comes through the process of education enervated, feeble, without courage or vigor, elasticity or strength. After a single summer's exhausting study, let sickness strike such a school, and they sink and die most fearfully. Do those who are so strenuous to educate ladies as long and as severely as men *must* be educated for their sphere, know what mortality awaits so many after they are educated? I wish they would examine this point. "Languid and nervous, easily dispirited, instead of feeling within themselves the freshness and buoyancy of youth, what wonder that they draw back, appalled, from their new responsibilities" at marriage. So says a lady writing to me from Minnesota. My unknown correspondent adds, "I have often wished for the tongue of an angel, or a pen of fire, that I might arouse parents, teachers, and school committees to a sense of the wrong they are inflicting on this generation and those to come. I glory in the opportunities for culture of American women, but I pray do not abuse them. Let the girls have time to *grow* as well as to study. If they are not finished scholars at eighteen, what matters it, if they are healthy in body and mind? The mania is a spreading one. Here even in Minnesota I see it." Alas! must we crowd education upon our daughters, and for the sake of having them "intellectual," make them puny, nervous, and their whole earthly existence a struggle between life and death? If it ministers to vanity to call a girl's school "a college," it is very harmless; but as for training young ladies through a long intellectual course, as we do young men, it can never be done—they will die in the process. Give woman all the advantages and all the education which her organization, so tender and delicate, will bear; but don't try to make the anemone into an oak, nor to turn the dove out to wrestle with storms and winds, under the idea that she may just as well be an eagle as a dove. We Americans belong to the Over-do family. We want to fish the brook dry if we fish at all. We mount hobbies easily because we are "spry"; and now that we have taken woman in hand, we are in danger of educating her into the grave; taking her out of her own beautiful, honored sphere, and making her an hermaphrodite, instead of what God made her to be.

The root of the great error of our day is, that *woman is to be made independent and self-supporting*—precisely what she never can be, because God never designed she should be. Her support, her dignity, her beauty, her honor, and happiness lie in her dependence as wife, mother, and daughter. Any other theory is rebellion against God's law of the sexes, against marriage, which it assails in its fundamental principles, and against the family organization, the holiest thing that is left from Eden.

O woman! your worst enemy is he who scouts at marriage; who tries to flatter you with honeyed words about your rights, while he sneers in his own circle, boasting that "it is cheaper to buy milk than to keep a cow"; who would cruelly lift you out of your sphere, and try to reverse the very laws of God; who tries to make you believe that you will find independence, wealth, and renown in man's sphere, when your only safety and happiness is in patiently, lovingly, and faithfully performing the duties and enacting the relations of your own sphere.

Women of my country! beloved and honored in your own sphere, can't you see that man, rough, stern, cold, almost nerveless, was made to be the *head* of human society; and woman, patient, quick, sensitive, loving, and gentle, is the *heart* of the world? where she may rule and move the world to an extent second to no human power, and where she becomes a blessing greater than we can ever acknowledge, because it is greater than we can measure!

I have spoken to you, gentle ones, kindly and faithfully. Very likely I may have a torrent of abuse poured upon me for it; but it is time that your real friends should no longer have utterance choked. I have tried to select smooth stones from the brook for my sling, and not to wound those whom I would defend; and having said this, I only add, that no provocation will force me to speak on this subject again.

NOTES

1. Sir Isaac Newton (1642–1727), pioneering British natural philosopher. Pierre Simon, Marquis de Laplace (1749–1827), French mathematician and astronomer who conceived the nebular hypothesis. Nathaniel Bowditch (1773–1838), American mathematician and astronomer.

2. The bloomer was an undergarment in the shape of trousers invented by Amelia Jenks Bloomer (1818–1894), American crusader for women's rights. It allowed greater freedom of movement than the petticoat, but was widely condemned as being immoral, radical, and "unfeminine."

3. "And the true goddess lay revealed by her gait." Virgil *Aeneid* 1.405.

2.

EVILS OF WOMAN'S REVOLT AGAINST THE OLD STANDARDS

(1927)

Hugh L. McMenamin

Hugh L. McMenamin (1871–1947) was, from 1908 until his death, rector of St. Mary's Church in Denver, Colorado. He was a monsignor of the Roman Catholic Church and, in 1933, became domestic prelate to the pope. In the following essay, published in a special issue of *Current History* (October 1927) devoted to the role of women in modern society, McMenamin relies on biblical teachings and conventionalized attitudes to condemn the political and sexual freedom of women.

What is woman's place in the social order? Is the modern woman, the so-called "New Woman," filling that place with credit? What may society justly demand from her? Is she supplying that demand?

A study of man reveals the fact that when God created men and

---

Source: Hugh L. McMenamin, "Evils of Woman's Revolt against the Old Standards," *Current History* 27, no. 1 (October 1927): 30–32.

women He made them the complement of each other, one supplying what the other lacked, mutually dependent, but both forming a perfect whole. That same study reveals the spiritual equality and the physical inequality of the sexes. It reveals that, while to man has been assigned the aggressive, progressive and governing power in the world, to woman has been assigned the conservative and refining power. Hers is the social and aristocratic influence, and following her divinely given impulse she shrinks from conflict, but entwining her affections around those she loves with tender devotion, she has filled the world with homes, the foundation stones upon which rests our present civilization. She has filled it with sweet and tender recollections, with elevated sentiments and religious impulse. She has been the friend, the companion, the affectionate counselor of man in every Christian age.

That same study reveals to me that woman is dependent upon her warrior husband for sustenance, and God and Christianity are averse to subjecting her to the brutalizing influence of competition with man. She is physically and temperamentally handicapped, and the result will be an injury to the race. It reveals to me that man shall rule over woman. "He shall rule over thee,"[1] was decreed not by man but by man's Creator, and before the Christian era, in pagan lands, man perverted that decree by making woman his slave. But with the passing of the centuries and the injunction, "Husbands, love your wives,"[2] there was born in the heart of man that love for woman which made her his companion—not his slave—that tenderness that threw the protection of his strong right arm around her frailer figure, that chivalry which caused him to stand aside and let a Titanic carry him to a watery grave while she rowed on to safety, that admiration, respect and esteem which placed her on a pedestal, before which he comes to learn lessons of culture, refinement and morality. For what reason, think you, did God give her those finer sensibilities, that higher moral tone, those loftier ideals, those gentle aspirations, if it be not that she should set the standard after which we should shape our conduct? We have the right to demand it from her. She has a duty to fulfill the demand.

While I write, two events are taking place near me, both of them indicative of the trend of thought that is developing the "New Woman." In Colorado Springs a national "Equal Rights for Women" convention is in session;[3] here in Denver a newspaper is conducting a "bathing beauty contest." In Colorado Springs a group of women are confusing an equality of rights with an equality or identity of duties and privileges. If woman is ever emancipated from the protecting care of man; if she insists upon being man's competitor; if she disregards the limitations of sex and claims the right to do all that man may do with equal propriety; if, in a word, she descends to man's plane and is considered merely as a rival, then it will not be long until the theory of companionship will be discarded and women will relapse into the pagan condition of servitude, for when woman forfeits the right to be ruled by the tender rod of love and guardianship, then will she be ruled by the iron rod of tyranny. Agitation, human legislation and modern paganism may attempt to place the sexes on the same political, commercial and social position, but it never can. Sex limitations forbid it.

We have defined woman's place in the social order. Is the so-called "New Woman" filling that place with credit and is she supplying society's just demands? Let us see. We hear a great deal in these days about the "double standard." It is undoubtedly true that a great many are influenced, led on perhaps unconsciously, by the sophism and false principles of the age which condones immorality in man and makes mere respectability his code of morals, but holds aloft to woman the sacred laws of God; which judges the enormity of the sin by the sex of the transgressor, as if forsooth sin had sex. Now, while we abhor such a condition of affairs, we breathe a prayer that the "double standard" remain, for, if it should be changed by the woman of the present generation, it will not be by lifting man to her standard, but by her descent to his. The tendency is downward, not upward. The "New Woman" has neither the influence nor the inclination to lift man up. She has forgotten that she has been fashioned by God and nature to be the refining influence in the world and that her standard of life and conduct should be such that there will always be something for man to strive for and to imitate.

Look about you. The theatre, the magazine, the current fiction, the ball room, the night clubs and the joy-rides—all give evidence of an ever-increasing disregard for even the rudiments of decency in dress, deportment, conventions and conduct. Little by little the bars have been lowered, leaving out the few influences that held society in restraint. One need be neither prude nor puritan to feel that something is passing in the hearts and in the minds of the women of today that is leaving them cold and unwomanly. I know it is said that if a man may indulge freely in alcohol so may she; if he may harangue a crowd from a corner soap box so may she; if he may go about half naked so may she. But the moment she does so she has stepped down from the pedestal before which man was accustomed to worship and he is left without an ideal.

There are many who would have us believe that she does not differ from her mother or her grandmother. It is significant that she is on the defensive, for she does not claim to be better. We may try to deceive ourselves and close our eyes to the prevailing flapper conduct. We may call boldness greater self-reliance, brazenness greater self-assertion, license greater freedom and try to pardon immodesty in dress by calling it style and fashion, but the fact remains that deep down in our hearts we feel a sense of shame and pity.

When women can gaze upon and indulge in the voluptuous dance of the hour; when young girls can sit beside their youthful escorts and listen to the suggestive drama of the day and blush not; when they spend their idle hours absorbed in sex-saturated fiction; when women, both married and single, find their recreation in drinking and petting parties; when mothers clothe their daughters in a manner that exposes their physical charms to the voluptuous gaze of every passing libertine; when they can enter the contract of marriage with the avowed purpose of having no children; then surely the "New Woman" is different, and it is a libel on the generation that has gone to hold the contrary. In the words of a prominent churchman, "If this be the 'New Woman,' then God spare us from any further development of the abnormal creature."

The "New Woman" has not yet reverted to the pagan practice of deifying the vices. She does not yet call them virtues; but how far has she not departed from the standards of twenty-five or fifty years ago, from that innate modesty, that reserve, that sense of delicacy which must ever be an essential characteristic of female excellence? In that other day woman retained at least a sense of shame, and though they fell, they found themselves ultimately on their knees sobbing out their broken-heartedness. The "New Woman" has no sense of shame and she endeavors to save her self-respect by putting a halo on her wickedness. She attempts to hide her sordidness under fine phrases—"Art for art's sake," "To the pure all things are pure," "*Honi soit qui mal y pense*" ("Evil to him who evil thinks"),[4] and the like. Having delivered herself of these platitudes, she proceeds to wallow in the turpitude of vice and then attempts to convince the world that it is the artistic, the beautiful, the esthetic in the play, the film, the dance, the dress, and not their vile suggestiveness that attract, but she succeeds in deceiving neither herself nor us.

The public sense of decency has been so perverted that spectacles like *The Black Crook*,[5] to which a few degenerates crept in shame a half century ago, are models of decency compared to those to which mothers take their sons and daughters today. We have now reached the condition that finds our modern sociologist condoning crime and endeavoring to give it respectability by the simple expedient of legalizing it and by teaching that "codes in morals are as changeable as style in dress"; that "sin, so-called, is but the tyranny of society." Witness the "companionate marriage"[6] discussion and its necessary adjunct, instruction in the use of contraceptives. Note their logic. Our modern sociologist observes a growing laxity in morals and an increased freedom between the sexes—a laxity which society frowns upon and a freedom which oftimes creates an embarrassing condition for the woman. But instead of bending his efforts to correct the laxity and curtail the freedom, our modern sociologist attempts to give the condition respectability by calling concubinage by a new name and prevent the possible embarrassment by teaching the use of contraceptives. Similarly, our modern sociologist observes that not a few married couples, unwilling to make the mutual sacrifice necessary for the permanence of any marriage, become dissatisfied and separate, and thus deprive their children of a home. So our modern sociologist conceives of a union in which there will be no children until the couple discover that they are going to be happy together, forgetting that it is impossible for any couple to endure the intimacy of married life without the bond of a babe. Ninety per cent of the divorces granted in the City of Denver last year were granted to childless couples. The fact that the most enthusiastic exponent of this new attack upon decency is the "New Woman" reveals her distorted nature at its very worst. Men will not turn to such for inspiration.

"BATHING BEAUTY" CRAZE

Witness the second event I referred to—the "bathing beauty contest." This contest will have been held before this article is in print. Nine out of ten of the "beauties" have never touched water deeper than that in their bath tubs. They are to be assembled in a public park, in the scantiest of attire, and will be exhibited on a platform to the gaze of the assembled libertines of the city. Denver has an annual stock show; I see no reason why the exhibitions should not be joined. This "bathing beauty" craze, together with present-day ballroom and street attire, reveals a dominant characteristic of the "New Woman." She would attract by the lure of her person rather than her personality, and men are accepting her at her own valuation—"Only a rag and a bone and a hank of hair."[7] Evidently the "New Woman" is not supplying the demand that society has the right to make of her. She is not a refining influence.

Modern economic conditions, with the mania for speedy profits, have been a powerful factor in producing the "New Woman," inasmuch as they have dragged her into the commercial world and made her economically independent. It is quite impossible for a woman to engage successfully in business and politics and at the same time create a happy home. A woman cannot be a modern and a typist at the same time, and unfortunately she elects to be merely a wife, and out of that condition have arisen those temples of race suicide—our modern apartment houses—and the consequent grinding of the divorce mills.

Modern conditions have made woman more independent, if you will, but that independence is not benefiting the race. The woman who goes off to work with her husband each morning and returns in the evening to keep house for him has assumed a burden too hard to carry and one that will make it impossible for her to make him happy. In addition to that, such an arrangement forces them into an unnatural, childless union which is disastrous to them and to the race.

NOTES

1. Gen. 3:16.
2. Eph. 5:25.
3. A convention of the National Woman's Party, advocating an equal rights amendment, was held in Colorado Springs, Colorado, in July 1927.
4. This is in fact the motto of the Most Noble Order of the Garter, the highest order of knighthood in Great Britain.
5. *The Black Crook* (1866), generally considered to be America's first musical, featured one hundred women scantily clad in ballet outfits. It ran for 475 performances and continued to be sporadically staged until 1903.
6. The notion of "companionate marriage"—marriage on a trial basis, with procreation held off until the couple has achieved genuine compatibility—was propounded by Judge Ben B. Lindsey (1869–1943) in the controversial volume *The Companionate Marriage* (1927; with Wainwright Evans).
7. Rudyard Kipling (1865–1936), "The Vampire" (1897), l.3.

3.

THE ENTRENCHMENT
OF THE AMERICAN WITCH

(1962)

George Frazier

George Frazier (1911–1974) was a widely published journalist and essayist. Early in his
career he had a column in *Mademoiselle*
(1936–1942), but he gained greatest celebrity
for his controversial columns in the *Boston
Herald* and *Boston Globe* in the 1960s and
1970s. An unrepentant chauvinist, he relentlessly criticized the feminist movement of his
time. In the following article, published in
Esquire (February 1962), Frazier begins by
spelling out a long list of desirable qualities
he seeks in the woman of his choice (but
failing to mention what virtues he plans to
bring to the relationship), then proceeds to
lambaste the American "witch"—the self-
assured, demanding woman who refuses to
subordinate her interests to that of her male
partner.

Source: George Frazier, "The Entrenchment of the American Witch," *Esquire* 57, no. 2 (February 1962): 100, 103, 138.

or a woman I ask the blessings of charm and chastity and a clear complexion; of wondrous wisdom and ready wit and a faint flame of color in her cheeks; of a voice bespeaking both the dark rustle of violins at dusk and the wild chiming of church bells crazy with Christmas cheer. All these I ask—and also such small miracles as patience with my procrastinations, indulgence toward my indiscretions, and interest enough in my involvements to be able to identify the infield-fly rule as well as to exult in the swift sweep of an end run impeccably executed. All these and, too, such eclectic endowments as being informed enough to genuflect to the grace and grit of such as Boom Boom Geoffrion,[1] and tasteful enough to be haunted by all the requiems of unrequited love by Rodgers and Hart.[2] These—and also such gladsome gifts as smelling good and smiling sunnily and, merely by her presence, making football games the autumn classics that sportswriters are accustomed to calling them; as trying a little tenderness in times of testiness, as participating, always and forever, in my passion. All these I ask for a woman—and, besides, that she never be a witch. For this is the greatest gift, the most bountiful blessing of all, for, without it, nothing can ever matter much—and that is why, quite often, men are made miserable.

Yet there was a time when the witch was so rare a breed in America that, reading about her, one felt assured that this could not, as it were, happen here. Mildred of *Of Human Bondage* seemed, for all her frightening feel of flesh-and-blood, a kind of freak.[3] We knew, of course, that such women existed, annihilating not only their men, but any one else who would hamper their hateful hedonism. And we knew, too, that they sanctified their selfishness, beatified their witchiness— but they did so, we told ourselves, mostly in books, and books of fiction at that—or, if not, then always elsewhere, never in our part of town. For it was inconceivable that we should ever meet a woman like that—as inconceivable as that we should ever meet, say, an ax murderer or a sex maniac. These were people one read about—the tabloids knew them well. Oh, they existed all right, but still and . . .

And this, of course—this fact of our acknowledging that somewhere there were undoubtedly women like Mildred—this was because Somerset Maugham was such a wonderful writer that he could create this character—this absolute witch!—with such spectacular skill that, for a little while, she was there in the room with us, giving us the creeps, making us long to strangle her with our bare hands. But then we would close the book and the image of infamy would gradually recede—and what a relief it was to realize that this had been but a story, merely make-believe. But that was in 1915 or thereabouts, which was in the age of our innocence.

Now, of course, we know better—as, for that matter, we have known better ever since the publication of "The Short Happy Life of Francis Macomber," which is Hemingway's story of a witch with bells on.[4] For though there can never be any pinpointing the beginning of any knowledge, it was obvious that something had occurred in the years between the appearances of *Bondage* and "Macomber." And it was simply this: In America, the witch had become, if not precisely prevalent, at least so common that a Mrs. Macomber, instead of striking us, as Mildred had, as a rare specimen, rather reminded us of certain women we either knew or had heard of. There was, in short, the rush of recognition. In the years since *Of Human Bondage* the witch had become sufficiently entrenched in America as to have prepared us for the arrival of Mrs. Macomber.

What we were not entirely prepared for was her appearance. For though witchiness has nothing whatsoever to do with any other characteristic—being, among other things, inviolably independent—it was not without a certain significance that Mrs. Macomber, unlike the physically unprepossessing Mildred, was immensely attractive, chic as well as sensual, both literate and lovely to look at, and as much at home in the bush as on Beekman Place. Not surprisingly, such attributes hardly made her witchiness any less insidious. Moreover, she could, when it served her purpose, command an almost irresistible charm—as, indeed, can any true witch. [. . .]

It is, in fact, one of the incongruities of American life that creature comforts do not always occasion contentment—nor, as far as that goes, enlightenment emoluments. For, with all its deprivations, life in frontier days was, on the whole, somewhat more relaxing than it is today in this modern age of affluences. Aspiration, it would seem, is apt to be more appealing than achievement. In the early years of this country, which were pre-suffrage-for-women, pre-pushbutton years, women, far from being ambivalent about their attitudes and ambitions, were, for better or worse, unequivocally feminine—and it had nothing at all to do with whether or not they ground corn, or fought Indians, or traveled by covered wagon. What mattered, as it will always matter, was their point of view, and their point of view was feminine beyond fault. For, notwithstanding their homespun clothes and unrouged cheeks, their hard day's work and their harassment by nature, they were born—and they recognized it and were more than merely reconciled to it—to love and to look up to their men—and, naturally, to bear their children too.

And now things are the other way around, for while the conveniences of American women are feminine, their motives are masculine, as masculine as the long pants in which they are seen increasingly at home and on the streets. It is a mirror of their confusion, with, on the one hand, their craving for rights equal to men's, stressing strength and self-sufficiency dreaming of their victories in chariot races and such, while dressed in their Maidenform bras; and, on the other, clutching the courtesies, desiring the delicate deferences, pleading for the prerogatives that are normally the weak's. Thus, the woman who demands not only a man's white-collar job, but also a man's wages for doing it, is, more likely than not, the same woman who feels most offended when no male gets up to give her his seat in the subway. For in America, as nowhere else in the world, women are forever demanding to be accepted as the equals of men without being willing to forfeit their franchise to be fawned upon as females. In varying degrees, these are the characteristics which, day after day, year after year, insure the entrenchment of the witch in our way of life.

The witch has been with us always, of course, and literature will so testify, all the shrewish way from Onan's wife and Cinderella's stepmother and Lady Macbeth to Craig's wife and Mrs. Francis Macomber. The difference is that now they seem to represent a way of life, an attitude, a philosophy, and not isolated specimens. Any number of arguments have been advanced in an effort to explain this, some of them sound, but most of them senseless.

"American woman is thoroughly spoiled," observed one psychiatrist. "She has plenty of pushbuttons, but not enough to satisfy her—so she also pushes her husband."

And that is the asinine air of so much of what has been advanced. On the other hand, there has been much serious thought given the matter, among it the theories set forth by Hendrik de Leeuw in *Woman, the Dominant Sex*.[5] It is de Leeuw's contention that the emancipation of the female began during the Civil War, when wives took over the jobs vacated by their husbands upon being mobilized. Then, finding it pleasant to be away from the home, the wives began to seek even more freedom. And de Leeuw may well be right, but I happen to place more credence in the sentiments of Father Norman O'Connor, a Paulist priest who is the Roman Catholic chaplain at Boston University.

In the course of five days a week of trying to solve the problems brought to him by both male and female students, Father O'Connor, a marvel of a man whose pursuits include a television program and a newspaper column devoted, with insight and informativeness, to jazz, is convinced that one of the major factors contributing to the entrenchment of the witch in America is the attitude of mothers when their daughters are about to go out on dates. In any number of instances, the mother instills the daughter with the determination to get everything she can out of her escort. And, as Father O'Connor annotates sadly, but with no visible surprise, "If that means having sexual relations with the boy, why, that's all right, according to the mother's point of view. The important thing is that the boy must be made to spend freely upon the girl. The terrifying thing is that the question of love or even of affection simply doesn't enter into the considerations. The boy is, purely and simply, a means to the girl's—or perhaps I should say the mother's—pleasure. And I'm not telling you about just one case. I hear the same sort of thing every day, although I'm inclined to think it happens less with college girls, who are away from parental supervision, than with the ones who live at home."

One consequence of this sort of thinking can, as Father O'Connor has reason to know, be Lesbianism, which, since it is a rejection of men, is not uncommon in the witch. Lesbianism, of course, is, like witchiness itself, essentially selfish, inasmuch as it precludes not only pregnancy, but the necessity of depending upon a male for gratification. Yet for all their innate dislike and disrespect for men, witches actually feel no more warmth for women. A witch, in fact, is, by her very nature, unable to be deeply interested in anyone but herself. When, for example, her assertive love for her children isn't sheer possessiveness, it is often a means of demeaning her husband by depriving him of their love. Yet for all their dim view of men, witches feel even more resentment toward members of their own sex who, in one way or another, are outstanding. And this, of course, is why female candidates for political office appear to be making relatively little headway in their efforts to gain eventual equal representation. As the number of witches increases, the votes by women for women diminish.

Paradoxically, though, a witch's best friend has proved to be the male lawmaker. If the witch is entrenched in America as she is nowhere else in the world, it is partly because men have so willed it by the laws they have enacted. The divorce court, for example, makes such a practice of punishing the husband in order to pander to the wife that no former husband is ever really free, mentally and morally as well as physically, unless his about-to-be-divorced so decrees. And it is none too often that she does, for here is a rare instance of the witch's thinking clearly, thinking only of herself and in terms that will hold up in court of law. [. . .]

Gentlemen, I demur. The witch may be upon us, and there may appear to be precious little we can do about it, but still we must try to do something. The open hostility between the sexes that has endured for centuries has turned now into a cold war, a battle of nerves that can be swung to our advantage only when we return with firmness to our historical position toward our women: to love them, comfort and honor them, to keep them in sickness and in health. That and nothing more.

NOTES

1. Bernard ("Boom Boom") Geoffrion (b. 1931), Canadian ice hockey player.

2. Richard Rodgers (1902–1979) and Lorenz Hart (1895–1943), renowned composers of musical comedies.

3. In *Of Human Bondage* (1915) by British novelist W. Somerset Maugham (1874–1965), Mildred Rogers is an unattractive, vain, and ignorant waitress who nonetheless exercises a baneful influence over the protagonist, Philip Carey.

4. Ernest Hemingway (1899–1961), "The Short Happy Life of Francis Macomber," first published in *Cosmopolitan* (September 1936) and collected in *The Fifth Column and the First Forty-nine Stories* (1938). It deals with a man on safari in Africa who panics at the sight of a wounded lion, prompting his wife to express contempt for him and leave him for a more courageous hunter.

5. Hendrik De Leeuw (1891–1977), *Woman, the Dominant Sex: From Bloomers to Bikinis* (1957).

Part 2

WOMAN'S "PLACE"

4.

WOMAN, IN HER SOCIAL AND DOMESTIC CHARACTER

(1831)

Elizabeth Sandford

> Little is known about the life of Elizabeth (Poole) Sandford (d. 1853). She was the wife of John Sandford (1801–1873), bishop of Edinburgh, and is the author of two much-reprinted volumes on women's conduct, *Woman, in Her Social and Domestic Character* (1831) and *On Female Improvement* (1836). In the following extract from the former volume, Sandford urges submissive conduct for women, recommending that they pay exclusive interest to home, family, children, and religion.

*A*ll that women do should be done modestly. They should not act the dictator in any thing, not even in matters of benevolence. It is very much the fashion to solicit their patronage, to give them the notoriety of office, and to invest them with a little authority. This may be politic on some accounts, and in some cases

---

Source: Elizabeth Sandford, *Woman, in Her Social and Domestic Character* (1831; 6th American ed., Boston: Otis, Broaders, 1842), pp. 163–67, 171–75.

necessary; but charity, in its most unobtrusive form, is what is more becoming to female character. Women, at least, should never be meddling or important; and if they must take the lead at female committees, or preside at tables at bazars, they should do so with the least possible display. We may some of us question altogether the propriety of young women offering their gay wares at a public mart, or exacting a guinea for every bauble; we may think that they might spend their time more profitably than in making hearts-ease pincushions or wafer-toys; but if they are to do these things, let them do them without effort or affectation. It is the importance assumed on such occasions that is the chief cause of offence.

It should be always considered the duty of women to be well and actively employed; and there is ample field for the most diligent. Let not, therefore, those who waste their time in doing nothing,—who sit at home in indolence, reading a novel, or drawing a flower, or embroidering a workbag,—excuse their own inertness by the officiousness of others. The one is far more defensible than the other; the one may be moderated or corrected, and its intention is its apology; but the other must be wholly overcome, for its principle is bad. The higher the rank, and the greater the wealth, the more important it is that sympathy should be expressed and charity exercised. Young women, of whatever degree, should never shrink from personal effort. Neither should they think, when they do enter a cottage, or teach school, that it is an act of condescension. It is certainly very right in them to be so employed, but it is an honor to them too; and they should ever remember that the greatest privilege that attaches to superiority of any kind is to render inferiors happy and at ease.

There is, perhaps, a greater sense of the duty now than there ever was. And if so why should there not be more effort? Why should not societies be every where established under ministerial sanction for the relief of the poor and the sick, and individual charity be thus concentrated and applied? In the detail of such societies, the assistance of women would often prove very valuable. They would, indeed, not be made the chief agitators; they would not be appointed to the most laborious or the most responsible offices; they would not be sent into districts where it is scarcely fit for modest women to appear;—but they would be directed in all cases of difficulty; and, instead of rambling about on a philanthropic crusade, they would have an assigned sphere of usefulness, and a proper and subordinate duty. The sweet Quakeress has shown what a woman can do. There would be found many such, if they were only judiciously called into action.

Yet it may not be in the power of all women to devote very much time to active efforts. Those who are married are not independent, though it is very much the fashion to consider them so; and to their duties at home all other social duties should be subordinate.

Obedience is a very small part of conjugal duty, and in most cases easily performed. Women have, indeed, not much cause to complain of their subjection; for, though they are apt very inconsiderately to deliver up their right of self-control, they suffer from this rashness, on the whole, less frequently than might be expected. Ill-assorted marriages are certainly too common; but, important as the union is, and thoughtlessly as it is often contracted, it is only wonderful that there should not be a great deal more unhappiness resulting from it than we see to be the case.

Much of the comfort of married life depends upon the lady; a great deal more, perhaps, than she is aware of. She scarcely knows her own influence; how much she may do by persuasion, how much by sympathy, how much by unremitted kindness and little attentions.

To acquire and retain such influence, she must, however, make her conjugal duties her first object. She must not think that any thing will do for her husband, that any room is good enough for her husband, that it is not worth while to be agreeable when there is only her husband, that she may close her piano, or lay aside her brush, for why should she play or paint merely to amuse her husband? No: she must consider all these little arts of pleasing chiefly valuable on his account,—as means of perpetuating her attractions and giving permanence to his affection. She must remember that her duty consists not so much in great and solitary acts, in displays of the sublimer virtues, to which she will be only occasionally called, but in trifles,—in a cheerful smile, or a minute attention, naturally rendered, and proceeding from a heart full of kindness and a temper full of amiability. [. . .]

The most anxious, however, if not the most important duty of married life, is that which is due to children, and which in their early years principally devolves upon the mother. None can supply her place, none can feel her interest; and as in infancy a mother is the best nurse, so in childhood she is the best guardian and instructress. Let her take what help she may, nothing can supersede her own exertions. She must give the tone to character; she must infuse the principle; she must communicate those first lessons which are never forgotten, and which bring forth fruit, good or evil, according as the seed may be.

Instruction is not without its trials. We have heard, in poetry, how delightful it is to "rear the tender thought";[1] but we doubt whether any of us can altogether sympathize with the beau ideal of the bard. In spite of Bell and Pestalozzi, it must ever be a work of patience to teach grammar and orthography.[2]

How needful then is a mother's interest. She may not be herself required to impart the elements of knowledge; but it is hers to give life to the system, to regulate the temper, to turn the little incidents of a child's life into so many useful lessons. It is hers to watch the early bias, to infuse into the lisping prattler a scrupulous regard to truth, to teach the first breathings of the infant spirit to ascend to heaven.

And well is her care repaid. On whom does the infant smile so sweetly as on its mother? To whom do the little boy and girl fly so naturally for sympathy as to their mother? And often, in afterlife, does not youth repose its confidence securely on a mother, and seek the counsel of a mother's faithful heats, and hide its griefs in a mother's tender bosom? It is a delightful relationship; and if mothers would secure the love and respect of their children, they must not grudge their attentions to them in their earliest years. They must be willing to sacrifice a little amusement, or a little company, or a little repose, for the sake of nursing their infants, or teaching their children, or fulfilling themselves offices which too frequently they devolve on servants.

To accomplish, however, these duties, a woman must be domestic. Her heart must be at home. She must not be on the look-out for excitement of any kind, but must find her pleasure as well as her occupation in the sphere which is assigned to her.

St. Paul knew what was best for woman when he advised her to be domestic.[3] He knew that home was her safest place, home her appropriate station. He knew especially the dangers to which young women are exposed, when, under any presence, they fly from home. There is composure at home; there is something sedative in the duties which home involves. It affords security not only from the world, but from delusions and errors of every kind. A woman who lives much at home hears the rumors merely of conflicts which perplex and agitate all who are involved in them. Opinions are presented to her, not dressed up with all the witchery of eloquence, and fresh from the mouth of their propounder, but divested of extrinsic attractions, and in their true garb. She entertains them with a mind not fevered by excitement nor athirst for stimulus, but prepared to weigh every thing impartially, and pre-occupied by important themes.

How preferable is the quiet lot of such a one, when really religious, to the most brilliant which this world can offer. She has set her footing on the Rock, and she will never be moved from it. Her faith is firm, as that on which it reposes. It is not that vague sentiment, which scarcely knows what it believes. It is not that fickle sentiment, which adopts the newest dogma, whatever it may be. It is not that vapid sentiment, which feels every thing or nothing, just as the world dictates. But it is a faith founded upon Scripture,—that bends to the authority of Scripture, however set at nought, that receives the doctrine of Scripture, however contemned, that recognises the obligations of Scripture, however mystified or explained away. It is a faith which, conscious of its own weakness, rests on Almighty strength,—feeling its own wants, flies to Infinite sufficiency,—which with filial confidence carries its cares to the mercy-seat of Heaven, and rests assuredly on Him in whom it has believed.

And how will such a faith be evidenced? By composure under

trials, by a modest fulfilment of duty, by a heavenly walk, by a happy death. Yes, it is then that the Christian really triumphs. The spirit that has animated for a while the tabernacle of clay, that has prompted to benevolence, that has stimulated to self-denial, that has striven and struggled and suffered under its load of flesh, then breaks from its prison and finds its repose. Then it meets with those with whom it long has held communion, whose temptations, and trials, and constancy, have been the same, and whose home will be the same forever.

And let it encourage the female Christian that many have preceded her in her godly course,—that Ruth, and Hannah, and Mary, and Dorcas, and Priscilla, and other holy women, have led the way,—that they have striven and have prevailed,—have believed, and been accepted,—that they have received their crown of glory, and are with the spirits of the just made perfect. And let her go, and be like them.

NOTES

1. James Thomson (1700–1748), *The Seasons* (1726–1730), "Spring," l.1149.

2. Andrew Bell (1753–1832), author of books on education, including *Mutual Tuition and Moral Discipline* (1823). Johann Heinrich Pestalozzi (1746–1827), German philosopher and author of numerous books on the education of children that were translated into several languages. Sandford probably refers to his *Letters on Early Education* (1827).

3. "[Women should be] discreet, chaste, keepers at home, good, obedient to their own husbands, that the word of God be not blasphemed." Titus 2:5.

5.

THE CURSE OF EVE

(1903)

Margaret Bisland

Little is known of Margaret Bisland, who wrote several articles on woman's issues in *Outing* and other magazines of the 1890s and 1900s. In "The Curse of Eve" (*North American Review*, July 1903), Bisland argues that women are being diverted from their "true" function (maternity) by education and employment, both of which render them unfit for childbearing.

The denial to woman of an equal share in man's intellectual and physical career is not, as the near-sighted advocates of feminine enfranchisement would have us believe, a useless relic of barbarism and savagery. It is not an indication of mere male covetousness, selfishness and blind prejudice, upheld and exercised through ages by force of sheer physical superiority, and serving now as a stumbling-block in the path of beneficent progress. True enough, perhaps, it is a tradition inherited from our barbaric and Asiatic ances-

Source: Margaret Bisland, "The Curse of Eve," *North American Review* 177, no. 1 (July 1903): 113–15, 120–22.

tors; nevertheless, it flows from an ancient and profound realization of and respect for an inexorable law of nature—a law that never fails to deprive intellectually developed woman of her fecundity. It flows also from a knowledge, gained through the tragedy of experience, that only in the domestic shelter does civilized humanity find the environment congenial to reproductivity and proper development.

Why this is so, only Nature herself can give us a satisfactory answer. Why, to fulfil her most obvious mission, that of maternity, all the best and freshest forces of the female are required, and why participation in the pleasures and responsibilities, exhilarations and labors of a non-domestic career renders fulfilment of this function repugnant and all but impossible to women, I do not assume here to make clear. It is my intention only to show that it is a fixed law, established for the preservation of human life. It was first outraged, then interpreted and accepted, by wise and patient Asia. Thence we receive our initial record of its operation; and strong historical evidence bears witness to the dire results meted out by avenging Nature to the European nation that attempted to gain a great civilization without duly guarding against the curse of Eve inevitably following upon feminine participation in the life of men.

Reading the third chapter of Genesis aright, is it difficult to pierce through its allegorical disguise, and perceive why the Fall was attributed to woman and the forbidden fruit? The legend comes to us from Asia. It is so evidently founded upon a tremendous race tragedy, which once imperilled the existence of the human family and the progress of its evolution out of savagery, that the wonder is we have failed to read it understandingly and take its meaning to heart. Few and simple as are the words of the relation, they show us, with startling severity of outline, the whole race pictured in the persons of one man and one woman. In Eden they stand on the threshold of those new dominions and desires that reveal themselves to humanity at every stage of its higher spiritual development. What else are we reasonably to interpret as the serpent, "more subtle than any beast of the field,"[1] but the evil whisper of a false ambition, calling woman away from her appointed and primordial task, to aid at this crisis in a short, swift struggle for the attainment of a dazzling intellectual and material aggrandizement?

But the fruit of knowledge, that talisman which insures the highest human power, when plucked by the feminine hand, proves so grievous an outrage upon the law of orderly and consistent evolution, that it all but destroys the race daring thus to refute Nature's processes and principles. Checked and crippled by this perversion of divinely appointed rules, reeling, in consequent enfeeblement of mind and body, back again well-nigh into the blackness of the savage state, the race, in Asia, was taught under the ban that fell upon it in Eden, to fear all influences that call the female from her normal mission.

In that drama of the Creation, can we fail then to perceive how Asia learned certain lessons and truths concerning the preservation of the human species? Asia populated the world. Today, should Europe, America and Oceania be robbed of their last inhabitant, she could populate them anew, for the Asiatic refuses all emancipation to his woman.

The laws and religions of that hoary continent lay terrible fetters upon any development of her individuality beyond her home, her wifehood and motherhood. Immured in the zenana,[2] her face covered, her feet crippled, the existence of a soul to save or a brain to educate often denied her; given in marriage in her infancy, enslaved to masculine authority from the hour of her birth and herded in polygamous wedlock, every means has been taken to confine the woman to her home and to her natural task. Yet, as we consider intelligently that Continent and her doctrine of female seclusion, we see no more nor less than the primitive but correct instincts of the mighty Queen-bee of the race, guarding with jealous care the fountain-head of civilized human life. [. . .]

We fail or refuse to perceive the violently reactionary influence upon the race of that tendency of our Occidental civilization, which, in withdrawing the woman more and more from her home, tends to destroy the true balance of the physical and moral forces between the sexes.

The most marked and deleterious effect of Americanization upon woman is the false energies and abnormal ambitions it excites in her life. Her endeavor is no longer toward the realization and glorification of her sex in its femininity. The education she receives tends to render her either contemptuous of or indifferent to her own peculiar forces and their normal expression. For them, she not only strives, but is encouraged, to substitute an individuality which is purely hybrid and unessential, a grotesque falsetto masculinity.

Yet, for this perversion of her true character and influence, she is no more directly responsible than was the woman of Rome. So long as she found honorable, independent, profitable employment in her domestic environment, she rested there supremely content. Her hopes and dreams, her pride and patriotism and her ambitions were realized in her children.

It was when the greedy current of commercialism tore out of her hands all her home employment, that she followed her tasks to the mills and factories. Then she first began to envy and grasp at the estates and prerogatives of men. As skilled hands are guided best by trained minds, it behooved men to give this willing, cheap, and efficacious feminine labor a fitting education. Forced thus to gain her support outside the home, it is no matter for wonder that she has found it necessary to demand legal and social privileges, property rights and new marriage laws.

So far-reaching and thorough has been her alienation from the true aims of her sex, so complete has been the hasty sacrifice made to the mere temporal and transitory prosperity of this Republic, that we now detect as a consequence certain tendencies to decay gnawing already at the roots of its new civilization.

First, in the diminution of the family; and, again, in the weakening of the marriage tie.

The prodigious increase in divorces among Americans of every class and religion is, perhaps, the most serious menace to the moral and physical stability of our race, that has resulted from the non-domestic avocations of the average woman.

By the last census, the increase in divorce is estimated as two and one half times greater than the increase in population. In the Western Reserve of Ohio, there is one divorce to every eleven marriages. For so appalling a social condition as this, we find no parallel save in the empire of the Romans. There "the law of divorce became more widely extended and more frequently resorted to, and nothing tended more to sap the morals of the Romans than the laxity which was thus introduced into the holiest and most delicate of all human relations."[3]

Vain and empty have been proven the hope and faith that from the highly educated mother profound advantages must accrue to the nation, in the consequently superior mental equipment of her child. The highly educated woman avoids or is incapable of maternity. The exhilaration of monetary profit in exchange for her physical and mental toil, and the pursuit of her purely selfish pleasure or fortune, lure her from the self-sacrifice of maternity and the restraints of wedded life. Or, when wedded, she brings forth few or no children.

Always, among our upper and middle classes, where the daughters and wives enjoy the broadest and most varied mental culture, and where their avocations are semi-masculine by choice, flourish that blight and dry rot of the race, numerical decline. On the superior vitality of the well-nigh illiterate European peasant woman do we now depend largely for the maintenance of our population. On her we shall depend more and more, as time and the pressure brought to bear upon the native-American woman widen the field of her own non-domestic interests.

Great as we appear in our wealth and strength, should Europe cease to nourish us with the warm blood of her vast maternity, who can doubt that we would fall an easy prey to the constitutional fragility and consequent vice that destroyed the ill-balanced and defemininized Roman Empire?

As a nation, we now stand most in need of a re-elevation and rejuvenescence of the precious and powerful motherhood ideal. This, and not new incentives to the spread of education or expansion of the spheres of public activities and influence among our women, is required to produce a permanent and powerful race of our own soil; a true autochthon, a stable, homogeneous and more noble type than Europe has yet created, and which as yet we only fondly imagine we see in the American of to-day. Wide as is the gulf which separates us from the East, the hand of Nature is still heavy upon us. Not yet, even in America, will she permit Eve to eat of the fruit of the tree of knowledge and at the same time allow the race to escape eviction from this latest Eden of mankind, this fair garden of ours, planted in the western world.

NOTES

1. Gen. 3:1.

2. A zenana is, in India and Persia, the part of a dwelling where the women of the family are secluded.

3. [Charles Merivale, *A General History of Rome* (1875).]

6.

THE HOME BUILDER

(1908)

Lyman Abbott

Congregational clergyman Lyman Abbott (1835–1922) initially entered the field of law but, influenced by Henry Ward Beecher, became a Congregational minister, becoming pastor at the Congregational church in Terre Haute, Indiana (1860–1965), and at the Plymouth Congregational church in Brooklyn, New York (1888–1899). In 1876 he became assistant editor, under Beecher, of the *Illustrated Christian Weekly*, and upon Beecher's death in 1881 took over the editorship of the magazine. In 1893, wishing to make the magazine less exclusively focused on religious matters, he changed its name to the *Outlook*, and under his guidance it reached a circulation of one hundred thousand. Abbott became a figure of national renown with his weekly editorials in the *Outlook* as well as with

---

Source: Lyman Abbott, *The Home Builder* (Boston: Houghton Mifflin, 1908), pp. 61–71.

such treatises as *The Evolution of Christianity* (1892) and *Christianity and Social Problems* (1896). Although urging a progressive, less rigidly doctrinal Protestantism, Abbott revealed himself, in such works as *The Home Builder* (1908), to be socially traditional in regard to woman's functions. In the following chapter from this work, titled "The Housekeeper," Abbott paints a portrait of the ideal wife, dutifully cleaning up after her husband and children.

She has a passion for cleanliness. She abhors dirt and justifies her abhorrence by the Scriptural command, "Abhor that which is evil."[1] If dirt be not evil, she knows not what it is. She is contributor to the Society for the Prevention of Cruelty to Animals; but she hates vermin as David hated the enemies of Jehovah, with a perfect hatred, and she pursues them with a persecution as conscientious and relentless as those that were waged by the mediæval inquisitor against the heretics. She is not a scientist; but she needs no scientist to tell her that the germs of insidious disease lurk in dirt and are carried by vermin, and the definition of dirt as "matter misplaced" does nothing to cool her vehement ardor.

But no such passion for order possesses her. Cleanliness is itself a virtue. Next to godliness? If she were quite frank with herself, she would probably change the order and say godliness is next to cleanliness.[2] Certainly she would prefer as a visitor a clean sinner to a dirty saint, and she can find no severer condemnation for coarse language which the boys sometimes pick up in the streets than to tell them with a frown that it is dirty, no severer rebuke for their occasional petty meannesses to each other than to say that they are acting in a nasty manner. But order is not itself a virtue: it is only a means to an end. The end is general comfort and general convenience, and she never sacrifices the end to the means. She endeavors to have a place for everything; she endeavors to train the children—but not her hus-band—to put each thing in its appointed place. But she does not nag. If she sometimes follows a careless husband or son, picking up after him, she never does it with an ostentatious patience, or with a sigh which says, "See how much trouble your carelessness is making me." Her rooms do not look as spick and span as her neighbors', and she sometimes chides herself for not being as good a housekeeper. But she is a better *homekeeper*, which is far more important. For neither her husband nor her boys go to clubs or to other homes for liberty; her home is as free as the club. If order is heaven's first law, liberty is its atmosphere; and if she finds it difficult, as she sometimes does, to pre-serve both the law and the liberty, she prefers the liberty.

So there are in her household hours for meals and meal hours and the two do not always coincide. The hour for breakfast is half-past seven; but if some morning the boys would make an early start for a fishing expedition, the breakfast hour is six; if another morning they can, without neglect of duty, sleep late and wish to do so, it changes to half-past eight or nine. This requires both tact and efficiency in dealing with the kitchen; but when a neighbor asks her if this is not very dif-ficult to manage, she replies cheerfully, "This is what I am for." Nei-ther husband nor children ever know and rarely guess what tact and toil are required. For she surmounts her obstacles without talking about them, except occasionally in a burst of confidence to her hus-band or her daughter, and then as a narrative of her triumphs, not as a history of her trials.

This subordination of time and place to comfort and convenience is a part of her quite unconscious and therefore unformulated theory that life is the end and that all household arrangements are means to that end. She therefore believes that things are for folks, not folks for things, and always and instinctively acts on that belief. When children from the city make a visit to her country home and ask whether they may run on the grass, she says, "Of course"; and when an older visitor, fearing the effect on the young spring-shoots, asks if that is good for the lawn, she replies smilingly, "No! but it is good for the children." She has no use for books that cannot be read, chairs that cannot be sat in, a piano that cannot be played, a room that cannot be used. She has some fine editions, for she is fond of books, but she does not keep them under lock and key. She would rather injure the book in teaching the child how to use it than injure the child by refusing him the book. If a careless boy or a still more careless visitor demolishes a parlor chair by trying to balance himself in it upon the two hind-legs, she blames the chair, not the sitter, and does not get another of so delicate a construction. The piano-tuner has to come to her house twice as often as to the house of her neighbor; but her children learn to play by playing. And though they may never become musicians, they learn to love music, and in after life a piano always brings to them thoughts of their home and their mother. She has no parlor with closed blinds and drawn curtains, from which the sun is carefully excluded lest it fade the precious carpet, and into which visitors are received in state with a sunless and frigid hospitality. Sometimes a critical visitor surprises an unusual disorder due to a misused liberty in the parlor, which Harry has for the nonce converted into a nursery, and the mother expresses the wish gently to herself that Harry were not so heedless. But to shut Harry out of the parlor she is quite certain would be no cure for his heedlessness, and that, not the disordered parlor, is what she wishes to cure.

Her servants gradually, very gradually, imbibe the spirit of their mistress. For she is more than mistress to her servants. She believes with Queen Victoria that a good servant is a good friend. If a servant refuses to become a friend and insists on remaining a bit of animated machinery, they part as soon as the housekeeper has become convinced that no friendly bond is possible between them. On the other hand, if the servant be loyal to the home, interested in her work, friend to her mistress and to the household, and willing to learn, the mistress has unfailing patience in teaching. She will endure neither disloyalty nor indifference, but she will endure everything else, even much unintentional impertinence to herself. She is not dependent upon her servants; she can keep house without them, and they are quite conscious of that fact. And because she will readily put herself out to accommodate them, they are ready to put themselves out to accommodate her. She keeps house, however, for her husband and her children, not for the servants, and she adjusts the affairs of her kingdom to meet the needs of her family, not of those who are employed to minister to it. To this rule there is one exception: the Sunday meals are so adjusted as to give her servants an opportunity for church, and they are encouraged to fulfill with fidelity all that their consciences, not hers, call on them to fulfill church-wise.

The doors of her home are always open to the friends of her husband and of her children. She is glad to see them and welcomes them right cordially to what she has to give. But she never strains endeavor to give them something better than she gives her own. She has not two standards, one for her family, another for the stranger. She makes no effort to conform her living to the accustomed standard of her visitors; she is glad to see them if they will adapt their life for a few days to her standards. It is perhaps for this reason that she is always more ready to welcome men than their wives. Critical herself, and sensitively conscious of what she calls the defects of her housekeeping, she dreads to exhibit them to the critical eyes of other housekeepers. Yet her guests feel a charm in the free air of her home, which they do not feel in that of homes that are kept with more military precision. If she has not a reputation among women of being a model housekeeper, she has the reputation among men of having a model home. She knows what the women think and laments her deficiencies; she does not know what the men think, and would not much care if she did know. She knows that her husband and her children are home-lovers and she is content. For love, not ambition, is the inspiration of her life and the reward of her endeavors.

NOTES

1. Rom. 12:9.

2. The axiom "Cleanliness is next to godliness" is found in the Hebrew fathers and was cited (as a quotation) by John Wesley (1703–1791) in "Sermon 93: On Dress."

7.

THE NORMAL AMERICAN WOMAN

(1908)

Charles W. Eliot

Charles William Eliot (1834–1926) came from a family long associated with Harvard University. He graduated from there in 1853 and was a professor of mathematics and chemistry from 1858 to 1863. He married Ellen Darby Peabody in 1858; they had four sons. She died in 1869, and in 1877 he married Grace Ellen Hopkinson, with whom he remained happily married until her death in 1924. After serving a brief stint as professor of chemistry at the Massachusetts Institute of Technology, Eliot was elected to Harvard's Board of Overseers in 1868 and, in an unexpected move, became president of the college the next year. He remained in that post until his retirement in 1909, and in that period he undertook numerous reforms, focusing chiefly on scientific research, graduate study, and professional

Source: Charles W. Eliot, "The Normal American Woman" (1908), in *Charles W. Eliot's Talks to Parents and Young People*, ed. Edward H. Cotton (Boston: Beacon Press, 1928), pp. 83–92.

education. Eliot thereby became one of the most prominent educational figures of his time. After his retirement from Harvard, he edited the Harvard Classics, the celebrated "five-foot shelf" of great literary and philosophical works of Western civilization. One of his last publications was *Charles W. Eliot's Talks with Young People* (1924), edited by Edward H. Cotton. In the following chapter from that work (first published in *Ladies' Home Journal* in January 1908), Eliot asserts that housekeeping and child-rearing require considerable intelligence and therefore comprise a suitable "job" for the educated woman.

*T*here is a common impression that to procure for herself a real intellectual life, as distinguished from a life of sentimental or mechanical routine, a woman needs to have some occupation similar to those of men—that is, she needs to keep a shop, carry on a business, have some trade or profession, be skillful in some art which has a commercial use, or be a professional writer, artist or student. The common life of woman in bearing and rearing children and making a home for a family is not thought of as affording the wife and mother the means and opportunity for an intellectual development. Is this a rational view? Does it conform to the real experience of a woman of good parts who marries at twenty-four, and thereabouts, and brings up a family of five or six children.

There is no question that a woman who does not pursue the natural and common vocation of women may enjoy an intellectual life in employments similar to those which procure for men a large and enjoyable intellectual development. Many such exceptional women can follow with satisfaction the ordinary professions for men, keep shops, carry on business, labor for churches, schools and charitable societies, and take active part in the various social movements which are furthered by public discussion and the active stimulation of public opinion; but these exceptional women will, as a rule, contribute far less to the real progress of mankind than the normal women, whose intellectual opportunities they are apt to underrate.

The normal girl who learns to read, write, and cipher at school, and acquires there a little knowledge of history and literature and a taste for reading, finds her means of intellectual development, outside of the schoolroom, in her practice of the household arts, in her study of clothes for herself and her family, in her enforced careful expenditure of money, in reading, and in her daily intercourse with father and mother, brothers and sisters, companions and acquaintances. From these things much intellectual training can be extracted by a girl who thinks; and the girl who does not think before she is twenty-four is not likely to think much at any time of her life. Suddenly this girl takes into her heart and brain the personality and interests of another human being—a young man. When courtship and marriage are taken thoughtfully, and neither as a matter of mere impulse and emotion nor as a business arrangement, there comes with them a strong intellectual stimulation, and in most cases a widening of the field of observation and thought.

Going to housekeeping under new conditions is also a valuable piece of mental training. The young woman has new duties, or new applications of arts which she learned from her mother. Her husband brings home many subjects for thought and speculation which are new to her. He probably has a different trade or occupation from her father, with different invitations, obstacles and prospects.

With the coming of children the mother not only experiences new joys and anxieties, but also has many new things to learn and new difficulties to contend with. Tenderness, sympathy and love are indispensable in the care of babies and the bringing up of young children; but there is a large opportunity also for careful thought and practical wisdom in addition to those natural sentiments, particularly if the family lives in the sparsely settled country, or is not rich enough to command the prompt services of all sorts of specialists and helpers.

The process of training several children in helpfulness, mutual forbearance and productive cooperation is one which requires much mental capacity in the trainer, and the trainer is usually the mother. In imparting this training the mother herself practices keen observation, the comparative study of her different children, patience, and a gentle decisiveness which is quite as much an intellectual as a moral trait. The mother of several children—four, five or six—has better opportunities of developing her own intellectual life than the mother of one child or two children; because in a large family there are always great differences of disposition and capacity among the children, and the children react on each other and on their mother in more ways, and more interesting ways.

As soon as the schooling of the children begins numerous intellectual problems are set from day to day for the parents. Any mother who follows the mental development of five or six children at school will get herself a second schooling greatly superior to her first. If a son or daughter goes on to college the sympathetic mother will find her mind enlarged and informed. Again, when her children begin in their turn to mate, all the intellectual force the mother possesses will come into play. It is a lively and profitable mental exercise to keep in touch with the successively developed interests of a group of children from five to twenty years of age. The mother should stimulate and direct their growing mental powers. She should train them in habits of order, industry and consideration for others. She should teach her children self-control and the spirit of cooperation. She cannot perform well the combined functions of mother and teacher unless she learns to be just. Now, to be just involves not only righteous purpose and good feeling, but also sound thinking. To command clearly, refuse firmly, and praise warmly require a ready mind.

Of course, to win most of these opportunities for mental exercise and growth it is by no means necessary that a woman should have been married. Many an unmarried woman wins them all by taking care of other people's children.

It generally falls to the share of the woman of the family to keep up what are called the social relations, and to decide on the families with which she will maintain friendly or intimate relations. This function is a laborious and interesting one in all the walks of life. Among well-to-do people it is well recognized that this function requires for its proper discharge much thought and industry in addition to natural gifts. It is just the same in the lowest layer of society and in all the layers between the highest and lowest, except that social discrimination and selection are expressed in different ways in the different layers. The grounds of discrimination, attraction and repulsion are different in the different layers; but they are quite as apt to be sound and edifying at the bottom as at what is called the top. In every walk of life it is a matter of active discrimination and constant care to secure for one's children associations which will be apt to improve and lift them as the years go on.

The competent mother of a properly ambitious family has in these days another high task before her in directing and stimulating the training of her entire family to the intelligent use of books and other reading matter. No matter where she lives, in city, or country, or on an island in the sea, she can use first-rate mental powers in exercising this influence over her children. The evening is the most available time for discharging this educational function; and many a family in the humblest walks of life secures in this way, through the intelligent action of the mother, a satisfaction which lasts all their lives, and is transmitted to their descendants.

There is another function of the home-maker which has its intellectual side, namely, the cultivation in children of the sense of beauty, and of the enjoyment of beautiful objects. In most families—rich and poor alike—this function falls to the woman. In the poorest houses one often sees in the southerly window some flowering plants raised in tin cans and broken pieces of crockery, but cultivated with remarkable success by the wife and mother. A single oleander bush will be tended a whole year by the old wife whose children have left home—with much labor in winter to protect it from frost, because the kitchen is the only tolerably warm room at night—just for the sake of its three weeks of flowers. It is generally the mother of the family who keeps flowers blooming in the village house lot, or in the grounds just about the solitary farmhouse.

How many people remember all their lives the peculiar fragrance of grandmother's garden, and the selection of flowers in which she delighted! In the scattered houses in the country it is the woman who buys of the travelling pedlar the illuminated text of Scripture and the chromos of foreign scenery for the decoration of her walls. The houses of the rich are adorned with beautiful fabrics, etchings, paintings, china and glass provided by and for women. Thinking of such objects, and working for such ends, is an intellectual pleasure, and a civilizing influence for the household and neighborhood. [. . .]

It may be thought that the means of intellectual life here described differ from those which men enjoy in their professions or trades in that they are more mixed with moral qualities and motives; but it may well be doubted if such is the fact. In every profession and occupation, whether ordinarily called intellectual or manual, there is a large moral element without which the mental training which the profession or occupation provides is hardly worth having. Indeed, many activities called intellectual are really sterile, whereas all intellectual achievement in the household or family is likely to be immediately serviceable and productive.

Because of the sacredness of family life and its supreme importance for the progress of the race, the admixture of holy sentiments and aspirations with the labors of a mother seems more intimate and essential than with any other human labors; but the fact has no tendency to diminish the value of the intellectual part of that occupation.

The value of any occupation, whether occupation of a million human beings or of one human being, is best judged by its product. If we apply this standard to the occupation of a normal woman who brings up four or five dutiful, thoughtful and loving children, shall we not conclude that her occupation is the most precious in the world, no matter how we settle the question whether heredity or environment is the more influential factor in determining the quality of each new generation? The woman exerts both these influences. This is as true for a million women as it is for one.

It is a solid fact, which has been but imperfectly apprehended by mankind, that this most precious occupation is full of opportunities for training the reasoning powers through practice in observing, comparing, discriminating and choosing. This is the reason that we may fairly judge the real civilization of any race by the way it has treated, and is treating, its women. This is the reason that we always ask about any unusually serviceable man or woman—Who was the mother? This is the reason that the Christian nations of the world have made more progress than the others toward public justice and public happiness. They have a higher estimate than the other nations have of the intellectual and moral capacities of women, and of the dignity and informing quality of their normal occupation.

Part 3

SCIENTISTS ON WOMEN

8.

WOMAN: PHYSIOLOGICALLY CONSIDERED

(1843)

Alexander Walker

The Scottish physiologist Alexander Walker (1779–1852) holds a notable place in the biological, physiological, and medical thought of his time. In 1809 he founded and edited *Archives of Universal Science*, and went on to write several noteworthy treatises on anatomy, including *The Nervous System* (1834) and *Documents and Dates of Modern Discoveries in the Nervous System* (1839). He wrote a trilogy of loosely connected works on women: *Beauty: Illustrated by an Analysis and Classification of Beauty in Woman* (1836), *Intermarriage* (1838), and *Woman: Physiologically Considered* (1839). In the following extract from this last work, preceded by the heading "Morals," Walker regards it as axiomatic that women are intellectually inferior to men and proceeds to outline what he believes to be other physio-

Source: Alexander Walker, *Woman: Physiologically Considered* (London: A. H. Baily, 1839), pp. 39–41, 48–50, 51–56, 67–68, 69–70, 71–74.

logical features of women's character—vanity, sympathy, love, friendship, and coquetry.

*T*he natural sensibility, feebleness and timidity of woman lead her instinctively, and with little aid from reasoning, to observe the circumstances which prompt mankind to act, inspire her with a SENSE OF WHAT IS FITTING, induce her imperceptibly to measure her procedure and graduate her language, and imbue her with the spirit of society.

Women are accordingly peculiarly sensible to ridicule, and attach great importance to little faults. They are less influenced by the great qualities that more than atone for these. Nay, they often laugh at them; and it is very probable, as St. Lambert observes, that Xantippe made fun of Socrates, and that the patrician women of Rome told very amusing tales of Cato.[1]

The further necessity of woman's placing her weakness in safety—a necessity perpetually felt, and therefore requiring little to be reasoned, leads her instinctively to regulate her language and actions more particularly for the purpose of pleasing, and renders her an adept in the art of POLITENESS.

It is natural, therefore, that, while the politeness of men is more officious, that of women should be more caressing, better calculated to soften even the most rugged character.—As to their politeness to each other, that is altogether a different affair.

As the faculties of women thus lead her instinctively to please, there arises in her a sentiment which induces her to seek approbation even by the influence of external appearances, to pay attention to her person and her dress, and to direct all the powers she can derive from these, to the purposes of combat and conquest. This sentiment is VANITY.

Even at an early age, girls become evidently interested about the impressions which they make on those around them. Not contented, says Rousseau, "with being pretty, they wish to be thought so; we see by their little airs that this care already occupies them; and scarcely are they capable of understanding what is said, when they may be governed by telling them what is thought of them. The same motive very indiscreetly proposed to little boys, has no such influence over them. Provided they are independent, and have their pleasure, they care very little about what may be thought of them. It is only time and suffering that subject them to the same law."[2]

A more striking illustration of the power of vanity in woman, can scarcely be given than that when a collection of three hundred and fifty pounds was made for the celebrated Cuzzona, to save her from absolute want, she no sooner got the money into her possession, than she laid out two hundred pounds of it in the purchase of a shell cap, which was just then in fashion![3]

So powerful is vanity in woman, that it is chiefly when her self-love is offended that her obstinacy becomes excessive, and this obstinacy yields the moment such offence is removed by deference and homage. [. . .]

It is doubtless from the sympathy instinctively incited by the sense of her weakness that woman derives her gentle AFFECTIONS, benevolence, pity, &c.; and these her organization is well calculated to express. Every one, as Roussel observes,[4] feels that a mouth made to smile, that eyes full of tenderness or sparkling with gaiety, that arms more beautiful than formidable, that a voice conveying to the mind only soft impressions were not made to ally themselves with violent and hateful passions.

How entirely it is instinctive sympathy that produces these affections, is illustrated by the well-known fact, that the poor and miserable are ever relieved by those who are but a little less poor and miserable: beggars swarm on the evening when the poor man gets his wages; and if the poor woman's hand is still opener than her husband's, it certainly is not because she reasons better but because her instinctive sympathies are greater.

Woman's pity is more tender, more indulgent, and even more constant than man's; and the acts which spring from it under the guidance of instinct, are almost instantaneous. So powerfully opposed is this feeling to cruelty, that, as Voltaire observes, "you will see one hundred hostile brothers for one Clytemnestra. Out of a thousand assassins who are executed, you will scarcely find four women."[5]

The same weakness, however, which, by sympathy, produces benevolence and pity, sometimes, by fear, produces revenge; and every body knows—

———"Furens quid fœmina possit."[6]

The SENTIMENTS of woman result from the union of these powerful instinctive affections with her feebler intellectual operations. These sentiments have accordingly been observed to be less connected with the operations of the mind of woman than with the impressions made on it by those who have suggested these operations. St. Lambert, therefore, makes Ninon say, "we must always appear to feel rather than to think. . . . A sentimental air is the most powerful of all our charms."

It is this which renders women unjust, and which leads the same writer to say, that "a just man is very rare, but a just woman still more so.

"Your pity and benevolence often interfere with your justice. When your own interest does not make you unjust, the interest of others makes you so. When you take part in any affair, you take the side, not of him who is right, but of him who pleases you most." [. . .]

Of the FRIENDSHIP of woman, little that is favourable, I believe, can be said. Let us first understand its nature.

Love, we know, implies difference of sex; friendship, I believe, implies, or supposes, its absence. Love is a vital passion; friendship, an intellectual one. Friendship, therefore, is little suited to the unintellectual and instinctive faculties of woman.

Love, therefore, exists toward woman alone; friendship toward man chiefly—in the highest degree toward man solely, because his mind renders him its suitable object. It indeed appears to me that when friendship exists toward woman, it is generally toward the least loveable—toward those who "have neither been the most beautiful nor the most gentle of their sex."

I frankly confess that the only kind of women with whom I ever formed any thing like friendship, were ugly and clever old maids, women whom it was impossible to love, women who more resembled men, because the absence of all erotic feeling had enabled them to employ what brain they had in a masculine way. I never could have dreamt of choosing, as a mere friend, a being with great sensitive and small reasoning faculties, and still less with vastly developed vital organs.

It appears to me, therefore, that a truly loveable woman is thereby unfitted for friendship; and that the woman fitted for friendship, is but little fitted for love.

But it may be said—what then is the bond between the husband and wife in whom the period of love has passed?—Habits endeared by all the recollections of past love; the wants, inseparable from existence, that spring out of these; and where there are also children, ties as powerful, perhaps, as those between parent and child.

It is in a spirit perfectly philosophical that Moore says:—

"When time, who steals our years away,
    Shall steal our pleasures too,
The memory of the past will stay,
    And half our joys renew."[7]

Rousseau adds, "When love hath lasted as long as possible, a pleasing habitude supplies its place, and the attachment of a mutual confidence succeeds to the transports of passion. Children often form a more agreeable and permanent connection between married people, than even love itself."

Between women themselves, there is little or no friendship, because they have but one object. It is well observed, that the only bonds sufficiently strong to retain them are love secrets, which each is fearful the other may disclose; and that their friendships never go to the length of sacrificing a passion to each other.

"The first necessity of a friendship amongst women," says Madame de Stael, "is habitually the desire of reposing confidence; and that is then only a consequence of love. A similar passion must occupy both of them; and their conservation is frequently only a sacrifice alternately made by her who listens, in the hope of speaking in her turn. The confidence made to each other of sentiments of a less exclusive nature, has the same character, and whatever refers solely to one is alternately tedious to each.

"As all women have the same destiny, they all tend to the same point; and this kind of jealousy, which is a compound of sentiment and self-love, is the most difficult to conquer. There is, in the greater number of them, an art which is not exactly falsehood but a certain arrangement of truth, the secret of which they all know, though they hate its being discovered. The generality of women cannot bear endeavouring to please a man in the presence of another woman: there is also a fortune common to all the sex in agreeableness, wit and beauty, and every woman persuades herself she gains something by the ruin of another."[8]

Montaigne regards woman as incapable of true friendship; deems her mind too weak and too much inflamed by trifling jealousies of other women; and thinks that it is only in men and children that the feeling rises to heroism.[9]

PHILANTHROPY, PATRIOTISM and POLITICS, not being matters of instinct, but of reason, are unsuited to the mind of woman, conducted as it best is by particular ideas, and incapable as it is of generalizing. It is by that faculty alone that man can pass from individuals to nations, and from nations to the human race, both at the present time and during the future. The mind of woman, on the contrary, rejects such extended views; and it has been truly said, that to her one man is more than a nation, and the day present than twenty future ages.

The public relations which arise out of this mental difference of the sexes, are noticed by Kaimes, when he says, "The master of a family is immediately connected with his country: his wife, his children, his servants, are immediately connected with him, and with their country through him only. Women accordingly have less patriotism than men; and less bitterness against the enemies of their country."[10]

The imprudent advocates of the rights of woman nevertheless contend for her right to legislate, &c.—"I really think," says Mrs. Wolstonecraft, "that women ought to have representatives, instead of being arbitrarily governed without having any share allowed to them in the deliberations of government."[11]

On this subject I have *elsewhere* observed that, as to those who actually desire to make representatives and senators of women, they surely forget that though, in such assemblies, an ugly woman might be harmless, a pretty one would certainly corrupt the whole legislation! To a certainty, the prettiest women would always be sent in as representatives, instead of the most intelligent ones; because, if they *would* but obey instructions, and *could* but understand them sufficiently to state them, their constituents might certainly, through them, command whatever they desired. The handsomest women, then, would infallibly be in requisition from all quarters as members; and, in consequence of the furtive glances and the whisperings of love, &c. &c., the house would soon merit a character still worse, if possible, than its present one.

This system would, moreover, be rendered very inconvenient by the little indescribable accidents which at all times attend the health of women, and more especially by some of the symptoms of pregnancy, by some of the slight diseases of gestation, or even occasionally perhaps by premature parturition, which might easily be occasioned by a variety of accidents. Were, moreover, a tendency to the latter to spread rapidly among the congregated female senators, as it does sometimes among the females of inferior animals, what a scene would ensue! A few midwives, to be sure, might be added to the officers of the house. Thus a man might have the glory, not merely of having died, like Lord Chatham, in the senate, but of having been born there![12]

The advocates of this system may mean, indeed, that no woman who is not ugly, and more than fifty, should be returned; but then one is at a loss to see what would be gained by that, for the honourable house has always been, to a vast extent, composed in that very way. [. . .]

Abandoning, therefore, all further consideration of subjects so remote from the nature of woman, as friendship, philanthropy, patriotism, and politics, (into which I have been led by their relation to friendship), and passing to such as are more connected with those acts of the mind which were previously noted, (politeness, vanity, affection and sentiment, which do naturally characterize her), we are first led to her DEPENDENCE ON AND KNOWLEDGE OF MAN, as preliminary to love, and her morals as related either to it or to its consequences.

Here again woman's sense of weakness and inability to act upon the objects around her by force, instinctively lead her to seek for means which are indirect, and to strengthen herself by the aid of man. Wants always felt, and acts almost unconsciously performed, preclude reason. To man, moreover, she discovers that she has other motives of attachment, for instinctive feelings also tell her, that she is the depositary of germs, and is destined for reproduction. [. . .]

The prevalence of the instinctive faculties in woman, is the reason why, as has been truly observed, "LOVE commences in her more promptly, more sympathetically, and with less apparently of rational motive"; and the great development of her vital system is the reason why "love, which is said to be only an episode in the life of man, becomes in that of woman the whole romance"—why, "when young, she fondles her doll; at maturity, attaches herself to her husband and children; in old age, when she can no longer hope to please men by her beauty, devotes herself to God, and heals one love by another, without being entirely cured of it."

It certainly is not wonderful that, in what they know so well, women should possess a thousand shades and delicacies, of which men are incapable.

Love, then, is the empire of woman. She governs man by the seduction of her manners, by captivating his imagination, and by engaging his affections. She ensures the assumption and some of the terms of power by reserving to herself the right of yielding.

For this purpose, some ARTIFICE is required. Dissimulation, indeed, is inherent in the nature not only of woman, but of all the feebler and gentler animals: and this illustrates its instinctive character. [. . .]

The consciousness of weakness in woman, then, leads her instinctively to her dissimulation, her finesse, her little contrivances, her manners, her graces—her coquetry.

By these means she at once endeavours to create love, and not to show what she feels; while by means of modesty she feigns to refuse what she wishes to grant.

How sweetly has this native diffidence been described by Milton!

—————————"She heard me thus:
Yet innocence and virgin modesty,
Her virtue, and the conscience of her worth,
That would be woo'd and not unsought be won,
Not obvious, not obtrusive, but retired,
The more desirable—or, to say all,
Nature herself, though pure of sinful thought,
Wrought in her so, that, seeing me, she turn'd;
I followed her; she what was honour knew,
And with obsequious majesty approved
My pleased reason. To the nuptial bower
I led her, blushing like the morn."[13]

This view of the meaning and use of these demonstrations in love, derives the most decided confirmation from the observation of the manners of animals, which at the same time show these demonstrations to be instinctive. Among them, the female also, though she place herself in the way of the male, pretends to submit reluctantly, especially among the polygamous species in order the more to excite the ardour of the other sex. In the genus canis, this is easily observed; the male always enduring the preliminary threats of the female.

It was wrongly, therefore, that the Cynics regarded modesty as a dangerous allurement, and made it a duty to do every thing that could possibly be done, to banish it from society.[14]

After all this, it is curious that Mrs. Wolstonecraft should say, "A man, when he undertakes a journey, has, in general, the end in view; a woman thinks more of the incidental occurrences, the strange things that may possibly occur on the road, the impression that she may make on her fellow-travellers, and above all, she is anxiously intent on the care of her finery that she carries with her, which is more than ever a part of herself, when going to figure on a new scene, when, to use an apt French turn of expression, she is going to produce a sensation.— Can dignity of mind exist with such trivial cares?"[15]—On which no other comment need be made than that women instinctively, or if you please, wisely, seek security, for the maintenance of the progeny which every year of their life is to be engaged in producing.

That this faculty may be abused is true. Hence Diogenes said:— Trust not to a woman, not even if she were dying.[16]

To the artifice of woman, her CAPRICE suggests many resources. It is nevertheless perfectly natural: extreme delicacy of organization is inseparable from fickleness of affections, and the inconsistency of conduct which it induces.

Hence Virgil says,

————Varium et mutabile semper
Fœmina.[17]

And Terence,

————Nosti mulierum ingenium?
Nolunt ubi velis: ubis nolis, cupiunt ultro.[18]

This fickleness and inconsistency, physiologists rightly explain by means of the numerous communications both between the various branches of the great sympathetic nerve, and between these and the branches of the cerebro-spinal system. Hence the sympathy of the lips, the nipples, and the mammae, with the clitoris, the ovaries, and the matrix. And hence, at critical periods especially, woman passes suddenly from tears to laughter, and from bursts of passion to transports of love.—This dependence on the vital system is a striking proof of the instinctive character of female caprice.

Women, accordingly, feel the need of frequent lively impressions, or even of serious agitation; and a French writer says that, among his countrywomen, he has known individuals, who unconsciously actuated by this thirst for emotion, provoked very lively scenes with their lovers, solely to obtain for themselves the pleasure of tears, reproaches and reconciliation: they go even so far as to derive a secret delight from their remorse and repentance.

But, as already said, caprice suggests resources to artifice, and is of great value in love. It represses desires only to render them more vivid, to make opportunity more valuable, to cause it to be profited by when it occurs. It delays the purpose only the better to attain it.

With all this is connected the adoption of those pleasant playful and sometimes infantile airs, which accompany courtship.

Thus it appears that all the faculties in which woman excels are those which depend chiefly upon instinct: and all those in which she is deficient require the exercise of reason.

NOTES

1. Xantippe was the wife of Socrates, frequently depicted as a shrew. Cato the Elder (234–149 BCE) was a stern moralist of republican Rome. The anecdotes are derived from Jean-François, Marquis de Saint-Lambert (1716–1803), *Principes des moeurs* (1796).

2. Jean Jacques Rousseau (1712–1778), *Emile* (1762), bk. 5.

3. Francesca Cuzzoni (1698–1770), Italian soprano and one of the first great prima donnas.

4. Gérard Roussel (d. 1555), French mystic and religious reformer. Walker probably refers to his *Familière exposition du simbole* (1549).

5. The quotation from Voltaire (François Marie Arouet, 1694–1778) has not been identified.

6. "What a maddened woman is capable of." Virgil *Aeneid* 5.6.

7. Thomas Moore (1760–1822), "Song," stanza 1.

8. Anne Louise Germaine (Necker), Baronne de Staël-Holstein (1766–1817), *De l'influence des passions sur le bonheur des individus et des nations* [The Influence of the Passions on the Happiness of Individuals and Nations] (1796), sec. 2, chap. 2.

9. Michel de Montaigne (1533–1592), *Essays*, bk. 1, no. 28 ("Of Friendship").

10. Henry Home, Lord Kames (1696–1782), British essayist and critic best known for *The Elements of Criticism* (1762). The quotation is from bk. 1, chap. 6 ("Progess of the Female Sex") of *Sketches of the History of Man* (1774–1775).

11. Mary Wollstonecraft (1759–1797), *A Vindication of the Rights of Women* (1792), chap. 9.

12. William Pitt the Elder (1708–1778), first Earl of Chatham, prime minister of England (1766–1768) and one of the leading British statesmen of his time, collapsed during a debate in the House of Lords and died a few weeks later.

13. John Milton (1608–1674), *Paradise Lost* (1667), 8.500–511 (of Eve).

14. The Cynics were an ancient Greek sect (whose leading exponent was Diogenes of Sinope) who practiced extreme asceticism, including the virtual discarding of all clothing, in the belief that such artificialities were a hindrance to the attainment of true virtue.

15. Wollstonecraft, *Vindication*, chap. 4.

16. The quotation has not been identified.

17. "Woman is always fickle and changeable." Virgil *Aeneid* 4.569–70 (spoken by Mercury to Aeneas as a means of urging him to desert Dido and leave Carthage).

18. "Do you know the mind of women? They won't when you would; when you wouldn't they want it the more." Terence *Eunuchus* 812–13.

9.

SEX AND CHARACTER

(1903)

Otto Weininger

The life of Otto Weininger (1880–1903) was as tragic as it was short. The son of nonreligious Jewish parents, Weininger was born in Vienna, Austria, where he spent the whole of his life. He entered the University of Vienna in 1898 and shortly afterward began collecting material for his doctoral thesis, which became the basis for the only work published in his lifetime, *Geschlecht und Charakter* (1903), translated into English as *Sex and Character*. In 1900 a friend of Weininger's reported to him Freud's theory of the bisexual disposition present in human beings; Weininger made this the basis of his work, maintaining that each individual possessed both male and female characteristics in varying degrees. (Freud later claimed, however, that Weininger's "principal thesis he got from me indirectly, and in a quite

Source: Otto Weininger, *Sex and Character* (London: William Heinemann; New York: G. P. Putnam's Sons, 1906), pp. 186–87, 188–89, 190–92, 194–99, 200–204, 205–208.

inaccurate way."[1]) Weininger met Freud in the fall of 1901, at which time Freud read the manuscript of his doctoral thesis and delivered an unfavorable opinion of it. Weininger received a PhD for the thesis on July 21, 1902, the same day he converted to Protestantism. The thesis served as part 1 of his book; he wrote part 2 in the fall of 1902. By this time he had lapsed into introspection and self-hatred, admitting to "not being able to love anybody." Tormented by the fear of death and by unresolved sexual tensions, Weininger committed suicide on October 4, 1903. His book, although initially received with indifference or hostility, became widely popular in the first two decades of the century, being translated into Italian, English, Spanish, Polish, Danish, and Hebrew. The following extract from *Sex and Character*, from a chapter titled "Male and Female Psychology," reveals Weininger's shortcomings as a social thinker: making arbitrary assumptions of what constitutes innately male and female behavior, and making broad generalizations based upon limited knowledge of women (Weininger was never romantically involved with a woman, and had sexual relations only with prostitutes), he concludes that women have no ego, soul, or moral sense. The final chapter of *Sex and Character* is also controversial in its anti-Semitism: it asserts that Jewish male behavior is essentially effeminate.[2]

S hortly speaking the matter stands as follows: I have shown that logical and ethical phenomena come together in the conception of truth as the ultimate good, and posit the existence of an intelligible ego or a soul, as a form of being of the highest superempirical reality. In such a being as the absolute female there are no logical and ethical phenomena, and, therefore, the ground for the assumption of a soul is absent. The absolute female knows neither the logical nor the moral imperative, and the words law and duty, duty towards herself, are words which are least familiar to her. The inference that she is wanting in supersensual personality is fully justified. The absolute female has no ego.

In a certain sense this is an end of the investigation, a final conclusion to which all analysis of the female leads. And although this conclusion, put thus concisely, seems harsh and intolerant, paradoxical and too abrupt in its novelty, it must be remembered that the author is not the first who has taken such a view; he is more in the position of one who has discovered the philosophical grounds for an opinion of long standing. [. . .]

But since the soul of man is the microcosm, and great men are those who live entirely in and through their souls, the whole universe thus having its being in them, the female must be described as absolutely without the quality of genius. The male has everything within him, and, as Pico of Mirandola put it, only specialises in this or that part of himself. It is possible for him to attain to the loftiest heights, or to sink to the lowest depths; he can become like animals, or plants, or even like women, and so there exist woman-like female men.

The woman, on the other hand, can never become a man. In this consists the most important limitation to the assertions in the first part of this work. Whilst I know of many men who are practically completely psychically female, not merely half so, and have seen a considerable number of women with masculine traits, I have never yet seen a single woman who was not fundamentally female, even when this femaleness has been concealed by various accessories from the person herself, not to speak of others. One must *be* (*cf.* chap. i. part I.)

either man or woman, however many peculiarities of both sexes one may have, and this "*being*," the problem of this work from the start, is determined by one's relation to ethics and logic; but whilst there are people who are anatomically men and psychically women, there is no such thing as a person who is physically female and psychically male, notwithstanding the extreme maleness of their outward appearance and the unwomanliness of their expression.

We may now give, with certainty, a conclusive answer to the question as to the giftedness of the sexes: there are women with undoubted traits of genius, but there is no female genius, and there never has been one (not even amongst those masculine women of history which were dealt with in the first part), *and there never can be one*. Those who are in favour of laxity in these matters, and are anxious to extend and enlarge the idea of genius in order to make it possible to include women, would simply by such action destroy the conception of genius. If it is in any way possible to frame a definition of genius that would thoroughly cover the ground, I believe that my definition succeeds. And how, then, could a soulless being possess genius? The possession of genius is identical with profundity; and if any one were to try to combine woman and profundity as subject and predicate, he would be contradicted on all sides. A female genius is a contradiction in terms, for genius is simply intensified, perfectly developed, universally conscious maleness.

The man of genius possesses, like everything else, the complete female in himself; but woman herself is only a part of the Universe, and the part can never be the whole; femaleness can never include genius. This lack of genius on the part of woman is inevitable because woman is not a monad, and cannot reflect the Universe.[3] [. . .]

The logical axioms are the foundation of all formation of mental conceptions, and women are devoid of these; the principle of identity is not for them an inevitable standard, nor do they fence off all other possibilities from their conception by using the principle of contradictories. This want of definiteness in the ideas of women is the source of that "sensitiveness" which gives the widest scope to vague associations and allows the most radically different things to be grouped together. And even women with the best and least limited memories never free themselves from this kind of association by feelings. For instance, if they "feel reminded" by a word of some definite colour, or by a human being of some definite thing to eat—forms of association common with women—they rest content with the subjective association, and do not try to find out the source of the comparison, and if there is any relation in it to actual fact. The complacency and self-satisfaction of women corresponds with what has been called their intellectual unscrupulousness, and will be referred to again in connection with their want of the power to form concepts. This subjection to waves of feeling, this want of respect for conceptions, this self-appreciation without any attempt to avoid shallowness, characterise as essentially female the changeable styles of many modern painters and novelists. Male thought is fundamentally different from female thought in its craving for definite form, and all art that consists of moods is essentially a formless art.

The psychical contents of man's thoughts, therefore, are more than the explicit realisation of what women think in henids. Woman's thought is a sliding and gliding through subjects, a superficial tasting of things that a man, who studies the depths, would scarcely notice; it is an extravagant and dainty method of skimming which has no grasp of accuracy. A woman's thought is superficial, and touch is the most highly developed of the female senses, the most notable characteristic of the woman which she can bring to a high state by her unaided efforts. Touch necessitates a limiting of the interest to superficialities, it is a vague effect of the whole and does not depend on definite details. When a woman "understands" a man (of the possibility or impossibility of any real understanding I shall speak later), she is simply, so to speak tasting (however wanting in taste the comparison may be) what he has thought about her. Since, on her own part, there is no sharp differentiation, it is plain that she will often think that she herself has been understood when there is no more present than a vague similarity of perceptions. The incongruity between the man and woman depends, in a special measure, on the fact that the contents of the thoughts of the man are not merely those of the woman in a higher state of differentiation, but that the two have totally distinct sequences of thought applied to the same object, conceptual thought in the one and indistinct sensing in the other; and when what is called "understanding" in the two cases is compared, the comparison is not between a fully organised integrated thought and a lower stage of the same process; but in the understanding of man and woman there is on the one side a conceptual thought, on the other side an unconceptual "feeling," a henid.[4] [. . .]

A being like the female, without the power of making concepts, is unable to make judgments. In her "mind" subjective and objective are not separated; there is no possibility of making judgments, and no possibility of reaching, or of desiring, truth. No woman is really interested in science; she may deceive herself and many good men, but bad psychologists, by thinking so. It may be taken as certain, that whenever a woman has done something of any little importance in the scientific world (Sophie Germain, Mary Somerville,[5] &c.) it is always because of some man in the background whom they desire to please in this way; and it is more often justifiable to say "cherchez l'homme" where women are concerned than "cherchez la femme" in the case of men.

But there have never been any great discoveries in the world of science made by women, because the facility for truth only proceeds from a desire for truth, and the former is always in proportion to the latter. Woman's sense of reality is much less than man's, in spite of much repetition of the contrary opinion. With women the pursuit of knowledge is always subordinated to something else, and if this alien impulse is sufficiently strong they can see sharply and unerringly, but woman will never be able to see the value of truth in itself and in relation to her own self. Where there is some check to what she wishes (perhaps unconsciously) a woman becomes quite uncritical and loses all touch with reality. This is why women so often believe themselves to have been the victims of sexual overtures; this is the reason of extreme frequency of hallucinations of the sense of touch in women, of the intensive reality of which it is almost impossible for a man to form an idea. This also is why the imagination of women is composed of lies and errors, whilst the imagination of the philosopher is the highest form of truth.

The idea of truth is the foundation of everything that deserves the name of judgment. Knowledge is simply the making of judgments, and thought itself is simply another name for judgment. Deduction is the necessary process in making judgments, and involves the propositions of identity and of contradictories, and, as I have shown, these propositions are not axiomatic for women.

A psychological proof that the power of making judgments is a masculine trait lies in the fact that the woman recognises it as such, and that it acts on her as a tertiary sexual character of the male. A woman always expects definite convictions in a man, and appropriates them; she has no understanding of indecision in a man. She always expects a man to talk, and a man's speech is to her a sign of his manliness. It is true that woman has the gift of speech, but she has not the art of talking; she converses (flirts) or chatters, but she does not talk. She is most dangerous, however, when she is dumb, for men are only too inclined to take her quiescence for silence.

The absolute female, then, is devoid not only of the logical rules, but of the functions of making concepts and judgments which depend on them. As the very nature of the conceptual faculty consists in posing subject against object, and as the subject takes its deepest and fullest meaning from its power of forming judgments on its objects, it is clear that women cannot be recognised as possessing even the subject.

I must add to the exposition of the non-logical nature of the female some statements as to her non-moral nature. The profound falseness of woman, the result of the want in her of a permanent relation to the idea of truth or to the idea of value, would prove a subject of discussion so exhaustive that I must go to work another way. There are such endless imitations of ethics, such confusing copies of morality, that women are often said to be on a moral plane higher than that of man. I have already pointed out the need to distinguish between the non-moral and the immoral, and I now repeat that with regard to women we can talk only of the non-moral, of the complete absence of a moral sense. It is a well-known fact of criminal statistics and of daily life that there are very few female criminals. The apologists of the morality of women always point to this fact.

But in deciding the question as to the morality of women we have to consider not if a particular person has objectively sinned against the idea, but if the person has or has not a subjective centre of being that can enter into a relation with the idea, a relation the value of which is lowered when a sin is committed. No doubt the male criminal inherits his criminal instincts, but none the less he is conscious—in spite of theories of "moral insanity"—that by his action he has lowered the value of his claim on life. All criminals are cowardly in this matter, and there is none of them that thinks he has raised his value and his self-consciousness by his crime, or that would try to justify it to himself.

The male criminal has from birth a relation to the idea of value just like any other man, but the criminal impulse, when it succeeds in dominating him, destroys this almost completely. Woman, on the contrary, often believes herself to have acted justly when, as a matter of fact, she has just done the greatest possible act of meanness; whilst the true criminal remains mute before reproach, a women can at once give indignant expression to her astonishment and anger that any one should question her perfect right to act in this or that way. Women are convinced of their own integrity without ever having sat in judgment on it. The criminal does not, it is true, reflect on himself, but he never urges his own integrity, he is much more inclined to get rid of the thought of his integrity, because it might remind him of his guilt: and in this is the proof that he had a relation to the idea (of truth), and only objects to be reminded of his unfaithfulness to his better self. No male criminal has ever believed that his punishment was unjust. A woman, on the contrary, is convinced of the animosity of her accuser, and if she does not wish to be convinced of it, no one can persuade her that she has done wrong.

If any one talks to her it usually happens that she bursts into tears, begs for pardon, and "confesses her fault," and may really believe that she feels her guilt; but only when she desires to do so, and the outbreak of tears has given her a certain sort of satisfaction. The male criminal is callous; he does not spin round in a trice, as a woman would do in a similar instance if her accuser knew how to handle her skilfully.

The personal torture which arises from guilt, which cries aloud in its anguish at having brought such a stain upon herself, no woman knows, and an apparent exception (the penitent, who becomes a self-mortifying devotee,) will certainly prove that a woman only feels a vicarious guilt.

I am not arguing that woman is evil and anti-moral; I state that she cannot be really evil; *she is merely non-moral.*

Womanly compassion and female modesty are the two other phenomena which are generally urged by the defenders of female virtue. It is especially from womanly kindness, womanly sympathy, that the beautiful descriptions of the soul of woman have gained most support, and the final argument of all belief in the superior morality of woman is the conception of her as the hospital nurse, the tender sister. I am sorry to have to mention this point, and should not have done so, but I have been forced to do so by a verbal objection made to me, which can be easily foreseen.

It is very shortsighted of any one to consider the nurse, as a proof of the sympathy of women, because it really implies the opposite. For a man could never stand the sight of the sufferings of the sick; he would suffer so intensely that he would be completely upset and incapable of lengthy attendance on them. Any one who has watched nursing sisters is astounded at their equanimity and "sweetness" even in the presence of most terrible death throes; and it is well that it is so, for man, who cannot stand suffering and death, would make a very bad nurse. A man would want to assuage the pain and ward off death; in a word, he would want to *help*; where there is nothing to be done he is better away; it is only then that nursing is justified and that woman offers herself for it. But it would be quite wrong to regard this capacity of women in an ethical aspect.

Here it may be said that for woman the problem of solitude and society does not exist. She is well adapted for social relations (as, for instance, those of a companion or sick-nurse), simply because for her there is no transition from solitude to society. In the case of a man, the choice between solitude and society is serious when it has to be made. The woman gives up no solitude when she nurses the sick, as she would have to do were she to deserve moral credit for her action; a woman is never in a condition of solitude, and knows neither the love of it nor the fear of it. The woman is always living in a condition of fusion with all the human beings she knows, even when she is alone; she is not a "monad," for all monads are sharply marked off from other existences. Women have no definite individual limits; they are not unlimited in the sense that geniuses have no limits, being one with the whole world; they are unlimited only in the sense that they are not marked off from the common stock of mankind.

This sense of continuity with the rest of mankind is a sexual character of the female, and displays itself in the desire to touch, to be in contact with, the object of her pity; the mode in which her tenderness expresses itself is a kind of animal sense of contact. It shows the absence of the sharp line that separates one real personality from another. The woman does not respect the sorrow of her neighbour by silence; she tries to raise him from his grief by speech, feeling that she must be in physical, rather than spiritual, contact with him.

This diffused life, one of the most fundamental qualities of the female nature, is the cause of the impressibility of all women, their unreserved and shameless readiness to shed tears on the most ordinary occasion. It is not without reason that we associate wailing with women, and think little of a man who sheds tears in public. A woman weeps with those that weep and laughs with those that laugh—unless she herself is the cause of the laughter—so that the greater part of female sympathy is ready-made.

It is only women who demand pity from other people, who weep before them and claim their sympathy. This is one of the strongest pieces of evidence for the psychical shamelessness of women. A woman provokes the compassion of strangers in order to weep with them and be able to pity herself more than she already does. It is not too much to say that even when a woman weeps alone she is weeping with those that she knows would pity her and so intensifying her self-pity by the thought of the pity of others. Self-pity is eminently a female characteristic; a woman will associate herself with others, make herself the object of pity for these others, and then at once, deeply stirred, begin to weep with them about herself, the poor thing. Perhaps nothing so stirs the feeling of shame in a man as to detect in himself the impulse towards this self-pity, this state of mind in which the subject becomes the object. [. . .]

Strong evidence of the want of modesty in woman is to be derived from the fact that women dress and undress in the presence of one another with the greatest freedom, whilst men try to avoid similar circumstances. Moreover, when women are alone together, they are very ready to discuss their physical qualities, especially with regard to their attractiveness for men; whilst men, practically without exception, avoid all notice of one another's sexual characters.

I shall return to this subject again. In the meantime I wish to refer to the argument of the second chapter in this connection. One must be fully conscious of a thing before one can have a feeling of shame about it, and so differentiation is as necessary for the sense of shame as for consciousness. The female, who is only sexual, can appear to be asexual because she is sexuality itself, and so her sexuality does not stand out separately from the rest of her being, either in space or in time, as in the case of the male. Woman can give an impression of being modest because there is nothing in her to contrast with her sexuality. And so the woman is always naked or never naked—we may express it either way—never naked, because the true feeling of nakedness is impossible to her; always naked, because there is not in her the material for the sense of relativity by which she could become aware of her nakedness and so make possible the desire to cover it.

What I have been discussing depends on the actual meaning of the word "ego" to a woman. If a woman were asked what she meant by her "ego" she would certainly think of her body. Her superficies, that is the woman's ego. The ego of the female is quite correctly described by Mach in his "Anti-metaphysical Remarks."[6]

The ego of a woman is the cause of the vanity which is specific of women. The analogue of this in the male is an emanation of the set of his will towards his conception of the good, and its objective expression is a sensitiveness, a desire that no one shall call in question the possibility of attaining this supreme good. It is his personality that gives to man his value and his freedom from the conditions of time. This supreme good, which is beyond price, because, in the words of Kant, there can be found no equivalent for it, is the dignity of man.[7] Women, in spite of what Schiller has said, have no dignity, and the word "lady" was invented to supply this defect, and her pride will find its expression in what she regards as the supreme good, that is to say, in the preservation, improvement, and display of her personal beauty. The pride of the female is something quite peculiar to herself, something foreign even to the most handsome man, an obsession by her own body; a pleasure which displays itself, even in the least handsome girl, by admiring herself in the mirror, by stroking herself and playing with her own hair, but which comes to its full measure only in the effect that her body has on man. A woman has no true solitude, because she is always conscious of herself only in relation to others. The other side of the vanity of women is the desire to feel that her body is admired, or, rather, sexually coveted, by a man.

This desire is so strong that there are many women to whom it is sufficient merely to know that they are coveted.

The vanity of women is, then, always in relation to others; a woman lives only in the thoughts of others about her. The sensibility of women is directed to this. A woman never forgets that some one thought her ugly; a woman never considers herself ugly; the successes of others at the most only make her think of herself as perhaps less attractive. But no woman ever believes herself to be anything but beautiful and desirable when she looks at herself in the glass; she never accepts her own ugliness as a pitiful reality as a man would, and never ceases to try to persuade others of the contrary.

What is the source of this form of vanity, peculiar to the female? It comes from the absence of an intelligible ego, the only begetter of a constant and positive sense of value; it is, in fact, that she is devoid of a sense of personal value. As she sets no store by herself or on herself, she endeavours to attain to a value in the eyes of others by exciting their desire and admiration. The only thing which has any absolute and ultimate value in the world is the soul. "Ye are better than many sparrows"8 were Christ's words to mankind. A woman does not value herself by the constancy and freedom of her personality; but this is the only possible method for every creature possessing an ego. But if a real woman, and this is certainly the case, can only value herself at the rate of the man who has fixed his choice on her; if it is only through her husband or lover that she can attain to a value not only in social and material things, but also in her innermost nature, it follows that she possesses no personal value, she is devoid of man's sense of the value of his own personality for itself. And so women always get their sense of value from something outside themselves, from their money or estates, the number and richness of their garments, the position of their box at the opera, their children, and, above all, their husbands or lovers. When a woman is quarrelling with another woman, her final weapon, and the weapon she finds most effective and discomfiting, is to proclaim her superior social position, her wealth or title, and, above all, her youthfulness and the devotion of her husband or lover; whereas a man in similar case would lay himself open to contempt if he relied on anything except his own personal individuality.

The absence of the soul in woman may also be inferred from the following: Whilst a woman is stimulated to try to impress a man from the mere fact that he has paid no attention to her (Goethe gave this as a practical receipt), the whole life of a woman, in fact, being an expression of this side of her nature, a man, if a woman treats him rudely or indifferently, feels repelled by her. Nothing makes a man so happy as the love of a girl; even if he did not at first return her love, there is a great probability of love being aroused in him. The love of a man for whom she does not care is only a gratification of the vanity of a woman, or an awakening and rousing of slumbering desires. A woman extends her claims equally to all men on earth.

The shamelessness and heartlessness of women are shown in the way in which they talk of being loved. A man feels ashamed of being loved, because he is always in the position of being the active, free agent, and because he knows that he can never give himself entirely to love, and there is nothing about which he is so silent, even when there is no special reason for him to fear that he might compromise the lady by talking. A woman boasts about her love affairs, and parades them before other women in order to make them envious of her. Woman does not look upon a man's inclination for her so much as a tribute to her actual worth, or a deep insight into her nature, as the bestowing a value on her which she otherwise would not have, as the gift to her of an existence and essence with which she justifies herself before others.

The remark in an earlier chapter about the unfailing memory of woman for all the compliments she has ever received since childhood is explained by the foregoing facts. It is from compliments, first of all, that woman gets a sense of her "value," and that is why women expect men to be "polite." Politeness is the easiest form of pleasing a woman, and however little it costs a man it is dear to a woman, who never forgets an attention, and lives upon the most insipid flattery, even in her old age. One only remembers what possesses a value in one's eyes; it may safely be said that it is for compliments women have the most developed memory. The woman can attain a sense of value by these external aids, because she does not possess within her an inner standard of value which diminishes everything outside her. The phenomena of courtesy and chivalry are simply additional proofs that women have no souls, and that when a man is being "polite" to a woman he is simply ascribing to her the minimum sense of personal value, a form of deference to which importance is attached precisely in the measure that it is misunderstood. [. . .]

If woman had a sense of her personal value and the will to defend it against all external attacks she could not be jealous. Apparently all women are jealous, and jealousy depends on the failure to recognise the rights of others. Even the jealousy of a mother when she sees another woman's daughters married before her own depends simply on her want of the sense of justice.

Without justice there can be no society, so that jealousy is an absolutely unsocial quality. The formation of societies in reality presupposes the existence of true individuality. Woman has no faculty for the affairs of State or politics, as she has no social inclinations; and women's societies, from which men are excluded, are certain to break up after a short time. The family itself is not really a social structure; it is essentially unsocial, and men who give up their clubs and societies after marriage soon rejoin them. I had written this before the appearance of Heinrich Schurtz' valuable ethnological work, in which he shows that associations of men, and not the family, form the beginnings of society.[9]

Pascal made the wonderful remark that human beings seek society only because they cannot bear solitude and wish to forget themselves.[10] It is the fact expressed in these words which puts in harmony my earlier statement that women had not the faculty of solitude and my present statement that she is essentially unsociable.

If a woman possessed an "ego" she would have the sense of property both in her own case and that of others. The thieving instinct, however, is much more developed in men than in women. So-called "kleptomaniacs" (those who steal without necessity) are almost exclusively women. Women understand power and riches but not personal property. When the thefts of female kleptomaniacs are discovered, the women defend themselves by saying that it appeared to them as if everything belonged to them. It is chiefly women who use circulating libraries, especially those who could quite well afford to buy quantities of books; but, as matter of fact, they are not more strongly attracted by what they have bought than by what they have borrowed. In all these matters the relation between individuality and society comes into view; just as a man must have personality himself to appreciate the personalities of others, so also he must acquire a sense of personal right in his own property to respect the rights of others.

One's name and a strong devotion to it are even more dependent on personality than is the sense of property. The facts that confront us with reference to this are so salient that it is extraordinary to find so little notice taken of them. Women are not bound to their names with any strong bond. When they marry they give up their own name and assume that of their husband without any sense of loss. They allow their husbands and lovers to call them by new names, delighting in them; and even when a woman marries a man that she does not love, she has never been known to suffer any psychical shock at the change of name. The name is a symbol of individually; it is only amongst the lowest races on the face of the earth, such as the bushmen of South Africa, that there are no personal names, because amongst such as these the desire for distinguishing individuals from the general stock is not felt. The fundamental namelessness of the woman is simply a sign of her undifferentiated personality.

An important observation may be mentioned here and may be confirmed by every one. Whenever a man enters a place where a woman is, and she observes him, or hears his step, or even only guesses he is near, she becomes another person. Her expression and her pose change with incredible swiftness; she "arranges her fringe" and her bodice, and rises, or pretends to be engrossed in her work. She is full of a half-shameless, half-nervous expectation. In many cases one is only in doubt as to whether she is blushing for her shameless laugh, or laughing over her shameless blushing.

The soul, personality, character—as Schopenhauer with marvellous sight recognised—are identical with free-will.[11] And as the female has no ego, she has no free-will. Only a creature with no will of its own, no character in the highest sense, could be so easily influenced by the mere proximity to a man as woman is, who remains in functional dependence on him instead of in free relationship to him. Woman is the best medium, the male her best hypnotiser. For this reason alone it is inconceivable why women can be considered good as doctors; for many doctors admit that their principal work up to the present—and it will always be the same—lies in the suggestive influence on their patients.

The female is uniformly more easily hypnotised than the male throughout the animal world, and it may be seen from the following how closely hypnotic phenomena are related to the most ordinary events. I have already described, in discussing female sympathy, how easy it is for laughter or tears to be induced in females. How impressed she is by everything in the newspapers! What a martyr she is to the silliest superstitions! How eagerly she tries every remedy recommended by her friends!

Whoever is lacking in character is lacking in convictions. The female, therefore, is credulous, uncritical, and quite unable to understand Protestantism. Christians are Catholics or Protestants before they are baptized, but, none the less, it would be unfair to describe Catholicism as feminine simply because it suits women better. The distinction between the Catholic and Protestant dispositions is a side of characterology that would require separate treatment.

It has been exhaustively proved that the female is soulless and possesses neither ego nor individuality, personality nor freedom, character nor will. This conclusion is of the highest significance in psychology. It implies that the psychology of the male and of the female must be treated separately. A purely empirical representation of the psychic life of the female is possible; in the case of the male, all the psychic life must be considered with reference to the ego, as Kant foresaw.

NOTES

1. Sigmund Freud, letter to David Abrahamsen, quoted in Abrahamsen's *The Mind and Death of a Genius* (New York: Columbia University Press, 1946), p. 43.

2. See *Jews and Gender: Responses to Otto Weininger*, ed. Nancy A. Harrowitz and Barbara Hyams (Philadelphia: Temple University Press, 1995).

3. The conception reflects Weininger's definition of a monad as "a potential or actual individuality." *Sex and Character*, part 2, chap. 12 (London: William Heinemann; New York: G. P. Putnam's Sons, 1906).

4. A henid is Weininger's coined term for a stage of primitive thought in which "it is impossible to distinguish perception and sensation as two analytically separate factors." *Sex and Character*, part 2, chap. 3.

5. Sophie Germain (1776–1831), French mathematician and philosopher. Mary Somerville (1780–1872), British scientist and author of *The Connection of the Physical Sciences* (1834) and other works.

6. Weininger refers to the opening chapter ("Antimetaphysische Vorbemerkungen") of Ernst Mach (1838–1916), *Beiträge zur Analyse der Empfindungen* (1886), translated as *Contributions to the Analysis of the Sensations* (1897).

7. Immanuel Kant (1724–1804), *Grundlegung zur Metaphysik der Sitten* (1785; translated as *Groundwork of the Metaphysics of Morals*), sec. 2.

8. Luke 12:7.

9. Heinrich Schurtz (1863–1903), *Altersklassen und Männerbünde* (1902).

10. Blaise Pascal (1623–1662), *Pensées* (1670), part 2, chap. 1 ("La misère de l'homme").

11. See Arthur Schopenhauer, *The World as Will and Representation* (1819), passim.

10.

THE INEVITABILITY
OF PATRIARCHY

(1973)

Steven Goldberg

Steven Goldberg (b. 1941) is a professor of sociology at City College of the City University of New York. In his controversial treatise *The Inevitability of Patriarchy* (1973), Goldberg argues that men are physiologically "driven to attain 'dominance.'" All human societies, in his estimation, have been based on this dominance, and there is a danger that a society will become extinct if social equality is pressed beyond certain limits. Goldberg therefore suggests that women should be trained not to compete with men, for this will only lead to frustration as they encounter a male's "natural" dominance.[1] Goldberg wrote a follow-up to this work, *Why Men Rule* (1993), largely devoted to a rebuttal of the critics of his first book. He has also written *When Wish Replaces Thought: Why So Much of What You*

Source: Steven Goldberg, *The Inevitability of Patriarchy* (New York: William Morrow, 1973), pp. 103–14.

Believe Is False (Prometheus Books, 1991) and
Fads and Fallacies in the Social Sciences (2003).
The following excerpt from *The Inevitability of
Patriarchy* appears in the chapter titled "Male
Aggression and the Attainment of Power,
Authority, and Status."

IF MALE AGGRESSION WERE THE ONLY DIFFERENCE . . .

*H*aving discussed the universality of patriarchy, male dominance, and male attainment of high-status roles and the biological factors that are relevant to these universals, we are
now prepared to examine the mechanisms that *require* these biological
factors to be manifested in these social institutions. In discussing these
mechanisms we shall proceed as if the only inherent difference
between men and women were their different hormonal systems, which
leads to an inherent aggression advantage for the male. This does not
imply that I doubt that there are positive female biological forces
underlying the woman's extraordinary sensitivity and emotional
powers or the mother's attentiveness to her infant and her protective
reaction to her infant's vulnerability. Eleanor Maccoby has suggested
that "if you try to divide child training among males and females we
might find out that females need to do it and males don't."[2] Such biological imperatives would have enormous significance in the development of male and female roles. Every society must care for its young
and, if the need to care for and protect the young is greater in the female
than the male, this would be reflected in the social expectations of men
and women. If one accepts this female biological factor, he could utilize it to explain the universal sex-role differences I explain by differences in aggression and could use the same lines of reasoning I do
without mentioning aggression. Likewise it is not unlikely that the
neural factors underlying the male's sexual dominance come into play
in social contacts between men and women; there may even be a

female desire for men to dominate ("take the lead") that is a secondary manifestation of the neural factors directly relevant to female sexuality. Biological evidence indicates that there is a strong possibility that such dominance and submission factors exist in male and female physiologies, but, since such factors need not exist for the theory presented here to be correct, we will assume that they do not exist. If they do exist, of course, the theory presented here can be only strengthened.

Quite possibly all of these factors lead to the universal institutions we have discussed. *Aggression, however, is the only sexual difference that we can explain with direct (as opposed to convincing, but hypothetical) biological evidence.* Nothing is lost because the inevitable social manifestations of sexual differences in aggression are sufficient to explain the inevitability of patriarchy, male dominance, and male attainment of high-status roles. If the other biological directives do exist we have an example of a situation in which a factor (hormonal aggression) is *sufficient* to describe a reality (institutionalized sex differences), but not *necessary*. Maternal attentiveness, a male need to dominate, or a female desire for male political dominance would be sufficient even if there were no hormonal aggression differences, but none of these need exist for the theory proposed here to be correct.

Therefore, *we are assuming throughout this chapter that there are no differences between men and women except in the hormonal system that renders the man more aggressive.* This alone would explain patriarchy, male dominance, and male attainment of high-status roles; for the male hormonal system gives men an insuperable "head start" toward attaining those roles which any society associates with leadership or high status as long as the roles are not ones that males are biologically incapable of filling.

AGGRESSION AND ATTAINMENT

In other words, I believe that in the past we have been looking in the wrong direction for the answer to the question of why every society rewards male roles with higher status than it does female roles (even when the male tasks in one society are the female tasks in another). While it is true that men are always in the positions of authority from which status tends to be defined, male roles are not given high status primarily *because* men fill these roles; men fill these roles because their biological aggression "advantage" can be manifested *in any non-child related area rewarded by high states in any society.* (Again: the line of reasoning used in this book demonstrates only that the biological factors we discuss would make the social institutions we discuss inevitable and does not preclude the existence of other forces also leading in the same direction; there may be a biologically based tendency for women to prefer male leadership, but there need not be for male attainment of leadership and high-status roles to be inevitable.) As we shall see, this aggression "advantage" can be most manifested and can most enable men to reap status rewards *not* in those relatively homogeneous, collectivist primitive societies in which both male and female must play similar economic roles if the society is to survive or in the monarchy (which guarantees an occasional female leader); this biological factor will be given freest play in the complex, relatively individualistic, bureaucratic, democratic society which, of necessity, must emphasize organizational authority and in which social mobility is relatively free of traditional barriers to advancement. There were more female heads of state in the first two-thirds of the sixteenth century than in the first two-thirds of the twentieth.

The mechanisms involved here are easily seen if we examine any roles that males have attained by channeling their aggression toward such attainment. We will assume for now that equivalent women could *perform* the tasks of roles as well as men if they could attain the roles.[3] Here we can speak of the corporation president, the union leader, the governor, the chairman of an association, or any other role or position for which aggression is a precondition for attainment. Now the environmentalist and the feminist will say that the fact that all such roles are nearly always filled by men is attributable not to male aggression but to the fact that women have not been allowed to enter the competitive race to attain these positions, that they have been told that these positions are in male areas, and that girls are socialized away from competing with boys in general. Women *are* socialized in this way, but again we must ask why. If innate male aggression has nothing to do with male attainment of positions of authority and status in the political, academic, scientific, or financial spheres, if aggression has nothing to do with the reasons why *every* society socializes girls away from those areas which are given high status and away from competition in general, then why is it never the *girls* in any society who are socialized toward these areas, why is it never the nonbiological roles played by women that have high status, why is it always boys who are told to compete, and why do women never "force" men into the low-status, nonmaternal roles that women play in every society?

These questions pose no problem if we acknowledge a male aggression that enables men to attain any nonbiological role given high status by any society. For one need merely consider the result of a society's *not* socializing women away from competitions with men, from its *not* directing girls toward roles women are more capable of playing than are men or roles with status low enough that men will not strive for them. No doubt some women would be aggressive enough to succeed in competitions with men and there would be considerably more women in high-status positions than there are now. But most women would lose in such competitive struggles with men (because men have the aggression advantage) and so most women would be forced to live adult lives as failures in areas in which the society had *wanted them to succeed*. It is women, far more than men, who would never allow a situation in which girls were socialized in such a way that the vast majority of them were doomed to adult lifetimes of failure to live up to their own expectations. Now I have no doubt that there is a biological factor that gives women the desire to emphasize maternal and nurturance roles, but the point here is that we can accept the feminist assumption that there is no female propensity of this sort and still see that a society must socialize women away from roles that men will attain through their aggression. For if women did not develop an alternative set of criteria for success their sense of their own competence would suffer intolerably. It is undeniable that the resulting different values and expectations that are attached to men and women will tend to work against the aggressive woman while they work for the man who is no more aggressive. But this is the unavoidable result of the fact that most men are more aggressive than most women so that this woman, who is as aggressive as the average man, but more aggressive than most women, is an exception. Furthermore, even if the sense of competence of each sex did not necessitate society's attaching to each sex values and expectations based on those qualities possessed by each sex, observation of the majority of each sex by the population would "automatically" lead to these values and expectations being attached to men and women.

SOCIALIZATION'S CONFORMATION
TO BIOLOGICAL REALITY

Socialization is the process by which society prepares children for adulthood. The way in which its goals conform to the reality of biology is seen quite clearly when we consider the method in which testosterone generates male aggression (testosterone's serially developing nature). Preadolescent boys and girls have roughly equal testosterone levels, yet young boys are far more aggressive than young girls. Eva Figes has used this observation to dismiss incorrectly the possibility of a hormone-aggression association.[4] Now it is quite probable that the boy is more aggressive than the girl for a purely biological reason. We have seen that it is simplistic to speak simply in terms of hormone levels and that there is evidence of male-female differences in the behavior of infants shortly after birth (when differential socialization is not a plausible explanation of such differences). The fetal alteration of the boy's brain by the testosterone that was generated by his testes has probably left him far more sensitive to the aggression-related properties of the testosterone that is present during boyhood than the girl, who did not receive such alteration. But let us for the moment assume that this is not the case. This does not at all reduce the importance of the hormonal factor. For even if the boy is more aggressive than the girl only because the society allows him to be, the boy's socialization still flows from society's acknowledging biological reality. Let us consider what would happen if girls have the same innate aggression as boys and if a society did not socialize girls away from aggressive competitions. Perhaps half of the third-grade baseball team would be female. As many girls as boys would frame their expectations in masculine values and girls would develop not their feminine abilities but their masculine ones. During adolescence, however, the same assertion of the male chromosomal program that causes the boys to grow beards raises their testosterone level, and their potential for aggression, to a level far above that of the adolescent woman. If society did not teach young girls that beating boys at competitions was unfeminine (behavior inappropriate for a woman), if it did not socialize them away from the political and economic areas in which aggression leads to attainment, these girls would grow into adulthood with self-images based not on succeeding in areas for which biology has left them better prepared than men, but on competitions that most women could not win. If women did not develop feminine qualities as girls (assuming that such qualities do not spring automatically from female biology) then they would be forced to deal with the world in the aggressive terms of men. They would lose every source of power their feminine abilities now give them and they would gain nothing. (Likewise, if there is a physiological difference between men and women which generates dimorphic behavior in the feelings elicited by an infant, social values and socialization will conform to this fact. They will conform both because observation by the population of men and women will preclude the development of values which ignore the physiological difference and because, even if such values could develop, they would make life intolerable for the vast majority of males, who would feel the tension between social expectation and the dearth of maternal feelings, and the vast majority of females, whose physiologically generated feelings toward the infant would be frustrated.)

DISCRIMINATION OF A SORT

If one is convinced that sexual biology gives the male an advantage in aggression, competitiveness, and dominance, but he does not believe that it engenders in men and women different propensities, cognitive aptitudes, and modes of perception, and if he considers it discrimination when male aggression leads to attainment of position even when aggression is not relevant to the task to be performed, then the unavoidable conclusion is that discrimination so defined is unavoidable. Even if one is convinced from the discussion in the following sections that the differing biological substrates that underlie the mental apparatus of men and women *do* engender different propensities, cognitive aptitudes, and modes of perception, he will probably agree that the relevance of this to male attainment of male roles is small when compared to the importance of male biological aggression to attainment. Innate tendencies to specific aptitudes *would* indicate that at any given level of competence there will be more men than women or vice versa (depending on the qualities relevant to the task) and that the very best will, in all probability, come from the sex whose potentials are relevant to the task. Nonetheless, drastic sexual differences in occupational and authority roles reflect male aggression and society's acknowledgment of it far more than they do differences in aptitudes, yet they are still inevitable.

In addition, even if artificial means were used to place large numbers of women in authority positions, it is doubtful that stability could be maintained. Even in our present male bureaucracies problems arise whenever a subordinate is more aggressive than his superior and, if the more aggressive executive is not allowed to rise in the bureaucracy, delicate psychological adjustments must be made. Such adjustments are also necessary when a male bureaucrat has a female superior. When such situations are rare exceptions adjustments can be made without any great instability occurring, particularly if the woman in the superior position complements her aggression with sensitivity and femininity. It would seem likely, however, that if women shared equally in power at each level of the bureaucracy, chaos would result for two reasons. Even if we consider the bureaucracy as a closed system, the excess of male aggression would soon manifest itself either in men moving quickly up the hierarchy or in a male refusal to acknowledge female authority. But a bureaucracy is not a closed system, and the discrepancy between male dominance in private life and bureaucratic female dominance (from the point of view of the male whose superior is a woman) would soon engender chaos. Consider that even the present minute minority of women in high authority positions expend enormous amounts of energy trying *not* to project the commanding authority that is seen as the mark of a good male executive. It is true that the manner in which aggression is manifested will be affected by the values of the society in general and the nature of the field of competition in particular; aggression in an academic environment is camouflaged far more than in the executive arena. While a desire for control and power and a single-mindedness of purpose are no doubt relevant, here aggression is not easily defined. One might inject the theoretical argument that women could attain positions of authority and leadership by countering the male's advantage in aggression with feminine abilities. Perhaps, but the equivalents of the executive positions in every area of suprafamilial life in every society have been attained by men, and there seems no reason to believe that, suddenly, feminine means will be capable of neutralizing male aggression in these areas. And, in any case, an emphasis on feminine abilities is hardly what the feminists desire. All of this can be seen in a considerably more optimistic light, from the point of view of most women, if one considers that the biological abilities possessed only by women are complemented by biologically generated propensities directing women to roles that can be filled only by women. But it is still the same picture.

FIFTY-ONE PERCENT OF THE VOTE

Likewise, one who predicates political action on a belief that a society is oppressive until half of the positions of authority are filled by women faces the insuperable task of overcoming a male dominance that has forced every political and economic system to conform to it and that may be maintained as much by the refusal of women to elect widespread female leadership as by male aggression and ability. No doubt an exceptional configuration of factors will someday result in a woman's being elected president, but if one considers a society "sexist" until it no longer associates authority primarily with men and until a woman leader is no longer an exception, then he must resign himself to the certainty that all societies will be "sexist" forever.[5] Feminists make much of the fact that women constitute a slight majority of voters but in doing so make the assumption that it is possible to convince the women who constitute this majority to elect equal female leadership. This is a dubious assumption since the members of a society will inevitably associate authority with males if patriarchy and male dominance are biologically inevitable. It would be even more dubious if there is an innate tendency for women to favor men who "take the lead." However, proceeding from this assumption and assuming that the feminists were successful, it is a sure bet that democracy—which obviously is not biologically inevitable (not patriarchy, which is)—would be eliminated as large numbers of males battled for the relatively small numbers of positions of power from which the rules that govern the battle are made. In any real society, of course, women can have the crucial effect of mobilizing political power to achieve particular goals and of electing those men who are motivated by relatively more life-sustaining values than other men just as mothers have the crucial effect of coloring and humanizing the values of future male leaders.

"OPPRESSION"

All of this indicates that the theoretical model that conceives of male success in attaining positions of status, authority, and leadership as *oppression* of the female is incorrect if only because it sees male aggressive energies as *directed toward* females and sees the institutional mechanisms that flow from the fact of male aggression as *directed toward* "oppressing" women. In reality these male energies are directed toward attainment of desired positions and toward succeeding in whatever areas a particular society considers important. The fact that women lose out in these competitions, so that the sex-role expectations of a society would have to become different for men and women even if they were not different for other reasons, is an inevitable byproduct of the reality of the male's aggression advantage and not the cause, purpose, or primary function of it. In other words, men who attain the more desired roles and positions do so because they channel their aggression advantage toward such attainment; whether the losers in such competitions are other men or women is important only in that—because so few women succeed in these competitions—the society will attach different expectations to men and women (making it more difficult for the exceptional, aggressive woman to attain such positions even when her aggression is equal to that of the average man). Perhaps one could at least begin to defend a model that stressed "oppression" if he dealt only with male dominance in dyadic relationships; here male energies are directed toward the female, but to call that which is inevitable "oppression" would seem to confuse more than clarify and, if one feels that male dominance is "oppressive," this model offers an illusory hope of change where there is no possibility of change. Male dominance is the emotional resolution (felt by both the man and the woman) of the difference between a man and a woman in the biological factors relevant to aggression; male authority in dyadic relationships, and the socialization of boys and girls toward this male authority, is societal confirmation to this biological difference and a result of society's attempting to most smoothly and effectively utilize this difference.

NOTES

1. For an incisive review of this book, see Eleanor E. Maccoby, "Sex in the Social Order," *Science* 182 (November 2, 1973): 469–71.

2. [Eleanor E. Maccoby, "Woman's Intellect," in *The Potential of Women*, ed. Seymour M. Earber and Roger H. Wilson (New York: McGraw-Hill, 1963), p. 44.]

3. [I assume this for the present in order to demonstrate that these will be male roles even if women can *perform* these roles as well as men when they can attain them. It should be pointed out, however, that the line between attainment and performance is not always clear in a bureaucratic society or in leadership in any society; much of the performance of an executive or leader concerns his ability to maintain the authority which his position gives him. Therefore, it is possible that the greater innate male aggression, particularly when opposed to the lesser innate female aggression, leads to *performance* by the male which is superior to that of the female. This does not, of course, mean that the male at any level of the hierarchy has an advantage over the exceptional woman who was aggressive enough to attain a comparable position, but it might indicate that men in general have an innate advantage over women in general which is relevant to the *performance* of bureaucratic and leadership roles.]

4. [Eva Figes, *Patriarchal Attitudes* (Greenwich, CT: Fawcett World, 1971), p. 8.]

5. [I grant that, since we have not hypothesized a direct male biological need to lead (but only an aggression advantage that can be manifested in this area), theoretically a situation could develop in which all leadership were given low status so that men chose not to use their aggression to attain positions of political leadership; in such a situation a nonpatriarchal society could develop. It is inconceivable that such a situation could ever develop, but if it did those who now complain that males fill the positions of leadership would then complain that women did not attain whatever roles males chose to attain by virtue of their superior aggression.]

Part 4
WOMEN AND INTELLECT

11.

MENTAL DIFFERENCES
BETWEEN MEN AND WOMEN

(1887)

George J. Romanes

George John Romanes (1848–1894) was born
in Canada but lived most of his life in England.
He studied natural science at Cambridge University and at University College, London,
where he became acquainted with Charles
Darwin. Family wealth allowed him to devote
all his energies to research. Romanes did pioneering work in invertebrate biology as well as
in the physiology and psychology of animals
(including human beings), embodied in such
works as *Animal Intelligence* (1882), *Mental
Evolution in Animals* (1883), and *Mental Evolution in Man* (1888). Much of his work was, however, criticized as lacking in scientific rigor and
was quickly superseded by more objective
studies. He became a leading advocate of the
theory of evolution and wrote the three-
volume treatise *Darwin, and After Darwin*

Source: George J. Romanes, "Mental Differences between Men and Women," *Nineteenth Century*
21, no. 5 (May 1887): 654–58, 659–60, 661–63, 664–66.

(1892–1897). In "Mental Differences between Men and Women" (*Nineteenth Century,* **May 1887), excerpted below, Romanes asserts that the intellectual inferiority of women is based upon a smaller than average brain-weight, that women are inferior in judgment and more under the sway of emotions, and that women's lack of distinguished intellectual and artistic achievement is the product of natural inferiority and not "artificial restraints."**

S eeing that the average brain-weight of women is about five ounces less than that of men, on merely anatomical grounds we should be prepared to expect a marked inferiority of intellectual power in the former.[1] Moreover, as the general physique of women is less robust than that of men—and therefore less able to sustain the fatigue of serious or prolonged brain action—we should also on physiological grounds be prepared to entertain a similar anticipation. In actual fact we find that the inferiority displays itself most conspicuously in a comparative absence of originality, and this more especially in the higher levels of intellectual work. In her powers of acquisition the woman certainly stands nearer to the man than she does in her powers of creative thought, although even as regards the former there is a marked difference. The difference, however, is one which does not assert itself till the period of adolescence—young girls being, indeed, usually more inquisitive than boys of the same age, as is proved by recent educational experiences both in this country and in America. But as soon as the brain, and with it the organism as a whole, reaches the stage of full development, it becomes apparent that there is a greater power of amassing knowledge on the part of the male. Whether we look to the general average or to the intellectual giants of both sexes, we are similarly met with the general fact that a woman's information is less wide and deep and thorough than that of a man. What we regard as a highly cultured woman is usually one who has read largely but superficially; and even in the few instances that can be quoted of extraordinary female industry—which on account of their rarity stand out as exceptions to prove the rule—we find a long distance between them and the much more numerous instances of profound erudition among men. As musical executants, however, I think that equality may be fairly asserted.

But it is in original work, as already observed, that the disparity is most conspicuous. For it is a matter of ordinary comment that in no one department of creative thought can women be said to have at all approached men, save in fiction. Yet in poetry, music, and painting, if not also in history, philosophy, and science, the field has always been open to both.[2] For, as I will presently show, the disabilities under which women have laboured with regard to education, social opinion, and so forth, have certainly not been sufficient to explain this general dearth among them of the products of creative genius.

Lastly, with regard to judgment, I think there can be no real question that the female mind stands considerably below the male. It is much more apt to take superficial views of circumstances calling for decision, and also to be guided by less impartiality. Undue influence is more frequently exercised from the side of the emotions; and, in general, all the elements which go to constitute what is understood by a characteristically judicial mind are of comparatively feeble development. Of course here, as elsewhere, I am speaking of average standards. It would be easy to find multitudes of instances where women display better judgment than men, just as in the analogous cases of learning and creative work. But that as a general rule the judgment of women is inferior to that of men has been a matter of universal recognition from the earliest times. The man has always been regarded as the rightful lord of the woman, to whom she is by nature subject, as both mentally and physically the weaker vessel; and when in individual cases these relations happen to be inverted, the accident becomes a favourite theme for humorists—thus showing that in the general estimation such a state of matters is regarded as incongruous.

But if woman has been a loser in the intellectual race as regards acquisition, origination, and judgment, she has gained, even on the intellectual side, certain very conspicuous advantages. First among these we must place refinement of the senses, or higher evolution of sense-organs. Next we must place rapidity of perception, which no doubt in part arises from this higher evolution of the sense-organs—or, rather, both arise from a greater refinement of nervous organisation. Houdin, who paid special attention to the acquirement of rapidity in acts of complex perception, says he has known ladies who, while seeing another lady "pass at full speed in a carriage, could analyse her toilette from her bonnet to her shoes, and be able to describe not only the fashion and the quality of the stuffs, but also to say if the lace were real or only machine made."[3] Again, reading implies enormously intricate processes of perception, both of the sensuous and intellectual order; and I have tried a series of experiments, wherein reading was chosen as a test of the rapidity of perception in different persons. Having seated a number of well educated individuals round a table, I presented to them successively the same paragraph of a book, which they were each to read as rapidly as they could, ten seconds being allowed for twenty lines. As soon as time was up I removed the paragraph, immediately after which the reader wrote down all that he or she could remember of it. Now, in these experiments, where every one read the same paragraph as rapidly as possible, I found that the palm was usually carried off by the ladies. Moreover, besides being able to read quicker, they were better able to remember what they had just read—that is, to give a better account of the paragraph as a whole. One lady, for example, could read exactly four times as fast as her husband, and could then give a better account even of that portion of the paragraph which alone he had had time to get through. For the consolation of such husbands, however, I may add that rapidity of perception as thus tested is no evidence of what may be termed the deeper qualities of mind—some of my slowest readers being highly distinguished men.

Lastly, rapidity of perception leads to rapidity of thought, and this finds expression on the one hand in what is apt to appear as almost intuitive insight, and on the other hand in that nimbleness of mother-wit which is usually so noticeable and often so brilliant an endowment of the feminine intelligence, whether it displays itself in tact, in repartee, or in the general alacrity of a vivacious mind.

Turning now to the emotions, we find that in woman, as contrasted with man, these are almost always less under control of the will—more apt to break away, as it were, from the restraint of reason, and to overwhelm the mental chariot in disaster. Whether this tendency displays itself in the overmastering form of hysteria, or in the more ordinary form of comparative childishness, ready annoyance, and a generally unreasonable temper—in whatever form this supremacy of emotion displays itself, we recognise it as more of a feminine than a masculine characteristic. The crying of a woman is not held to betray the same depth of feeling as the sobs of a man; and the petty forms of resentment which belong to what is known as a "shrew," or a "scold," are only to be met with among those daughters of Eve who prove themselves least agreeable to the sons of Adam. Coyness and caprice are very general peculiarities, and we may add, as kindred traits, personal vanity, fondness of display, and delight in the sunshine of admiration. There is also, as compared with the masculine mind, a greater desire for emotional excitement of all kinds, and hence a greater liking for society, pageants, and even for what are called "scenes," provided these are not of a kind to alarm her no less characteristic timidity. Again, in the opinion of Mr. Lecky, with which I partly concur:

> In the courage of endurance they are commonly superior; but their passive courage is not so much fortitude which bears and defies, as resignation which bears and bends. In the ethics of intellect they are decidedly inferior. They very rarely love truth, though they love passionately what they call "the truth," or opinions which they have derived from others, and hate vehemently those who differ from them. They are little capable of impartiality or doubt; their thinking is chiefly a mode of feeling; though very generous in their acts, they are rarely generous in their opinions or in their judgments. They persuade rather than convince, and value belief as a source of consolation rather than as a faithful expression of the reality of things.[4]

But, of course, as expressed in the well-known lines from *Marmion*,[5] there is another side to this picture, and, in now taking leave of all these elements of weakness, I must state my honest conviction that they are in chief part due to women as a class not having hitherto enjoyed the same educational advantages as men. [. . .]

So much, then, for the intellect and emotions. Coming lastly to the will, I have already observed that this exercises less control over the emotions in women than in men. We rarely find in women that firm tenacity of purpose and determination to overcome obstacles which is characteristic of what we call a manly mind. When a woman is urged to any prolonged or powerful exercise of volition, the prompting cause is usually to be found in the emotional side of her nature, whereas in man we may generally observe that the intellectual is alone sufficient to supply the needed motive. Moreover, even in those lesser displays of volitional activity which are required in close reading, or in studious thought, we may note a similar deficiency. In other words, women are usually less able to concentrate their attention; their minds are more prone to what is called "wandering," and we seldom find that they have specialised their studies or pursuits to the same extent as is usual among men. This comparative weakness of will is further manifested by the frequency among women of what is popularly termed indecision of character. The proverbial fickleness of *la donna mobile*[6] is due quite as much to vacillation of will as to other unstable qualities of mental constitution. The ready firmness of decision which belongs by nature to the truly masculine mind is very rarely to be met with in the feminine; while it is not an unusual thing to find among women indecision of character so habitual and pronounced as to become highly painful to themselves—leading to timidity and diffidence in adopting almost any line of conduct where issues of importance are concerned, and therefore leaving them in the condition, as they graphically expressed it, of not knowing their own minds. [. . .]

I will now pass on to consider the causes which have probably operated in producing all these mental differences between men and women. We have already seen that differences of the same kind occur throughout the whole mammalian series, and therefore we must begin by looking below the conditions of merely human life for the original causes of these differences in their most general form. Nor have we far to seek. The Darwinian principles of selection—both natural and sexual—if ever they have operated in any department of organic nature, must certainly have operated here. Thus, to quote Darwin himself:—

> Amongst the half-human progenitors of man, and amongst savages, there have been struggles between the males during many generations for the possession of the females. But mere bodily strength and size would do little for victory, unless associated with courage, perseverance, and determined energy. . . . To avoid enemies or to attack them with success, to capture wild animals, and to fashion weapons, requires reason, invention, or imagination. . . . These latter faculties, as well as the former, will have been developed in man partly through sexual selection—that is, through the contest of rival males—and partly through natural selection—that is, from success in the general struggle for life; and as in both cases the struggle will have been during maturity, the characters gained will have been transmitted more fully to the male than to the female offspring. . . . Thus man has ultimately become superior to woman. It is, indeed, fortunate that the law of the equal transmission of characters to both sexes prevails with mammals; otherwise it is probable that man would have become as superior in mental endowment to woman as the peacock is in ornamental plumage to the pea-hen.[7]

Similarly, Mr. Francis Galton writes:—

> The fundamental and intrinsic differences of character that exist in individuals are well illustrated by those that distinguish the two sexes, and which begin to assert themselves even in the nursery, where all children are treated alike. One notable peculiarity in the woman is that she is capricious and coy, and has less straightforwardness than the man. It is the same with the female of every species. . . . [Were it not so] the drama of courtship, with its prolonged strivings and doubtful success, would be cut quite short, and

the race would degenerate through the absence of that sexual selection for which the protracted preliminaries of love-making give opportunity. The willy-nilly disposition of the female is as apparent in the butterfly as in the man, and must have been continually favoured from the earliest stages of animal evolution down to the present time. Coyness and caprice have in consequence become a heritage of the sex, together with a cohort of allied weaknesses and petty deceits, that men have come to think venial, and even amiable, in women, but which they would not tolerate among themselves.[8]

We see, then, that the principles of selection have thus determined greater strength, both of body and mind, on the part of male animals throughout the whole mammalian series; and it would certainly have been a most unaccountable fact if any exception to this rule had occurred in the case of mankind. For, as regards natural selection, it is in the case of mankind that the highest premium has been placed upon the mental faculties—or, in other words, it is here that natural selection has been most busy in the evolution of intelligence—and therefore, as Mr. Darwin remarks, we can only regard it as a fortunate accident of inheritance that there is not now a greater difference between the intelligence of men and women than we actually find. Again, as regards sexual selection, it is evident that here also the psychologically segregating influences must have been exceptionally strong in the case of our own species, seeing that in all the more advanced stages of civilisation—or in the stages where mental evolution is highest, and, therefore, mental differences most pronounced—marriages are determined quite as much with reference to psychical as to physical endowments; and as men always admire in women what they regard as distinctively feminine qualities of mind, while women admire in men the distinctively masculine, sexual selection, by thus acting directly as well as indirectly on the mental qualities of both, is constantly engaged in moulding the minds of each upon a different pattern.

Such, then, I take to be the chief, or at least the original, causes of the mental differences in question. But besides these there are sundry other causes all working in the same direction. For example, as the principles of selection have everywhere operated in the direction of endowing the weaker partner with that kind of physical beauty which comes from slenderness and grace, it follows that there has been everywhere a general tendency to impart to her a comparative refinement of organisation; and in no species has this been the case in so high a degree as in man. Now, it is evident from what has been said in an earlier part of this paper, that general refinement of this kind indirectly affects the mind in many ways. Again, as regards the analogous, though coarser, distinction of bodily strength, it is equally evident that their comparative inferiority in this respect, while itself one of the results of selection, becomes in turn the cause of their comparative timidity, sense of dependence, and distrust of their own powers on the part of women, considered as a class. Hence, also, their comparative feebleness of will and vacillation of purpose: they are always dimly conscious of lacking the muscular strength which, in the last resort, and especially in primitive stages of culture, is the measure of executive capacity. Hence, also, their resort to petty arts and petty ways for the securing of their aims; and hence, in large measure, their strongly religious bias. The masculine character, being accustomed to rely upon its own strength, is self-central and self-contained: to it the need of external aid, even of a supernatural kind, is not felt to be so urgent as it is to the feminine character, whose only hope is in the stronger arm of another. "The position of man is to stand, of woman to lean"; and although it may be hard for even a manly nature to contemplate the mystery of life and the approach of death with a really stoic calm, at least this is not so impossible as it is for the more shrinking and emotional nature of a woman. Lastly, from her abiding sense of weakness and consequent dependence, there also arises in woman that deeply-rooted desire to please the opposite sex which, beginning in the terror of a slave, has ended in the devotion of a wife. [. . .]

We see [. . .] that with advancing civilisation the theoretical equality of the sexes becomes more and more a matter of general recognition, but that the natural inequality continues to be forced upon the observation of the public mind; and chiefly on this account—

although doubtless also on account of traditional usage—the education of women continues to be, as a general rule, widely different from
that of men. And this difference is not merely in the positive direction
of laying greater stress on psychological embellishment: it extends
also in the negative direction of sheltering the female mind from all
those influences of a striving and struggling kind, which constitute the
practical schooling of the male intellect. Woman is still regarded by
public opinion all the world over as a psychological plant of tender
growth, which needs to be protected from the ruder blasts of social life
in the conservatories of civilisation. And, from what has been said in
the earlier part of this paper, it will be apparent that in this practical
judgment I believe public opinion to be right. I am, of course, aware
that there is a small section of the public—composed for the most part
of persons who are not accustomed to the philosophical analysis of
facts—which argues that the conspicuous absence of women in the
field of intellectual work is due to the artificial restraints imposed upon
them by all the traditional forms of education; that if we could suddenly make a leap of progress in this respect, and allow women everywhere to compete on fair and equal terms with men, then, under these
altered circumstances of social life, women would prove themselves
the intellectual compeers of man.

But the answer to this argument is almost painfully obvious.
Although it is usually a matter of much difficulty to distinguish
between nature and nurture, or between the faults of inborn faculty
and those of acquired knowledge, in the present instance no such difficulty obtains. Without again recurring to the anatomical and physiological considerations which bar *à priori* any argument for the natural
equality of the sexes, and without remarking that the human female
would but illustrate her own deficiency of rational development by
supposing that any exception to the general laws of evolution can have
been made in her favour—without dwelling on any such antecedent
considerations, it is enough to repeat that in many departments of
intellectual work the field *has* been open, and equally open, to both
sexes. If to this it is answered that the traditional usages of education

lead to a higher average of culture among men, thus furnishing them with a better vantage-ground for the origin of individual genius, we have only to add that the strong passion of genius is not to be restrained by any such minor accidents of environment. Women by tens of thousands have enjoyed better educational as well as better social advantages than a Burns, a Keats, or a Faraday; and yet we have neither heard their voices nor seen their work.

If, again, to this it be rejoined that the female mind has been unjustly dealt with in the past, and cannot now be expected all at once to throw off the accumulated disabilities of ages—that the long course of shameful neglect to which the selfishness of man has subjected the culture of woman has necessarily left its mark upon the hereditary con-stitution of her mind—if this consideration be adduced, it obviously does not tend to prove the equality of the sexes: it merely accentuates the fact of inequality by indicating one of its causes. The treatment of women in the past may have been very wrong, very shameful, and very much to be regretted by the present advocates of women's rights: but proof of the ethical quality of this fact does not get rid of the fact itself, any more than a proof of the criminal nature of assassination can avail to restore to life a murdered man. We must look the facts in the face. How long it may take the woman of the future to recover the ground which has been lost in the psychological race by the woman of the past, it is impossible to say; but we may predict with confidence that, even under the most favourable conditions as to culture, and even supposing the mind of man to remain stationary (and not, as is probable, to advance with a speed relatively accelerated by the momentum of its already acquired velocity), it must take many centuries for heredity to produce the missing five ounces of the female brain.

NOTES

1. [This is proportionally a greater difference than that between the male and female organism as a whole, and the amount of it is largely affected by

grade of civilisation—being least in savages and most in ourselves. More-over, Sir J. Crichton Browne informs me, as a result of many observations which he is now making upon the subject, that not only is the grey matter, or cortex, of the female brain shallower than that of the male, but also receives less than a proportional supply of blood. For these reasons, and also because the differences in question date from an embryonic period of life he con-cludes that they constitute "a fundamental sexual distinction, and not one that can be explained on the hypothesis that the educational advantages enjoyed either by the individual man or by the male sex generally through a long series of generations have stimulated the growth of the brain in the one more than in the other."]

2. [The disparity in question is especially suggestive in the case of poetry, seeing that this is the oldest of the fine arts which have come down to us in a high degree of development, that its exercise requires least special education or technical knowledge, that at no level of culture has such exer-cise been ostracised as unfeminine, that nearly all languages present several monuments of poetic genius of the first order, and yet that no one of these has been reared by a woman.]

3. Jean Eugène Robert-Houdin (1805–1871), French magician and pres-tidigitator. The anecdote is found in Houdin's autobiography, *Confidences d'un prestidigitateur* (1858), translated as *Memoirs of Robert-Houdin* (1859).

4. W. E. H. Lecky (1838–1903), British historian and philosopher. The quotation is from *History of European Morals* (1869), chap. 5.

5. Romanes alludes to the lines from Sir Walter Scott's *Marmion* (1808): "O Woman! In our hours of ease, / Uncertain, coy, and hard to please, / And variable as the shade / By the light quivering aspen made; / When pain and anguish wring the brow, / A ministering angel thou!" (Canto 6, stanza 30).

6. "The fickle woman." The celebrated aria "La donna è mobile" is from Verdi's *Rigoletto* (1851).

7. Charles Darwin (1809–1882), *The Descent of Man* (1871), chap. 19.

8. Sir Francis Galton (1822–1911), British statistician and cousin of Charles Darwin who founded eugenics with the treatise *Hereditary Genius* (1869). The quotation is from *Inquiries into Human Faculty and Its Devel-opment* (1871).

12.

ON THE ABSENCE OF THE CREATIVE FACULTY IN WOMEN

(1891)

Molly Elliot Seawell

Molly Elliot Seawell (1860–1916) was born in Virginia but moved to Washington, DC, with her family around 1880; for much of her life, after the death of her father, she supported her mother and sister by her prolific writings. The author of numerous popular novels—including the much-reprinted *The Berkeleys and Their Neighbors* (1888) and *The Loves of Lady Arabella* (1898)—Seawell revealed herself as markedly hostile to women's intellectual, political, and social advancement. The following article, first published in the *Critic* (November 29, 1891), gained national attention for its relentless assertion of women's inferiority in literary and artistic creation. A later work, *The Ladies' Battle* (1911), is a polemic against woman suffrage. It evoked a quick response in Adele Clark's *Facts vs. Fal-*

Source: Molly Elliot Seawell, "On the Absence of the Creative Faculty in Women," *Critic* (November 29, 1891): 292–94.

lacies (1912). *The Diary of Molly Elliot Seawell 1900–1916* was published in 1990.

*I*t may be stated, as a general proposition, that no woman has ever done anything in the intellectual world, which has had the germ of immortality. This is equivalent to saying that the power to create is entirely lacking in women. This, in turn, may be taken to mean that genius—which differs from talent in being creative—has been totally denied the feminine sex. If these propositions can be proved, it establishes the fact that genius exists in almost every man; for as all the arts and sciences, and the whole material civilization of the world are due to men, this creative power must have been very generally distributed among them—so much so, that it would scarcely be overstating the case to say that all men possess genius in some form, and no woman ever possessed it in any form.

At this stage in the argument, it may be expected that attention will be vehemently called to George Eliot. But it must be remembered that no cycle of literature has passed without producing at least one woman, who has been as highly ranked by her contemporaries as George Eliot is by hers. Indeed, a few women have had a much loftier place accorded them than the author of "Adam Bede"; but they have never been able to keep it. Sappho was considered by long odds the greatest lyric poet among the Greeks. Men like Ovid pronounced her immortal, and for hundreds of years her claim to immortality was undisputed. But a lot of men, whose work did not make half as much noise in the world as Sappho's, still survive, and it is only through their praises that we know of Sappho at all. Her work was not creative, and, consequently, it did not have the germ of immortality. It withered away, and nothing practically survives. Not a page has come down to us, except about forty lines, which do not, by any means, bear out the immense reputation of their author. These lines could easily be surpassed, and have very often been surpassed, by Miss Edith Thomas or Miss Helen Gray Cone.[1]

A list of the women who, in their time, have been classed as high as George Eliot or George Sand—for both of these eminent women of the century stand or fall together—would bring a smile to the countenances of the very irrational persons who think that one or the other of these writers is to set at naught the precedent of thousands of years. Mme. Scudéry was counted not only the greatest romancist of her age, but she actually exerted a commanding influence upon the literature of the time.[2] Mme. Scudéry, however, was as dead as a door-nail fifty years after she ceased to write. Nobody had the hardihood to deny genius to Mme. de Staël, although George Eliot's claim to genius has been called in question by some astute critics, among them Mr. Algernon Charles Swinburne.[3] But does anybody in this year of grace consider "Corinne" as a great work of fiction? or "L'Allemagne" as a powerful philosophic description?[4] Better books than "Corinne" are printed every day, and "L'Allemagne" exists only upon its past reputation. It is a singular fact, that all women whose claims to genius have been seriously considered, have had an enormous contemporary reputation—and it is strikingly true that posterity has not in a single instance endorsed this contemporary verdict. Nor, although it has often reversed the contemporary verdict of men writers, and has placed them upon a pinnacle to which they probably never aspired, it has never done so with any woman writer. The people, in Shakspeare's day, thought him a clever playwright, an admirable poet and a jolly good fellow—but it was another age and another generation that declared him to be the mightiest literary genius the world ever saw. Thackeray's contemporaries esteemed him as an amusing satirist, a writer of clever novels that were not particularly popular. It was when Thackeray was dust and ashes that the English-speaking world pronounced him to be Saul among his brethren.

Perhaps the greatest praise from the greatest men that was ever bestowed on any woman, except Sappho, was lavished on Jane Austen; and it is not extravagant to say that, if the whole intellectual order is to be reversed, she is the woman to do it. Macaulay, in sober earnest, wrote of her that Shakespeare had no equal and no second, but that Miss Austen did some things in the master's manner.[5] Sir Walter

Scott declared that she had certain great literary qualities which he had never seen equalled, and he read "Pride and Prejudice" three times running.[6] Mr. Andrew Lang, in his "Letters to Dead Authors," places her among the immortals because, as he quaintly says, her admirers "are apt somewhat to abate the rule, or shake off the habit of temperate laudation."[7] She is the only woman that Mr. Lang puts among the immortals. But not even Jane Austen has that universality which is the mark of genius. Cultivated minds adore her—*The Athenaeum* declares that to like her is a test of true literary taste; but she is caviare to the general. One needs a certain quality of enlightenment, a certain perception of the most delicate and subtle humor, to appreciate this exquisite writer. But the great masters can make themselves intelligible to all kinds and conditions of men. The most absolute lout, as well as the best trained intelligence, can understand the fury of Othello's jealousy, the madness of Macbeth's remorse. One does not need to be well-read in the best literature to laugh at Becky Sharp[8] hiding the pie in the bed, and Don Quixote tilting at the windmill. So that, regretfully it must be said, not even Jane Austen can withstand the universal law that no woman can create—that she can only describe, and hence her work must always lack the catholicity of genius.

And this catholicity is indicated by the way in which the types created by men become part and parcel of the everyday knowledge of the world, and their words become part and parcel of the vernacular. Everyone who can read and write knows something of Becky and Othello and Mr. Micawber and Ivanhoe and Robinson Crusoe and Pantagruel and Don Quixote and Faust, and all the other creations. But no woman has contributed to this glorious company of immortals. Spring Jane Bennett[9] upon an unsuspecting crowd, and how many persons ever heard of her? Quote Tito;[10] and how many fairly educated persons can place him? But Tito is never quoted. Just as no woman has ever created a character that stands for a type, so no woman has ever uttered a sentence that has passed into the common currency of conversation, like Sancho Panza's "Blessed be the man who first invented sleep,"[11] Macaulay's celebrated illustration about the traveller from

New Zealand,[12] and thousands of others. In order to utter words and ideas that are so apt that the whole world appropriates them, genius must exist in the utterer; and no woman has ever written or spoken a word that has become immortal. Every civilized language is full of these phrases, some of which were made yesterday, and some were made thousands of years ago. But they were all, without exception, made by men.

But although women have done nothing in literature accounted worthy to live, yet that their work is good, and supplies something to every age which is unique and delightful, cannot be denied. Women excel in certain fine forms of literary art. They are like the French cooks described by Sterne, who can make ten dishes out of a burdock leaf, and would make the finest cooks in the world if they had some butcher's meat.[13] If, with their natural gift of expression, they possessed the creative power, they would drive men out of the field of literature entirely. As it is, none would willingly part with George Eliot, or George Sand, or Jane Austen, or Charlotte Brontë, or would give up such idyls of the soul as dear "Jackanapes," that loveliest of stories, about the bravest of boys.[14] These are all beautiful, charming, inspiring—but these things are not genius. They have neither universality nor immortality.

It may be urged with some speciousness, though not soundly, that woman's failure to create anything in other regions of work and thought than literature is due to her limited opportunities. But this theory has not a leg to stand upon as regards literature. Nothing is necessary, in order to write, except pen, paper and "the mind to," as Charles Lamb remarked when Wordsworth said he could write like Shakespeare if he had a mind to.[15] All the universities in the world cannot supply a single creative thought. The superiority of genius over talent is, that genius requires nothing—it creates something out of nothing. Women have been scribbling quite as long as men have, and as the first result of civilization always is to give leisure to a certain class of women, they have had time enough, heaven knows, to do immortal work. But neither time, nor opportunity, nor transcendent knowledge, can supply one single spark of that magnetic flame which is superior to all of these things. Shakespeare, the wool-carder's son, had nothing to learn from the schools: the schools must learn from him.

As regards the power of acquiring facts, women are perhaps not behind men, and this acquisitive power is commonly confounded with the creative power. But it has no relation to it whatever. Miss Fawcett topped the senior wrangler at Cambridge, but she did not add one iota to the sum of human knowledge, nor did she create one single idea. She only proceeded upon a path whereof every step was as regularly ordered as the squares upon a chessboard.[16]

But if woman's failure to create anything in literature is obvious upon very slight examination, her failure to create anything else whatever is perfectly overwhelming. In music, which is the most creative of all the arts, and indeed, the only one which does not copy nature, her failure is complete and conspicuous. In many ages and countries, women have had a monopoly of music, and in all they have had an equal chance with men. Yet, not only have they never produced a single great composer, but not even a single great composition. They are, by far, and always have been, the largest class of interpreters of music, but they have absolutely contributed nothing to the world's stock of music—for the feeble claim of a few third-rate compositions cannot be considered for a moment. In painting, the same may be said, although painting, being merely an imitative art, they have done somewhat better than in music. However, including Rosa Bonheur and Angelica Kauff-mann, and Mme. Le Brun,[17] and a few others, no woman has ever risen to the front rank of painters, or has founded a school, or has contributed a masterpiece to the world's stock of masterpieces.

As regards manufactures and inventions, women would still be pounding corn between two stones if men had not provided mills to grind it. Their utter inability to invent the smallest labor-saving machinery in their domestic concerns is as striking as their failure to create anything in music. For thousands of years women did all the baking and washing and sewing done on this planet—and yet every contrivance to lighten their labor has been put into their hands by men.

Billions of women sewed for ages with needles invented by men, but to no one of them came the idea of the sewing machine.

There is some claim made to inventions by women, based chiefly upon patents granted at Washington. But these do not bear close investigation. None of them can be classed as great inventions, and they are, without exception, simple applications of well-known principles, and without the smallest right to be considered as creative, or even highly original.

In considering this peculiar and universal lack of creative power in all women, the highest, intellectually, as well as the lowest, one is brought to the conclusion that women left to themselves would have remained in utter barbarism, owing to their inability to create anything whatever. They could supply the civilization of the emotions, but men had to supply material civilization; and a law as inexorable as the law of gravity shuts women out from the highest forms of intellectual life. As with every other woman's gift, her intellect seems given to please, and that it can both please and improve is as true as it is good. In so far as her mental make-up goes, she seems to have a wider field for it than man—for while a man seldom follows but one calling, and that requires only one set of ideas, woman has a kingdom within four walls, when there is ample scope for the very highest intellectual effort. To be the home maker requires the first order of executive ability, and there is no grace, gift or accomplishment which has not its place and its beauty in a home. Nowhere on earth is the enormous superiority of a sensible woman over a silly one so sharply defined as in the widely different homes they make. There is a common delusion that brilliant women are for society, while a very ordinary woman can fill the domestic role. Never was there a more grotesque fallacy. Society is a republic where there is no more chance for the display of great talents than for the display of great virtues. A commonplace woman, if she be well-dressed and presentable, is at her best in society. But it is at home, it is in the midst of wasted opportunities, of unused possibilities, that a commonplace woman becomes unendurable. It takes a woman of superior intelligence to see that the conduct of an agreeable home for herself or for somebody else is a much larger, freer, fuller life, than entering into the unequal contest outside with men. What is more charming than the home life of a sensible and refined woman? And what is more wearisome than the "demnition grind," as Mr. Mantalini says,[18] of the domestic life of a silly woman, no matter how refined she may be; for a woman may be perfectly refined and as stupid as an old cow besides. An intelligent woman, who is well balanced, realizes that the theatre of her life is at home. Nor is she forbidden excursions outside—but she must always return to her nest; she is incapable of those boundless flights that only the wing of genius can sustain.

It is unpopular, and worse, it is unfashionable, to say that women are naturally, radically, and mentally inferior to men intellectually. The old cry is raised: Women have not had a fair chance. But if the sexes were originally created equal, when did they first begin to differentiate? And if they lost their equality in the dawn of the ages, what chance have they now of regaining it? Educate them, we are told. But the education of men proceeds as fast as the education of women, and ensures that men will keep the long lead they have gained, besides being originally of stronger fibre.

It would seem that the old-fashioned view is right—men have the power of the intellect, women of the emotions. It is not meant at all that women have no intellect and men no emotions, but only that in the normal man, his intellect is superior to his emotions, and in the normal woman, her emotions are superior to her intellect. Nor is it meant that the ideal man shall not be strong emotionally, nor that the ideal woman shall not be gifted intellectually, merely the relative order of their gifts is in question.

In conclusion: what woman can do in art and literature has not only its beauty, but its usefulness—it has not, however, any essentiality. If all that women have ever done in those two branches of human endeavor were swept out of existence, the world would not lose a single masterpiece. To crib Lord Tennyson's metaphor about the sunlight and the moonlight,[19] the books and pictures and artistic performances of women have the value that the moonlight has—tenderly beautiful, unmatched and unique. If, however, the moon's light were forever quenched, it would make no perceptible difference in the destiny of the human race. But man's intellect is the sun—the great life-giver. Put out the sun, and all humanity would cease to exist.

It therefore behooves women who attempt intellectual achievements to be extremely modest, and to forbear claiming for their sex an equal place, or even a very high place. This view will be politely controverted by men, but secretly they all know it is true, and will wink knowingly at each other, while civilly disagreeing with it. A woman becomes inevitably ridiculous when she imagines that she has a purely intellectual mission. All the abstract intellect in the world is in possession of the ruthless masculine sex. There is a perilous resemblance to "phenomena" in all intellectual achievements of women, like the feat of the dog that stood so remarkably well on its hind legs, so Bozzy told Dr. Johnson. "Sir," thundered the Doctor, "the only remarkable thing about it is, that the dog could stand on its hind legs at all!"[20]

NOTES

1. Edith Thomas (1854–1925) and Helen Gray Cone (1859–1934), minor American poets.

2. Madeleine de Scudéry (1608–1701), the most prolific French novelist of the seventeenth century.

3. British poet and critic Algernon Charles Swinburne (1837–1909) wrote harshly of George Eliot in *A Note on Charlotte Brontë* (1877), referring to her as "an Amazon thrown sprawling over the crupper of her spavined and spur-galled Pegasus."

4. Madame de Staël, *Corinne* (1807), a novel; *De L'Allemagne* (1810–13), a study of German culture that was banned by Napoleon Bonaparte.

5. British historian and critic Thomas Babington Macaulay (1800–1859) wrote of Jane Austen in the essay "Madame d'Arblay" (*Edinburgh Review*, January 1843; in Macaulay's *Critical and Historical Essays*, 1860).

6. The comment on Jane Austen by Scottish novelist Sir Walter Scott

(1771–1832) can be found in his review of *Emma* in the *Quarterly Review* 14 (1815): 188–201.

7. See Andrew Lang (1844–1912), "To Jane Austen," in *Letters to Dead Authors* (1886).

8. The protagonist of William Thackeray's *Vanity Fair* (1847–1848).

9. Jane Bennet is the protagonist of Jane Austen's *Pride and Prejudice* (1813).

10. The reference is to Tito Melema, the husband of Romola in George Eliot's novel *Romola* (1863).

11. See Miguel Cervantes, *Don Quixote* (1605–1615), part 2, bk. 4, chap. 68.

12. "She [the Roman Catholic church] may still exist in undiminished vigour when some traveller from New Zealand shall, in the midst of a vast solitude, take his stand on a broken arch of London Bridge to sketch the ruins of St. Paul's." Macaulay, "Von Ranke" (*Edinburgh Review*, October 1840; in *Critical and Historical Essays*).

13. See Laurence Sterne, *A Sentimental Journey* (1768).

14. Juliana Horatia Ewing (1841–1885), *Jackanapes* (1883), a popular boys' book of the period.

15. "Wordsworth . . . says he does not see much difficulty in writing like Shakspeare [*sic*], if he had a mind to try it. It is clear, then, nothing is wanting but the mind." Charles Lamb, letter to Thomas Manning (February 26, 1808).

16. Dame Millicent Fawcett (1847–1929), British feminist, suffragist, and author of *Political Economy for Beginners* (1870) and other works.

17. Rosa Bonheur (1822–1899), French painter and sculptor. Angelica Kauffmann (1741–1807), Swiss painter and etcher. Elisabeth-Louise Vigée Le Brun (1755–1842), French painter.

18. Alfred Mantalini is a character in Charles Dickens's *Nicholas Nickleby* (1838–1839).

19. "Woman is the lesser man, and all thy passions, matched with mine, / Are as moonlight unto sunlight, and as water unto wine." Alfred, Lord Tennyson (1809–1892), "Locksley Hall" (1842), 11.151–52.

20. See James Boswell, *Life of Johnson* (1791), under the date July 31, 1763.

13.

THE WEAKER SEX:
A SCIENTIFIC RAMBLE

(1926)

James H. Leuba

James Henry Leuba (1868–1946) was born in
Switzerland but came to the United States in
1887. He received a PhD in psychology from
Clark University and was a longtime professor
of psychology at Bryn Mawr College (1899–
1933), where, one would imagine, he would
have had abundant opportunities to observe
women's intellects in action. Leuba wrote a
number of psychological analyses of religion—
A Psychological Study of Religion (1912), *The
Belief in God and Immortality* (1916), *The Psychology of Religious Mysticism* (1925), *God or
Man? A Study of the Value of God to Man* (1933)—
along with numerous popular articles,
including the following, first published in the
Atlantic Monthly (April 1926). Nervously aware
that women's intellectual inferiority could no
longer be plausibly maintained, Leuba none-

Source: James H. Leuba, "The Weaker Sex: A Scientific Ramble," *Atlantic Monthly* 137, no. 4 (April
1926): 455–57.

theless finds a way to assert women's inferiority by maintaining their weakness in energy.

$\mathcal{U}$ nder the goad of imputed general inferiority, women have claimed not only political but also mental equality. It has seemed to them that nothing short of the full recognition by the dominant male of their mental capacity would bring to them the sense of worth and dignity before which the complex and its baleful effects would vanish. Unfortunately, whatever success they may have obtained in the realization of their political demands, the facts continue to be, or seem to be, against their claim of mental equality.

With regard to the past, they have found it sufficient to plead social disabilities as an explanation of their inferior performance in every or almost every form of activity. How could woman have attained eminence when the institutions of higher learning were closed to her, and when society in general refused to help her to gratify any of her ambitions if it led beyond the home?

Science, in the form of mental tests, has seemed to come to the support of this uncertain argument. No significant differences have been found to exist between schoolboys and schoolgirls or even between adult men and women. Unfortunately, the mental tests so far available are applicable to only certain parts of the mental life: the functions of the sense organs (acuity of perception, fineness of discrimination, and so forth), memory, certain forms of imagination, of comparison, of judgment, and some other aspects of what makes up "intelligence." No adequate test of the dynamic aspect of the mind— that is, of interest, persistency, energy—has as yet been devised. When it is realized that the intellectual abilities are useless without motive power, the impossibility of deducing from the possession of equal intellectual abilities equal life-achievements becomes obvious. Little may be expected of a person finely gifted intellectually, if he be not also well endowed with mental energy. The talents of the artist, without the power of ceaseless work, are of little avail.

Unfortunately, again, for the peace of mind of women, the extensive removal of social disabilities, which has recently taken place, has not yielded the fruits expected by the believers in equality of mental ability. It is true that even now, in many professions and activities, women enjoy neither the encouragement nor the freedom given to men. Nevertheless, it may well seem to dispassionate observers that the degree of liberation gained by women during the last fifty years has not been followed by the fruits which equality of ability would have produced. Feminine musical composers and performers of the first rank are remarkably few, though public opinion and social customs place no obstacle in the way of the female musician.

Equality of opportunity and of intelligence can ensure equality of mental achievement only if energy also is equal. Are there reasons for referring to less mental energy the inferior performance of women? I think there are.

It is with trepidation that I engage in so delicate a venture as the demonstration of the inferiority of women in mental energy. Claiming a purely scientific interest in these matters would, I fear, not spare me a storm of protest. But may I not at least contend that the reference of women's deficiency to energy, and not to intelligence, constitutes a favorable change of venue? Is it not easier to confess to fatigue than to lack of wits? So it almost seems that success in this attempt means ridding womankind of the dreadful inferiority complex. They may, therefore, perhaps bear with me. In any case, I trust to their fairness—a trait which, I am glad to say, is not impugned in the following pages. [. . .]

The ascription of superior performance to superior intellectual endowment when it is due, in fact, to superior energy is one of the common confusions besetting a muddle-headed humanity. The much-performers in business, in politics, and even in the arts and sciences, are often ranked far above their true place in the scale of intellectual talents—talents to observe, to remember, to understand, to appreciate, to reason. The very quality of their achievements conspires with their quantity to produce the deception. For quality also is improved by long-sustained effort. In my student days, I boarded for a while in the same house with a young woman said to have a remarkable gift for the piano. Yet, as time passed. she seemed more and more discouraged. Her professor was not satisfied with her progress; he complained that she did not practice enough. As she told me that she added, "I play six hours a day; I can do no more—I am done up." Has it not been said that Paderewski, during his apprenticeship, had been known to sit at the piano twelve hours a day?[1] The promise of this young woman's talent was frustrated by insufficient energy.

Even in the fields of endeavor involving, as we say, purely mental work,—mathematics, for instance,—energy, and not only intellectual talent, determines the quality of achievement. Other things being equal, the person who in the attempted solution of a problem wearies last is the one who has the best chances of success. But the problem of the advantages due in this field to greater energy must not be considered with reference to a brief period of time. The energy-factor operates throughout life. The greater store of mathematical knowledge accumulated throughout his school and college years by the less easily fatigued person will give him such an advantage over his more easily tired competitor that now, even in the same space of time, he will readily surpass him, not in amount of work merely, but also in its quality: the problems he will be able to solve will be beyond the present attainments of the other. The world is full of men of vast achievements, reputed of transcendent intelligence, who owe their success to a surpassing energy actuating a mediocre brain. Not their intellectual talents but their ceaseless use of them is their distinction. [. . .]

We may, then, say that, other things being equal, the greater the difference in energy, the greater the difference in mental achievements, both in quantity and in quality. The inferiority in the mental performance of women, however great it may be in quantity or quality, can therefore be explained without the assumption of inferior intelligence.

NOTE

1. Ignacy Jan Paderewski (1860–1941), Polish pianist and composer.

Part 5

WOMEN AND EDUCATION

14.

SEX IN EDUCATION; OR, A FAIR CHANCE FOR THE GIRLS

(1873)

Edward H. Clarke, MD

Edward Hammond Clarke (1820–1877) graduated from Harvard University in 1841 and
received his MD from the University of Pennsylvania Medical School in 1846. He opened a private practice in Boston, Massachusetts, and at
one point was thought to have the largest such
practice in the city. From 1855 to 1872 he was
professor of materia medica at Harvard, spe-
cializing in the effects of drugs on animals and
human beings. His major treatise, *Sex in Education; or, A Fair Chance for the Girls* (1873), was a
best seller, receiving nineteen printings by
1892. It urged radically different methods of
secondary education for boys and girls
because, in Clarke's opinion, overeducation of
girls in their teenage years would adversely
affect their burgeoning reproductive organs
and render them unfit mothers, thereby

Source: Edward H. Clarke, MD, *Sex in Education; or, A Fair Chance for the Girls* (Boston: James R. Osgood, 1873), pp. 118–31, 134–40, 154–58.

causing a decline in the overall health of the American population. The treatise was immediately rebutted by numerous book-length studies, and Clarke himself followed it up with *The Building of a Brain* (1874). The following excerpt appears in the chapter "Co-Education."

$\mathcal{G}$uided by the laws of development which we have found physiology to teach, and warned by the punishments, in the shape of weakness and disease, which we have shown their infringement to bring about, and of which our present methods of female education furnish innumerable examples, it is not difficult to discern certain physiological principles that limit and control the education, and, consequently, the co-education of our youth. These principles we have learned to be, three for the two sexes in common, and one for the peculiarities of the female sex. The three common to both, the three to which both are subjected, and for which wise methods of education will provide in the case of both, are, 1st, a sufficient supply of appropriate nutriment. This of course includes good air and good water and sufficient warmth, as much as bread and butter; oxygen and sunlight, as much as meat. 2d, Mental and physical work and regimen so apportioned, that repair shall exceed waste, and a margin be left for development. This includes out-of-door exercise and appropriate ways of dressing, as much as the hours of study, and the number and sort of studies. 3d, Sufficient sleep. This includes the best time for sleeping, as well as the proper number of hours for sleep. It excludes the "murdering of sleep,"[1] by late hours of study and the crowding of studies, as much as by wine or tea or dissipation. All these guide and limit the education of the two sexes very much alike. The principle or condition peculiar to the female sex is the management of the catamenial function,[2] which, from the age of fourteen to nineteen, includes the building of the reproductive apparatus. This imposes upon women, and especially upon the young woman, a great care, a corresponding duty, and compensating privileges. There is only a feeble counterpart to it in the male organization; and, in his moral constitution, there cannot be found the fine instincts and quick perceptions that have their root in this mechanism, and correlate its functions. This lends to her development and to all her work a rythmical or periodical order, which must be recognized and obeyed. "In this recognition of the chronometry of organic process, there is unquestionably great promise for the future; for it is plain that the observance of time in the motions of organic molecules is as certain and universal, if not as exact, as that of the heavenly bodies."[3] Periodicity characterizes the female organization, and develops feminine force. Persistence characterizes the male organization, and develops masculine force. Education will draw the best out of each by adjusting its methods to the periodicity of one and the persistence of the other.

Before going farther, it is essential to acquire a definite notion of what is meant, or, at least, of what we mean in this discussion, by the term co-education. Following its etymology, *con-educare*, it signifies to draw out together, or to unite in education; and this union refers to the time and place, rather than to the methods and kinds of education. In this sense any school or college may utilize its buildings, apparatus, and instructors to give appropriate education to the two sexes as well as to different ages of the same sex. This is juxtaposition in education. When the Massachusetts Institute of Technology teaches one class of young men chemistry, and another class engineering, in the same building and at the same time, it co-educates those two classes. In this sense it is possible that many advantages might be obtained from the co-education of the sexes, that would more than counterbalance the evils of crowding large numbers of them together. This sort of co-education does not exclude appropriate classification, nor compel the two sexes to follow the same methods or the same regimen.

Another signification of co-education, and, as we apprehend, the one in which it is commonly used, includes time, place, government, methods, studies, and regimen. This is identical co-education. This means, that boys and girls shall be taught the same things, at the same time, in the same place, by the same faculty, with the same methods, and under the same regimen. This admits age and proficiency, but not sex, as a factor in classification. It is against the co-education of the sexes, in this sense of identical co-education, that physiology protests, and it is this identity of education, the prominent characteristic of our American school-system, that has produced the evils described in the clinical part of this essay, and that threatens to push the degeneration of the female sex still farther on. In these pages, co-education of the sexes is used in its common acceptation of identical co-education.

Let us look for a moment at what identical co-education is. The law has, or had, a maxim, that a man and his wife are one, and that the one is the man.[4] Modern American education has a maxim, that boys' schools and girls' schools are one, and that the one is the boys' school. Schools have been arranged, accordingly, to meet the requirements of the masculine organization. Studies have been selected that experience has proved to be appropriate to a boy's intellectual development, and a regimen adopted, while pursuing them, appropriate to his physical development. His school and college life, his methods of study, recitations, exercises, and recreations, are ordered upon the supposition, that, barring disease or infirmity, punctual attendance upon the hours of recitation, and upon all other duties in their season and order, may be required of him continuously, in spite of ennui, inclement weather, or fatigue; that there is no week in the month, or day in the week, or hour in the day, when it is a physical necessity to relieve him from standing or from studying,—from physical effort or mental labor; that the chapel-bell may safely call him to morning prayer from New Year to Christmas, with the assurance, that, if the going does not add to his stock of piety, it will not diminish his stock of health; that he may be sent to the gymnasium and the examination-hall, to the theatres of physical and intellectual display at any time,—in short, that he develops health and strength, blood and nerve, intellect and life, by a regular, uninterrupted, and sustained course of work. And all this is justified both by experience and physiology.

Obedient to the American educational maxim, that boys' schools and girls' schools are one, and that the one is the boys' school, the female schools have copied the methods which have grown out of the requirements of the male organization. Schools for girls have been modelled after schools for boys. Were it not for differences of dress and figure, it would be impossible, even for an expert, after visiting a high school for boys and one for girls, to tell which was arranged for the male and which for the female organization. Our girls' schools, whether public or private, have imposed upon their pupils a boy's regimen; and it is now proposed, in some quarters, to carry this principle still farther, by burdening girls, after they leave school, with a quadrennium of masculine college regimen. And so girls are to learn the alphabet in college, as they have learned it in the grammar-school, just as boys do. This is grounded upon the supposition that sustained regularity of action and attendance may be as safely required of a girl as of a boy; that there is no physical necessity for periodically relieving her from walking, standing, reciting, or studying; that the chapel-bell may call her, as well as him, to a daily morning walk, with a standing prayer at the end of it, regardless of the danger that such exercises, by deranging the tides of her organization, may add to her piety at the expense of her blood; that she may work her brain over mathematics, botany, chemistry, German, and the like, with equal and sustained force on every day of the month, and so safely divert blood from the reproductive apparatus to the head; in short, that she, like her brother, develops health and strength, blood and nerve, intellect and life, by a regular, uninterrupted, and sustained course of work. All this is not justified, either by experience or physiology. The gardener may plant, if he choose, the lily and the rose, the oak and the vine, within the same enclosure; let the same soil nourish them, the same air visit them, and the same sunshine warm and cheer them; still, he trains each of them with a separate art, warding from each its peculiar dangers, developing within each its peculiar powers, and teaching each to put forth to the utmost its divine and peculiar gifts of strength and beauty. Girls lose health, strength, blood, and nerve, by a regimen that ignores the periodical tides and reproductive apparatus of their organization. The mothers and instructors, the homes and schools, of our country's daughters, would profit by occasionally reading the old Levitical law.[5] The race has not yet quite outgrown the physiology of Moses.

Co-education, then, signifies in common acceptation identical co-education. This identity of training is what many at the present day seem to be praying for and working for. Appropriate education of the two sexes, carried as far as possible, is a consummation most devoutly to be desired; identical education of the two sexes is a crime before God and humanity, that physiology protests against, and that experience weeps over. Because the education of boys has met with tolerable success, hitherto,—but only tolerable it must be confessed,—in developing them into men, there are those who would make girls grow into women by the same process. Because a gardener has nursed an acorn till it grew into an oak, they would have him cradle a grape in the same soil and way, and make it a vine. Identical education, or identical co-education, of the sexes defrauds one sex or the other, or perhaps both. It defies the Roman maxim, which physiology has fully justified, *mens sana in corpore sano*.[6] The sustained regimen, regular recitation, erect posture, daily walk, persistent exercise, and unintermitted labor that toughens a boy, and makes a man of him, can only be partially applied to a girl. The regimen of intermittance, periodicity of exercise and rest, work three-fourths of each month, and remission, if not abstinence, the other fourth, physiological interchange of the erect and reclining posture, care of the reproductive system that is the cradle of the race, all this, that toughens a girl and makes a woman of her, will emasculate a lad. A combination of the two methods of education, a compromise between them, would probably yield an average result, excluding the best of both. It would give a fair chance neither to a boy nor a girl. Of all compromises, such a physiological one is the worst. It cultivates mediocrity, and cheats the future of its rightful legacy of lofty manhood and womanhood. It emasculates boys, stunts girls; makes semi-eunuchs of one sex, and agenes[7] of the other.

The error which has led to the identical education of the two sexes, and which prophesies their identical co-education in colleges and universities, is not confined to technical education. It permeates society.

It is found in the home, the workshop, the factory, and in all the ramifications of social life. The identity of boys and girls, of men and women, is practically asserted out of the school as much as in it, and it is theoretically proclaimed from the pulpit and the rostrum. Woman seems to be looking up to man and his development, as the goal and ideal of womanhood. The new gospel of female development glorifies what she possesses in common with him, and tramples under her feet, as a source of weakness and badge of inferiority, the mechanism and functions peculiar to herself. In consequence of this wide-spread error, largely the result of physiological ignorance, girls are almost universally trained in masculine methods of living and working as well as of studying. The notion is practically found everywhere, that boys and girls are one, and that the boys make the one. Girls, young ladies, to use the polite phrase, who are about leaving or have left school for society, dissipation, or self-culture, rarely permit any of Nature's periodical demands to interfere with their morning calls, or evening promenades, or midnight dancing, or sober study. Even the home draws the sacred mantle of modesty so closely over the reproductive function as not only to cover but to smother it. Sisters imitate brothers in persistent work at all times. Female clerks in stores strive to emulate the males by unremitting labor, seeking to develop feminine force by masculine methods. Female operatives of all sorts, in factories and elsewhere, labor in the same way; and, when the day is done, are as likely to dance half the night, regardless of any pressure upon them of a peculiar function, as their fashionable sisters in the polite world. All unite in pushing the hateful thing out of sight and out of mind; and all are punished by similar weakness, degeneration, and disease. [. . .]

The identical education of the sexes has borne the fruit which we have pointed out. Their identical co-education will intensify the evils of separate identical education; for it will introduce the element of emulation, and it will introduce this element in its strongest form. It is easy to frame a theoretical emulation, in which results only are compared and tested, that would be healthy and invigorating; but such theoretical competition of the sexes is not at all the sort of steady, untiring, day-after-day competition that identical co-education implies. It is one thing to put up a goal a long way off,—five or six months or three or four years distant,—and tell boys and girls, each in their own way, to strive for it, and quite a different thing to put up the same goal, at the same distance, and oblige each sex to run their race for it side by side on the same road, in daily competition with each other, and with equal expenditure of force at all times. Identical co-education is raging in the latter way. The inevitable results of it have been shown in some of the cases we have narrated. The trial of it on a larger scale would only yield a larger number of similar degenerations, weaknesses, and sacrifices of noble lives. Put a boy and girl together upon the same course of study, with the same lofty ideal before them, and hold up to their eyes the daily incitements of comparative progress, and there will be awakened within them a stimulus unknown before, and that separate study does not excite. The unconscious fires that have their seat deep down in the recesses of the sexual organization will flame up through every tissue, permeate every vessel, burn every nerve, flash from the eye, tingle in the brain, and work the whole machine at highest pressure. There need not be, and generally will not be, any low or sensual desire in all this elemental action. It is only making youth work over the tasks of sober study with the wasting force of intense passion. Of course such strenuous labor will yield brilliant, though temporary, results. The fire is kept alive by the waste of the system, and soon burns up its source. The first sex to suffer in this exhilarating and costly competition must be, as experience shows it is, the one that has the largest amount of force in readiness for immediate call; and this is the female sex. At the age of development, Nature mobilizes the forces of a girl's organization for the purpose of establishing a function that shall endure for a generation, and for constructing an apparatus that shall cradle and nurse a race. These mobilized forces, which, at the technical educational period, the girl possesses and controls largely in excess of the boy, under the passionate stimulus of identical co-education, are turned from their divinely-appointed field of operations, to the region of brain activity.

The result is a most brilliant show of cerebral pyrotechnics, and degenerations that we have described.

That undue and disproportionate brain activity exerts a sterilizing influence upon both sexes is alike a doctrine of physiology, and an induction from experience. And both physiology and experience also teach that this influence is more potent upon the female than upon the male. The explanation of the latter fact—of the greater aptitude of the female organization to become thus modified by excessive brain activity—is probably to be found in the larger size, more complicated relations, and more important functions, of the female reproductive apparatus. This delicate and complex mechanism is liable to be aborted or deranged by the withdrawal of force that is needed for its construction and maintenance. It is, perhaps, idle to speculate upon the prospective evil that would accrue to the human race, should such an organic modification, introduced by abnormal education, be pushed to its ultimate limit. But inasmuch as the subject is not only germain to our inquiry, but has attracted the attention of a recent writer, whose bold and philosophic speculations, clothed in forcible language, have startled the best thought of the age, it may be well to quote him briefly on this point. Referring to the fact, that, in our modern civilization, the cultivated classes have smaller families than the uncultivated ones, he says, "If the superior sections and specimens of humanity are to lose, relatively, their procreative power in virtue of, and in proportion to, that superiority, how is culture or progress to be propagated so as to benefit the species as a whole, and how are those gradually amended organizations from which we hope so much to be secured? If, indeed, it were ignorance, stupidity, and destitution, instead of mental and moral development, that were the *sterilizing* influences, then the improvement of the race would go on swimmingly, and in an ever-accelerating ratio. But since the conditions are exactly reversed, how should not an exactly opposite direction be pursued? How should the race *not* deteriorate, when those who morally and physically are fitted to perpetuate it are (relatively), by a law of physiology, those least likely to do so?"[8] The answer to Mr. Greg's inquiry is obvious. If the culture of the race moves on into the future in the same rut and by the same methods that limit and direct it now; if the education of the sexes remains identical, instead of being appropriate and special; and especially if the intense and passionate stimulus of the identical co-education of the sexes is added to their identical education,—then the sterilizing influence of such a training, acting with tenfold more force upon the female than upon the male, will go on, and the race will be propagated from its inferior classes. The stream of life that is to flow into the future will be Celtic rather than American: it will come from the collieries, and not from the peerage. Fortunately, the reverse of this picture is equally possible. The race holds its destinies in its own hands. The highest wisdom will secure the survival and propagation of the fittest. Physiology teaches that this result, the attainment of which our hopes prophecy, is to be secured, not by an identical education, or by an identical co-education of the sexes, but by *a special and appropriate education, that shall produce a just and harmonious development of every part.* [. . .]

It may be well to mention two or three details, which are so important that no system of *appropriate* female education, separate or mixed, can neglect them. They have been implied throughout the whole of the present discussion, but not distinctly enunciated. One is, that during the period of rapid development, that is, from fourteen to eighteen, a girl should not study as many hours a day as a boy. "In most of our schools," says a distinguished physiological authority previously quoted, "the hours are too many for both boys and girls. From a quarter of nine or nine, until half-past two, is with us (Philadelphia schools for girls) the common schooltime in private seminaries. The usual recess is twenty minutes or half an hour, and it is not filled by enforced exercise. In certain schools,—would it were the rule,—ten minutes' recess is given after every hour. To these hours, we must add the time spent in study out of school. This, for some reason, nearly always exceeds the time stated by teachers to be necessary; and most girls between the age of thirteen and seventeen thus expend two or three hours. Does any physician believe that it is good for a growing girl to be so occupied seven or eight hours a day? or that it is right for her to use her brains as long a time as the mechanic employs his muscles? But this is only a part of the evil. The multiplicity of studies, the number of teachers,—each eager to get the most he can out of his pupil,—the severer drill of our day, and the greater intensity of application demanded, produce effects on the growing brain, which, in a vast number of cases, can be only disastrous. Even in girls of from fourteen to eighteen, such as crowd the normal school in Philadelphia, this sort of tension and this variety of study occasion an amount of ill-health which is sadly familiar to many physicians."[9]

Experience teaches that a healthy and growing boy may spend six hours of force daily upon his studies, and leave sufficient margin for physical growth. A girl cannot spend more than four, or, in occasional instances, five hours of force daily upon her studies, and leave sufficient margin for the general physical growth that she must make in common with a boy, and also for constructing a reproductive apparatus. If she puts as much force into her brain education as a boy, the brain or the special apparatus will suffer. Appropriate education and appropriate co-education must adjust their methods and regimen to this law.

Another detail is, that, during every fourth week, there should be a remission, and sometimes an intermission, of both study and exercise. Some individuals require, at that time, a complete intermission from mental and physical effort for a single day; others for two or three days; others require only a remission, and can do half work safely for two or three days, and their usual work after that. The diminished labor, which shall give Nature an opportunity to accomplish her special periodical task and growth, is a physiological necessity for all, however robust they may seem to be. The apportionment of study and exercise to individual needs cannot be decided by general rules, nor can the decision of it be safely left to the pupil's caprice or ambition. Each case must be decided upon its own merits. The organization of studies and instruction must be flexible enough to admit of the periodical and temporary absence of each pupil, without loss of rank, or necessity of making up work, from recitation, and exercise of all sorts. The periodical type of woman's way of work must be harmonized with the persistent type of man's way of work in any successful plan of co-education.

NOTES

1. "Methought I heard a voice cry 'Sleep no more! / Macbeth does murder sleep.'" Shakespeare, *Macbeth*, 2.2.34–35.

2. I.e., pertaining to catamenia, or the menstrual discharge.

3. [<Henry Maudsley,> *Body and Mind* <1870>, p. 178.]

4. See William Blackstone's *Commentaries on the Laws of England* (pp. 247–51 in this book).

5. Presumably a reference to chap. 12 of Leviticus, which prescribes various courses of action after a woman has given birth.

6. "A sound mind in a sound body." Juvenal *Satires* 10.356.

7. Evidently a noun form of *agenesic* ("characterized by absolute sterility").

8. [*Enigmas of Life.* By W. R. Greg, p. 142.]

9. S. Weir Mitchell (1829–1914), *Wear and Tear; or, Hints for the Overworked* (Philadelphia: J. B. Lippincott, 1871), pp. 33–34.

15.

HIGHER EDUCATION OF WOMEN AND RACE SUICIDE

(1905)

A. Lapthorn Smith

Arthur Lapthorn Smith (b. 1855) was a physician residing in Montreal, Canada, and is the author of numerous papers on gynecology and obstetrics, as well as of the treatise *How to Be Useful and Happy from Sixty to Ninety* (1922). In the following essay, first published in *Popular Science* of March 1905, Smith combines misogyny and racism in maintaining that higher education for women will endanger their physical constitutions, making them unfit for childbearing and thereby engendering the "race suicide" of the "original American people" (i.e., Anglo-Saxons). Smith further asserts that overeducated women will be dissatisfied with husbands of their own class and impatient of housework and child rearing.

Source: A. Lapthorn Smith, "Higher Education of Women and Race Suicide," *Popular Science Monthly* 66, no. 5 (March 1905): 466–73.

Education on the continent of America, and more especially in the United States, has reached a point of perfection which hardly leaves room for any further development.[1] At first sight, this would seem to be a very satisfactory state of affairs and, to the ordinary observer, the question of still higher education would seem to be deserving of all praise. "You can not have too much of a good thing," they say, and the very highest possible degree of education for women is none too good or too great for them. But to those who look beyond the present and only a little way into the future a great danger is gradually arising, a danger which will go on increasing until it brings about a revolution the signs of which are already beginning to be seen and which will effectually put an end to the evil which is to form the subject of this paper. The author will limit himself principally to a discussion of the harm resulting from too high an education of women, because on that part of the subject he has had exceptional opportunities for observation and for drawing accurate conclusions; but, incidentally, he will take the liberty of questioning the advisability of affording *higher* education freely to the people at large, of the male, as well as of the female sex.

The author regrets to be like a voice crying in the wilderness, a note of warning against what the majority of people consider to be an unalloyed blessing; and some will no doubt say that he is going back to the time of the great preacher who said "he that increaseth knowledge increaseth sorrow."[2] And yet all the facts on which his conclusions are based are known to many thousands, and even millions, of people in America, and even, though to a lesser extent, in England, where the same disastrous results are following the same apparently innocent cause. The author would crave the indulgence of his readers, if, at times, he is obliged to speak of delicate matters in rather a plain way; but where this has to be done he will endeavor to do it in such a manner as not to offend the sensibilities of any scientific reader.

In the human race, as among every species throughout creation, as every well-informed person knows, there is constantly going on a struggle for existence—not only for the existence of the particular individual, but for that of his progeny, which is of far greater importance in nature, because when the individual is wiped out, only one person disappears; but when his progeny ceases to exist, an end is put to countless thousands, who are thus prevented from ever being born. He will endeavor to show, as he believes to be the case, that the higher education of women is surely extinguishing her race, both directly by its effects on her organization, and, indirectly, by rendering early marriage impossible for the average man.

First of all, is education being carried on at present to such a degree as to at all affect the bodily or physical health of women? This is a very important question, because the duties of wifehood, and still more of motherhood, do not require an extraordinary development of the brain, but they must absolutely have a strong development of the body. Not only does wifehood and motherhood not require an extraordinary development of the brain, but the latter is a decided barrier against the proper performance of these duties. Any family physician could give innumerable cases out of his experience of failures of marriage, directly due to too great a cultivation of the female intellect, which results in the scorning to perform those duties which are cheerfully performed, and even desired, by the uneducated wife. The duties of motherhood are direct rivals of brain work, for they both require for their performance an exclusive and plentiful supply of phosphates.[3] These are obtained from the food in greater or less quantity, but rarely, if ever, in sufficient quantity to supply an active and highly educated intellect, and, at the same time, the wants of the growing child. The latter before birth must extract from its mother's blood all the chemical salts necessary for the formation of its bony skeleton and for other tissues; and in this rivalry between the offspring and the intellect how often has not the family physician seen the brain lose in the struggle. The mother's reason totters and falls, in some cases to such an extent as to require her removal to an insane asylum, while in others, she only regains her reason after the prolonged administration of phosphates, to make up for the loss entailed by the growth of the child. Sometimes, however, it is the child which suffers, and it is born defectively nourished or rickety, and, owing to the poor quality of the mother's milk, it obtains a precarious existence from artificial foods, which at the best are a poor substitute for nature's nourishment. The highly educated woman seems to know that she will make a poor mother, for she marries rarely and late and, when she does, the number of children is very small. The argument is sometimes used that it is better to have only one child and bring it up with extraordinary care than to have six or eight children brought up with ordinary care because in the latter case the mother's attention is divided. But this is a fallacy. Everybody knows that the one child of the wealthy and highly educated couple is generally a spoiled child and has, as a rule, poor health; while the six or eight children of the poor and moderately educated woman are exceedingly strong and lusty. But even supposing that the highly educated woman were able and willing to bear and rear her children like any other woman, she has one drawback from having a fairly large family, and that is the lateness at which she marries, the average being between twenty-six and twenty-seven years. Now, as a woman of that age should marry a man between ten and fifteen years older than herself, for a woman of twenty-seven is as old as a man of forty for the purpose of marriage, both she and her husband are too old to begin the raising of an ordinary sized family. Men and women of that age are old maids and old bachelors. They have been living their own lives during their best years; they have become set in their ways, they must have their own pleasures; in a word, they have become selfish. And, after having had one or at the most two children, the woman objects to having any more, and this is the beginning of the end of marital happiness. The records of our divorce courts show in hundreds of instances, that there was no trouble in the home while the woman was performing her functions of motherhood, but that trouble began as soon as she began to shirk them. Hundreds of thousands of men at the present day are married, but have no wives; and while this sad state of affairs occurs occasionally among the moderately educated, it exists very frequently among the highly educated.

Is the health of the women at the present day worse than it was in the time of our grandmothers? Are the duties of wifehood and mother-hood really harder to perform now than they were one hundred years ago? Without hesitation the answer to both questions is "Yes." Not only are the sexual and maternal instincts of the average woman becoming less and less from year to year; the best proof of which is later and later marriages and fewer and fewer children; but, in the writer's opinion, the majority of women of the middle and upper classes are sick and suffering before marriage and are physically dis-abled from performing physiological functions in a natural manner. At a recent meeting of a well-known society of specialists for obstetrics and diseases of women, one of the fellows with the largest practise in the largest city on this continent stated that it was physically impos-sible for the majority of patients to have a natural labor, because their power to feel pain was so great, while their muscular power was so little. On these two questions the whole profession is agreed, but I am bound to say that there is a difference of opinion as to the reason. Sev-eral of the most distinguished fellows of the above society claim that the generally prevalent breakdown of women is due to their inordinate pursuit of pleasure during the ten years which elapse between their leaving school and their marriage. This includes late hours, turning night into day, insufficient sleep, improper diet, improper clothing and want of exercise. The writer claims that most of the generally admitted poor health of women is due to over education, which first deprives them of sunlight and fresh air for the greater part of their time; second, takes every drop of blood away to the brain from the growing organs of generation; third, develops their nervous system at the expense of all their other systems, muscular, digestive, generative, etc.; fourth, leads them to live an abnormal single life until the age of twenty-six or twenty-seven instead of being married at eighteen, which is the latest that nature meant them to remain single; fifth, raises their requirements so high that they can not marry a young man in good health.

There is another aspect of the question, which is not often dis-cussed, but which has an important bearing upon it. The very essence of cultivation of intellect to its highest point consists in raising the standard of one's requirements. A contented mind makes a man happy. Does a high education make one's mind contented, or does it make it discontented with the present, and ever struggle towards a higher ideal in the future? Is the woman who is versed in art and literature contented with a simple home, or must she be surrounded with objects of art and more or less costly books; and, if so, is she satisfied with her lot when she marries an average man, who is able to provide for her all the necessaries of life, but is not possessed of sufficient wealth to provide those things which would be useless luxuries to a woman of ordinary education, but which are necessities for her? Not only must the highly educated woman have an artistic home, large enough to hold her artistic and literary collections, and roomy enough in which to entertain her artistic friends, but she must have a certain number of expensive and highly trained assistants, to keep these large collections in proper order. In plain language, she must have servants to clean them and move them about without destroying them. Can such a woman, anxious and worried over the care of several thousands or hundreds of objects of art, devote the same care to the bearing and bringing up of her family as the woman whose ordinary education has made her feel no need of possessing such objects, but who, on the contrary, is content with a home and furniture which she herself is oftentimes alone capable of taking care of?

We all want to be happy, and to that end we all want to be good; and, I have already said, we want our children, especially our boys, to be good and happy. But those who know anything about virtue in the male know that the marriage of our young men under twenty-five, to a woman with a sound body about eighteen years of age, is almost, if not the only means of preserving the virtue of the rising generation of men. People, and even mothers, speak lightly of their daughters at twenty-six or twenty-seven marrying men who have sown their wild oats; but one must reap what he sows and do they realize what an awful misfortune such a harvest has brought to the character of the man, and will almost surely bring to the health of the innocent woman? If one has any doubts on this subject they would soon be set right by the testimony of any physician who has made a specialty of attending men, or who has devoted his practise especially to women.

Just as there are occasionally cases where a divorce becomes necessary, but very much fewer than those actually granted, so, occasionally, the life of an unborn child must be sacrificed to save the life of the mother. But will anybody pretend for a moment that there is any excuse for the two million of child-murders which is a fair estimate of the number occurring annually on the North American continent? The crime has become so general that public opinion has ceased to condemn it, and among the few who do condemn it we certainly do not find those women who claim that wifehood and motherhood are degrading and should be reserved to the lowest class of the population. It is well known that were it not for the enormous immigration pouring into America day by day and week by week, the population of this continent would have died out ere now. And it is generally admitted that the original American people have almost died out. Even the foreigners who are so quickly assimilated soon learn the practise of race-suicide, although never to the appalling extent of the native-born Americans. As far as my experience goes, the crime is most prevalent among the highly educated classes, while it is almost unknown among those with an ordinary education.

Another way in which the higher education is making people unhappy is in the cultivation of the powers of analysis and criticism. When the power of analysis is applied to one's own self it is especially unfortunate, for then it becomes introspection, a faculty which is carried so far with some women that their whole life is spent in looking into themselves, caring nothing for the trials or troubles of those about them. This produces an intense form of egotism and selfishness. These people are exceedingly unhappy, very often suffering from what is wrongly called "nervous prostration," but which could rather be called "nervous prosperity." When the wonderful power of criticizing is applied to others it takes the form of fault-finding. Such a woman must have many victims; will she make them happy?

One of the greatest objections to the higher education of women, namely, the interference with outdoor exercise, no longer can be raised, because the universities and boarding-schools have within the last ten years foreseen this danger and met it by special courses of instruction in athletics and the encouraging of girls to spend a good deal of time in outdoor sports. But even these universities and schools cannot avoid the charge of fostering a condition of intellectual pride, which is in exact proportion to the success of the school or college. There is no doubt that women can do everything that men can do, and a great deal more; but the knowledge of their ability brings with it an aggressive, self-assertive, independent character, which renders it impossible to love, honor and obey the men of their social circles who are the brothers of their schoolmates, and who in the effort to become rich enough to afford the luxury of a highly educated wife have to begin young at business or in the factory, and for whom it is impossible to ever place themselves on an intellectual equality with the women whom they should marry. These men are, as a rule, refused by the brilliant college graduate, and are either shipwrecked for life and for eternity by remaining single, or are only saved by marrying a woman who is their social inferior, but who, by reason of her contented mind, in the end makes them a much better helpmate than the fault-finding intellectual woman who is looking for an impossible ideal.

The catholic church has, for many centuries, realized the importance of marriage and maternity in the upbuilding and strengthening of religious life in the community; and if the protestant churches are not to be emptied of their male attendance, the protestant clergy must speak out in no uncertain tone against the present methods of education, which are turning out women by the thousands, with requirements so varied and so great that no young man can afford to marry them; a step, moreover, which he is deterred from taking by the discouraging report of those of his friends who have ventured to marry the women of their own class, and who have advised them, in the words of Punch: "To those about to marry, don't." Whether a man should marry or not is too often spoken of lightly and as a joke. But to those who believe in the immortality of the soul, and that the whole world avails nothing to a man if he loses it, the possibility of early and happy marriages becomes a question of the vastest importance and one which students of sociology, and the fathers of the nation should study with the most intense anxiety and care.

Occasionally a college graduate goes through the ordeal of a high education, which has developed her intellect without ruining either her body or her natural instincts; but, as far as the writer can see, she is decidedly an exception. To the average highly intellectual woman the ordinary cares of wifehood and motherhood are exceedingly irksome and distasteful, and the majority of such women unhesitatingly say that they will not marry, unless they can get a man who can afford to keep them in luxury and supply them with their intellectual requirements. The gradual disappearance of the home, which any thoughtful observer must deplore, is, to a large extent, the result of the discontentment of the educated woman with the duties and surroundings of wifehood and motherhood, and the thirst for concerts, theaters, pictures and parties, which keep her in the public gaze, to the loss of her health and the ruin, very often, of her husband's happiness.

Fortunately, nature kills off the woman who shirks motherhood, but, unfortunately, it takes her a generation to do it; and in that short lifetime she is able to make one or many people unhappy.

What about the supply of female school teachers? Is not the very highest education possible necessary for them? From the writer's point of view most of the women who are now teaching school should have been married at eighteen and in a house of their own which might have been the schoolmaster's home. The profession of teaching was once exclusively in the hands of the men, and it can not be denied that they have achieved some great results. But as education rendered an everincreasing number of women unsuited for marriage, that is, unwilling to marry the available men, they invaded the schoolmaster's rank to such an extent that his salary has been cut down one half, and now he is unable to marry at all. Two well-known consequences have followed this state of affairs; first it is impossible to get men in sufficient numbers to become teachers for the boys' schools; and secondly, even big boys being taught by women, the effeminization of our men is gradually taking place. Although there are some instances of a mother alone having formed her son into a manly man, yet as a rule the boys require the example of a man's character to make them manly men. This subject has recently been dealt with in several elaborate papers by well-known educationalists, to whom it appears to be a real danger to the coming generation.

What about the men? If the higher education prevents the women from being good wives and mothers, will it not prevent the men from being good husbands and fathers? To some extent it does, and in so far it is a misfortune, but to a much less extent than among women, for the simple reason that the man contributes so little towards the new being; while, on the other hand, high intellectual training enables him to win in the struggle for existence much better than if he were possessed of mere brute force. But nature punishes the man who has all the natural instinct cultivated out of him, just as it does the woman, namely, by the extinction of his race. For the struggle for existence among the highly educated men has become so keen, because there are so many of them, that great numbers of them are unable to earn a living even for themselves; while the supporting of a highly educated woman, with her thousand and one requirements, is simply out of the question. A president of a great company recently informed the writer that he had, in one month, applications from eighty-seven university graduates for a position equivalent to that of an office boy at fifteen dollars a month while out of one hundred millionaires, at least ninety-five of them are known not to have been highly educated; but, on the contrary, to have left school between fourteen and sixteen years of age. So there is such a thing as learning too much, without knowing how to do anything. Just as athletes may be overtrained, so men may be overeducated.

This great question has received the attention of one of the brightest men of our age—no less than the chief magistrate of the United States;[4] while quite recently, in the British House of Lords, the Right Reverend Dr. Boyd-Carpenter, Bishop of Ripon, from his seat in that august assemblage, has called attention to the lateness of the age for marriage and the diminishing birth-rate, foreseeing, no doubt, that these two factors would soon be followed by the emptying of the churches and the lowering of the high standard of British morals and character.

The writer feels certain that, before long, this subject will receive the attention which it deserves from those who love their country and have the forming of its destiny in their hands. If he succeeds, by this or any other means, in drawing their attention to it, he will have fulfilled the object of his paper.

NOTES

1. [The American boy is generally admitted to be the *smartest* on earth, while the American girl is still more clever and brilliant than her brother.]

2. Eccles. 1:18.

3. Phosphates are the salts of phosphoric acid, found in many food groups. They are, of course, only one of many nutrients required to preserve health. See Ricardo A. Molins, *Phosphates in Food* (Boca Raton, FL: CRC Press, 1991).

4. Theodore Roosevelt (president of the United States, 1901–1909) gave much attention to the notion of "race suicide" (i.e., the small number of children being born to Anglo-Saxon parents). See such essays and reviews as "Kidd's 'Social Evolution'" (*North American Review*, July 1895), "Race Decadence" (*Outlook*, April 8, 1911), and "Twisted Eugenics" (*Outlook*, January 3, 1914).

16.

WOMANLY EDUCATION FOR WOMEN

(1915)

John M. McBryde Jr.

John McLaren McBryde Jr. (1870–1956) was the
son of the celebrated Southern educator John
M. McBryde (1841–1923), who was president of
South Carolina College and the Agricultural and
Mechanical College of Virginia (later Virginia
Polytechnic Institute). McBryde Jr. received his
PhD in English from Johns Hopkins University
and was chairman of the English department at
Tulane University. He is the author of a text-
book, *Profitable Company in Literature and Science* (1934). He also served as editor of the
Sewanee Review (1910–1919), where the following article appeared in the July 1915 issue. In
the extract presented below, McBryde proposes
that women's college education should specialize in "domestic economy" and other fields
that will produce the kind of Southern women
prevalent before the Civil War.

Source: John M. McBryde Jr., "Womanly Education for Women," *Sewanee Review* 15, no. 3 (July 1915): 473–76, 478–84.

*T*wo questions naturally present themselves:

First: Should the courses offered in colleges for women be different from those given in men's colleges?

Second: Should the studies pursued in women's colleges follow along exactly the same lines as the corresponding studies in colleges for men?

The answer to the first question involves a discussion of woman's work in life. Does woman's work lie in exactly the same sphere with man's? The answer to the second question concerns the development of woman's character. Is her ideal type to be the same as that of man?

Let us consider now the first question. It is generally conceded, I believe, that what constitutes a liberal education for man should furnish a liberal education for woman also. No single study that is considered a part of man's collegiate course is now omitted from the curricula of women's colleges, and all departments of knowledge are open to women. This is as it should be, for we want a type of woman as broad and liberal as possible in knowledge of the world and of all phases of humanity. For with knowledge usually comes sympathy. But in the education of women attention should, as far as possible, be centered on those studies which touch more closely women's work and women's lives, and which are most likely to develop their highest and truest womanly qualities. Now, if you ask me what is woman's work, I should find it hard to give you a very definite answer, for of recent years women have found a place in almost every field of manual labor and of intellectual activity. I would not make a plea for the narrowing of women's influence, for a limiting of the field, but for a deepening of the channel. Educated purely as woman, with all her qualities of modesty, sympathy, patience, endurance, hope, courage, faith, loyalty, devotion to duty developed to the full, she is an untold power for good. Educated as man, with her intellectual side developed at the expense of these gentler, finer qualities, she becomes unsexed, and is robbed of more than half her strength and influence.

Hence I should say that, without sacrificing the necessary intellectual training and careful discipline without which no education is complete, our college courses for women should lay special stress on the study of literature, music and art (including the so-called arts and crafts), domestic economy, and economics, or social science.

The importance of the study of literature in English and in the modern languages is now so clearly recognized as an essential part of any collegiate training, that I shall need to place little emphasis upon it. What I should like to make a plea for, however, is the study of literature as an art and not as a science. Our young women of to-day need to be brought into sympathetic, vital touch with the thoughts and feelings of the great masters of literature, rather than to be drilled in laboratory methods of dissecting and anatomizing. And in a day when so many women enter upon literature as a profession, they need less formal rhetoric and more practical work in composition.

Music and art should occupy a prominent place in all college courses for women as a necessary part of culture, and both the practical and theoretical work should be placed on a high plane. In many of the Northern colleges for women there is a tendency to crowd out both branches or to reduce the study to the theory and history of each subject. In some of our Southern institutions, on the other hand, they are regarded as extras or as mere accomplishments, and too great emphasis is laid upon parlor performances. It is always extremely difficult to adjust music and art to the more strictly academic studies, so that a proper balance may be preserved. Instead of being regarded as extras, they are now, in all of the leading colleges, placed in line with other studies and count towards a degree. This is a decided gain.

In addition to its purely cultural value, the study of art in its practical application to life has opened up new and delightful fields of work for women. The whole problem of house furnishing and house decoration, for example, should be in the hands of women, and, I believe, will eventually be considered as their special work. The colleges, recognizing the opportunity for women along this line, have, in many instances, included in their art courses the study of designs for wall papers, and patterns for carpets, for curtains, and for furniture. The making of china and pottery, too, should be a part of women's work, and Sophie Newcomb, in New Orleans, is a pioneer among our Southern colleges in this special line. Such work, however, is usually considered purely for its commercial value, and is generally left to the separate industrial schools. But, to my mind, such training is equally essential to every woman that has or hopes to have a home of her own, and I think all of our colleges for women should include in their art courses practical work in the furnishing and decoration of the house.

This leads me to the question of domestic economy, or the practical management of household affairs, another line in which the courses for women should diverge from those for men. In this day of minute specialization we have, as I have already indicated, separate industrial schools for women, where they may prepare themselves for professional work. But such schools are apt to be lacking in that broader outlook so essential to true culture, and the courses are usually directed to purely practical ends, with a view to the student's earning her own livelihood. I cannot stop here to go into the whole question of industrial education for women. It is a broad subject, and I do not pretend to an intimate acquaintance with it. But I do wish to say, with all the emphasis I am capable of, that every well-educated woman should know a good deal about that complex and perplexing subject, domestic economy.

Our college girls are far too busy with their studies to learn house-keeping at home, and they certainly don't learn anything about it at college, except to make fudge, or scrambled eggs, or Welsh rabbit for midnight feasts. The home training for girls is not what it used to be, and the college does not supply the lack. Our public schools, it is true, now have in nearly all cases practical work in cooking, and I think our colleges should continue this work along both theoretical and practical lines, and broaden and deepen it and give it true dignity. It is argued, however, that such work should be done at home, and that at college it interferes with the more serious intellectual studies. But the home, as I have just said, does not nowadays supply the training, and though at college the problem is to adjust the two lines of study, it can be done with judicious management, as laboratory investigations in chemistry or field experiments in agriculture are made to illustrate and enforce the theoretical work. For a long time it was thought that agriculture, too, could be learned far better at home on the farm in the furrow behind the plow. And if this work in domestic economy does interfere with the more serious intellectual training, what of that? Every mother will agree with me that she can spare in her daughter a little intellectuality for the sake of a little more domesticity.

In the complex life of to-day, we need women that can manage the household and make the wheels run without a hitch and without noise. And this task of household management seems to be becoming each year increasingly difficult, calling for women developed along every line. The servant problem throws heavier burdens than ever upon the mistress of the house, and yet, in spite of all this, many a young bride takes charge of a home with absolutely no experience in the management of the household. It is pitiable. It is wrong. Though our Western colleges are paying great attention to this line of women's work, our Southern colleges are doing little or nothing to help solve the problem. They could and should do much. [. . .]

For any kind of charitable work we need women who realize the necessity of studying social conditions, of investigating carefully all the facts of a given case, the influences of heredity and environment, for example, before they venture to take a single step for reform. With many such movements in the South the great difficulty has been the lack of trained leaders. Excellent as is the work already accomplished and now being done by the Van Dyke League in Lynchburg, the members of that organization will tell you that what they need just now more than all else is trained leadership along certain lines. There, as in every such undertaking, they need leaders who can diagnose social evils and suggest a remedy, just as in case of an epidemic we need a specialist to search out the cause and tell us how to improve the conditions and stamp out the disease. Such work requires something more than sentiment, more than good will, more than loving kindness and mercy and charity, more even than money, though all these we must have. In solving all practical social problems what we need is tact, training, and experience. Our colleges, then, should develop the natural tact of our young women, should furnish them with the necessary training and experience, and should send out each year enthusiastic workers, to take their places as leaders in the task of civic and social improvement wherever they may be needed in town or country throughout the State and Nation.

And now I have taken up so much time with the first question and its answer that I have little space left for the second: Should the studies for men and for women follow along exactly the same line? Are we to develop women as women or as men? This question is so closely connected with the first, that I have already anticipated and indicated the answer in much that I have said before. Whatever may be urged as to woman's intellectual equality with man, I believe with all my heart that that education which takes no account of differences of sex is misdirected and mischievous. And that education which fills a woman's soul with foolish notions of a glorious independence apart from man and apart from home is, I am convinced, equally pernicious. Because some women have to struggle alone for a livelihood—more's the pity—it does not follow that all women are to be educated for strenuous competition with men, shoulder to shoulder in business relations. It can never be too strongly emphasized or too often repeated that home is the centre of woman's influence and the source of her power, and the instruction in every subject of study should be directed with that important fact ever in view.

Yet no one can deny, it appears to me, that modern college education makes away from the home rather than toward it. Let us ask ourselves, Are our colleges sending out young women that fulfill all our hopes and expectations? Of course every mother thinks her daughter the absolute norm of perfection, but looking at what we may call the abstract type of modern college graduate, may we consider her altogether satisfactory? From the teacher's point of view, I must confess frankly I do not. It is difficult and somewhat dangerous to particularize, but, according to my observation, the two chief faults of the modern college girl are her extravagance and her lack of poise and of definite purpose. Now I wish to make no sweeping charges and no hasty, broad generalizations to draw forth indignant protests. What I mean to say is that these two faults are exceedingly common in our girls' schools in the South. It is but just to add, however, that these faults are characteristic of American social life to-day, and that they originate in the home, and the burden of them rests upon the shoulders of the parents themselves. In the average home of to-day there are to be seen the extravagance and lack of restraint and lofty ideal purpose which are reflected in the daughters at college.

One other criticism may be made of college life for women, and that is, it has become in every way too strenuous both in study and in athletics, resulting often in lifelong injury to health. Women are more conscientious than men, and in their studies subject themselves to far greater nervous strain, and the college course leaves little time for relaxation or repose. Even games for women are now exciting and dangerous. Basket ball is played with the same nervous intensity with which football is played at men's colleges, so that the atmosphere of most colleges for women is pervaded with a spirit of worry and haste and restless activity. In a forceful article in the *Atlantic* for January, 1892, entitled "The Greatest Need of College Girls," Miss Annie Payson Call draws attention to this unwholesome spirit and urges the absolute necessity for greater repose:

"No one who has been an inmate of a large college for women will deny the general state of rush and hurry which prevails there. 'No time,' is the cry from morning until night. Worry and hurry mark the average condition of the schoolgirl. If she is not hurried or worried herself, through the happy possession of a phlegmatic temperament, she cannot entirely resist the pressure about her. The spirit of the place is too strong for an individual to be in it and not of it. The strain is evident in the faces of students and teachers. It is evident in the number who annually break down from overstudy. More pitiably evident is it in those who have not wholly broken down, but are near enough the verge of disaster to have forgotten what a normal state of mind and body is. We can only think in the presence of such an one, What a magnificent specimen of womanhood that might have been, with a constitution that holds its own through such daily strain, and does not give in completely! This greatest physical need among studious women is so evident that those who will can see it. Those who will not see it are living in so abnormal a state that they do not recognize the want because of their necessity."

This was written fifteen years ago, and matters have grown worse instead of mending. Neither our college girls nor our college boys have learned the meaning and necessity of absolute rest or nerve-resting repose. Few ever seem to enjoy an hour of undisturbed, quiet contemplation, when with mind and heart emptied of worry and care, the whole physical and intellectual being seems to relax, become passive, and open itself to the beneficent influences of nature, or to silent communion with God. How many of our college men or women have ever entered into that mood of Wordsworth–

> . . . that serene and blessed mood
> In which the affections gently lead us on—
> Until, the breath of the corporeal frame
> And even the motion of our human blood
> Almost suspended, we are laid asleep
> In body, and become a living soul:
> While with an eye made quiet by the power
> Of harmony, and the deep power of joy,
> We see into the life of things.[1]

Such a mood of apparently meaningless mysticism to the casual reader seems foreign to our strenuous age, yet we need more of it among our young women, as an antidote against the frivolity and shallowness of modern society life.

Instead of teaching our college girls that they have intellects equal to men's, and that they must declare their independence and prove their equality, we should seek to open their eyes and give them something of that spiritual vision that Ruskin speaks of:

"The more I think of it, I find this conclusion more impressed upon me, that the greatest thing a human soul ever does in this world is to see something. Hundreds of people can talk for one who can think, but thousands can think for one who can see. To see clearly is poetry, prophecy, and religion—all in one."[2]

What, then, finally is the type of college woman that we should seek to send forth from our Southern colleges? I think we need to revert more to the ideal of womanhood in the Old South before the Civil War, which remains in nearly all respects the finest type that the modern world has seen. Let me bring that ideal before you in the words of a man[3] a who had intimate knowledge of it and who knew how to paint it clearly and truthfully, without one exaggerated line:

"She was . . . the key-stone of the domestic economy which bound all the rest of the structure and gave it its beauty. From early morn till morn again the most important and delicate concerns of the plantation were her charge and care. She gave out and directed all the work of the women. From superintending the setting of the turkeys to fighting a pestilence, there was nothing which was not her work. She was mistress, manager, doctor, nurse, counsellor, seamstress, teacher, housekeeper, slave, all at once. She was at the beck and call of everyone, especially of her husband, to whom she was 'guide, philosopher, and friend.'[4] . . .

"Her life was one long act of devotion—devotion to God, devotion to her husband, devotion to her children, devotion to her servants, to her friends, to the poor, to humanity. Nothing happened within the range of her knowledge that her sympathy did not reach and her charity and wisdom did not ameliorate. She was the head and front of the church; an unmitred bishop *in partibus*,[5] more effectual than the vestry or deacons, more earnest than the rector; she managed her family, regulated her servants, fed the poor, nursed the sick, consoled the bereaved. . . . With her own hands administering medicines or food; ever by her cheeriness inspiring new hope, by her strength giving courage, by her presence awaking faith; telling in her soft voice to dying ears the story of the suffering Saviour; with her hope soothing the troubled spirit, and lighting with her own faith the path down into the valley of the dark shadow. What poor person was there, however inaccessible the cabin, that was sick or destitute and knew not her charity! Who that was bereaved that had not her sympathy!

"The training of her children was her work. She watched over them, inspired them, led them, governed them; her will impelled them; her word to them, as to her servants, was law. She reaped the reward. If she admired them, she was too wise to let them know it; but her sympathy and tenderness was theirs always, and they worshipped her."

We must remember that there were no women's colleges in those days to teach the relative food values of potatoes and cabbages, the percentage of proteids in milk, the science of relieving the necessities of the poor, or the proper method of managing a household and rearing children according to sound pedagogical principles. And yet, does the modern college girl, with all her advantages and training, surpass this type, or even measure up to it?

Though I haven't quite reached that grandfatherly age that leads me to exalt the past unduly at the expense of the present, I do believe that in the rapid social revolution that followed immediately after the Civil War, and in the marvellous commercial development of the South in recent years, there has been too violent a breaking away from good old social traditions. Radicalism that cuts loose completely from the past is even more dangerous than conservatism that clings too closely to it. Among our young women of to-day we miss that exquisite grace, that refinement, rare tact, wonderful directing power, calm dignity, and absolute self-possession which characterized the women of the Old South. Our social code is too lax, our manners too free, and our young women are not sufficiently subjected to discipline and restraint. To check this growing spirit of restiveness we need in our college courses for women, to make a careful, loving investigation of the social and economic life of the Old South; we need to give our young women full and accurate information as to the beauty of family life and as to the characters and achievements of their grandmothers in the gracious days of old. Such a study of the past cannot fail to be helpful in restoring a finer feeling for tradition and in cultivating a proper appreciation of proportion and perspective.

It is, of course, natural that, having been kept back all these years and even denied their rights, women should now assert their independence and rejoice in their fancied freedom, rebelling at every restriction that draws a line between their liberty and men's privileges. But women should bear in mind that they form, or ought to form, the conservative, restraining, purifying, ennobling element in our society. To them we men must look for guidance and inspiration in our struggle against the growing commercialism and materialism of the day; and to this end we must see to it that our college training, by laying greater stress on womanly modesty, reserve, and repose, shall, along with and in addition to intellectual development, ever keep alive and foster more and more of the old-time grace and charm and winning force of the Southern woman.

NOTES

1. ["Lines Composed a Few Miles above Tintern Abbey" (41–49).]

2. John Ruskin (1819–1900), *Modern Painters* (1843–1856), vol. 3, part 4, chap. 16.

3. [Thomas Nelson Page, *Social Life in Old Virginia before the War* <1897>.] Page (1853–1922) was a leading Southern novelist of the period who nostalgically sought to carry his readers imaginatively back to the antebellum South.

4. Alexander Pope, *An Essay on Man* (1733–1734), 4.1.390.

5. I.e., *in partibus infidelium*, "in the realms of the infidels."

Part 6

WOMEN AND WORK

17.

WOMEN'S MISTAKES
ABOUT WORK

(1879)

Anonymous

In the later nineteenth century, *Lippincott's Magazine* emerged as a forceful opponent of women's rights. The following article, written by a woman and appearing in the August 1879 issue, broaches several of the standard objections to women's full participation in the workforce, specifically noting that women do not apply themselves to their work and that their proper "profession" is housekeeping.

The subject of women's work—what they shall do, how they shall do it, and how much they shall get for it when done—is one which has become of late personally and intensely interesting to many of the women in our own and other countries of the world. The pressure of the recent financial troubles,[1] so widely felt and coming upon so many persons and families who never before knew what it was to have a want unsupplied, has been, no doubt, partly responsible for the restless desire of the women of the present day to

Source: Anonymous, "Women's Mistakes about Work," *Lippincott's Magazine* 24, no. 2 (August 1879): 236–37, 239–40.

be up and doing something, they scarcely seem to know what themselves, but at all events something—if possible, something new, and which shall open to them a larger field of action than that formerly attainable by their sex.

There is no denying that in our grandmothers' days the position of women with regard to the active business of the world was very different from that which they now occupy, and which, while they are sometimes, no doubt, thrust into it by necessity, is often the result of their own desire and efforts for a larger sphere, and also of their inability to dispense with the luxuries to which they have been accustomed. Seventy years ago, women of the better class were beings to be sheltered, protected, worked for. Men so regarded them, and the idea of the female portion of a family being expected or allowed to provide in any way for its support or their own never seems to have occurred to any one except in case of direst necessity. A great deal of economy was practised, much self-denial quietly borne, before the domestic, home-loving woman of that time sallied forth to make her own way in the world. Not that she was at all a useless member of the family firm, or hung a helpless weight on her protectors. She managed with thrifty care the household concerns; she knew what her servants ought to do, and made them do it; she prevented waste and practised a wise and discriminating economy, the result of which was that families were but seldom broken up and scattered from want of means to keep together —a thing which in our day has become sadly familiar to us all.

Past times are past times, however, and we may as well acknowledge that this dear domestic divinity has vanished for ever, taking with her her commonplace virtues, her sweet contentment with her appointed lot, and her cheerful performance of the small daily duties which added so much to the comfort of those around her, and which filled her life to its peaceful close. The life of the woman of the present is as different from all this as it well can be, and she would regard with scorn unspeakable the uneventful existence which her forebears found so busy and pleasant. She demands her full share of the excitements of modern life, its pleasures and indulgences which have become necessities to her; and if her father, brother or husband cannot supply her with them, she forthwith proceeds to obtain them for herself. Nor does she generally meet with any decided opposition to her doing so, for the horror which the idea of women's work excited in the men of other days has departed with the women who shared the feeling and called it forth.

But let us see whether women have gained or lost by the changed position in which they now stand before the world. *"Stava bene, ma per star meglio, sto qui,"* says an old Italian epitaph with doleful frankness ("I was well, but tried to be better, and here I am!"); and this saying is certainly applicable in some degree, though not entirely, to the present state of affairs with regard to women.

Women-workers may be divided into two classes—those who choose to work, and those who are obliged to. With the latter sadly-numerous corps of the noble army of martyrs we may presently have a few words, but our concern just now is with the first-named class, those who, tiring of the routine of their daily lives, and desirous of obtaining more luxuries than their income will permit without addition, betake themselves to some occupation more or less lucrative as a means to the desired end. We can all number among our acquaintances women who have done this rather than dress quietly, live inexpensively or economize on a moderate income. They know nothing of sewing, and neither can nor will make or renovate any part of their own wardrobe; they utterly contemn and ignore any sort of household labor; but they are quite willing to devote a portion of their time to the manufacture of dreary tidies and melancholy wax flowers, or picture-cards whereon a humpbacked bird appears roosting among the inevitable apple-blossoms which seem to be the beginning and end of their artistic capabilities in the vegetable line.

For here we immediately come upon one of the reasons why women so seldom rise to great excellence in what they undertake when they leave their own special domain. They will not plod. Severe study, really hard, sustained effort, is what they will not consent to. They are, with some rare exceptions, smatterers, looking for the

quickest and easiest way of attaining such a small amount of proficiency as will enable them to throw off some kind of work that will
pass muster and bring money. A few women here and there who have
undertaken to rank themselves with men really study hard, and perhaps achieve a degree of success in their chosen profession or career.
At least these exceptions should have credit for the energy and perseverance which they have shown in the attainment of their object, in
spite of many difficulties and the obstacles which Nature mercifully
interposes to the transformation of the household goddess into a
second-rate doctor or lawyer, and man's intended helpmeet into his
intrepid if somewhat over-confident competitor.

But these scattered cases are rare, and likely to remain so; and in
spite of many experiments, successful or otherwise, in the education of
women, we consider it highly improbable that the lords of creation will
ever have to dispute with the ladies their precious privileges of cutting
off people's legs and arms and wrangling over their lawsuits. And until
women understand that there is no royal road to real success, and that
patient labor is necessary if they would do any work which will bear
criticism, the studio and the concert-room will have scarcely more to
fear from them than the court-room and the dissecting-table. [. . .]

We will venture to say that there are but few women who cannot
add very materially in some way to the comfort of the household of
which they are a part. We are not alluding, of course, to those exceptionally placed in any way, as by poor health or the great misfortune
of being alone in the world. But we speak of the larger class of
women, who have homes and families whose welfare is or ought to be
inexpressibly dear to them, and can be largely affected by their supervision or neglect. To particularize. Is it any disgrace to the wife of a
professional man with a moderate income or a clerk on a small salary
that she should dispense with the services of a nurse and faithfully and
patiently take care of her child herself? or to the daughter of such a
man that she should learn to make and remake her own clothes and
those of her little brothers and sisters, or take a part in the nicer
cooking or up-stairs work of the house? Many a family could be com-

fortably and pleasantly supported and save a provision for the future by such a course, who are now struggling along with wasteful, over-paid servants and an anxious, toiling master, who knows that when he is gone little indeed will remain for those he leaves behind him, who will find that the amateur performances which did well enough for the supply of superfluities are but a poor dependence when it comes to making a living.

Let us not be understood as advocating the suppression of talent where it really exists. On the contrary, let it be cultivated and encour-aged with all the care and labor which its possessor can honestly bestow upon it, and not destroyed by slovenly, careless work and an effort to reap the harvest of success without having ploughed the ground or sown the seed. If a woman has a fine voice or a decided talent and love for music, by all means let her cultivate it as far as she can consistently with the comfort of those around her, and let her plod patiently onward and upward, mastering the principles and *technique* of her art and knowing thoroughly what she knows. She will find her reward for every hour of honest toil in her sense of power over her voice or instrument, and her far keener and more subtle, because intel-ligent, enjoyment of the divine gift. Music so cultivated becomes the blessing and comfort it was meant to be, instead of being degraded into a mere pastime of the ignorant and the torture of all within hearing of it, as it too often is. We doubt, however, if even poor music can ever do as much harm by vitiating and lowering the public taste as poor per-formances in other branches of art, for the reason that it is a less mar-ketable commodity. A woman who cannot read music at sight more or less well, and whose execution is poor, will have to confine her efforts to the edification of her family circle, as she will be unlikely to get a place in a choir or to be encouraged to appear in the concert-room; but many a plaque, which would be better designated if it were spelt with a *g* instead of a *q*, is sold for a price which, however small, is beyond its worth, and hangs on the wall it is far from decorating, an example of the reverse of the saying, "A thing of beauty is a joy for ever."[2]

The number of women who possess a decided talent for any

branch of the fine arts, and who feel an irresistible desire to exercise it, is, and always will be, small, compared to those not endowed with any great powers of mind, and are not calculated to shine intellectually, but who have a good supply of common sense, if they would only use it, and often an amount of executive ability, energy and practical skill which would, if brought into play, raise them to great eminence in their own particular profession.

For they have a profession as old as time itself, and certain to last till time shall be no more—one which is open to little or no competition from the other sex, and which almost every woman is called upon to engage in, at some period of her life and in some capacity, whether that of daughter, sister, wife or mother. We mean just the old, humdrum and often despised one of housekeeping, which began with the first dainty which our common mother provided for our first father, though with what, we are bound to admit, were somewhat disastrous results, and which will continue down to the final meal which the last woman will prepare for the last man and which, if it is a good one, he will doubtless, after the manner of his healthy, hungry sex, do full justice to, even with the crack of doom itself imminently impending over his head.

The woman cannot have seriously studied this profession who considers it unworthy of her time and attention or unimportant in its results: its duties are often the most obvious and unavoidable ones of her life, and extend their influence to many a future career. For housekeeping, in its fullest sense, means the keeping the house together, and includes much that is passed over and forgotten in the ordinary use of the term. It has its different branches—the useful, the æsthetic, sometimes the sympathetic—its upper and lower departments, exercising almost every faculty of the brain, and often of the heart, and embracing a constant ministration to the needs of a household in every possible way. It does not mean only a vigilant watch over the flour-barrel and the coal-bin, a crusade against cobwebs and the circumventing of Bridget in her meditated bestowal of the cold meat on her cousin. The influence of the keeper of the house is felt in things moral as well as things actual; and the refinement and fitness of its arrangements compatible with its means, the order which reigns in it, and, above all, the spirit which pervades it, must all depend on her to a great degree. Who else must set the example of forbearance to the different members of a family, often so necessary when all cannot be amply provided for? Who must watch over and train the children whose father is away earning their daily bread, and teach them to be honorable men and sweet, sensible women? And who must keep up the courage of that father, and speak the cheerful, sympathetic word he needs when he comes home, often disheartened by failure or irritated by his struggle with the hard outer world? Who but the woman who understands her profession, and considers it, as it is, one of the most ancient and honorable callings in the world?

And, though there are of course exceptions, the man who has such a home is apt to appreciate it fully, and the children brought up in it generally do honor to their early training. And the woman who has made it and kept it together will have something better to look back upon, when she comes to the twilight hour and sits with folded hands taking her well-earned rest, than an existence which might be summed up in the words which record, we presume, the entire virtues of a deceased lady of rank: "She was bland, passionate and religious; also painted in water-colors, and sent three pictures to the Exhibition; and of such is the kingdom of heaven!"

NOTES

1. The United States suffered a severe depression in 1873–1877 as a result of excessive speculation in railroad expansion.
2. John Keats (1795–1821), *Endymion* (1818), 1.1.1.

18.

THE EDUCATION AND EFFICIENCY OF WOMEN

(1910)

Emily Greene Balch

Emily Greene Balch (1867–1961) graduated at the head of her class from Bryn Mawr College in 1889 and subsequently studied sociology at the Sorbonne, Paris, where she learned of the "settlement houses" being established for the poor and for immigrants. Returning to her native Boston, she opened her own settlement house, Denison House, in 1892. She quickly befriended the reformer Jane Addams, who was undertaking similar work; they remained lifelong associates. Balch also organized labor unions, including the Women's Trade Union League. She began teaching at Wellesley College in 1897. During World War I, Balch vigorously supported pacifism and world peace; one of the organizations she helped found at this time later became the American Civil Lib-

Source: Emily Greene Balch, "The Education and Efficiency of Women," *Proceedings of the Academy of Political Science* 1, no. 1 (1910): 61–66, 69–70.

erties Union. Her pacifism led to her dismissal from Wellesley in 1918. After the war she helped found the Women's International League for Peace and Freedom. In the 1930s she modified her pacifist views, coming to believe that fascist aggression must be met by force. Throughout World War II she assisted refugees and spoke of the need for international cooperation after the war. Her work led to her receiving the Nobel Peace Prize in 1946. Balch wrote numerous studies in economics and sociology. In the following essay, first published in the *Proceedings of the Academy of Political Science* in 1910, in a special issue titled "The Economic Position of Women," Balch maintains that women are "misfits" in the industrial economy because they are unable to fulfill their functions as mothers.

*W*omen in modern production are a misfit. They are like the dog that puzzled the expressman in the classic story. "*He* don't know where he wants to go, and *we* don't know where he wants to go; he's eat his tag."

Is not this sense of misadjustment, of being astray, due to the fact that, industry being arranged to meet its end of private profits, human nature has to adjust itself as best it can to industrial conditions, instead of industrial conditions adjusting themselves to human nature? The troubles that result from this system make themselves felt everywhere, among men as well as women, but most seriously among the weakest competitors, and especially among wage-earning children and women.

My subject is education and efficiency, but I do not propose to go over the well-worn arguments to show that we ought at once to establish schools for trade training. It is now pretty generally understood that this is true. I want to raise a more far-reaching question—can women be economically efficient in production, production being organized as it now is?

The lives of both men and women have certain permanent aspects; whether in the stone age or in the twentieth century they must rear their descendants, they must between them produce material support for themselves and for the growing generation, they must lead their own personal lives and feed and discipline and "invite" their own souls and minds. There is always this trinity of their racial, their economic, and their inner life.

But while both men and women have this three-fold function, the differences in their racial life involve far-reaching economic consequences. Motherhood is an occupation as fatherhood is not, and this deeply affects woman's industry. Even in the primitive world, where industry is largely a household matter for all, woman's activity is bound to the hearthstone more closely than man's, for the bearing and rearing of children is intertwined with all her other business, and conditions it. This makes housework with all its ramifications and outlying branches the great feminine profession throughout the ages.

Consequently when industry, passing from the control of the worker to that of the owner of the business, assumed its modern specialized form and took work and workers out of the home into the factory and workshop, this change, carried out with no regard for the results on the workers themselves, affected the lives of women in ways which are not paralleled in those of men. Besides other consequences, it greatly lessened woman's efficiency both as mother and as worker.

Under the old régime there was an effective unity in women's lives, an organic harmony of function with function. The claims of motherhood and of work upon woman harmonized, because she herself was in control and arranged the conditions of her industry to fit her duties and disabilities as wife and mother. For herself and for her household she planned the various tasks with a view to strength, convenience and training for development. Besides the unity of motherhood and industry, there was unity of education and industry, of preparation and practice. The girl was essentially an apprentice of the housekeeper, whether mother or mistress. Her lessons were indistinguishable from her labor. From a little child she was working as well as learning, and also till she was at the head of her own home she was learning as well as working. Read Solomon's description, or even better, Xenophon's charming sketch in his *Economicus*, for a picture of feminine household industry on a rather large scale.[1] We need not conceive this stage as ideal. The point is that there was a natural adjustment of work to worker which modern industry undermines in three ways—in separating work from the home, in separating work from education, and in shaping the conditions and concomitants of work without regard to the powers, tastes, or needs of the workers.

Before endeavoring to analyze these effects let us consider various types of modern women in whose lives all the different difficulties interact, shaping their fate, too often, in most strange and inharmonious fashion.

First let us take the professional woman. If she leads a single life she cuts the Gordian knot of the incompatibility of work and marriage. This is simple, certainly, but quite abnormal. While it is doubtless a happy solution in many cases, it is certainly undesirable that large numbers of women should adopt it, especially if we may suppose that a class of celibate professional women withdraw from the race the inheritance of some degree of picked intellectual ability. It has been argued, by Sidney Webb[2] if I remember rightly, that the rule disqualifying married women for public-school teaching tends to keep a selected group of women out of marriage; a practical exclusion from marriage of women who succeed in medicine, law, architecture, art and business would be, from this point of view, at least an equally serious loss as regards quality if not quantity.

If a woman is able to combine professional activity with marriage and motherhood, as some have been so brilliantly successful in doing, this is because professional work is often more like the old housework than is factory work as regards elasticity and the possible adjustment of time and amount of work to personal convenience.

As our second group let us take well-to-do married women who command domestic service and nursery assistance. Such a woman has the maximum of freedom in ordering her own life, yet, even so, under the mould of the general situation, how chaotic her life history is likely to be. Suppose that she is at a finishing school till she "comes out" in society, or that she goes to college and at twenty-two comes home again to live, not choosing a professional career. Although she is only half conscious of the situation she practically waits for a few years to see whether or not marriage is to be her lot. Probably her natural mates are not yet financially able to offer marriage, and, again, more or less conscious of her rather humiliating situation, she becomes seriously and definitely interested in some specialized activity. By distinct preparation or simply by practice she fits herself for the work that she has found to do; then, just as she is well engaged in this work, the critical moment arrives and she marries. For some years her profession is motherhood, though this is the last thing for which she has thought of fitting herself; and then again her life takes a new turn. Her children are no longer children; they are at college or at work or married; or her daughter at home, perhaps without liking to say so, yearns to be intrusted with the home administration, for a while at least. Whether or not the mother resigns any of her housekeeping duties, motherhood is no longer a business that fills her days and gives adequate employment to her powers; again she seeks for occupation.

Such women, with the unmarried women of leisure, make the most disposable force in our society, but one very variously disposed. Some of them, the spenders, live purely parasitic lives, absorbing the services of others and consuming social wealth without rendering any return. Others, at the opposite extreme, perform work that is unpaid and that could not be paid for, work that demands experimentation, initiative and devotion. The work of a man or woman who combines with the chance gift of economic freedom the chance gift of genius consecrated to service—the work of a Charles Darwin, a William Morris, a Josephine Shaw Lowell, or a Jane Addams[3]—is a pearl beyond price, but probably common people (that is, most of us) work better under a reasonable degree of pressure.

Our next social class is the married women who do their own work, as we say. For them life retains in the main its primitive harmony, except that they are less likely than women of old to come to their life work adequately prepared to carry on a household on the highest plane practicable with the resources available under contemporary conditions.

Our last class is the working women. The woman who does her own work is not, in the curious development of our phraseology, a working woman, though we may believe that the mother of a brood of children for whom she cleans, cooks, sews, washes and nurses does some work. On the other hand, the working woman is not, in our common phrase, occupied in "doing her own work," and truly, the work at which she is set might appear to be almost anybody's rather than hers, if its unsuitability to her needs and powers is any criterion. While her school, however imperfect it may have been, was designed to meet her needs, was administered with the object of advancing her interests, her workshop, on the contrary, seeks quite a different end— the owner's profits. If she prospers or suffers through its conditions, that is a wholly alien consideration. The work is not her own, both because the product is not hers and because the conditions under which the work is carried on have no relation to her needs.

The education of the girl who is to enter industry generally fails as yet, however well intended, to fit her effectively for her working career. Most working girls, indeed, leave school at fourteen, when they are in any case too young to be efficient. Then come the proverbial wasted years of casual and demoralizing employment, till at eighteen or so the young workers find their footing and for five years, it may be, rank as working women. Then to most of them comes marriage. They entered industry untrained, now they enter married life untrained, if not unfitted, for such life, and at a less adaptable age than earlier. To a considerable extent the economic virtues of the factory are virtues that the girl cannot carry over into her housework, and its weaknesses are weaknesses that lessen her success as wife and mother. Industry tends to unfit her for home making if it tends to make her a creature of mechanical routine, unused to self-direction, unplastic, bored by privacy and not bored by machine monotony; if it accustoms her to an inapplicable scale and range of expenditure which assigns too much money to clothes (which are necessary to the status and earning power of the worker as they are not to mothers and children) and too little to adequate nourishment which, important to the adult, is fundamental to the health of children. Worst of all, the employments of working women tend, as has now been shown, more commonly and more seriously than has been at all generally understood, to unfit women, nervously and physically, for bearing children.

When we try to disentangle the confusions illustrated in these varying types of lives we see that one of the main causes of trouble is the fact that modern industry is largely incompatible, while work lasts, with the functions of wife and mother or that at least it militates against them. We have seen some of the ways in which this simple fact of the incompatibility of two fundamental functions distracts and deforms women's lives.

A result of this divorce of industrial and married life is the fact that it is impossible to predict whether a given girl will spend her life in the home or in the working world, commercial, industrial or professional, and that consequently she commonly fails to prepare for either. We have indeed some professional training, some business training, and are just beginning to have some trade training; training for the home vocations has hardly got commonly beyond some cooking and sewing in the grades—most desirable as far as it goes. In Utopia, I dare say that every girl when she becomes engaged to be married, receives, besides her general education and her trade training, six months of gratuitous and compulsory vocational preparation for homemaking, and that this training for the bride, and a course in the ethics and hygiene of marriage for both bride and groom, is there required before a marriage license can be issued; moreover, I imagine that there every woman expecting her first child is given a scholarship providing instruction and medical advice for some months before and after the child is born, the conditions depending upon individual circumstances.

In the real world some of our grossest evils are related to the lack of preparation for the most vital relations of life. Uncertainty as to her vocation not only prevents a girl's being trained for either household or industrial life, but it makes her a most destructive element in competitive wage earning. She does not care to make herself efficient in industry, for she hopes soon to marry, and meanwhile the semi-self-supporting woman drags down the pay of women wholly dependent on their own earnings and also that of men, perhaps including that of the man who might marry her but cannot afford it, thus increasing the chances against her in the lottery of marriage. [. . .]

As regards married women in industry, the situation is much the same as the situation with regard to children. They should stay out wholly because it is disastrous to the family for them to go in wholly and unreservedly, because their subsidized competition is likely to be injurious, and finally because the conditions of work are apt to be ruinous to their health. And yet for women after marriage to abstain from all employment outside the household is often wasteful and altogether undesirable. If married women could work some hours a day, or some days a week, or some months a year, or some years and not others, as circumstances indicated (as they conceivably might do under a more elastic and adaptable organization of employment), and if they could do so without damage to wage standards or workshop discipline, it would seem advantageous, in more ways than one, for them not to drop out of industry at marriage. Both marriage and employment might become sufficiently universal to make it usual to train every girl for both, at least in a general way. If marriage did not appear to girls (quite fallaciously in most cases) as a way of getting supported without working, their interest in increasing their earning power would be greater; if wives were normally and properly contributors in some degree to the money income of the family, marriage would be more general and, above all, earlier, especially if the giving of allowances to mothers, of which Mr. Wells dreams, ever came into practice.[4]

NOTES

1. Xenophon, *Oeconomicus* (c. 362 BCE), 7.36–42, discussing the role of a wife in the management of an estate.

2. Sidney Webb (1859–1947), British social and political reformer who, in collaboration with his wife, Beatrice Webb (1858–1943), wrote numerous works on politics and economics.

3. The last two names refer to Josephine Shaw Lowell (1843–1905), American charity worker and reformer, and Jane Addams (1860–1935), American social reformer.

4. In numerous works in the first decade of the century, such as *A Modern Utopia* (1905), British novelist and philosopher H. G. Wells (1866–1946) proposed tax subsidies for mothers.

19.

THE PSYCHOLOGY OF SUPERVISING THE WORKING WOMAN

(1942)

Dr. Donald A. Laird and Eleanor C. Laird

Donald Anderson Laird (1897–1969) received his PhD in psychology from the State University of Iowa in 1923 and taught at numerous universities, including Yale and Northwestern. He was the author of many popular treatises on psychology, several of them specifically relating to the psychology of business; among them are *The Psychology of Selecting Men* (1925), *Increasing Personal Efficiency* (1925), *How to Increase Your Brain Power* (1939), and *Practical Business Psychology* (1951). In the following extract from *The Psychology of Supervising the Working Woman* (1942), written in collaboration with his wife, Eleanor Childs Laird, Laird suggests that many women secretly yearn to be men, and that their behavior in the office can be accounted for by noting this "striving for completeness." This excerpt appears in the

Source: Dr. Donald A. Laird and Eleanor C. Laird, *The Psychology of Supervising the Working Woman* (New York: McGraw-Hill, 1942), pp. 109–21, 123–25.

chapter "Striving for Completeness—The Key to Woman's Emotional Life."

*T*o get an understanding of the more inclusive effects of these changes and differences on woman's make-up, we shall examine the findings of the psychoanalysts who have studied the end results.

Women take all these differences in physique and make-up seriously—much more seriously than they will admit, except under the skilled ferreting of psychoanalysts. They feel, perhaps unconsciously, that they have been cheated in the lottery of Nature. This gives a clue to the secret of managing women:

Tell them they are doing better than men! Quite likely they are— but they crave reassurance. Tell them, and keep on telling them.

Of the application of this to selling, we wrote in "What Makes People Buy":

> Today woman can vote, but, until Nature makes it possible for her to be a father, she will continue to feel that she has been shortchanged and will want to have and to do many things in a futile, yet ceaseless effort to show that, after all, she can do anything a man can. So, if she is a city girl, she smokes cigarettes; if she is a hillbilly, she chews a cud of "'backer."
>
> The highest flattery that can be given her when she is deciding on an investment is to say, "You are reasoning this through better than most men do." And one of the most telling things that can be said to the recalcitrant man consumer is, "Now, let's talk this over, man to man." Especially is this true of the hard-boiled purchasing agent, as we shall see.
>
> In many superficial psychological respects women are different from men, but at heart, in their unconscious minds, they want to be like men. Perhaps they sense this mental difference which may reinforce the unconscious irritability over the more obvious physical differences.
>
> The woman consumer's unconscious mind feels keenly, but inarticulately, that she has been cheated, that she is not quite up to man's par.[1]

This ineradicable desire of women to be treated as men, if they cannot be truly masculine, leads to many problems. Dr. Eleanor Rowland Wembridge, referee of the Juvenile Court at Cleveland, Ohio, has devoted her life to helping straighten out the jams in which girls and young women get caught. She finds that girls do many foolish, even dangerous things just because they are tired of being treated as girls.

They get "fed-up" on being told that girls cannot do this or that, and many of them finally decide to do whatever they wish in order to show that they are just as good as their brothers. It is for no better reason than envying brothers their independence that many girls leave home and go away to take a job where they may make their own living and be their own boss. Others, Dr. Wembridge finds, make sudden marriages to worthless men they have known only a few days in order to get away from their parents' home and into a home—usually a much less comfortable one—of their own where they can do as they like.

These, of course, are rebellious girls, those recognized as the hard-to-handle kind, but mental analysts in hundreds of places find out that even grown-up women the world over are, in the majority of instances, still inwardly rebellious because of envy over man's greater physical strength and greater freedom to go and to do as he pleases.

Women periodically envy men their freedom from the worries and problems of the "curse" of menstruation. This is an open masculine protest, as compared with some of the more subtle forms of its manifestation.

"Women envy men to an extent far beyond ordinary recognition," says Dr. Karl A. Menninger, the Midwestern mental specialist.[2] The old saw about the better grass in the other pasture is very true here. Women are frequently conscious of it and protest bitterly against the superarrogation of males.

"To play the normal passive feminine role seems to them a kind of humiliation which they cannot bear. They envy all male prerogatives; they envy man his physique, his strength, even his sexual organs. They sometimes show this by ostentatious demonstrations of their own abilities; 'Look, I am just as capable as any man,' some of them like to say.

"Of course, such women are very neurotic; they do not realize that they are renouncing their biological superiority over men in exchange for play-acting which is dictated by childish enviousness."

This is why many husbands are henpecked, bossed around unmercifully by some wives. By dominating her husband, the woman gains the feeling that she is not, after all, the weaker sex, and that by limiting the freedom of one man, she is getting even with the world for the way her freedom was limited as a child.

Women, as a rule, make poor bosses in a factory or office—or even with their domestic help—because of this tendency to become too "bossy." Professor Harry W. Hepner, for example, found that being too dictatorial was a fault in only 8 per cent of men, but in more than twice as many women.[3]

Not only may a woman boss her husband around shamefacedly to show who is superior, but in a strange quirk of mind, some women are capricious in love for the same reason. They will encourage the man and then unexpectedly turn him down and have nothing further to do with him in order to keep from becoming enslaved to a person they envy. That is why the great majority of single women are not worried about finding a man; only 16 per cent of single women worry about not finding the right life-mate—84 per cent are apparently content to stay single so they will not be under the bondage of the envied male.

This protest against the envied sex shows itself in many minor, but yet interesting ways. College girls wear men's overalls and mannish hats to imitate the envied male. Many mannish women are that way for no more serious reason than imitating the envied sex. They still have the fingerprint of true and lovable femininity, but they apparently wish they did not have it and try to be more like men.

Other women who overvalue the importance of being masculine try to become interested in amusements which are typically masculine. The typically masculine amusements are fishing, hunting, driving an automobile, boxing matches, billiards, mechanical puzzles, sleight-of-hand tricks, vaudeville, and detective stories. Women who go in for some of these amusements do so largely in protest at not being men, not necessarily because of any deep interest in the recreation. Or the dainty nurse may specialize in taking care of men patients because her ministrations to the helpless male convince her how dependent great hulks of men are upon a wisp of a woman.

All in all, this striving for completeness is perhaps the greatest single force, next to dire necessity, that leads women to go to work.

It is a force to be reckoned with in the management of women workers. An elderly, or at least older, man boss causes less of this surging resentment, for he rather naturally takes the place, in her thinking, of her father with whom she is likely to be secretly in love.

Buoying up her own self-respect, her feeling that after all it is the men who are the world's fools, also helps. This can be done subtly and effectively. One large concern, for instance, has the walls of its spacious lounge for women workers decorated with cartoon-like murals of high artistic merit which portray the embarrassments of that complete male ninny—Ichabod Crane, of headless horseman fame. The girls lounging there must feel that womankind is not so bad after all—look what a fool that Crane boy turned out to be. In a clever fashion, and without stirring up dangerous resentment, this series of wall decorations helps the girls restore their own egos to a more healthy condition.

But with some girls, the inner turmoil over not having been a man, and not being treated like a man, has taken on proportions far too large to be given such benign treatment.

It is the quiet little woman who is most likely to have this internal resentment at not being a man, says Dr. Beatrice Hinkle.[4] This so-called "introverted" type has the more sensitive feelings, is more likely to break down and cry when "bawled out" by a man, and is more inclined to notice and to brood over the unfairness of the world in making men stronger and giving them more freedom.

In those few women who are men-haters, it is obvious that their envy is bitter. There are women who avoid meeting men or who are embarrassed when with men because of the foolish notion that men are superior to women.

The tomboys, those young girls who run around wildly and play at boy's games, usually before they are old enough to go to high school, show how early in life this feeling of resentment develops in womankind. The tomboy, instead of having envy turn into hate, tries seriously to be as much like a boy as she can. [. . .]

Dr. Arthur T. Jersild, of Columbia University, recently made a study of 200 girls from five to twelve years of age. He found that 10 per cent of the girls consciously desired to be changed to the opposite sex. Among a like number of boys in the same places and ages, he found only one who wished he had been born a girl.

At Buffalo, N. Y., nearly 500 high-school seniors were studied along similar lines by Drs. Herman J. P. Schubert and Mazie Earle Wagner. They discovered that 32 per cent of the girls wished they had never been born. Not quite half as large a percentage of the boys had the same negative wish.

Why women become so disturbed over the thought that men may be superior is a puzzler. There is no real basis in scientific fact. True, men are stronger of body than women are, and can carry heavier weights and throw a ball farther. But in intelligence men and women are equal. In ability to use the senses—eyes, ears, nose, etc.—women are superior to men. Women are also superior to men in getting along with people, in schoolwork, and in resistance to disease and illness.

But many women still think they have to be like men to be appreciated. "Unaware that the mannish woman is a credit neither to her true sex nor to the one she simulates, the female dons the masculine dress, and takes up smoking with a vim, in order to convince men that what they can do, she can do also," observes Dr. Wayland F. Vaughan of Boston University. "Intoxicated with the success of her assertiveness, she demands equal pay for equal work. She must leave home and enter business where she can outdo man in his own lines. The very noise of her masculine protest is evidence of her inferiority feelings. In all her mannish pretensions, she reveals her inconsistency—for if she is the equal to man, why should she not be content with being feminine, instead of attempting to convince the other sex that she is competent to play the manly role?"

Science cannot say that one sex is inferior to the other. They are just vastly different in many respects; that is all that can be said, without praise or censure for either. Nature has evolved men and women to be different in many ways, so that one complements the shortcomings of the other. Looked upon as a cooperative pair, Nature has done a good job, although each sex may have its weaknesses. These are not weaknesses, however, when one sex understands the distinctive traits and their organic basis in the other.

But womankind is still goaded on by the feeling that she is incomplete. From this feeling—which might be looked upon as resentment—arise a number of problems in managing women workers. Teamwork, for instance.

NOTES

1. Donald A. Laird, *What Makes People Buy* (New York: McGraw-Hill, 1935), p. 68.

2. Karl A. Menninger (1893–1990), renowned American psychiatrist and author of *The Human Mind* (1930), *Love against Hate* (1942), and other treatises.

3. Harry Walker Hepner (1893–1984), professor of psychology at Syracuse University and author of several works on marketing, business, and psychology.

4. Beatrice (Moses) Hinkle (1874–1953), psychiatrist and author of *The Re-creating of the Individual* (1923) and other works.

20.

MEMO TO
THE AMERICAN WOMAN

(1966)

Patricia Coffin

Patricia Coffin (1912–1974) is the author of a children's book, *The Gruesome Green Witch* (1969), and of *1, 2, 3, 4, 5, 6: How to Understand the Years That Count* (1972), a manual on childcare. She also served for many years as editor of *Look* (1942–1971) and *Life* (1971–1974). In the following essay, published in *Look* (January 11, 1966), Coffin reacts to the feminist movement of the early 1960s by criticizing women for abandoning their homes for work, given that "women have less intellectual acumen than men." Instead, she says, women should consider themselves "lucky to have a man to lean on."

$\mathcal{F}$rustrated? So they say. Your case has been hash-browned and French-fried in the press, on the air, among the best-sellers, and is still being dished up. The case of the American Woman with a capital "W," that is. How you are trying to find yourself. How

Source: Patricia Coffin, "Memo to the American Woman," *Look* (January 11, 1966): 15–17.

you want to fulfill yourself as a homemaker *and* career girl. Or how, to use a homey homily, you want to have your cake and eat it too.

Well, try. It is a tricky cake mix. You will find that no matter how you bake it, you will come out with two careers: homemaker and would-be world shaker. U.S. Children's Bureau chief Katherine Oettinger flatly states: "The most difficult task a human being can face is being a working mother." To lead this double life, you need the strength of two. As author Marya Mannes[1] puts it: The career woman has no *wife to come home to.* Your intuition must be tuned to two wavelengths: home and office. Your emotional resilience will get a brutal workout.

The average married woman with the usual complement of children is being discussed. For frustrated single girls, disillusioned divorcées, embattled daughters, and even happy housewives, see the following stories.

According to Betty *The Feminine Mystique* Friedan,[2] the feminist who found "home and peace in the bustling, noisy life of the big city . . . after eight years in suburbia," women should *take action, enter the outside world, achieve a fourth dimension.* She seems to feel that intelligent women, especially those with college degrees, have a moral obligation to get out of their homes. Furthermore, she suggests that woman's work should be *creative,* even *richly satisfying.* You should be free to be yourself, in fact, to be *out* for yourself. Who is going to help you? Not your husband.

Well, now, let's evoke a bit of masculine "mystique." How many men have jobs in which they feel "fulfilled"? Is Friedan trying to imply that women must never be frustrated, even on the job? It is a rare human being, never mind which sex, who is completely satisfied with his or her manner of earning a living.

But assuming both you and your husband have absorbing, interesting, demanding jobs—who runs the home? Sharing household responsibilities becomes an artificial situation beyond a certain point. Your husband cannot *habitually* cope with laundry, supper, blowing the children's noses—and keep his masculinity.

Besides, what mother can go to the office when her child is taken seriously ill? You are the one who calls the doctor and stays home. Not your husband. If you are determined to take on the responsibilities of an executive position, you must be just as willing to help your child with his homework and cook (or plan) your husband's dinner, or you will be a failure as a woman and, therefore, as a human being. You must make up your mind to fish or cut bait.

If you are going to fish, you should prepare to join the ranks of the professions with more seriousness. American women want jobs rather than careers. And those who yearn for careers are, in most cases, not prepared for them. I am not speaking of America's many woman doctors, lawyers and merchant chiefs, but of the hordes of yammerers who wish they were. [. . .]

If you are in a top spot, competing against men, how can you expect wolf noises after five o'clock? If you are working *with* and for men, are you willing to admit that you will never beat them at their game? On the whole, women have less intellectual acumen than men (the remark is deliberately hedged). Your thinking is less analytic, less direct, more intuitive, more global. Generally speaking, you are not good at high (or even low) finance. Some of you have made great generals. Look at Joan of Arc. Some would have made great presidents. Look at Mrs. FDR. Others have been leaders in fields as diverse as science and fiction. But what woman has ever achieved the greatness of Einstein, Dostoevski, Beethoven or Buddha?

You should not try to equal man, for you are a different creature. You are complex. He is simple. You function best behind the scenes, as a mover and manipulator, bolsterer and ego-builder, a talented receiver of confidences and favors. Your insistence on competing with men is leading to what *The Insider's Newsletter* reported as "The Creeping Femininity." Helen Lawrenson asks in *Esquire:* If a male transvestite wants to look like a woman, does he wear pants and boots?[3] How confused can things get?

You Americans walk all over your husbands as no other women dare. The most hag-ridden Cockney or Paris fishwife's spouse has more rights in his home than does many a U.S. businessman. You are spoiled. You won your "rights" 45 years ago, but you are like a new African nation: You don't know what to do with them. Has everyone forgotten how much women like to be bossed? Or how pathetically swift they are to respond to gallantry? Men have.

In the early days, you pioneered with your husbands. In the '20's, you proved that you could smoke and drink with the boys. In the '30's and '40's, you went to work, and you went to war. In the '50's, you stayed home in a college-educated attempt to "fulfill" yourselves. Besides, the boys were back, and they wanted their jobs again. It was a big do-it-yourself bore. So, in the '60's, you went back to work. You don't *need* to. But you are still trying to "find" yourselves. Where? In an office file?

Too many American women are self-centered drags. You are unsure of yourselves. You have many reasons to be, including the malaise of the Atomic Age. You are being taken in by too many intellectual success symbols. You are overimpressed by the college degrees you insist that your sons and daughters earn. There is a case for *not* going to college, you know. Your values are topsy-turvy. [. . .]

The climate is phony. You don't really want to look like a tinker toy or a little boy. You are a gender apart, and lucky to have a man to lean on. If you don't work to support your husband, no eyebrows are raised. Nor does your husband lead a double life because he has children and a job. You would have to.

You ought to go back to being a woman.

You are losing out on a lot of nice things—like being loved. It is you who sets the emotional pace in marriage. You can ease or increase the tension at home with the tone of your voice. "There is no equality in marriage," says writer Leila Hadley, a mother of four. "It is up to the woman to make it go."[4] How strong you have to be! How wise! And what power you have! Woman could bring about on-site atomic inspection. [. . .]

So, have your cake and eat it too—but let's not hear about any indigestion syndromes. If you can find your way back to true womanhood—at home, in bed—in the deep, beautifully illogical female sense, the American man will recover his pride and his manhood. Which is a way of saying that you should never underestimate the importance of that four-letter word spelled l-o-v-e. It may save the world.

NOTES

1. Marya Mannes (1904–1990), American novelist, journalist, and commentator on women's issues.

2. Betty Friedan (b. 1921), *The Feminine Mystique* (1963).

3. Helen Lawrenson, ". . . Androgyne, You're a Funny Valentine," *Esquire* 63, no. 3 (March 1965): 80–81, 83.

4. Leila Hadley (b. 1925), American travel writer and journalist.

Part 7

WOMEN AND SEX

21.

FEMINISM:
ITS FALLACIES AND FOLLIES

(1916)

John Martin

John Martin (1864–1956) was director of the
City Housing Corporation in New York City
and a member of the New York City Board of
Education (1908–1916). Later in life he was a
lecturer on international relations at Rollins
College, and is the author of *Dictators and
Democracies Today* (1935) along with numerous papers on politics and economics. In the
following extract from *Feminism: Its Fallacies
and Follies* (1916), from the chapter "Feminism
and Free Love," Martin frankly claims that
feminism leads to free love and the abandonment of marriage and children. Part 2 of the
treatise, written by Martin's wife, Prestonia
Mann Martin, echoes many of his views.

Source: John Martin, *Feminism: Its Fallacies and Follies* (New York: Dodd, Mead, 1916), pp. 112–21.

*D*oes Feminism lead toward Free Love? Conservative women suffragists resent the imputation that their principles involve approval of changes in the marriage laws or any condonation of laxer sexual relationships. Yet literary exponents of Feminism, more concerned with philosophy than practical policies, declare unequivocally that implicit in feminist doctrine lies the advocacy of radical readjustments of sexual relations. So long as the woman's movement is merely instinctive, a childish revolt, not sustained by any thoughtful reasoning, so long it escapes the vision of its own destiny. But "wherever the conscious striving to elevate, to educate and to secure the rights of woman has been profound, it has been united with the desire to reform the position of women in love and marriage," declares Ellen Key,[1] the acute observer whose eye, from her Swedish eyrie, follows the sweep of the woman's movement the wide world over.

In America "the conscious striving" has not been so "profound" as in Scandinavia and Germany, and "the desire to reform the position of woman in love and marriage" is therefore not so intense and subversive; though in America also, writes Mrs. Coolidge, "the emphasis upon freedom from the moral domination of man, made by the first female insurgents, is now transferred to a readjustment of the marriage relation and the question of economic responsibility."[2] Another exponent exclaims: "The free power of Selection in Love. Yes! That is the true Female Franchise. It must be regained by woman. Existing marriage is a pernicious survival of the patriarchal age."[3] "Free Power of Selection in Love" or "Freedom in Love" (Ellen Key's phrase), is a euphemism for what simple people call free love. Yet these extreme doctrines, as another American historian of the woman's movement testifies, "have been the logical outgrowth of the self-same faith" held by the "more conservative spirits" in the women's ranks.[4]

Their logical lineage can be traced through the emphasis made at all stages of Feminism upon freedom as the supreme aim. The key word of Feminism is freedom. It seeks to make each woman the arbitress of her own destiny, to rid her step by step of the restraints which laws and customs impose upon her. "Women are striving for legal, political and sexual independence," explains a woman doctor.[5]

But woman cannot enjoy freedom—so runs the argument—so long as she accepts economic support from her father or husband. Dependence means subjection. So she must win economic independence before marriage, that is, be free from the domination of her father, and retain it after marriage, that is, be free from the domination of her husband. Her higher education must be directed to prepare her for winning economic independence and she must win the vote mainly that she may use it to aid her in her economic struggle. Accepting the support of her children's father is "being dependent on her sex functions for a means of livelihood"—a revolting slavery.[6] And "danger lurks for woman and her freedom when, to safeguard her independence, she has no other resources than the seduction of her beauty to gain and to hold the love she is able to inspire. Sex becomes the defensive weapon and one she must use for self-protection if she is to live. It seems to me that this economic use of sex is the real cancer at the very root of the sexual relationship. It is but a step further and a perfectly logical one that leads to prostitution."[7] To preserve themselves from this fate married women and mothers must jealously guard their self-support through wage earning.

Freedom from her husband's support, we are told, would be of little worth, however, did it not enable a woman to grant or withhold conjugal rights at her pleasure, and even to cast off a husband who was no longer congenial. Of all forms of enslavement enforced subjection to marital embraces is one of the most odious. Married women must win and assert "possession of their own bodies." They must be allowed by law and custom to determine whether they will bear one child or none, whether their wedded life shall be virginal or conjugal; none of which is feasible so long as the husband is the breadwinner. They must be free to return to single life whenever the husband insists on entrenching upon their privacy. So economic independence is recognised and advocated as preliminary to sexual independence.

As Mrs. Gallichan says, with respect to the Burmese women, who do most of the business of the country and throng the streets at all hours of the day: "Given such complete economic freedom of woman, it is self-evident that the sexual relationship will also be free." Not necessarily loose or licentious, but free. "Very striking are the conditions of divorce. The marriage contract can be dissolved freely at the wish of both or even of one of the parties." And, it should be remembered, a large part of women suffragists approve the economic self-support of both single and married women, though usually they do not realise that, "given the complete economic freedom of women and the sexual relationship will also be free."[8] A few not only recognise the outcome but openly announce their intention. One of the founders of the Equality Alliance in New York City, an organisation led by writers, editors and artists, formed mainly to prevent the withdrawal of women teachers from their salary-earning upon marriage or motherhood, announced, in the writer's hearing, to an applauding audience of feminists: "We mean to be monogamous, but reasonably monogamous; not always monogamous with the same person."

"In the main," explains another candid advocate in the *Atlantic Monthly*, "we are opposed to the indissoluble Christian marriage. The present increase in the divorce rate is of course gratifying; but it is not enough. Personally I believe that the ultimate aim of Feminism is the suppression of marriage and the institution of free alliance. It may be that only thus can woman develop her own personality."[9]

For, the argument proceeds, if divorce and frequent matings are to be common and easy, and if economic support of the husband is repudiated as a disgrace why go through all the fuss and fettering of marriage at all? Why not accept an "affinity" during your pleasure and his good behaviour, assuming, yourself, the responsibility for any offspring, and retaining to the full, without even temporary sacrifice, your soul's chief joy,—freedom? Especially where there are not enough men to give every woman a husband why should a woman be debarred from motherhood unless she find a husband? Why should her freedom be so grievously curtailed in the deepest concern of her life? Discussion of "Free Motherhood," as this claim for a child outside of wedlock is styled, is heard among the younger feminists in American cities, but is most open in England and Germany, where the slaughter of the future husbands in the Great War is likely to make it in the future, indeed, a vital issue. In both countries, as one of the rebels asserts, "Very gallant and very young are the rebels of this class for the most part, seeking joy and self-expression, individualistic, assured, capable. To the younger generation of rebels the potential mother crying for the prohibited baby is become the central figure of life's tragedy."[10]

Another advocate avers: "As indicating the extent of the present sex revolt we see a type of woman arising who believes in a state of society in which man will not figure in the life of woman except as the father of her child."[11]

While these conclusions are startling, the chain of reasoning which leads to them is continuous. All the consequences follow from the fundamental assumption of Feminism that so long as woman's fate is knit up with that of the family she cannot attain proper individual development and that her salvation demands that she disentangle herself from the family relationship. And, if the freedom and self-expression of the woman be exclusively considered, the claim of Feminism must be granted. Surely, if her satisfaction be isolated from all other considerations, each woman is entitled to command over her own body and to escape from an uncongenial husband; she is entitled to free maternity and to an independent economic status. This female Anarchism is impossible simply because woman is an essential part of the social organism. Her freedom and self-expression cannot be exclusively regarded. Her destiny is bound up with the destiny of the child. Woman must sacrifice even part of her freedom for the sake of the race.

At each stage in the desired process towards sexual independence for her there is an inalienable conflict between woman's freedom and the child's well-being. If, before marriage, she must win economic independence, the result is too often that her strength is exhausted and her maternal powers are deranged. If, after marriage, she continue to earn money that she may be economically independent of her husband, the outcome is again injurious to the next generation. The tale of baby deaths in factory towns, the slaughter of the innocents wherever the mother daily deserts the home, demonstrate the cost to the race of the mother's specious freedom. If the mother be free to part from her husband so soon as he becomes uncongenial and be free also to accept a new comrade, the child is again the victim. Also "Free Motherhood" is to be repudiated, because the child needs two parents, its training a masculine as well as a feminine hand.

It must be admitted that there is an ideal aspect to the proposal to marry with the understanding that any cooling of affection shall dissolve the bonds. "Love alone consecrates marriage," pleads the ardent young soul. "If Reginald ceases to love me or I to love Reginald, we shall dissolve our marriage." But society, concerned for its own permanence and solicitous for the care of the next generation, cannot permit Reginald and Angela to be the sole judges in their difficulty. Not merely they, but society, not merely the present but the future, must be considered. So divorce can be granted only by legal process upon serious grounds.

In the end woman herself would suffer from the effects of "freedom." Were Feminism's programme to succeed, it would ultimately, despite the seeming temporary advantage, inflict incalculable injury on her.

First. Woman, struggling against man, throughout life, in the industrial world, is robbed of that affectional satisfaction in her work which is her steadiest joy. Normally a woman, to be contented, must be working for some person she loves. With a child or a relative to serve, she can endure prolonged effort without succumbing. She cannot win satisfaction, as man can, from building up a business, improving a firm's credit, increasing the output, enlarging the nation's exports and the like. Tending a machine, even if it demands less muscular strength, is more wearing to her than tending a baby. The machine exhausts her energy and gives back no joy; the baby replenishes her energy and gives back comfort for effort. As well try to further the satisfaction of a musician by "freeing" him from slavery to piano and violin that he may revel in the din of a boiler factory as to further the satisfaction of woman by "freeing" her from personal service to those she loves that she may revel in impersonal, economic independence.

Second. It would release man from the restraints and obligations to which, through the ages, he has gradually been subjected. Were the wife to become customarily the bread-winner, the husband, set free from drudgery, might return to the hunting and fishing and fighting which engaged his savage ancestor whose squaw fed the household. As man attained a settled life and began to till the soil he took the field work from the woman's shoulders and assumed an ever-increasing share of the responsibility for feeding the family. But, if woman insists on taking back that responsibility, his will be the release and hers the burden.

Third. If, in addition, she should make the marriage tie so loose that either partner could easily slip the noose, she would find that man's fancy roams more lightly than woman's and she would most often be left deserted. Her affection for the child and, through the child, for the father, is naturally deeper rooted than the husband's. Man, as yet, is but "imperfectly monogamous." But the best protection of mother and child will be secured by enforcing paternal obligation ever more stringently, by demanding from the husband a stricter and stricter fidelity.

Woman, like man, must choose between freedom and duty. Her yearning for freedom is not discreditable. It has been shared by the world's noblest spirits. It is, indeed, say the philosophers, an intimation of immortality. But freedom, pursued after it parts company with duty, leads to destruction. And duty to the child is the supreme duty for woman, since, if she abandon that duty, the race must decline.

NOTES

1. [*Love and Marriage*, p. 62.] Ellen Key (1849–1926) was a Swedish feminist and author of several tracts proposing a variety of radical measures regarding the role of women in society. *Love and Marriage* (1911) is a translation of *Kärleken och äktenskapet* (1911).

2. Mary Roberts Coolidge (1860–1945), *Why Women Are So* (New York: Henry Holt, 1912), p. 269. Coolidge was a social worker and professor of sociology at Stanford University and Mills College.

3. [*The Truth about Woman* <1913>, by G. Gasquoine Hartley <Mrs. Walter M. Gallichan, 1867–1928>, p. 256.]

4. [*Feminism in Germany and Scandinavia* <1915>, by Katharine Anthony <1877–1965>, p. 10.]

5. [*Woman, Marriage and Motherhood* <1913>, by Elizabeth S. Chesser, p. 257.]

6. [Ibid.]

7. [*The Truth about Woman*, by C. G. Hartley, p. 215.]

8. [*The Truth about Woman*, p. 157.]

9. [W. L. George, <"Feminist Intentions,"> *Atlantic Monthly*, December, 1913.] Later incorporated into George's *The Intelligence of Women* (1916).

10. [Candida, <"The Right to Motherhood,"> in *The New Statesman*, June 27, 1914.]

11. [W. L. George, *Atlantic Monthly*, December, 1913.]

22.

FEMALE SEXUALITY

(1931)

Sigmund Freud

The views on women by the pioneering Vien-
nese psychoanalyst Sigmund Freud (1856–
1939) are immensely complicated.[1] His general puzzlement over women's character and
motivation can be summed up in his poignant
query, *Was will das Weib?* ("What does woman
want?").[2] As a child Freud was dominated by
his mother and five younger sisters. He married Martha Bernays after a passionate love
affair. Many of Freud's views of woman were
undoubtedly shaped by his treatment of such
figures as Anna O. (one of the subjects of his
Studies in Hysteria, 1895),[3] and Dora, a sexually
confused woman whom he analyzed begin-
ning in 1898. Although Freud deserves credit
for recognizing, in such works as *Three Essays
on the Theory of Sexuality* (1905), that women
are sexual beings as much as men are, he

Source: Sigmund Freud, "Female Sexuality" (1931), *Collected Papers*, vol. 5, ed. James Strachey
(London: Hogarth Press, 1950), pp. 255–58, 271–72.

otherwise adopted many prevailing stereo-
types about women—that they should be
shielded from discussions about sex and are
sexually passive. But Freud later came to see a
girl as a kind of failed boy: man is the sexual
model, and women are devastated at their
failure to equal men by possession of the
phallus. The following essay, first published in
German in 1931, enunciates the celebrated
concept of "penis envy" as a means of
accounting for female behavior.

*F*irst of all, there can be no doubt that the bisexual disposition
which we maintain to be characteristic of human beings manifests itself much more plainly in the female than in the male.
The latter has only one principal sexual zone—only one sexual
organ—whereas the former has two: the vagina, the true female organ,
and the clitoris, which is analogous to the male organ. We believe that
we may justly assume that for many years the vagina is virtually non-
existent and possibly remains without sensation until puberty. It is
true, however, that recently an increasing number of observers have
been inclined to think that vaginal stirrings are present even in those
early years. In any case female genitality must, in childhood, centre
principally in the clitoris. The sexual life of the woman is regularly
split up into two phases, the first of which is of a masculine character,
whilst only the second is specifically feminine. Thus in female development there is a process of transition from the one phase to the other,
to which there is nothing analogous in males. A further complication
arises from the fact that the clitoris, with its masculine character, continues to function in later female sexual life in a very variable manner,
which we certainly do not as yet fully understand. Of course, we do
not know what are the biological roots of these specific characteristics
of the woman, and we are still less able to assign to them any teleo-
logical purpose.

Parallel with this first great difference there is another, which concerns the love-object. The first love-object of the male is the mother, because it is she who feeds and tends him, and she remains his principal love-object until she is replaced by another which resembles her or is derived from her. With the female too the mother must be the first object, for the primary conditions of object-choice are the same for all children. But at the end of the girl's development it is the man—the father—who must come to be the new love-object; *i.e.* as she changes in sex, so must the sex of her love-object change. What we now have to discover is how this transformation takes place, how radical or how incomplete it is, and all the different things that may happen in this process of development.

We have already observed that there is yet another difference between the sexes in their relation to the Oedipus complex. We have the impression that what we have said about that complex applies in all strictness only to male children, and that we are right in rejecting the term "Electra complex" which seeks to insist that the situation of the two sexes is analogous. It is only in male children that there occurs the fateful simultaneous conjunction of love for the one parent and hatred of the other as rival. It is thereupon the discovery of the possibility of castration, as evidenced by the sight of the female genital which necessitates the transformation of the boy's Oedipus complex, leads to the creation of the super-ego and thus initiates all the processes that culminate in enrolling the individual in civilized society. After the paternal function has been internalized so as to form the super-ego, the next task is to detach the latter from those persons of whom it was originally the psychical representative. In this remarkable course of development the agent employed to restrain infantile sexuality is precisely that narcissistic genital interest which centres in the preservation of the penis.

One residue of the castration complex in the man is a measure of disparagement in his attitude towards women, whom he regards as having been castrated. In extreme cases this inhibits his object-choice, and, if reinforced by organic factors, it may result in exclusive homosexuality. Very different is the effect of the castration complex on the girl. She acknowledges the fact of her castration, the consequent superiority of the male and her own inferiority, but she also rebels against these unpleasant facts. So divided in her mind, she may follow one of three lines of development. The first leads to her turning her back on sexuality altogether. The budding woman, frightened by the comparison of herself with boys, becomes dissatisfied with her clitoris and gives up her phallic activity and therewith her sexuality in general and a considerable part of her masculine proclivities in other fields. If she pursues the second line, she clings in obstinate self-assertion to her threatened masculinity; the hope of getting a penis sometime is cherished to an incredibly late age and becomes the aim of her life, whilst the phantasy of really being a man, in spite of everything, often dominates long periods of her life. This "masculinity complex" may also result in a manifestly homosexual object-choice. Only if her development follows the third, very circuitous path does she arrive at the ultimate normal feminine attitude in which she takes her father as love-object, and thus arrives at the Oedipus complex in its feminine form. Thus, in women, that complex represents the final result of a lengthy process of development; castration does not destroy but rather creates it, and it escapes the strong hostile influences which, in men, tend to its destruction—in fact, only too often a woman never surmounts it at all. Hence too the cultural effects of the break-up of this complex are slighter and less important in women than in men. We should probably not err in saying that it is this difference in the interrelation of the Oedipus and the castration-complexes which gives its special stamp to the character of woman as a member of society.[4] [. . .]

Some authors are inclined to disparage the importance of the child's first, most primal libidinal impulses, laying stress rather on later developmental processes, so that—putting this view in its extreme form—all that the former can be said to do is to indicate certain trends, while the amounts of energy [*Intensitäten*] with which these trends are pursued are drawn from later regressions and reaction-formations. Thus, for example, K. Horney (1926)[5] is of opinion that we greatly over-estimate the girl's primary penis-envy and that the strength of her subsequent striving towards masculinity is to be attributed to a *secondary* penis-envy, which is used to ward off her feminine impulses, especially those connected with her attachment to her father. This does not agree with the impressions that I myself have formed. Certain as it is that the earliest libidinal tendencies are reinforced later by regression and reaction-formation and difficult as it is to estimate the relative strength of the various confluent libidinal components, I still think that we must not overlook the fact that those first impulses have an intensity of their own which is greater than anything that comes later and may indeed be said to be incommensurable with any other force. It is certainly true that there is an antithesis between the attachment to the father and the masculinity-complex—this is the universal antithesis between activity and passivity, masculinity and femininity—but we have no right to assume that only the one is primary, while the other owes its strength merely to the process of defence. And if the defence against femininity is so vigorous, from what other source can it derive its strength than from that striving for masculinity which found its earliest expression in the child's penis-envy and might well take its name from this?

NOTES

1. For further reading on this subject, see the following (arranged chronologically): Marie Bonaparte, *Female Sexuality* (1951); Hendrik M. Ruitenbeck, ed., *Psychoanalysis and Female Sexuality* (1966); Mary Jane Sherfey, *The Nature and Evolution of Female Sexuality* (1972); Juliet Mitchell, *Psychoanalysis and Feminism* (1974); Jean Strouse, ed., *Women and Analysis: Dialogues on Psychoanalytic Views of Femininity* (1974); Harold P. Blum, ed., *Female Psychology: Contemporary Psychoanalytic Views* (1977); Lucy Freeman and Herbert S. Strean, *Freud and Women* (1981); Estelle Roith, *The Riddle of Freud: Jewish Influences on His Theory of Female Sexuality* (1987); Peter Gay, *Freud: A Life for Our Time* (1988), chap. 10; Eli Sagan, *Freud, Women, and Morality: The Psychology of Good and Evil* (1988); Teresa Brennan, *The Interpretation of the Flesh: Freud and*

Femininity (1992); Marie-Christine Hamon, *Pourquoi les femmes aiment-elles les hommes?* (1992); Lisa Appignanesi and John Forrester, *Freud's Women* (1993); Samuel Slipp, *The Freudian Mystique: Freud, Women, and Feminism* (1993).

2. An undated remark to his disciple Marie Bonaparte, as quoted in Ernest Jones, *The Life and Work of Sigmund Freud* (New York: Basic Books, 1953–57), 2.421.

3. Titles of Freud's works are supplied in English, but the dates refer to their first publication in German.

4. [It is to be anticipated that male analysts with feminist sympathies, and our women analysts also, will disagree with what I have said here. They will hardly fail to object that such notions have their origin in the man's "masculinity complex," and are meant to justify theoretically his innate propensity to disparage and suppress women. But this sort of psycho-analytic argument reminds us here, as it so often does, of Dostoevsky's famous "knife that cuts both ways." The opponents of those who reason thus will for their part think it quite comprehensible that members of the female sex should refuse to accept a notion that appears to gainsay their eagerly coveted equality with men. The use of analysis as a weapon of controversy obviously leads to no decision.]

5. Freud refers to Karen Horney's "The Flight from Womanhood," *International Journal of Psycho-Analysis* 7 (1926): 324–39. Horney (1885–1952) was a German-born psychoanalyst who severely criticized Freud's antifeminism in *The Neurotic Personality of Our Time* (1937) and other works.

23.

HOW TO GET AND KEEP A HUSBAND

(1957)

Kate Constance

Little is known about Kate Constance, author of *How to Get and Keep a Husband* (1957). Written explicitly from the standpoint of a "Christian businesswoman," this manual of conduct deprecates sex before marriage as ultimately harmful to a happy marriage. The chapter below is titled "Your Chances with Free Love and Pre-Marital Sex."

*A*t various times in our history of modern sophistication we have fostered faddisms of "free love" and "trial marriage," but since World War II sexual laxity has assumed proportions of a national attitude tantamount to that existing in Europe and Asia today. It is more than the hot flare of the rebellious youth of a generation, for it has dared to become a neo-morality emanating from the pressures of a vast sociological change that has overtaken our people.

Whether you are married or unmarried, this change holds a per-

Source: Kate Constance, *How to Get and Keep a Husband: A Christian Businesswoman's Answer to One of the Most Perplexing Problems of Our Time* (Philadelphia: Dorrance, 1957), pp. 183–95.

sonal significance for you if you are interested in that institution responsible for holding together our way of life.

This great change is the higher ratio of females to males in our population. A drastic trend toward easy sex comes about when women, finding it more difficult to win a husband, resort to every available physical means to arouse—and satisfy—the most basic animal appetite of the males within their orbit of attraction. Failing to achieve marriage they snatch whatever they can steal in male attention. And being susceptible (otherwise described as polygamous and "weak"), men are worried and fretted, surrounded and pressured by a superabundance of feminine allurements which tempt them into destroying the very codes and standards by which they prefer to live.

There are three questions which every woman should ask herself, and to which she should add complete answers regarding illicit love, these three questions being:

1. Why does a woman enter into a relationship of this kind?
2. What does she really get out of it if it does not materialize into marriage?
3. What are the dangers if it does materialize into marriage?

There are a number of pseudo-reasons for a woman becoming a party to illicit sex but they almost always converge to the one and only answer: she is trying to get and/or hold a man. We will not dignify the matter by saying she is trying to get and/or hold the love of a man, for it is highly questionable whether a man really and truly cares for a woman with whom he desecrates the finest relationship existing between the sexes.

In this age of much talk about marriage compatibility, there is a type of young modern who says that she wants to prove to herself that complete sexual mating exists between her and the man of her choice before she enters into the marital contract. She has heard so much about the intense importance of sexual harmony she believes that it must be achieved at any price. She believes that by the trial method she can arrive at a satisfactory relationship before marriage and thereby dispense with the biggest adjustment to be made during the honeymoon. This theory, of course, precludes any sacred element surrounding the union of a man and a woman. It holds only to the idea that what you don't like you can dispense with, ignoring the fact that physical satisfaction deepens and intensifies to its ultimate in the favorable, temperate zone of convention and law, and that it is more likely to sicken and die in the unfavorable, chilling zone of lawlessness.

In reality, the reason that a woman enters into an illicit relationship most times is fear—fear of her own capabilities, fear of loss of love, fear of losing out matrimonially. When her fiancé momentarily loses his head during a pre-nuptial embrace, she accedes to his importunities, later resorting to trumped-up excuses such as the wish to insure sexual compatibility. She is afraid to insist on a "chaste" relationship until their wedding night, for she does not want to seem old-fashioned; she does not want to take the chance of losing him to another woman in his aroused condition; she wants to keep her hold on him at all risks.

Then there is that other type of sophisticate who believes herself passionately in need of sexual satisfaction. Yes, there are nymphomaniacs, those females beset with uncontrolled sexual desire, but they are pathologically few. For the most part, the sexual desire of the average woman is intensified, oddly enough, by unfavorable factors as well as favorable factors—loneliness, too much alcohol, self-pity, emotionalism, and most of all, a desire to assert her femaleness. She cannot satisfy this latter yearning without the attentions of a male. Therefore, her "passion" is primarily psychological.

We cannot overlook that type of woman who is so callous to morality she engages in sexual intercourse with almost any man, married or single, any time, any place, and under any circumstances, as casually as she accepts a drink at the soda fountain—and goes her way. She is not the prostitute variety—she is a whore, one of the most serious blocks to marriage. More often she does not ask even for an evening's entertainment in exchange. She is indeed a cheap outlet, with a cheap set of values if you can call them values at all, her interests concerned with a few animal gratifications. She is the kind who can spawn her young and walk off and leave it to the care of public charity or to starve in an ash can. She is the type that takes up with a drifter as his common-law wife, quite often wandering away into another and another shady relationship, almost as stolidly as the bovine grazing in the fields. Men call her a "sex machine." Her motive? Nothing more than having an interest in her shiftless pattern.

Then there is that big majority of women who become involved sexually with the primary objective of winning a husband. They understand the theory of moral right and wrong, but if it does not conform to their objectives they do exactly as they wish. In self-defense and conscience-assuaging they resort to the triteness that anything which does not suit their easy way of life is "old-fashioned." They laugh at the words chastity, adultery, fornication, ruined women and seduction, which is another reason we now employ such soothing terms as "free love" and "pre-marital sex," but these violations are still adultery in the case of a married person sharing sexual intercourse with one other than his or her married mate, or fornication in the case of a single person sharing sexual intercourse out of wedlock, and in both cases it is violation of the very laws of our Christian concepts that have dragged us upward and onward in social advancement in spite of our errant natures. This type of woman calculatingly envisions two results and one conclusion: 1. Binding a man to her physically by satisfying his desires, and 2. preying upon his sense of honor to reward her with marriage for "lowering" herself for his sake. Usually, this type is not concerned with long-lasting spiritual love, just so long as she has a chance at a marriage license. What damage she perpetrates to law and order is of no concern to her while she is busy with the quest. However, she becomes painfully aware of the results of her lax morals if she loses out and does not win the man to marriage. Also, she can become just as sensitive to her errantry after marriage takes place and when repercussions of her fornicacious past start taking effect. Of that possibility we shall speak a little later on.

And so we come to the last and most pathetic type of woman who shares illicit sex. She is the one that is easily deluded by a man—often any man—who professes "love" for her. She is making a great "sacrifice" for him because she "loves" him and wants to do anything he desires. Of course she possesses his heart! Ah! So romantic, this great, overpowering passion that starts at her front door and winds up on the seat of his car or in some secluded roadside motel. She knows she should not—but what is a girl to do when the one and only man loves her and needs her?

Many, many women naively confuse animal passion with love. Most men can become passionate with any number of women without caring for or even liking them. In the majority of men, it takes little to arouse eroticism. A younger woman particularly is deceived by this misinterpretation when a boy while pawing over her whines that he has got to have her. She thinks it is "love" when the truth is that he has "got to have" any female and any female will do. Does he marry her? Sometimes—most times not. And if he does marry her, it is her particular type that pays hell in the after-effects. And if he doesn't marry her, she goes through another type of emotional inferno which has much more to do with self-respect and remorse than with regrets over loss of the man.

Now we come to the second question, what does a woman really get out of illicit sex if it does not materialize into marriage? Well, while it's going on she shares a kind of precarious companionship, with perhaps some social activity. Then there is the physical intimacy which cannot by any stretch of the imagination be called completion.

But she gets a lot of other results from free love when her partner to the act steps out of her life. Unless she is of that near-brutish temperament to which we previously referred, she is cast into varying degrees of repercussions.

Some of these after-effects are:

Galling bitterness, her outlook on religion and morality cynical. Her personality, reflecting this acridity, repels and displeases and removes her still further from sincere attentions of other men.

A hardened attitude toward the best human standards, probable aggressiveness in pursuit of men as she determines to attract and then to hurt in every way possible to "get even" for the injury to her ego. In this frame of mind she is likely to take on any shoddy attention, her moral stamina degenerating with each episode until she has little if any fortitude left.

Excessive drinking, smoking and spending accompanying the down-grade process.

Cheapening of her language, dress and mannerisms.

Smudged-up reputation. Even in this sophisticated era, morality still counts. Women might shy away from her and men probably become either overly familiar and vulgar in their approaches or curtly distant.

Of course, most of these degeneracies result from her injured vanity. She broods over the galling thought that what she considered her best gift (her body and her passion) was not enticing enough to win and keep an enduring love. Women who have been hurt in this way—and mind you through their own foolhardiness or selfish aims—often try to compensate for the shame and belittlement by resorting to various panaceas: exclusive prostitution, perversion (the bitterest anger), retiring to a non-social existence, enslavement to a job or profession, alcoholism, gambling, and dabbling in various fads and cults ranging from overeating to Yoga.

These women have only themselves to blame. Regardless of their motives, they shared and encouraged the violation of rules set for their very own protection. How could they expect to get away with it unharmed? Just because one or two males want them to go to bed with them some women take on ideas of sexual grandeur. They have read some best sellers extolling women who swayed kingdoms, won legions of men and gained great wealth with flaunted bad behavior. All of which makes juicy reading for the vulgarized mind. In truth, only a few kings' mistresses ever attained any sort of happiness and well-being, most of them having to slave sexually, steal, lie enormously, and even murder during the prime of their beauty and power, and in most cases they were finally cast off into poverty and oblivion if they were lucky; and if unlucky, they were handed over to the executioner for the severance of their heads from their overly used bodies.

Today men seldom kill off their excess females. They dismiss them with a kiss and often with less than a kiss.

These women who lose out in the sex gamble should realize that when they serve the desires of men in the hope of winning them to marriage they only reduce their personal chances to win a husband. Besides, they contribute to a weakening of our national standards of morality which in turn affects their lives as individuals. For a man who enjoys free sexual satisfaction is not prone to seek marriage and its responsibilities, and if he does it is going to be for reasons other than sex.

I was reared in a home full of men—four brothers older than I. Our house was a meeting place for teenagers and young men in their early twenties before marriage finally took them away. Although much younger, I was impressed by the conversation of those young males as they played cards or other games in our big, fire-lit dining room. From my corner chair where I would be reading I could hear their quips and slurs about girls they knew—"fancy" girls, "fast" girls, "easy" girls. They said a lot of things and did a lot of laughing about certain girls and I soon learned to think seriously about these young females of our acquaintance. As the years brought inevitable developments into their lives, I was able to piece together most telling facts. A couple of the "fast" ones were diseased; they gave birth to a blind child and an imbecile. Another committed suicide when one of our college friends eloped with another girl. A fourth was shot by the wife of a businessman.

And so we come to the third question that a woman should answer satisfactorily regarding free love and pre-marital sex. What are the dangers if the illicit relationship does materialize into marriage?

First, we must admit that a man is a marvelous creature—when and as long as a woman demands that he be a marvelous creature. She sets the example by her character, her strengths, her objectives. A man really wants to love a woman—his very own type of woman—with all his heart and being. No matter how low or how high he becomes, he envisions his type of woman being better than he. If only she would fulfill his desires and help him to realize his dream of a woman who is tender, warmly human in emotion but oh so much bigger and stronger than he in protecting the sacred rules of conduct. Only when she is stronger than he in this respect can he be fully convinced of her merits.

Any way you look at it, courtship is a dangerous period when emotions stimulate sexual desire. For that reason engagements should be of short duration, even at the sacrifice of material considerations.

Dr. Clifford R. Adams, professor of psychology in charge of marriage counselling, School of Education of Pennsylvania State College, deals with pre-marital controls in his book *Looking Ahead to Marriage*, in which he says:

"As their love and their need for each other grow, the engaged couple have an awakening and deepening of their sexual feelings. Were this not to occur, many engagements would be broken. If the couple have normal feelings, they will have strong desires for the full intimacy of marriage. That is one reason why an engagement of three to six months is more desirable than one that is longer. Oftentimes, the man has stronger feelings than does the girl. For him to take advantage of her love or to persuade her into a course of action that she disapproves of or will feel guilty about, is neither sensible nor a mark of real love.

"Pre-marital intercourse is never approved. Aside from moral or religious considerations, the very real possibility of pregnancy cannot be escaped. And there is no more unfortunate person than the unmarried pregnant girl. In most cases such behavior will leave feelings of guilt for both the man and the girl, and it should always be avoided. Otherwise, the couple may never be sexually adjusted in marriage."[1]

Divorce lawyers and medical doctors often deal with results of pre-marital intimacies. A prominent attorney from the East, whom I met in Nevada while he was out there handling a divorce case, told me that one of the unrecorded complaints of many divorce-seekers concerns rehashed insults about pre-marital indiscretions hurled back and forth during heated arguments. These insults, of course, stem from a sense of guilt and are used as a weapon to hurt pride and sting conscience because both parties know that they are law-breakers. This sense of guilt takes the following forms of expression:

Suspicion on the part of both husband and wife. They have reason to think that if they cheated the moral rules once they are likely to cheat them again with some other woman, some other man when opportunity comes along.

This suspicion leads the woman particularly to nag her husband, accusing him of real and imagined defections if he is late for dinner or if he forgets an anniversary, and particularly if he fails to tell her often that he loves her. She harbors a deep harassing sense of insecurity about his love. She cannot trust him.

Whenever he hurts her, she drags out the old resentment toward him for inducing her to lower her standards to an illicit affair before marriage.

Contempt for each other that flares up from its smoldering suppression whenever an argument arises.

A sense of cheapness and weakness. Often a man feels that he has been "roped in" by his sense of honor. Outwardly they are supposed to defend high standards of morality, and at the same time they carry a sense of guilt which perpetuates itself in morbid concern over the conduct of their children.

One of the repercussions of pre-marital intimacy is the sharp let-down in a man's ardor after marriage. One of my medical doctor friends related several instances of such sexual fizzling. One woman who came to him for advice explained that her husband became disturbingly indifferent several months after marriage for no reason she could designate. In a roundabout way she disclosed that they had had intercourse for several months before marrying during which period of time his love-making sustained a fever-pitch. A few weeks after the wedding he hardly kissed her goodnight.

The excitation of stolen love, which to some men is the greatest sex stimulant, was removed. He had to adjust a legalized situation to an illicit background, which is difficult for many men to do. His sense of consistency was confused.

A complete feeling of let-down ensues. At the beginning of the marriage there does not exist that excitement of a new sexual experience to ease other adjustments; therefore money, household chores, restraints on freedom, and other lesser factors take on mountainous proportions to cause disagreements.

This is an age of unlimited freedoms for the individual, and therefore it calls for greater self-discipline, more self-control. All of us must answer for our proportionate contribution to the upgrade or downgrade of the human race. Are we for decency and honor and morality—or against them? We cannot be both for and against. What we do attests to our code regardless of what we say or pretend. Suppose that every woman subscribed to a life of uncertain morals. Suppose that every man had an affair with every woman he looked upon with desire. The structure of personal morals would crumble with ensuing chaos in the relations of the sexes. The orderliness of our social system would collapse. We decry that possibility. Yet the conduct of a disturbingly large number of men and women would indicate that they do not care if their conduct is contributing to such a state of affairs.

I know—you know—very few people, if any, who are towers of impregnable strengths. Such is not humankind. I do know many whose moral stamina is tremendous because they have striven mightily to build the strength to overcome. We cannot build strength one day and dissipate it the next by wilfully courting temptation. I for one am neither brave nor strong. My defenses have been of a preventive nature and I think that any woman who earnestly seeks to uphold the pattern of morality is safer by side-stepping temptation.

If sex is the all too common commodity today and the market is glutted with it, if too many women are too easy to get, then what will distinguish a woman among her sisters and set her up as desirably different in the eyes of men? Men are natural hunters, forever seeking that which is hard to get, rare in kind, or just enough unattainable to spark their interest. Men want something different. There is very little that is different about sex *per se.*

The woman who is different in the evaluation of men is the woman with high moral standards.

NOTE

1. Clifford R. Adams (b. 1902), *Looking Ahead to Marriage* (Chicago: Science Research Associates, 1949), pp. 34–35.

Part 8
WOMEN AND MARRIAGE

24.

COMMENTARIES ON THE LAWS OF ENGLAND

(1765–1769)

Sir William Blackstone

Sir William Blackstone (1723–1780) was the first professor of English law at Oxford University (1758–1766) and was also a member of Parliament before becoming justice of common pleas in 1770. His *Commentaries on the Laws of England* (1765–1769), excerpted below, was immensely influential as an exposition and analysis of English law. It was immediately popular in the United States as well: an edition published in 1771–1772 sold 1,557 subscription copies, a large number for so scholarly a work. Blackstone's interpretation of the legal status of women in marriage—whereby they effectively cease to exist as legal entities—was endorsed by the American scholar James Kent's *Commentaries on American Law* (1826–1830), and many of the

Source: Sir William Blackstone, *Blackstone's Commentaries*, vol. 2, ed. St. George Tucker (Philadelphia: William Young Birch & Abraham Small, 1803), pp. 441–45.

statutes governing the function of wives remained embodied in American law until well into the nineteenth century.

*B*y marriage, the husband and wife are one person in law: that is, the very being or legal existence of the woman is suspended during the marriage, or at least is incorporated and consolidated into that of the husband: under whose wing, protection, and *cover*, she performs every thing; and is therefore called in our law-french *feme-covert, foemina viro co-operta*; is said to be *covert baron*, or under the protection and influence of her husband, her *baron*, or lord; and her condition during her marriage is called her *coverture*. Upon this principle, of an union of person in husband and wife, depend almost all the rights, duties, and disabilities, that either of them acquire by the marriage. I speak not at present of the rights of property, but of such as are merely *personal*. For this reason, a man cannot grant any thing to his wife, or enter into covenant with her: for the grant would be to suppose her separate existence; and to covenant with her would be only to covenant with himself: and therefore it is also generally true, that all compacts made between husband and wife, when single, are voided by the intermarriage. A woman indeed may be attorney for her husband; for that implies no separation from, but is rather a representation of, her lord. And a husband may also bequeath any thing to his wife by will; for that cannot take effect till the coverture is determined by his death. The husband is bound to provide his wife with necessaries by law, as much as himself: and if she contracts debts for them, he is obliged to pay them; but, for any thing besides necessaries, he is not chargeable. Also, if a wife elopes, and lives with another man, the husband is not chargeable even for necessaries; at least if the person, who furnishes them, is sufficiently apprised of her elopement. If the wife be indebted before marriage, the husband is bound afterwards to pay the debt; for he has adopted her and her circumstances together. If the wife be injured in her person or her property, she can bring no action for redress without her husband's concurrence, and in his name, as well as her own: neither can she be sued, without making the husband a defendant. There is indeed one case where the wife shall sue and be sued as a feme sole, *viz.* where the husband has abjured the realm, or is banished: for then he is dead in law; and, the husband being thus disabled to sue for or defend the wife, it would be most unreasonable if she had no remedy, or could make no defence at all. In criminal prosecutions, it is true, the wife may be indicted and punished separately; for the union is only a civil union. But, in trials of any sort, they are not allowed to be evidence for, or against, each other: partly because it is impossible their testimony should be indifferent; but principally because of the union of person: and therefore, if they were admitted to be witnesses *for* each other, they would contradict one maxim of law, *"nemo in propria causa testis esse debet"*;[1] and if *against* each other, they would contradict another maxim, *"nemo tenetur seipsum accusare."*[2] But, where the offence is directly against the person of the wife, this rule has been usually dispensed with: and, therefore, by statue 3 Hen. VII, c. 2, in case a woman be forcibly taken away, and married, she may be a witness against such her husband, in order to convict him of felony. For, in this case, she can with no propriety be reckoned his wife; because a main ingredient, her consent, was wanting to the contract: and also there is another maxim of law, that no man shall take advantage of his own wrong: which the ravisher here would do, if by forcibly marrying a woman, he could prevent her from being a witness, who is perhaps the only witness, to that very fact.

In the civil law, the husband and the wife are considered as two distinct persons; and may have separate estates, contracts, debts, and injuries: and, therefore, in our ecclesiastical courts, a woman may sue, and be sued, without her husband.

But, though our law in general, considers man and wife as one person, yet there are some instances in which she is separately considered; as inferior to him, and acting by his compulsion. And, therefore, all deeds executed, and acts done, by her, during her coverture, are void; except it be a fine, or the like matter of record, in which case she must be solely and secretly examined, to learn if her act be voluntary. She cannot by will devise lands to her husband, unless under special circumstances; for at the time of making it she is supposed to be under his coercion. And in some felonies, and other inferior crimes, committed by her, through constraint of her husband, the law excuses her: but this extends not to treason or murder.

The husband also (by the old law) might give his wife moderate correction. For, as he is to answer for her misbehaviour, the law thought it reasonable to intrust him with this power of restraining her, by domestic chastisement, in the same moderation that a man is allowed to correct his apprentices or children; for whom the master or parent is also liable in some cases to answer. But this power of correction was confined within reasonable bounds, and the husband was prohibited from using any violence to his wife, *aliter quam ad virum, ex causa regiminis et castigationis uxoris suae, licite et rationabiliter pertinet.*[3] The civil law gave the husband the same, or a larger, authority over his wife: allowing him, for some misdemesnors, *flagellis et fustibus acriter verberare uxorem;*[4] for others, only *modicam castigationem adhibere.*[5] But with us, in the politer reign of Charles the second, this power of correction began to be doubted: and a wife may now have security of the peace against her husband; or, in return, a husband against his wife. Yet the lower rank of people, who were always fond of the old common law, still claim and exert their antient privilege: and the courts of law will still permit a husband to restrain a wife of her liberty, in case of any gross misbehaviour.

These are the chief legal effects of marriage during the coverture; upon which we may observe, that even the disabilities, which the wife lies under, are for the most part intended for her protection and benefit. So great a favourite is the female sex of the laws of England.

NOTES

1. "No one ought to be a witness in his own cause."
2. "No one should be compelled to accuse himself."

3. ". . . except as lawfully and reasonably pertains to the man, for the purpose of management and of the chastisement of his wife."

4. ". . . to beat his wife sharply with whips and cudgels."

5. ". . . to apply moderate chastisement."

25.

THE YOUNG WIFE

(1837)

William A. Alcott

William Andrus Alcott (1798–1859) was the cousin of Louisa May Alcott's father, Amos Bronson Alcott. Early in life he devoted his attention to teaching, establishing model schools at Wolcott and Southington, Connecticut, and making numerous reforms in teaching procedure. He later wrote of his experiences in *Confessions of a School Master* (1839). Alcott, plagued by ill health in his early years, also studied medicine, receiving a diploma from Yale Medical School. He was an editor at the *American Annals of Education* as well as two of the earliest periodicals devoted to children, the *Juvenile Rambler* and *Parley's Magazine*. In his later years he was a prolific author, writing numerous handbooks of conduct for adults and young people. Among those relating to women and marriage are *The*

Source: William A. Alcott, *The Young Wife; or, Duties of Woman in the Marriage Relation* (Boston: G. W. Light, 1837), pp. 25–32.

Young Mother (1836), *The Young Husband* (1839), *Letters to a Sister; or, Woman's Mission* (1850), *The Physiology of Marriage* (1856), and *The Moral Philosophy of Marriage* (1857). In *The Young Wife* (1837)—one of Alcott's most popular works, receiving twenty printings by 1855—Alcott appeals to the Bible and to physiology in urging wives to submit to their husbands. The following excerpt is from the chapter titled "Submission."

An opinion still prevails, even in civilized countries, that woman should be little more than the mere instrument of her husband; that on many points she is not expected to have a voice; that she should have even no opinion; and that her duty consists in submitting, without a question, to the dictates of her "lord."

Now I am of opinion that woman is made to supply, in some measure, the defects in her husband's character—thus making him a more perfect man than otherwise he would be. But I hold, also, that the same duty is required of the husband toward the wife, and with the same view and end; and that in this respect, the husband has little, if indeed any superiority. I hold, moreover, that God has required of each party, in the married state, though the union be ever so close or so perfect, to preserve the individual character of each. No female has a right, were she disposed to do it, so to merge her own character in that of her husband, as to lose her own individuality.

Still I cannot help thinking that there is a species of submission to the husband sometimes required of the wife. Not that I would ever claim it myself, or recommend it to any one else to make the claim. If a wife has not good sense enough to yield, voluntarily, what I suppose ought to be yielded, it is probably of little importance for the husband to claim anything. Perhaps I would say, "That is my opinion; you will, of course, do or act as you please."

And yet something of submission is certainly due. There was a time, in the history of our world, when woman did not exist. Man was not only alone—without a companion—but destitute of a "help-meet"—an assistant. In these circumstances, almighty Power called forth, and, as it would seem, for this very purpose, that modified, and in some respects improved form of humanity, to which was afterwards given the name of woman, and *presented her to man*. She was to be man's assistant.

This distinction is recognized throughout the Bible. Man is always considered as the head of the family, and woman as the helper. The man is not created for the woman—so the matter is represented—but the woman for the man.

It is true that this does not, of necessity, imply an intellectual and moral inferiority on the part of woman. It does not preclude the idea that in morals she may even be the superior. The concession is that of physical prowess, rather than of moral influence.

It is a concession, however, whose necessity stands as prominent in the pages of the great book of nature as in those of revelation. The exercise of that physical force which seems necessary in many of the arts and employments of life, is scarcely compatible with woman's distinguishing characteristics and her peculiar prerogative, had it been assigned her.

Heaven has accordingly withheld it. No form of education will give to woman a masculine development. No circumstances will impart to her muscular system, as a whole, that power which is so constantly developed in the other sex. Even in those countries, and among those tribes, where the ruder and coarser employments have been partially or wholly allotted her, she still retains the more striking physical traits of character which God in nature has assigned. They may indeed be modified, slightly, but never wholly overcome. A skilful anatomist could still distinguish the sexes, at any age, by a mere hasty inspection of an arm or a face, after the lapse of a thousand successive generations.

Let me not hence be set down as an enemy to female athletic exercises. What muscular exercise, in degree, woman does demand, is demanded still more imperiously than in man. She needs muscular exercise during her growth and after maturity, both to develope her form, internal and external, and to maintain her health. But no muscular exercise whatever—and this is the burden of my present argument—will essentially and permanently alter her structure, to render it more masculine in future generations. Say what we will, therefore, God in nature must have imposed on her a physical inferiority. She is thus obviously fitted to be an assistant to her husband in the work of self-improvement, and the improvement of others.

Perhaps all this inquiry is utterly needless. Perhaps very few readers entertain a single doubt on any one of these points. But it was necessary to make the statement, preliminary to what follows in other chapters.

Indeed, in one point, the agitation of this question would certainly seem needless. Matrimony cannot exist, without concession on both sides. Each party gives up certain natural rights, for the sake of certain privileges to be acquired. On which side lies the balance of concession, we need not inquire; it is sufficient if it is shown that it must be made, and that matrimony cannot exist without it.

I say, then, that the very act of entering into the married state is, on the part of the woman, a concession. It matters little whether this fact is recognized in the external forms of celebrating this rite or not; it is essential to, and inherent in its nature.

Leaving home, as a general rule, involves concession and submission. What female ever quits the circle in which she is brought up, in the expectation of retaining every privilege and every right to which she has been accustomed? Does she not, on the contrary, even diminish her own personal enjoyment?

In addition to the physical comforts of which she voluntarily deprives herself, does she not subject herself to numerous cares, and responsibilities, and trials? Does she not submit, at least prospectively, to a long train of circumstances and consequences which, in her father's house, she would be able to escape? Does she not even merge her own name in that of her husband? And is there no concession in all this? Is there no submission?

How much soever of his own natural rights the husband is required to yield, the concessions of the wife are still more numerous, and justify the inevitable conclusion that matrimony involves, as a matter of the plainest necessity, not only a greater degree of dependence on her part, but also a species of inferiority.

Let me here say again, that I would be the last person in the world to justify a tyrannical assumption of superiority on the part of our own sex. Let nothing be claimed by man, except what the necessity of the circumstances requires; and let even this be done in the most gentle manner. But if reason, nature and revelation unite in affirming that the balance of concession does actually devolve on woman, it is proper to say so. I may also add, that the more cheerful and voluntary the submission, the happier the results.

This was the conclusion of a newly married couple, among my own acquaintance. Each respected the rights of the other, but both saw how much more numerous the points were in which woman was required to yield; and both saw, too, the necessity of an umpire, in certain cases. It was therefore mutually agreed that it belonged to the husband to decide, in all matters of dispute. This point, once settled, has never, thus far, been questioned by either party.

But besides the numerous general concessions which a well regulated matrimonial state requires of the wife, and which, from its very nature, it involves, she is called to a series of smaller concessions, on which depend, much more than on all else, her comfort and happiness.

No woman can suppose herself perfect in opinions, habits or manners. But whether hers are right or wrong, she finds them daily, and perhaps hourly conflicting with those of her husband. He has been trained differently from herself. He has been accustomed to view things through a medium somewhat different. He is more ignorant on many points than she; and it unfortunately happens that when a difference of opinion arises among mankind—and between husband and wife, no less than elsewhere—those who are most ignorant will usually be most positive, and most tenacious of their sentiments.

He is often more tenacious of habits and manners than of opinions;

and especially of small habits. But what shall be done? Shall she set herself firmly against every habit of which she has reason to believe is not the very best? Shall she not rather, for the sake of peace, often concede or yield a point, at least for the time?

Perhaps there is no one thing on which domestic happiness so much depends as this; here, too, as in the matters already mentioned, the balance of concession devolves on the wife. Whether the husband concede or not, she must. If she insists too long or too strenuously for what she deems to be truth or right in small matters, she does it at the expense of her own comfort and peace. I do not say that she must express her assent to what she does not believe; but I do say that she must not dispute too long about it. She must endeavor to waive the whole subject. By contending, she will probably gain nothing, but only confirm him in his habits or opinions. By a temporary concession, that is, by suspending the question, she may possibly lead him to reflect farther, and to change his views or conduct.

So valuable is the disposition to make temporary concessions in matters of opinion or habit, that an aged friend of mine, in giving directions in reference to matrimony prior to marriage, represented the whole question of domestic happiness or misery as turning upon this single point. After giving the reasons for her opinions, she concluded by observing—"If you are both wise in this respect, you cannot but be prosperous and happy."

26.

THESE WOMEN

(1925)

William Johnston

William Andrew Johnston (1871–1929) was, for
much of his career, a reporter for a variety of
New York newspapers, including the *Journal*,
the *Herald*, and, most notably, the *World*
(1900–1927). He wrote an account of the
Spanish-American War, *History Up to Date*
(1899), along with several novels. Johnston published a series of articles on women in *Cosmopolitan* from 1923 to 1925; they were gathered in *These Women* (1925). The following
article, appearing in the February 1925 issue,
discusses the new phenomenon of "hemigamy"
—women half married to their husbands and
half married to their jobs. It evidently does not
trouble Johnston that most men are similarly
half married to their jobs.

Source: William Johnston, *These Women* (New York: Cosmopolitan Book Corp., 1925), pp. 40–65.

$\mathcal{Y}$es, that's the word, h-e-m-i-g-a-m-y, with the accent on the "ig," hemigamy.

Probably you never have heard it before. It isn't in the dictionary yet, except disguised as a botanical adjective. It is a new word describing a new condition.

Every time anything happens that changes the habits and customs of people a new vocabulary is born. Until automobiles came into use you were unfamiliar with such words and phrases as "tonneau," "blow-out," and "inner tube." Airplanes introduced "hangar" and "joy-stick," and now that so many people have radio sets, new terms like "broadcasting" and "tuning in" are in daily use.

Presently, too, you will find everyone talking about hemigamy, for it accurately describes a new condition of affairs. It defines with exactitude the amazing and perplexing plight in which a lot of us men find ourselves without quite knowing how we got there.

Hemigamy is the state in which a husband lives when he has a wife half married to him and half married to a job.

In derivation it's perfectly sound. It comes from the Greek words meaning "half" and "marriage." Botanists apply the word "hemigamous" to plants "having one of two florets on the same spikelet neuter." It is cognate in derivation to polygamy, the state of a man with many wives, and bigamy, the state of a man with two wives. If these two words are properly used, then when a man has only half a wife, he must be in a state of hemigamy.

And hemigamy today is far more prevalent than you might suspect. We men have a habit of keeping our domestic troubles to ourselves. Far more men these days have half a wife than anyone realizes. Each year more and more married women are going out and getting jobs for themselves, and the number of these half-wives is increasing in alarming degree. I doubt whether many of us men realize how far we have slipped and how fast we still are slipping from our former proud and lofty position when each of us had one wife that was all his own. Even those of us whose wives have not yet deserted home for an occupation, must, if we stop to think about it, sense our peril, for at least once a week under our own roof-tree we hear the wifely threat made:

"I'm going to strike out one of these days and get a job for myself. Every woman I know is doing something for herself."

Once any wife gets a job, all masculine domination ends. Such a thing as a mere husband has at once to take a back seat. Husband's opinions, husband's ideas, husband's welfare, husband's future, at once cease to be matters of prime importance to the wife. Let us put the matter in the form of a concrete example.

A married man in Detroit is earning fifty dollars a week. His wife who is also employed there is earning seventy-five. The man is offered a job in Seattle that will pay him a hundred dollars a week. Can you imagine him going home to tell his wife of the wonderful offer he has had? Do you suppose for a minute that she is at once going to volunteer to give up HER job and go with him to Seattle? She is NOT. It is a hundred to one that she will calmly tell him to go to Seattle and take the position offered if he wishes to. As for her she is going to stay right where she is in Detroit. Hasn't she been promised a raise at the first of the year? Surely he is not selfish enough to expect that she is going to give up her job and her future just for the sentimental idea of sticking to a husband.

It is a lamentable fact that once any of our wives begin to earn money of their own, we men no longer command the feminine respect and adulation that used to be ours in the good old days when the husband was the only wage-earner. Turn back to the pages of your own childhood. Do you remember what an important personage in the household your father was, infinitely more respected, reverenced, feared and looked up to by his wife and by his children than you are by your wife and family? Nothing ever was done by any of the family without first ascertaining father's ideas on the subject. If he was a Methodist they all went to the Methodist church. If he was a Democrat they all wore Cleveland buttons. Mother would not think of going anywhere, doing anything, or buying anything, without first consulting him. If when you were a youngster and there was to be a church sociable, or a straw ride, or if the circus came to town, and you asked mother for permission to go, there was but one invariable answer:

"Wait and see what your father says about it."

In those forgotten days, before hemigamy became prevalent, we men were some pumpkins. The whole household was organized to ensure our comfort and every member of the family catered to our whims. If there were any pleasant little vacations to be taken it was we men who took them. We went off fishing and hunting, attended the trotting races and took occasional little trips to the city. Woman's place was in the home and generally we left her there. It was we men who ventured forth to enjoy the world's pleasures. If there was any money to be spent, we men spent it. If there was any money to be bequeathed, it went to the male members of the family. Women a generation or two ago were not supposed to need money nor to know how to spend it if they had it. Mother got a new dress and daughter a new hat when father thought it was time for her to have one, or felt in the humor of getting it, and as likely as not it was father himself who selected the dress or the hat.

In those times we men had a good thing of it. The womenfolk all respected us and for the most part obediently did what we told them to. It was a rare occasion indeed when a woman would think of disputing a man's judgment or disputing his opinions. But now, almost without our knowing it, somebody has come along and pulled the legs of our comfortable easy chair from under us.

Don't think for a minute, however, that I am inclined to blame the tragedy that has overtaken us husbands on the women. If they have upset our easy chair, they didn't mean to do it. They, as much as we, are victims of circumstance. Hemigamy, as I see it, has been the inevitable result of that dubious blessing called Progress.

In the days of a more simple life it was possible for any average man by working reasonably hard, to earn money enough to provide for his wife and family such of the comforts and luxuries of life as they needed or as he thought they needed. But into this happy home life entered a new snake—the snake of Progress. Science and invention, in a new-born mechanical, chemical, electrical, commercial age, began to invent and discover a hundred new and wonderful things to make life easier and pleasanter. Rather, the expectation and prophecy was that these things would make life easier and pleasanter. The fact is that today in order to procure the things that make life easier, everybody has to work harder than ever to get the money to pay for them.

Progress has made daily necessities out of a hundred things that a previous generation had never heard nor dreamed of: telephones, elevators, kitchen cabinets, automatic sweepers, dish-washing machines, automobiles, radio sets, motion pictures, fur jacquettes, golf outfits, silk stockings, lipsticks, permanent waves, complexion clays. One by one the daughters of the household began slipping out of the home to earn money to buy these wonderful new things that father's income could not be stretched sufficiently to procure.

The new phrase "woman's economic independence" became current, and swiftly its virus has spread in the home, infecting all of our wives. The married woman, envying the girl at work the money she has to spend on feminine fripperies, an income that is hers to do as she pleases with, has gone forth from the home, and is going each year in larger numbers, to get a job for herself. If she has a position before she marries she is insisting on retaining it after marriage.

And how is this condition of hemigamy affecting us husbands? How are we faring with a wife half married to us, and half married—in some cases a good deal more than half married—to her job? Look around you in the circle of your own acquaintances and you will quickly discover that the position of us men in relation to domestic life, under hemigamy, is not nearly as important, nor as imposing, nor as soul-satisfying, as it used to be when we were the sole wage-earners. Read the newspapers and the magazines and you will hear of movements for married women to retain their own names, of self-supporting wives who insist on maintaining separate establishments.

These half-married wives, for the most part still resolutely clinging to the special rights and privileges that were theirs in the bygone days of chivalry, glorying in the new-found independence that the sense of earning and spending their own money has brought to them, no longer even try to keep up the pretense of properly respecting us husbands and our rights, and dignities.

Rather our wives are delighting in flaunting their emancipation in the face of the world. At the theater the other evening I actually saw one of these job-holding wives sitting in the aisle seat, with her husband on the inside. Her money had paid for the tickets. Why should she not sit on the aisle if she wished, and proclaim to the audience that it was she who had financed the evening's entertainment? Frequently I have seen these self-important half-wives, accompanied by their husbands, do the calling of the taxicab and the paying of the driver. I have even seen them in restaurants ordering the dinner, paying the check and tipping the waiter, to their husband's open shame. What are the feelings of any mere husband compared to the importance of a woman publicly proclaiming her economic independence?

Whether this wrecking of masculine comfort, this wanton destruction of masculine self-respect, is a real or is only an imagined evil, of this one thing I am certain—hemigamy is destructive of a happy home life.

The tradition of centuries has been that the wife's place was in the home, to look after her husband's comfort, to do or to supervise the cooking, the cleaning, the washing and the mending, to entertain such guests as her husband might bring home, to take care of and rear the children if there were any. This tradition has been ruthlessly shattered by the fascinations of a woman having a job of her own. Ask any employed wife about housekeeping and home-making and she will calmly assure you that they do not interest her in the least.

Many a husband whose wife is employed knows all too well the cold comfort of entering his home, after his day's work, to find no one there to greet him. Instead of a welcoming kiss and an enticing meal awaiting him there is a telephone message from his wife's place of business that she has been unexpectedly detained at the office and will he please go out to a restaurant and get his dinner? Even when he is fortunate enough to find his wife at home when he gets there, as likely as not she has brought home to dinner a couple of "girls"—our wives call them girls even when they're hatchet-faced and fifty-five—a couple of "girls" from the office and all through the evening meal the trio of women sit and discuss affairs at their office in which the husband is not in the least interested or concerned. When under such circumstances we husbands try to assert ourselves we get nowhere. All attempts to switch the conversation to us and our affairs quickly languish under the cold air of indifference with which our remarks are received. In these homes of hemigamy what has happened to the husband during the day is never a topic of conversation. Possibly when we men held the reins we often may have bored our wives talking about ourselves and what had happened to us since we left home in the morning; but, if we did, these employed wives now are more than making up for it.

Housework and cooking cease to interest a wife once she gets a job. In fact, I have one male friend who insists that women never were really interested in cooking. He points out that cooking is an art, and that for generations women have been doing their utmost to reduce it to a mere trade. We men, he says, turned over the art of cooking to the women, and they immediately went and hired other women to do it, women too ignorant to get any other sort of job, or too homely to get husbands. And to prove his case he points out that while for thousands of years women have been doing most of the cooking the only cooks that have achieved fame have been men. Whether or not he is right in his contentions, the fact is certain that none of these half-married wives are willing to cook.

In every city and town all over the country there are springing up innumerable little restaurants and cafeterias where employed couples get their meals. There are coming into popularity delicatessen stores and rotisseries where cooked food may be purchased and carried home by the wife as she returns from her job. Since our wives have gone to work we men are being fed out of brown paper parcels and cans. Scientists tell us that men are what they eat. What are we men going to become if our employed wives continue to keep us on a delicatessen diet?

Equally distasteful to these half-wives of ours is the matter of having a family. The young married woman who goes into business, or who, having a job, stays in it after marriage, with her maternal instincts smothered by her ambitions to succeed, dreads the prospect of children interfering with her career. If she has children, as soon as she can possibly do it she turns them over to hired nurses or plants them for the day in a "crèche"[1] and gets back to her job. It will not be long before the famous old poems about mother, motherhood, and mother love will have to be all rewritten. "The hand that rocks the cradle" stuff is getting out of date. Babies don't have cradles any more, and if they had them, mother's hand wouldn't be rocking them. It would be pounding typewriter keys, or selling soap in a department store. Can you imagine anyone today writing pretty little mother jingles like:

> Who ran to help me when I fell,
> And would some pretty story tell,
> Or kiss the place to make it well?
>> My Mother.

Mother can't do this sort of thing and be at the office—and she prefers to be at the office. The ballad singers of the next generation will not be able to make the men in the audience snuffle and choke with "Home and Mother" songs. Most of the men, twenty or thirty years from now, if they remember their mothers at all, will remember them as hustling creatures with permanent waves who were always in the act of rushing off to business.

But the most serious peril of hemigamy from the viewpoint of us husbands is its dire effect not on our wives, but on us. Apparently hemigamy is turning us men into parasites.

The strong, forceful type of he-man still wants the soft, sweet old-fashioned feminine sort of girl for a wife. The woman that appeals most to him is the kind that is content to stay in the home and let him do the wrestling with the cruel world for the cash they need. He wants a wife that will be in the house to greet him, when he comes in, that will go into raptures over the presents he brings her, that will be at his beck and call when he wants her, that will ornament his dinner table, entertain his friends, comfort him when he is tired, cheer him when he is depressed. If she'll do these things he is ready to give her all the money she wants, and if he hasn't enough, he'll hustle to get some more. This he-man type of husband simply will not listen to the idea of his wife getting a job. No half-wife for him.

Women with jobs never have husbands like this. The employed woman's husband generally is a lemon, and the bigger and better paid her job is, the more of a lemon her husband is likely to turn out. It goes against masculine pride to have a wife helping support the household, and once a man's pride is shattered, anything can happen to him.

Not infrequently it happens that some ambitious youth with the makings of a real he-man in him, temporarily blinded by the love delirium, is beguiled by the pleadings of his bride into letting her continue at work after marriage. Occasionally you will find couples who continue to live happily and congenially while each goes ahead in a job. But there are not many of these couples. The few that there are, are constantly being exploited in newspaper and magazine articles.

Sometimes there is a happy marriage with both husband and wife at work, but the risk is great. Suppose the wife develops more business ability than the husband, and presently begins to earn more money than he does. Every one of us husbands knows it is hard enough to keep our wives in their proper place when it is we who provide the money and support the household. The minute a wife begins earning more than a husband she sets herself up as the head of the family and the trouble starts. If the husband hasn't sufficient self-respect left to get out and let her get a divorce, he's sure to break under the strain of having to look up to and take orders from his wife. His whole moral fiber seems to collapse, and he starts rapidly slipping back.

I've seen it time and again. Just as surely as a married woman begins to be successful in business, her husband starts going in the other direction. There was a couple I once knew in Chicago. At the time of their marriage the husband was earning $5,000 a year. Two years after marriage the wife went to work, and presently was making more than her husband. His home became a desolate place, for his wife's job required her to travel to other cities. Driven to seek companionship to escape from the loneliness of home the man became addicted to drink. Today they are divorced. The woman is a notable business woman, and the man a drunken drifter.

But, the women will comment, the husband drank. What of it? No husband drinks to excess unless there's a reason for it. If the truth were known there are many men who began drinking because their wives took to work.

But the marriage habit is far too strongly rooted in the feminine sex to be readily given up. If the strongly masculine type will not be satisfied with women of the half-wife type, the employed woman nevertheless feels that she must have some sort of husband; so these wage-earning women marry the weakling men—men who are hardly able to earn a living for themselves. In fact, under hemigamy, these money-earning wives prefer having husbands who will look up to them and will come to them for money for a hat or a new overcoat.

In this aspect hemigamy presents a far graver evil than polygamy ever did, for weakling fathers must mean a degenerating race. Polygamy, on the other hand, however the women may denounce it, according to most of the historians was an important factor in bringing about race progress. In the early tribal times the strongest men took all the women away from the weaker ones, so each strong man had many wives and many children. Thus it happened that in each generation far more children had strong fathers than had weak fathers. Gradually by this means the tribe became taller, stronger mentally and physically, and moved on toward civilization. Under hemigamy the opposite threatens. With all the women employed, there will be fewer children, and those that are born will be of weak paternal stock; so the race will quickly deteriorate.

Nor is there any question that if hemigamy continues there must soon come about an entire recasting of the marriage relations. Don't think I am talking through my hat about this. If you watch the papers and the magazines and the reviews, you'll find many students of human affairs prophesying it. Gray-whiskered conservatives, like dear old Dr. Henry van Dyke,[2] who was formerly our minister to Holland, speak of it guardedly as "a readjustment of the social relation." Women themselves recognize the approaching change: women like Anna Strunsky,[3] who, although she believes that the sanctity of matrimony is too deep-rooted for reformation, says:

"We are rapidly advancing to a time when all women who marry will retain their own names. There will come a time, too, when more special marriage contracts will be made between men and women."

And Jeffery Farnol[4] with the keen vision of the novelist prophesies more boldly thus:

"Women are growing more powerful. I look for them to abolish the double standard of morals and substitute the single standard. By that I mean that women will set up a code that women should be forgiven where man is forgiven."

How, I ask you, are we husbands going to abide such a condition should it ever come about? It has been the masculine creed for centuries that there were many things a man might properly do, but that if a woman did them she would be damned forever. The wife with a job, with money in her pocket, or wherever she carries it, with the knowledge that she is dependent on no man for financial support, with the feeling that she can buy lobster and lipsticks, no matter what happens, isn't going to let herself be damned. It's only a question of a short time till these hemigamous wives are going to assert themselves. "Whatever is right for men to do is right for us" will be their cry.

A few years ago a woman would not have even thought of getting her shoes shined in public. Now in public places she smokes, dances, puts on her rouge, constantly demonstrating her increasing self-assurance.

Now, men, just among ourselves, think over the things we husbands have been getting away with all these years, taking too much to drink, swearing whenever we felt like it, gambling far more than we could afford, staying out all night and lying brazenly about where we have been, flirting with pretty girls, running around with other women.

What are we husbands going to do and say if our self-supporting wives begin acting the way we have been accustomed to act? What is there we *can* do, if our wives continue to have jobs and earn money?

We husbands, under hemigamy, are assuredly up against it. Vanity always has been one of the qualities of femininity. Woman, even when she stayed in her place in the home, took the compliments and flattery of us men seriously. She came to believe that she was a wonderful creature and to have most extravagant ideas about her own importance and the part she played in man's existence. Now that she has gone out into the world and got herself a job and an income, her good opinion of herself has been enhanced still more. No wall seems too high to her for her to scale, no flight too hazardous to attempt. She is invading the factory, the office, law, finance, business, politics. She's organizing a National Party—a big woman's union. Delusions of grandeur possess her as to her place in the universe. The women of today—our wives— our half-wives—ride the world triumphant. Yet, let them beware!

The law of compensations about which wise old Dr. Emerson used to talk and write still prevails. With each gain there must be a corresponding loss. Our wives, under hemigamy, cannot achieve for themselves money, independence, successful careers, without in some way paying for it.

Let every wife, before she considers deserting the home for a place in the business world, write down these words, put them in the side of her mirror and say them over slowly three times before breakfast each day for a week:

No woman succeeds in business without losing something, something of feminine charm and loveliness, something of sentimentality, something of romance, something of the capacity for loving and being loved.

Far be it from me to say there are no good-looking women in the business world, for there are many; but this I will say: business hardens a woman's face. The business woman may wear carefully tailored suits in the daytime, and costly and becoming dinner gowns at night. She may, and generally does, keep herself well coiffured and manicured and daintily shod. She may be and often is handsome, but never is she as handsome, never is she as feminine, never is she as lovely, never is she as appealing to men, as she might have been had she remained at home, satisfied with the love of a husband and children.

Very likely the battle of us husbands against hemigamy will be in vain. The army of women going into business each year is likely to increase. The time may come before we know it when all the good places in business will have been taken and held by the women, when we men, if we work at all, will have to work under women directors, women general managers, women managing clerks. Presently there may be no place left for us husbands in the world of work and business. Home eventually may be our only refuge, while our wives earn the money to support us. Then indeed will our wives wake up to the horrors of hemigamy.

In every one of us men there are latent instincts that we have carefully suppressed. We, too, are fond of personal adornment and of idleness and ease. We, too, are susceptible to flattery. When the time comes that our wives support us, we'll make them support us in a far more extravagant style than ever we provided for them.

We never really have liked working. It has been all pretense on our part. Often in the midst of big affairs, we have been seized with an almost irresistible desire to run off and play, to drop everything and roam the world in search of pleasure, to let ourselves drift with the tide. Only a few of us ever have had the courage to do it, to become loafers and tramps, even though the instinct is in all of us. We've gone off and played golf instead. But wait, just wait, till women are doing all the money-earning and we'll be the greatest idlers the world has ever known.

And what we'll do in the way of dressing will astonish our wage-earning wives beyond measure. We men always have liked pretty clothes. It was only two or three centuries ago, remember, that it was we men who went about with our hair curled, wearing silk and laces, using powder and rouge.

Working as we've had to work the last few generations, we've suppressed our clothes complex fairly well. Only in the matter of neckties, and waistcoats, and golf trousers have we let our tastes manifest themselves. But wait—just wait till the women have all the jobs and all of the money, and we husbands are supported by them, instead of supporting them and ourselves. What gorgeous clothes we'll wear—what wonderful times we'll have!

Our wives some day will find out that this hemigamy business is expensive. Maybe then they'll think about those wonderful lines dear old Sir Alfred wrote in "The Princess":

"Man for the field and woman for the hearth;
Man for the sword, and for the needle she;
Man with the head and woman with the heart;
Man to command and woman to obey;
All else confusion."[5]

NOTES

1. I.e., a public nursery for infants; a daycare center.

2. Henry van Dyke (1852–1933), Presbyterian clergyman and American author of numerous popular essays, short stories, and poems.

3. Anna Strunsky (1878–1964), Russian-born American socialist and coauthor with Jack London of *The Kempton-Wace Letters* (1903), an epistolary novel on love and marriage in which London wrote the letters from Herbert Wace, and Strunsky the letters from his mentor, Dane Kempton.

4. Jeffery Farnol (1878–1952), popular British historical novelist of the period.

5. Alfred, Lord Tennyson, *The Princess: A Medley* (1847), 5.437–41.

27.

MEN AND MARRIAGE

(1986)

George Gilder

George Gilder (b. 1939) graduated from Harvard University and rapidly gained ascen-
dancy in Republican political circles, becoming a speechwriter for Nelson A. Rockefeller,
Richard Nixon, and Bob Dole. Since 1981 he
has been program director of the Manhattan
Institute for Policy Research. Among his
numerous books are several treatises antici-
pating the "men's movement" of the 1980s,
including *Naked Nomads: Unmarried Men in
America* (1974) and *Visible Man* (1978). *Wealth
and Poverty* (1981) is a "theology" or moral
defense of capitalism; it was quickly endorsed
by President Ronald Reagan. It was followed
up by *The Spirit of Enterprise* (1985). In 1973
Gilder published the controversial *Sexual Suicide* (1973), later revised as *Men and Marriage*
(1986). In this work, Gilder lashes out at femi-

Source: George Gilder, *Men and Marriage* (Gretna, LA: Pelican, 1986), pp. 167–77.

nists, linking them with pornographers and sexologists as promoting sexual license and undermining "civilized society." Claiming that childbearing and child rearing are the most emotionally satisfying roles a woman can have, Gilder worries about the increasing number of childless couples and concludes that "[t]he woman's place is in the home, and she does her best when she can get the man there too." The following is excerpted from the chapter "The Home Front."

omen's activities are far richer in intellectual and social challenges than most academic writers comprehend. It is foolish to imagine that these complex roles and relationships can be abolished or assumed by outside agencies. The woman's role is nothing less than the hub of the human community. All the other work—the business and politics and entertainment and service performed in the society—finds its ultimate test in the quality of the home. The home is where we finally and privately live, where we express our individuality, where we display our aesthetic choices, where we make and enjoy love, and where we cultivate our children as individuals.

The central position of the woman in the home parallels her central position in all civilized society. Both derive from her necessary role in procreation and from the most primary and inviolable of human ties, the one between mother and child. In those extraordinary circumstances when this tie is broken—as with some disintegrating tribes—the group tends to sink to a totally bestial and amoral chaos.[1]

Most of the characteristics we define as humane and individual originate in the mother's love for her children. Men have no ties to the long-term human community so deep or tenacious as the mother's to her child. Originating in this love are the other civilizing concerns of maternity: the desire for male protection and support, the hope for a stable community life, and the aspiration toward a better long-term future. The success or failure of civilized society depends on how well the women can transmit these values to the men.

This essential female role has become much more sophisticated and refined in the modern world. But its essence is the same. The woman assumes charge of what may be described as the domestic values of the community—its moral, aesthetic, religious, nurturant, social, and sexual concerns. In these values consist the ultimate goals of human life—all those matters that we consider of such supreme importance that we do not ascribe a financial worth to them. Paramount is the worth of the human individual life, enshrined in the home, and in the connection between a woman and child. These values transcend the marketplace. In fact to enter them in commercial traffic is considered a major evil in civilized society. Whether proposing to sell a baby or a body or a religious blessing, one commits a major moral offense.

This woman's role is deeply individual. Only a specific woman can bear a specific child, and her tie to it is personal and unbreakable. When she raises the child she imparts in privacy her own individual values. She can create children who transcend consensus and prefigure the future: children of private singularity rather than "child-development policy." She is the vessel of the ultimate values of the nation. The community is largely what she is and what she demands in men. She does her work because it is of primary rather than instrumental value. The woman in the home with her child is the last bastion against the amorality of the technocratic marketplace when it strays from the moral foundations of capitalism.

In recent years, the existence of a distinctive feminine role in ethics has been discovered by feminists. Seeking to answer male psychologists who regard masculine defense of justice and equality as the highest level of moral development, female scholars have offered a contrary case for the moral perceptions of women. The leading work in this field is *In a Different Voice*, by Carol Gilligan of Harvard.[2] She postulates a uniquely feminine moral sense rooted in webs of relationship and responsibility, in intimacy and caring, rather than in rules and abstractions.

Gilligan's point is valuable and true and her book is full of interesting evidence for it. But contrary to her egalitarian vision, women's moral sense is not merely an equal counterpoint to masculine ideals. Stemming from her umbilical link to new life itself and from a passionate sense of the value and potential of that life, the woman's morality is the ultimate basis of all morality. The man's recognition of the preciousness and equality of individuals is learned from women and originates with the feminine concern for relationships, beginning in the womb and at the breast. This concern contrasts sharply with his own experience of hierarchy and preference, aggression and lust, and the sense of sexual and personal dispensability he experiences as a single man. Just as outside male activity is regarded in all societies as most important in instrumental terms, women's concerns are morally paramount, by the very fact that they are female, part of the unimpeachable realm of life's creation and protection.

What is true for individual moral issues is also true for the practical needs of a nation: the maternal role remains paramount. There is no way to shunt off child care to the "society" or to substantially reduce its burdens. If children lack the close attention of mothers and the disciplines and guidance of fathers, they tend to become barbarians or wastrels who burden or threaten society rather than do its work. Raising children to be productive and responsible citizens takes persistent and unrelenting effort. The prisons, reformatories, foster homes, mental institutions, and welfare rolls of America already groan under the burden of children relinquished to "society" to raise and support. In the sense of becoming self-sufficient, all too many of these children never grow up at all. To reproduce the true means of production—men and women who can uphold civilization rather than subvert it—the diligent love of mothers is indispensable. In fact, the only remedy for the "overpopulation" in female-headed families is the creation of a larger population of children brought up by two active and attentive parents.

Crucial to the sexual liberals' dream of escape from family burdens is zero population growth. Because each individual no longer depends on his children to support him in old age, many observers seem to imagine that children are less important than they were in the past. But substantially fewer offspring are a possibility only for a while in modern welfare states. No less than in the past, the new generations will have to support the old. The only difference is that now the medium is coercive taxation and social security rather than filial duty.

With some 15 percent of couples infertile and others child-free by choice, in order to raise enough workers to support the social programs of retirees, each fertile woman must still bear more than two children. In order to prevent a substantial decline in the quality of children—their willingness to work hard and contribute to society in the face of high taxes and a generous dole—women must devote long hours to raising and disciplining the new generation. The decline in the quantity of children demands a rise in the quality of their contributions to society—a rise in their diligence and productivity.

This female responsibility, as Gilligan observes, entails difficult sacrifices of freedom and autonomy.[3] Other researchers, notably Jessie Bernard, have noted that these sacrifices produce a significantly elevated incidence of emotional stress and neurosis among full-time housewives, particularly when their children are young.[4] Some of this anxiety clearly reflects the sharp rise in expenses and tax burdens incurred by families raising children. Some of the problem is simply hard and grueling work. Part of the distress, though, may derive from the media's widespread disparagement of traditional women. Margaret Mead found that women are most contented not when they are granted "influence, power, and wealth," but when "the female role of wife and mother is exalted." A devaluing of "the sensuous creative significance" of woman's role, she wrote, makes women become unhappy in the home.[5] But regardless of the source of this stress, Gilligan's point is correct. Women do make great sacrifices, and these sacrifices are essential to society.

Some theorists list sexual restraint high among these sacrifices.

But women's sexual restraint is necessary for the fulfillment of their larger sexuality in families, which cannot normally survive the birth of children by men other than the family provider. In general, a man will not support a woman while she philanders.

Contrary to the assumption of most analysts, it is men who make the major sexual sacrifice. The man renounces his dream of short-term sexual freedom and self-fulfillment—his male sexuality and self-expression—in order to serve a woman and family for a lifetime. It is a traumatic act of giving up his most profound yearning, his bent for the hunt and the chase, the motorbike and the open road, the male group escape to a primal mode of predatory and immediate excitements. His most powerful impulse—the theme of every male song and story—this combination of lust and wanderlust is the very life force that drives him through his youth. He surrenders it only with pain. This male sacrifice, no less than the woman's work in the home, is essential to civilization.

Just as the female role cannot be shared or relinquished, the male role also remains vital to social survival. For centuries to come, men will have to make heroic efforts. On forty-hour weeks, most men cannot even support a family of four. They must train at night and on weekends; they must save as they can for future ventures of entrepreneurship; they must often perform more than one job. They must make time as best they can to see and guide their children. They must shun the consolations of alcohol and leisure, sexual indulgence and flight. They must live for the perennial demands of the provider role.

Unlike the woman's role, the man's tends to be relatively fungible and derivative. He does not give himself to a web of unique personal relationships so much as to a set of functions and technologies. Just as any particular hunter might kill an animal, so within obvious bounds any workman can be trained to do most jobs. The man makes himself replaceable. For most of his early years at the job site, individuality is an obstacle to earnings. He must sacrifice it to support his wife and children. He must eschew his desire to be an athlete or poet, a death-defying ranger or mountaineer, a cocksman and Casanova, and settle down to become a functionary defined by a single job, and a father whose children are earned by his work. Not his own moral vision but the marketplace defines the value of that work.

Extraordinary men transcend many of these constraints early in their careers and many men eventually rise to significant roles of leadership and self-expression. But even then jobs rarely afford room for the whole man. Even highly paid work often creates what Ortega y Gasset called "barbarians of specialization."[6] One may become a scientist, a doctor, an engineer, or a lawyer, for example, chiefly by narrowing the mind, by excluding personal idiosyncrasies and visions in order to master the disciplines and technicalities of the trade. In some cases, exceptionally successful specialization may bring some of the satisfactions won, for example, by the great athlete. Nevertheless, this process usually does not make a man interesting or whole. In fact, he is likely to succeed precisely to the extent that he is willing to subordinate himself to the narrow imperatives of his specialty, precisely to the extent that he forgoes the distractions and impulses of the full personality.

Among men, the term *dilettante* is a pejorative. Yet, because the range of human knowledge and experience is so broad, the best that most people can ever achieve, if they respond as whole persons to their lives, is the curiosity, openness, and eclectic knowledge of the dilettante. Most men have to deny themselves this form of individual fulfillment. They have to limit themselves, at great psychological cost, in order to fit the functions of the economic division of labor. Most of them endure their submission to the marketplace chiefly in order to make enough money to sustain a home, to earn a place in the household, to be needed by women. This effort most of the time means a lifetime of hard labor.

As with the woman's role, what is true in most specific cases is still more true on the level of general rules and expectations across the entire society. On forty-hour weeks the world dissolves into chaos and decay, famine and war. All the major accomplishments of civilization spring from the obsessions of men whom the sociologists would now disdain as "workaholics." To overcome the Malthusian trap of rising populations, or to escape the closing circle of ecological decline, or to control the threat of nuclear holocaust, or to halt the plagues and famines that still afflict the globe, men must give their lives to unrelenting effort, day in and day out, focused on goals in the distant future. They must create new technologies faster than the world creates new challenges. They must struggle against scarcity, entropy, and natural disaster. They must overcome the sabotage of socialists who would steal and redistribute their product. They must resist disease and temptation. All too often they must die without achieving their ends. But their sacrifices bring others closer to the goal.

Nothing that has been written in the annals of feminism gives the slightest indication that this is a role that women want or are prepared to perform. The feminists demand liberation. The male role means bondage to the demands of the workplace and the needs of the family. Most of the research of sociologists complains that men's work is already too hard, too dangerous, too destructive of mental health and wholeness. It all too often leads to sickness and "worlds of pain," demoralization and relatively early death. The men's role that feminists seek is not the real role of men but the male role of the Marxist dream in which "society" does the work.

"Women's liberation" entails a profound dislocation. Women, uniquely in charge of the central activities of human life, are exalting instead the peripheral values—values that have meaning only in relation to the role they would disparage or abandon. In addition, sexual liberals ask society to give up most of the devices and conventions by which it has ensured that women perform their indispensable work and by which men have been induced to support it. As a result, in many of the world's welfare states that have accepted the feminist vision, the two sexes are no longer making the necessary sacrifices to sustain society.

Shunning the responsibilities of family support, men are rejecting available jobs and doing sporadic work off the books and stints on unemployment insurance. Shunning the role of wife and mother, many women are forgoing marriage. Consequently many Western nations are far overshooting the mark of zero population growth. With the average couple bearing scarcely more than one child, most of Northern Europe now shows a fertility rate about 60 percent of the replacement level.[7] If this rate continues, dictated by the pressures of excessive welfare programs, it would mean near-extinction of the genetic stock within four generations. To a less but still dangerous degree, the same pattern is evident in America. The U.S. also is under the replacement level of reproduction.

A nation may gain the illusion of a rising standard of living by raising and supporting fewer children. To paraphrase Allan Carlson, a society may consume for a while the ghosts of the unborn.[8] More specifically, we may eat the meals that would have gone to our prevented or aborted babies. But these gains are rapidly lost. In a vicious circle well known in Europe, smaller generations of workers find themselves devoting ever larger portions of their pay to supporting the child-free aged. Soon the young workers begin reducing their efforts in the face of rising tax rates and their wives themselves begin bearing still fewer children. This is the final contradiction of the welfare state. To the extent that it deters work and childbearing, it ultimately self-destructs.

There is a way out, however. It is to export the woman's role and import people through immigration. In more positive terms, this policy can be seen as extending the higher and more abstract role of motherhood and home into the world. In recent years, as much as a third of America's economic growth and technological progress has stemmed from such an opening of the arms of Lady Liberty to the refugees of socialism. For example, in California's Silicon Valley, the fount of the worldwide computer revolution, immigrants play key roles on assembly lines, in making major innovations, in performing laboratory research, and even in the entrepreneurial launching of major companies, from Intel in the 1970s to Tandon and Xicor in the 1980s. Immigrants may yet save the American social-security system.

The immigration option works to save the welfare state, however, only on one condition: the immigrants must stay off welfare. The dangers are clear from the U.S. experience with Puerto Ricans, who once showed far better family stability and work effort than American blacks. In two generations, the U.S. welfare state has turned hundreds of thousands of hard-working Puerto Rican families into fatherless units dependent on the state. European social democrats who prate about their compassion for the poor know well that they must mostly exclude their own poor and the world's real poor—i.e., immigrants—from welfare. If immigrants were allowed on the dole they would throng from around the world to the welfare states of the West and bankrupt them. The choice is clear. The welfare state must either bar immigration or create a second-class citizenship.

The Europeans, and to a lesser extent the U.S. with its illegal aliens, are already in the process of creating such a two-tiered society. At the top will be the leisured peers with full entitlement to be supported by others. On the bottom are laboring newcomers: a new serfdom imported to save the child-free socialism of the rich. The assertion of a new morality of caring for the world thus leads to a rejection of the dream of equal justice at the foundation of the welfare state.

Rather than face the full implications of their policy, the Europeans have also been toying with the ultimate form of protectionism: not only barring the products of poor people overseas but also barring the people themselves. Several European governments have recently been paying some of their immigrants to leave. Before long, though, Europe will have to invite them back, but without full access to the benefits of socialism. With this decision will collapse the last pretense that socialism can provide equality or compassion for the truly poor, as opposed to the welfare state's entitled peers.

In an important essay, "Two Cheers for ZPG," Norman Ryder illustrates some of these ironies in the current stance of sexual liberals. "A collective commitment to population replacement," he writes, "is a defensible posture only if we assume that whatever it is that we are proud of must be transmitted biologically." He suggests that we fulfill our "thrust toward immortality . . . by efforts to ensure that future generations share our values, whether or not they share our genes."[9] As

Carlson comments: "In the end, we learn that the final consequence of the existing welfare state is biological extinction. The grim humor lies in Ryder's belief that he could find self-respecting immigrants who would want to 'share values' with a decadent intelligentsia presiding over a self-inflicted genocide."[10]

Sexual liberalism is the cause, not the solution, of the problem of the West. But the error of the liberals comes not only in their fantasies of flight from work and children—not only in their illusion that full-time work and child care have declined in importance to modern society. They also deeply misunderstand what makes people happy. The pursuit of promiscuous sexual pleasures which many of them offer as an alternative to the duties of family leads chiefly to misery and despair. It is procreation that ultimately makes sex gratifying and important and it is home and family that gives resonance and meaning to life.

The woman's place is in the home, and she does her best when she can get the man there too, inducing him to submit most human activity to the domestic values of civilization. Thus in a sense she also brings the home into the society. The radiance of the values of home can give meaning and illumination to male enterprises. Male work is most valuable when it is imbued with the long-term love and communal concerns of femininity, when it is brought back to the home. Otherwise masculine activity is apt to degenerate quickly to the level of a game; and, unless closely regulated, games have a way of deteriorating into the vain pursuit of power.

It is the judgment of women that tames the aggressive pursuits of men. Men come to learn that their activity will be best received if it partakes of the values of the home. If they think the work itself is unworthy, they try to conceal it and bring home the money anyway. Like the legendary Mafiosi, they try to please their women by elaborate submission to domestic values in the household, while scrupulously keeping the women out of the male realm of work. But in almost every instance, even by hypocrisy, they pay tribute to the moral superiority of women.

In rediscovering for the secular world this feminine morality, rooted in "webs of relationship," Gilligan has written an important book. What she and the male moralists she criticizes do not see is that the self-sacrifice of women finds a perfect complement in the self-sacrifice of men. On this mutual immolation is founded the fulfillment of human civilization and happiness. For just as it is the sacrifice of early career ambitions and sexual freedom that makes possible the true fulfillment of women, it is the subordination of male sexuality to woman's maternity that allows the achievement of male career goals, that spurs the attainment of the highest male purposes. In his vaunted freedom and sexual power, the young single man may dream of glory. But it is overwhelmingly the married men who achieve it in the modern world. They achieve it, as scripture dictates and women's experience insists, by self-denial and sacrifice.

The fact is that there is no way that women can escape their supreme responsibilities in civilized society without endangering civilization itself. The most chilling portent of our current predicament, therefore, is the conjuncture of a movement of female abdication with a new biochemistry, which shines direct and deadly beams of technocratic light on the very crux of human identity, the tie between the mother and her child.

NOTES

1. [See the story of the Ik tribe in Colin Turnbull, *The Mountain People* (New York: Simon & Schuster, 1972), pp. 290–95 and passim.]

2. [Carol Gilligan, *In a Different Voice: Psychological Theory and Women's Development* (Cambridge, MA: Harvard University Press, 1982). In attacking the shallow notions of male maturation and male moral superiority offered by developmental psychologists, Gilligan performs an important service. But her alternative moral view comes perilously close to a slough of situational ethics. In her interesting comparison of George Eliot's *Mill on the Floss* (1860) with Margaret Drabble's retelling of the tale in *The Waterfall* (1969), Gilligan can even condone the stealing of another woman's husband. The most telling female offense against the sexual constitution, this violation

is at the root of the princess's problem in chapter 5 of this book and a source of the breakdown of monogamy that causes so many problems for women in modern society.]

3. [Ibid., pp. 70–71 and passim.]

4. [Jessie Bernard, *The Future of Marriage* (New York: World, 1972), pp. 336, 338, 339.]

5. [Margaret Mead, *Male and Female: A Study of the Sexes in a Changing World* (New York: Morrow, 1949), quoted from the paperback (New York: Dell, 1968), p. 110.]

6. [Jose Ortega y Gasset, *The Revolt of the Masses* (New York: Norton, 1932), pp. 94–95.]

7. [Allan Carlson, "Toward 'The Working Family': The Hidden Agenda behind the Comparable Worth Debate," *Persuasion at Work*, Rockford Institute, Rockford, Ill., July 1984, p. 5.]

8. [Carlson, "The Time Bomb within Social Security," *Persuasion at Work*, September 1985, p. 7.]

9. [Norman Ryder, "Two Cheers for ZPG," *Daedalus: Journal of the American Academy of Arts and Sciences*, Fall 1974, pp. 45–62.]

10. [Carlson, "Time Bomb," p. 7.]

Part 9

WOMEN AND RELIGION

28.

FEMALE INFLUENCE, AND THE TRUE CHRISTIAN MODE OF ITS EXERCISE

(1837)

Jonathan F. Stearns

The little-known clergyman Jonathan French Stearns (1808–1889) spent most of his career as pastor of the First Presbyterian Church in Newark, New Jersey. He is the author of numerous sermons, including one on the death of Abraham Lincoln two days after his assassination. In an early sermon, *Female Influence, and the True Christian Mode of Its Exercise* (1837), delivered at the First Presbyterian Church in Newburyport, Massachusetts, on July 30, 1837, Stearns cites biblical passages on the submission of wives to their husbands and maintains that these directives are designed to shield women from "rude exposure in public life."

Source: Jonathan F. Stearns, *Female Influence, and the True Christian Mode of Its Exercise* (Newburyport, MA: John G. Tilton, 1837), pp. 15–21.

*L*et us turn to the Bible for a moment, and see what we can gather from the teachings of inspiration. The principles and precepts of the Bible, be it remembered, first released woman from her thraldom, and gave her that elevated rank in society which she is now beginning to hold. Let us see how the same sacred document would define and regulate the exercise of her privilege. I will quote a few passages, some of which contain general principles, and others, specific directions and positive commands.

In the first Epistle to the Corinthians, 11th chapter, the apostle enjoins upon females to be covered, when they engage in the public exercises of religion. Not that he would depreciate their worth, for he adds—"Nevertheless, neither is the man without the woman, nor the woman without the man in the Lord. For as the woman is of the man, even so is the man also by the woman; but all things of God." And then he proceeds—"Judge in yourselves; is it comely that a woman pray unto God uncovered? Doth not even nature herself teach, that if a man have *long hair* it is a shame unto him; but if a *woman* have long hair it is a glory to her, for her hair is given her for a covering."[1] In the Epistle to Titus, he directs a young minister what principles he should teach on this subject—"That the aged women be in behaviour as becometh holiness, not false accusers, not given to much wine, teachers of good things. That they may teach the young women to be sober, to love their husbands, to love their children, to be discreet, chaste, keepers at home, obedient to their own husbands, that the word of God be not blasphemed."[2] In the first Epistle to the Corinthians, 14th chapter, the apostle enters at large into the subject of order and propriety in the public assemblies of christians, for mutual instruction and devotion. In this chapter he has given a variety of specific directions, ending with those memorable words—"Let all things be done decently and in order."[3] Among other precepts are the following— "Let your women keep silence in the churches, for it is not permitted unto them to speak, but they are commanded to be under obedience, as also saith the law. And if they will learn any thing, let them ask their husbands, (*their own men,* it is in the original,) at home; for it is a shame for women to speak in the church."[4] And again, in the second chapter of his first Epistle to Timothy, he says—"I will also that women adorn themselves in modest apparel, with shamefacedness and sobriety, not with broidered hair, or gold, or pearls, or costly array, but, as becometh women professing godliness, with good works. Let the woman learn in silence with all subjection. But I suffer not a woman to teach, nor to usurp authority over the man, but to be in silence."[5]

The apostle speaks in these passages in a tone of authority, as it was proper he should do, in his office, as commissioned ambassador of Christ. And his precepts, did they stand unsupported by any perceptible reasons, would doubtless be sufficient to command the conduct of christians. But I apprehend it will not appear difficult, to one who duly considers the nature of the case, as well as the history of the world, to see *reasons* sufficient to establish the wisdom of these precepts, independent of apostolic authority. I am confident no virtuous and delicate female, who rightly appreciates the design of her being, and desires to sustain her own influence and that of her sex, would desire to abate one jot or tittle from the seeming restrictions imposed upon her conduct in these and the like passages. They are designed, not to *degrade*, but to *elevate* her character,—not to cramp, but to afford a *salutary* freedom, and give a useful direction to the energies of the feminine mind. A prominent object of the apostle seems to have been, to protect those peculiar traits of character, which are the chief source of woman's influence over society, from the injury they are likely to sustain from rude exposure in public life. Let woman throw off her feminine character, and her power to benefit society is *lost*; her loveliness, her dignity, her own chief protection is *lost*.

I have met in an old Grecian author with a sentiment like this:— "Nature has given to all classes of creatures their appropriate defences. She has given horns to the bullock, hoofs to the horses, swiftness to the hares, fins to the fishes, wings to the birds. For woman she had none of these; and instead of them, gave her *beauty*, which was to her in place of shields and spears."

The sentiment was worthy of a heathen poet. Let us christianize it

and adopt it as our own. For *beauty* let us substitute *delicacy*—CHRIS-
TIAN DELICACY. This is woman's defence and her glory. Let her lay
aside delicacy, and her influence over our sex is gone; all the benefits
she is now so peculiarly fitted to confer on the church and the world are
sacrificed, and her own honor and safety exposed to the greatest danger.

And for what object should she make sacrifices? That she may do
good more extensively? Then she sadly mistakes her vocation. But why
then? That she may see her name blazoned on the rolls of fame, and
hear the shouts of delighted assemblies, applauding her eloquence?
That she may place her own sex on a fancied equality with men, obtain
the satisfaction of calling herself *independent*, and occupy a station in
life which she can never adorn? For *this* would she sacrifice the almost
magic power, which, in her own proper sphere, she now wields over the
destinies of the world? Surely *such privileges*, obtained at *such cost*,
are unworthy of a wise and virtuous woman's ambition.

When I see ladies of talent, and learning, and refinement,—ladies
whose accomplishments and virtues would have fitted them to stand in
the first rank among their own sex, stepping out of their sphere, to
enter upon stations and offices which have heretofore been regarded as
appropriate to men, it forcibly reminds me of the parable of Jotham
contained in the ninth chapter of Judges—"The trees of the wood went
forth on a time to anoint a king over them. And they said unto the olive
tree, Reign thou over us. But the olive tree said unto them, Should I
leave my fatness, wherewith by me they honor God and man, and go
to be promoted over the trees? And the trees said unto the fig tree,
Come thou and reign over us. But the fig tree said unto them, Should
I forsake my sweetness and my good fruit, and go to be promoted over
the trees? Then said the trees unto the vine, Come thou and reign over
us. And the vine said unto them, Should I leave my wine, which
cheereth God and man, and go to be promoted over the trees? Then
said all the trees unto the *bramble*, Come thou and reign over us. And
the bramble said unto the trees, If in truth ye anoint me king over you,
then come and put your trust in my shadow."[6]

Let the ladies of this assembly decide which example is most worthy of their imitation. Shall they *condescend* to leave a station, which they may cheer and adorn, and forego an influence which has been, ever since the dawn of christianity gave scope to it, so powerful and salutary, that they may enter the sphere and imitate the conduct of men, and attempt to convince the world that there is no distinction of character?

That there are ladies who are capable of public debate, who could make their voices heard from end to end of the church and the senate house,—that there are those who might bear a favorable comparison with others as eloquent orators, and who might speak to better edification than most of those on whom the office has hitherto devolved, I am not disposed to deny. The question is not in regard to *ability*, but to *decency*, to order, to christian *propriety*. Of one thing I am certain, they would find it hard to convince most of those whom they would emulate, that the course was either amiable or becoming. For if an effeminate man is always despised, no less so, as nature herself teaches, must be a masculine woman.

My hearers must pardon me for speaking thus explicitly. The advocates of such principles and measures have, in times past, been confined principally to the ranks of unbelievers, whom no pious and respectable female would desire to encourage. But when popular female writers, and women professing godliness, begin to take the same ground, it is time for the pulpit as well as the press to speak plainly. I verily believe, that should the practice I have censured become *prevalent*, and the consequent change in the treatment of females, already anticipated by some of its advocates, take place in the community, the influence of ladies, now so important to the cause of philanthropy and piety, would very speedily be crushed, and religion, morality and good order, suffer a wound from which they would not soon nor easily recover.

Far be it from me to insinuate that any ladies in this assembly, would transcend the bounds of christian modesty and propriety. I trust they have not so learned the teachings of Christ and his apostles. Nay, your own sense of delicacy, which none are able to impeach, I am confident will be a sufficient guard against any such temptation. Nor can

I doubt that the main principles at least of the foregoing discourse, will commend themselves at once to your undivided approbation. Surely, she who is to society the *teacher* of delicacy and of all its kindred virtues, should desire to preserve her own unsullied and entire.

NOTES

1. 1 Cor. 11:11–15.
2. Titus 2:3–5.
3. 1 Cor. 14:40.
4. 1 Cor. 14:34–35.
5. 1 Tim. 2:9–12.
6. Judg. 9:8–15.

29.

WOMAN'S PROFESSION AS MOTHER AND EDUCATOR

(1872)

Catharine E. Beecher

Catharine Esther Beecher (1800–1878) was the eldest child of Lyman Beecher, celebrated Presbyterian clergyman, and the sister of Congregational clergyman Henry Ward Beecher and of Harriet Beecher Stowe. Throughout her life she advocated enhanced education for women, although that education was, in her mind, to be devoted chiefly to making women into good wives and mothers. She initiated schools for "young ladies" in Hartford, Connecticut, and in Cincinnati, Ohio, and founded colleges for women in Burlington, Iowa; Quincy, Illinois; and Milwaukee, Wisconsin. But she also became an early leader of the anti–woman suffrage movement, maintaining that the vote would take women away from their "proper sphere." She wrote prolifically; among her works are *The Duty of Amer-*

Source: Catharine E. Beecher, *Woman's Profession as Mother and Educator* (Philadelphia & Boston: Geo. Maclean; New York: Maclean, Gibson, 1872), pp. 175–89.

ican Women to Their Country (1845), *The Evils Suffered by American Women and American Children* (1846), and *Woman Suffrage and Woman's Profession* (1871). In the following extract from *Woman's Profession as Mother and Educator* (1872), Beecher emphasizes the role of women in inculcating religion into their children, maintaining that women's submission to men is parallel to men's submission to the state.

ow the family state is instituted to educate our race to the Christian character,—to train the young to be followers of Christ. Woman is its chief minister, and the work to be done is the most difficult of all, requiring not only intellectual power but a moral training nowhere else so attainable as in the humble, laborious, daily duties of the family state.

Woman's great mission is to train immature, weak, and ignorant creatures, to obey the laws of God; the physical, the intellectual, the social, and the moral—first in the family, then in the school, then in the neighborhood, then in the nation, then in the world—that great family of God whom the Master came to teach and to save. And His most comprehensive rule is, "Thou shalt love the Lord thy God with all thy heart," and "this is the love of God that ye keep His commandments."[1] And next, "Thou shalt love thy neighbor as thyself."[2] These two the Master teaches are the chief end of man and includes all taught by Moses and the prophets. This then is woman's work, to train the young in the family and the school *to obey God's laws* as learned partly by experience, partly by human teaching and example, and partly by revelations from God.

But the most solemn duty of the Christian woman is the *motives* she is to employ in training to this obedience. The motives used by the worldly educator are the gain or loss of earthly pleasures, honors, and comforts. But the truly christian woman feels and presents as the grand motive, the dangers of the future life from which our Lord came to save us, and these so dreadful that all we most value in this life are to be made secondary and subordinate, while the chief concern is, not mainly to save self, but rather to save ourselves by laboring to save others from ignorance of God's laws and to secure the obedience indispensable to future eternal safety.

And this is to be done at a period when this great motive of Christ's religion is more and more passing out of regard, even in the Christian church. So much is this the case, that the world has good reason to say that while most creeds and preachers teach it in words, few really believe it. For "it is actions that speak louder than words," as to what is believed.

For example, if a company of amiable persons were told that a shipwreck was close at hand and help needed to save the struggling passengers, and yet, after a few enquiries, all went on as before, it would justly be said that these persons do not believe in the messenger and his message. But suppose another company, on hearing the news, rush out amid the darkness and danger, to help; this would prove their *faith* in the messenger and his story.

Now no earthly danger can compare with those revealed by our Lord as threatening every child born into this life; and He also teaches that *the number saved depends on the self-denying labors of His followers.* With small exceptions, all the Christian churches profess to believe this, and that the first concern of Christian life is to *save as many as possible.* And yet where is the *practical* evidence that this is believed?

If these teachings of Christ were fully and practically believed, would it not so divide the church from the world that there could be no mistake as to who are christians and who are not? And is there any such marked divisions in most of our churches?

It may be urged that this doctrine has been set forth with such hideous detail and additions entirely unwarranted by the Bible and so abhorrent to the best feelings of humanity, that the more men become humane and Christ-like the more they revolt from it.

Yet if this be so, the fact remains that Jesus Christ, the only reliable messenger from the invisible world, has in the strongest language both literal and figurative, set forth these dangers and enjoined on his followers as their *first* concern, to save as many as possible, by training them to a knowledge of God's laws and to habitual obedience to them. And is there not a want of *belief* in this—that is, a want of that *practical faith* in Christ and his message, which it is the greatest and chief mission of woman to secure by her ministry in the family and school? She it is who daily is to train all under her care to become *righteous*, that is, to *feel and act right* according to the rules of right revealed by Jesus Christ. She is to teach that "repentance" which consists in such sorrow for wrong doing as involves turning from it, and such love as secures obedience to the Lord and Savior.

Now the Christian woman in the family and in the school is the most complete autocrat that is known, as the care of the helpless little ones, the guidance of their intellect, and the formation of all their habits, are given to her supreme control. Scarcely less is she mistress and autocrat over a husband, whose character, comfort, peace, and prosperity, are all in her power. In this responsible position is she to teach, by word and example, as did Jesus Christ? Is she to set an example to children and servants not only of that of a ruler, but also of obedience as a subordinate? In the civil state her sons will be subjects to rulers who are weak and wicked, just as she may be subject to a husband and father every way her inferior in ability and moral worth. Shall she teach her children and servants by her own example to be humble, obedient, meek, patient, forgiving, gentle, and loving, even to the evil and unthankful, or shall she form rebellious parties and carry her points by contest and discord? God has given man the physical power, the power of the purse, and the civil power, and woman must submit with Christian equanimity or contend. What is the answer of common sense, and what are the teachings of Christ and His Apostles?

Let every woman who is musing on these questions, take a reference Bible and examine all the New Testament directions on the duties of the family state, and she will have no difficulty in deciding what was the view of Christ and His Apostles as to woman's position and duties. She is a *subordinate* in the family state, just as her father, husband, brother, and sons are subordinate in the civil state. And the same rules that are to guide them are to guide her. She and they are to be obedient to "the higher powers"[3]—those that can force obedience—except when their demands are contrary to the higher law of God, and in such a conflict they are "to obey God rather than man,"[4] and take the consequences whatever they may be. And a woman has no more difficulty in deciding when to obey God rather than man in the family state than her husband, father, and sons have, in the civil state. And obedience in the family to "the higher power" held by man, is no more a humiliation than is man's obedience to a civil ruler.

If this be so, then the doctrine of woman's subjugation is established and the opposing doctrine of Stuart Mills[5] and his followers is in direct opposition to the teachings both of common sense and of Christianity.

There is a moral power given to woman in the family state much more controlling and abiding than the inferior, physical power conferred on man. And the more men are trained to refinement, honor, and benevolence, the more this moral power of woman is increased. This is painfully illustrated in cases where an amiable and Christian man is bound for life to an unreasonable, selfish, and obstinate woman. With such a woman reasoning is useless, and physical force alone can conquer, and this such a man cannot employ. The only alternatives are ceaseless conflicts, at the sacrifice of conscience and self-respect, or hopeless submission to a daily and grinding tyranny.

The general principles to guide both men and women as to the duties of those in a subordinate station, have been made clear by discussions relating to civil government. But the corresponding duties of those invested with power and authority have not been so clearly set forth, especially those of the family state. While the duties of subordination, subjection, and obedience, have been abundantly enforced on woman, the corresponding duties of man as head and ruler of the family state have not received equal attention either from the pulpit or the press. And this is not because they are not as difficult, as important and as clearly taught by the Master and the Apostles of Christianity.

St. Paul, who, while he dwelt in retirement in Arabia, received the direct instructions of Jesus Christ, claims to have full authority from the Master to instruct on this important and fundamental topic, and in his Epistle to the Ephesians we have his express and full teachings. In this most interesting passage we find that the family state is the emblem to represent Jesus Christ and the Church—the Church "which is the great company of faithful people" in all ages and all lands— those who are appointed to guide and save the world—the true educa- tors of our race, who, by self-denying labors are to train men for Heaven. Of this body the Apostles teaches that Jesus Christ is the head—those whom He has redeemed by His labor and sacrifice, and who are to train as His children all whom they can rescue from igno- rance and sin, by similar labor and sacrifice.

It is in this connection that he sets forth the duties of the family state, Ephesians v:22 to 33, "Wives submit yourselves unto your own husbands *as unto the Lord*. For the husband is head of the wife, even as Christ is head of the Church: Therefore, as the Church is subject to Christ so let the wives be to their own husbands in everything.

"Husbands love your wives even as Christ also loved the Church and gave Himself for it, that He might sanctify and cleanse it with the washing of water by the word, that He might present it to Himself, a glorious Church, not having spot or wrinkle or any such thing, but that it should be holy and without blemish. So ought men to love their wives as their own bodies. He that loveth his wife loveth himself. For no man ever yet hated his own flesh, but nourisheth and cherisheth it even as the Lord the Church. For we are members of His body, of His flesh, and of His bones. For this cause shall a man leave his father and mother and shall be joined unto his wife, and they two shall be one flesh."

No wonder these directions close with "this is a great mystery"; for the most advanced followers of Christ have but just begun to understand the solemn relations and duties of the family state—man the head, protector, and provider—woman the chief educator of immortal minds—man to labor and suffer to train and elevate woman for her high calling, woman to set an example of meekness, gentleness, obedience, and self-denying love, as she guides her children and servants heavenward.

It is this comprehensive view of the family state as organized to train immortal minds for the eternal world that indicates the reason for the stringency of the teachings of our Lord as to the indissoluble union of man and wife in marriage.

> And he said unto them, Moses, *because of the hardness of your hearts*, suffered you to put away your wives; but from the beginning it was not so. And I say unto you, whosoever shall put away his wife, except it be for fornication, and shall marry another committeth adultery; and whosoever marrieth her that is put away doth commit adultery.[6]
>
> Have ye not read that He which made them at the beginning made them male and female, and said, For this cause shall a man leave a father and mother and shall cleave to his wife, and they twain shall be one flesh. What therefore God hath joined together let not man put asunder.[7]

This then is "the higher law" which abrogates all contrary human statutes and forbids to marry more than once, except when death or adultery breaks the bond. This statute brings all the advocates of free divorce in direct antagonism with the teachings of Jesus Christ. And it is a striking fact that the great body of those who advocate free divorce and free love, deny the authority of Jesus Christ as the authorized teacher of faith and morals.

In the discussions as to woman's rights and wrongs, it is assumed on one side that she is not to take a subordinate position either in the family or the State. And the apparent plausibility of the claim is owing to a want of logical clearness in the use of words. When it is said that "all men are created free and equal and equally entitled to life, liberty, and the pursuit of happiness,"[8] and that women as much as men are included, it is true in one use of terms and false in another. It is true in this sense, that woman's happiness and usefulness are equal in value to man's, and ought to be so treated. But it is not true that women are and should be treated as the equals of men in *every* respect. They certainly are not his equals in physical power, which is the final resort in *government* of both the family and the State. And it is owing to this fact that she is placed as a subordinate both in the family and the State. At the same time it is required of man who is holding "the higher powers" so to administer that woman shall have equal advantages with man for usefulness and happiness.

Hitherto the laws relating to women in the civil state have been formed on the assumption that society is a combination of families, in each of which the husband and father is the representative head, and the one who, it is supposed, will secure all that is just and proper for the protection and well being of wife and daughters. And if the teachings of Christianity were dominant, and every man loved his wife as himself, and was ready to sacrifice himself and suffer for her elevation and improvement, even as Christ suffered to redeem and purify the Church, there would be no trouble.

But both men and women have been selfish and sinful, neither party having attained the high ideal of Christianity, and very many have not even understood it so as to aim at it. But it is woman's mission as the educator of the race to remedy the evil, not by giving up the ideal but by striving more and more to conform herself and all under her care to its blessed outlines. And in past times those families have been the most peaceful and prosperous where the wife and mother has most faithfully aimed to obey the teachings of Christ and His Apostles, in this as in every other direction.

The principle of subordination is the great bond of union and harmony through the universe. At the head is the loving Father and Lord whom all are to obey with perfect faith and submission. Then revelation teaches that in the invisible world are superior and subordinate ranks, each owing obedience to superiors in station and described as "thrones, dominions, principalities, and powers."[9] Again, in this world are also superiors and subordinates, not only in the family state but in all kinds of business where heads of establishments and master workmen demand implicit faith and obedience.

This being so, one of the most important responsibilities of a woman in the family state is to train the young in this duty, not only by precept but also by example. And a woman who clearly understands the importance of this, will pride herself on her implicit obedience to the official head of the family state, as much so as the citizen or soldier does to his superior officer, or the subordinate operator to his master-workman.

But at the same time, such a woman will demand and expect a return for this submission, that the husband and father fulfil his corresponding and more difficult duties; to love his wife as himself; to honor her as *physically* the weaker vessel needing more tender care and less exposure and labor; to suffer for her in order to increase her improvement, usefulness, and happiness, even as the Lord suffered to elevate and purify his followers.

The duty of subordination, though so fundamental and important, is one to which all minds are naturally averse. For every mind seeks to follow its own judgment and wishes rather than those of another. Especially is this the case with persons of great sensibilities and strong will. It is owing to this that so many women of this class are followers of Stuart Mills' doctrine that a wife is not a subordinate in the family state. And it is for want of clear instruction on this subject from the pulpit and the press that this doctrine spreads so fast and so widely.

NOTES

1. Matt. 22:37; 1 John 5:3 ("we keep . . .").
2. Matt. 19:19 (and elsewhere).
3. Rom. 13:1.
4. Acts 5:29.
5. The reference is to *The Subjection of Women* (1869), a pioneering feminist tract by British philosopher John Stuart Mill (1806–1873).
6. Matt. 19:8–9.
7. Mark 10:6–9.
8. A loose paraphrase of the opening of the Declaration of Independence.
9. Colossians 1:16.

30.

"THE WAR OF THE SEXES"

(1896)

John Paul MacCorrie

Little is known about John Paul MacCorrie, author of "'The War of the Sexes,'" published in *Catholic World* (August 1896). In this article, MacCorrie declares that "God himself" has declared that "woman is not, and in the eternal fitness of things never can be, unqualifiedly man's co-equal or superior." He claims that abandonment of scriptural teachings regarding women's subordinate place in society would lead to "social disorder pure and simple."

The chief aim of the New Woman, in so far as she can be accused of having any definite purpose in view, is, we believe, the equality of sex. From certain points of observation this is surely a laudable ambition. Before God, for example, all rational beings are equal. There is no distinction between sex and sex in view of unity of origin and destiny. In the participation of eternal reward or punishment

---

Source: John Paul MacCorrie, "'The War of the Sexes,'" *Catholic World* 63, no. 5 (August 1896): 605–607, 612–15.

they are one. Again, there is no intrinsic reason why the intellectual capacities of woman should not equal, and in some instances even outstrip, those of her sterner brothers; although the distinction is sometimes made that the one is more quick and the other more judicious; the former remarkable for delicacy of association, while the latter is characterized by stronger power of attention. And advancing still further, we would aver that in its own proper sphere the female sex is not only equal but often decidedly the superior of the male. But, unfortunately, none of this forms the basis of contention. The New Woman lays claim not only to what we have herein gladly granted her, but, over and beyond that, she would fain step out of the natural modesty of her sex and strive to become man's equal in his special and peculiar province, his rival in the struggle for what at best are but doubtful honors.

A DECLARATION OF WAR

She tells us, "there is no intellectual, social, or professional advancement for woman except as she asserts her independence of man and arrays herself against him as the enemy of her sex." That "marriage under the existing conditions is unmitigated slavery." That the barriers begotten of masculine selfishness and conceit, "excluding woman from the more serious avocations of life, must be abolished."

Henceforth we must have female lawyers, surgeons, clergymen (clergywomen?), apothecaries, and justices of the peace; and if needs be, she will "avail herself of the convenience of male attire in order to give her greater facility in the practice of her profession."

She will "no longer receive her religious creeds from men, but will construct her own on a new and improved basis."

She must be actively represented in the government of the state.

In short, every right and liberty enjoyed by men, whether political, moral or religious, must be forthwith and univocally extended to women.[1]

Now that is where the New Woman becomes unpardonably ridiculous, for, unconsciously we trust, she launches forth her tiny javelin at the very corner-stone of the social edifice, which demands that for its preservation there always exist a suitable subordination of powers, the essential principle of all right order in heaven or on earth.

There are a great many things which we take for granted in our daily intercourse with men and women which, while merely implied, are fair and seemly enough; but once expressed by indirect hint or open avowal, assume at once an air of marked unkindness. If a man were to address the first plain-faced, plain-dressed young woman whom he chanced to meet, and tell her bluntly that she was neither handsome nor rich enough for him, and that he could never marry her, we should wish that he were thoroughly castigated for his ill manners. The young woman was sufficiently, perhaps painfully conscious of the unwelcome truth already, and if she were at all a reasonable person, she would never dream of making it the ground of controversy or discussion. And so it is not without much provocation—and even then we hate ourselves for doing it—that we are constrained to remind the "new" sisterhood that woman is not, and in the eternal fitness of things never can be, unqualifiedly man's co-equal or superior. God himself has said it, and for most people his word is sufficient. [. . .]

"According to the Christian idea the husband and wife are two in one flesh. They are united by an intimate and mutual love in God, and should edify each other in peace, in fidelity, and mutual support. The husband is the head of the wife, whom he should love, esteem, and protect. The wife is, within the circle of her duties, at the side of the man, not subject to him as the child is subject to its father or as the slave to the master; but as the mother, side-by-side with the father, having, no less than he, sacred and imprescriptible rights. But as in every company or corporation it is necessary that some hold superior rank and authority that order and peace may prevail, so in that association of man and woman called marriage, in which the parties are bound one to the other, there must be a superior while each according to rank has necessities, duties, and rights. The woman, thus raised above that condition of absolute subjection and low esteem which she occupies outside of Christendom, takes honorable and imposing rank by the side of her husband. Nevertheless, she is in certain respects subject to his authority. She should, according to Christian law, obey her husband, not as if in slavery, but freely in the same way that the church obeys Christ, her head.

"A loving, pious, moral, interior, laborious life is the glory of woman" (Rev. L. A. Lambert).[2]

And the duties of the husband, on the other hand, are admirably epitomized from St. Paul by the same writer: "'But yet neither is the man without the woman, nor the woman without the man, in the Lord. For as the woman is of the man, so also is the man by the woman: but all things of God'" (I. Cor. xi. 11, 12). Again: "'Husbands, love your wives, as Christ also loved the church, and delivered himself up for it. . . . So also ought men to love their wives as their own bodies. He that loveth his wife loveth himself. For no man ever hateth his own flesh, but nourisheth it and cherisheth it, as also Christ doth the church. Because we are all members of his body, of his flesh, and of his bones. For this cause shall a man leave his father and mother: and shall cleave to his wife, and they shall be two in one flesh. . . . Nevertheless, let every one of you in particular love his wife as himself'" (Eph. v. 25–33).

These are the doctrines which have stricken the bonds of heathen servitude from the trampled neck of woman and raised her to that lofty eminence which she now enjoys in the presence of the Church of Christ. The next step above and beyond that point is social disorder pure and simple. [. . .]

It makes one uncomfortably mindful of that peculiar type of infantine anomaly that cries and cries incessantly, not because it has suffered any injury, or because it desires anything in particular, but since becoming tired of its rattle and finding time rather burdensome, it decides that it would be good form to have a cry, and so it sobs and screams and yells—refusing all the while to be comforted.

For what do those women mean by "rights" and "liberties"? They have not as yet agreed among themselves, nor have any, to our knowledge, attempted to define their limits. The words themselves have no fixed or determined meanings, whether we regard their etymologies or general acceptation among mankind. We suppose there are no two of

their present advocates who would accept entirely any given defini-
tions. What are called rights or liberties in one age or set of circumstances would be called slavery in a new order of things.

And yet it must be manifestly clear to all that they are used to no purpose whatever until we arrive at a clearly defined and accurate understanding of what the terms mean. Until then, like toy balloons in the
hands of children, they stretch until they explode into empty nothingness,
or contract into insignificance at the whim of those employing them.

Our attention, for example, has been directed at the "absolute
freedom" enjoyed by Greek women. Now, the very concept of a social
condition, however crude, implies some restraint on individual liberty;
but this obviously can never co-exist with an "absolute freedom."
What, then, can this writer mean?

If the expression be intended to convey a notion of total lack of
restraint either on person or action—and what else can the words
imply, twist them as we may?—it must at once be accepted as a nonen-
tity, for while it may be thought that such conditions might be possible
in the wilds of the savage jungles—*de facto*, in the present order of
creation they never can exist.

That women have "rights" quite as sacred and inalienable as men,
no one in sound judgment will pretend to deny; but that many of the
things which are now demanded are in all good prudence manifestly
"wrongs" must be equally in evidence. There are, moreover, certain
things which, technically considered, are unquestionably "rights," but
which it would be neither wise nor expedient for man or woman in the
present time and circumstances to exercise—rights the vindication of
which would adduce a positive injury to the community, as the community is here and now maintained.

WOMAN'S TRUE DUTY AND PRIVILEGES

We contend, and we regret not without some opposition, that in the
home and family are concentrated woman's first and highest "rights."

"Let her learn first to govern her own house,"[3] says St. Paul; and whatever else she may claim in common with man must be after her duty has been fully acquitted in this respect. For each sex, because it is a sex, has its own specific and peculiar appointments which cannot be delegated to the other, and which being abandoned by those to whose care Providence has entrusted them, must remain for ever unaccomplished.

Say what we will, woman was created to be a wife and a mother; that is, after a special religious calling to the service of God, her highest destiny. To that destiny all her instincts are fashioned and directed; for it she has been endowed with transcendent virtues of endurance, patience, generous sympathies, and indomitable perseverance.

To her belongs the special function of moulding the youthful mind, of scattering the seeds of virtue, love, reverence, and obedience among her children, that her sons may become upright and loving husbands, and her daughters modest and affectionate wives, tender and judicious mothers, careful and prudent housekeepers. This the best of men can never do, for the office demands the sympathetic touch with children, the strong maternal instinct which is peculiar to the female heart. And the instant woman neglects that duty, for the exercise of other occupations, howsoever virtuous, in the sight of all reflecting men and women she is false to the first and most sacred principle of her existence—her life is a shameful lie. For women were not intended by the Creator to be men; they are needed not for that which men can do as well as they, but for that which man cannot accomplish.

Given, then, the faithful performance of this the grandest and most ennobling of woman's work, unwavering fidelity and devotion to the home, a responsibility sacred and above all things else, there are surely none more willing and anxious than we to accord to her every legitimate right which is hers, every liberty that can in any way contribute to the sum of her personal happiness.

NOTES

1. [See reports of conventions at Washington and elsewhere.]

2. Louis Aloisius Lambert (1835–1910), Catholic priest and author of numerous polemical works defending religion, including *Notes on Ingersoll* (1883) and *Christian Science before the Bar of Reason* (1908).

3. This sentence is not found in the Bible.

31.

THE INFLUENCE OF WOMEN AND ITS CURE

(1936)

John Erskine

John Erskine (1879–1951) received a PhD in English from Columbia University and taught for many years at Amherst College (1903–1909) and Columbia University (1909–37). The author of many books of poetry, criticism, and fiction, Erskine achieved celebrity with *The Private Life of Helen of Troy* (1925), *Adam and Eve* (1927), and other iconoclastic retellings of ancient myths. He was also an accomplished pianist and president of the Juilliard School of Music (1928–1937) and the Juilliard Music Foundation (1948–1951). He speaks of his musical career in *My Life in Music* (1950). In the unrelentingly hostile tract *The Influence of Women and Its Cure* (1936), Erskine blames women for making the church "passive" and thereby driving men away from it.

Source: John Erskine, *The Influence of Women and Its Cure* (Indianapolis: Bobbs-Merrill, 1936), pp. 85–89.

*I*f women have interfered, with unfortunate results, in our education, and have canceled from our political inheritance some
of the most creative ideas, they are perpetrating a still more
tragic mischief in the field of religion. Again I must hasten to define
my terms. It is sometimes said that the churches owe their survival in
America to faithful women, and certainly the ladies are active in
parish work and they form the largest proportion of the attendance on
services. That this should be so is for me an occasion of regret. I wish
the men went to church in greater numbers. I am not one of those who
believe that the function of religion in general and of public worship
in particular has withered up and come to an end. Every human being
has some kind of religion, and all kinds need some sort of expression.
If the women are now the principal church-goers, I count it to their
credit, and am sorry that the spiritual life of the male has for the
moment taken to cover. I don't doubt he still has a spiritual life. The
men who stay away from church are not necessarily skeptics; they just
stay away.

Why do they? My answer would be that the women are taking
the masculine element out of religion, so that the men can't find in
the churches what they need. You can state the problem in few
words. The male element in religion is positive, the female is passive. You can turn to religion either to give something or to get
something. You either are aflame with a vision and wish to utter it,
or you are looking for comfort, for a spiritual salve, a bandage or a
plaster. The masculine form of religion is aggressive, it would build
an empire, it would spread its gospel; the feminine form is intro-
spective, it is occupied with its own sensations in the presence of a
ritual or a discipline, it would rather conform than push ahead.

In this sense the religion of St. Paul, of St. Augustine or of any
other Fathers of Christianity was masculine, and their guarded attitude
toward women in the church was justified at least by instinct. In this
sense also the economic faith of Russia today is a religion, as much so
as the cult of patriotism in Japan. If Russia turned from the old church,
the profound reason probably is that the church had become femi-

nine—that is, passive. For the same reason, though they may not have thought it through, the men of America are now lukewarm toward organized Christianity. The churches have ceased to throw light on our destiny. Priests do indeed become voluble over the radio, but they bring no priestly message there, merely one more lay opinion in the fields of economics and finance, where we suspect they have had no special training.[1]

For this development it would be unfair to blame those women whose religion is genuine, and whose good lives give the churches much of the authority they still possess. But we may well blame those less simple ladies who make of religion a pathway to political or social prestige, who are concerned less about their souls or about the welfare of mankind than about their right as females to be elected elder or vestryman, even their right to preach and to administer the sacraments.

I know, as you do, that in many ancient religions there were priestesses as well as priests, but I hope the sacred office was won by personal qualifications rather than as the result of a minor skirmish in the sex war. Theoretically I can find no argument against women evangelists and sermonisers, but practically I'm stopped by the fact that those who aspire to this spiritual leadership don't look at all like priestesses. Actresses, rather, or showmen, or business executives. I'm further discouraged by the failure of the woman preacher to add anything to what religion already possesses.

To get to the heart of the matter, America is the country of priestesses and prophetesses, who build temples and found religions. I don't know them personally, but if I did I should probably admire their natural gifts even more than I do now. Certainly they must be endowed with rare talents for attracting and organizing the loyalty of masses. It remains, however, to ask what they have contributed, and I don't see how the answer can be very reassuring. They usually summon us to a side-stepping of trouble, rather than to a conquest of evil. They annihilate evil altogether, either by emotional hysteria or by definition. They make of religion not a pillar of fire to lead the exalted pilgrims, but a celestial apothecary's shop, where the sick soul may purchase drugs.

Yet they seem to be just about what the American women want. At least, every third woman you meet is now equipped with a formula for jaunty cheerfulness, a superiority over facts, an excuse for saving the world by thought rather than by work. "I'd like to tell you what my philosophy has done for me!" How often have you heard the testimony! Do they ever tell you what they've done for their philosophy?

Personally I prefer the advice of the Quakers, "When you pray, move your feet."

I'm still talking, you see, about those women in our country who wish to be supported and carried along, who exert wide influence, but who want others to work for them. In religion they want heaven or nature to do the work. They don't comprise all of their sex, but unfortunately they are laying upon our spiritual life the same enervating blight which they contribute to our educational system. Their influence penetrates even the traditional churches, sapping the intellectual fabric, blunting the moral edge. It penetrates also our economic philosophy. Many of us fall victims to the seductive fallacies which they like to spread; those who once had backbone and a little sense may now be playing with the notion that every man's business is to be happy, and the state should support him. It's unkind to ask who the state is, that it can support so much. In the passive religion of America, the feminine religion, the state is another kind of husband or another form of God, an infinite source of supply who delights to clothe and feed us, and whose divinity reveals itself most benignly by providing an armor of complacency against the shock of our own ignorance and folly.

If I am not altogether wrong in this account of our religious collapse, under the influence of the kind of woman who is a spoiled child, it is worth noting, by the way, that our country seems destined to represent the West in the coming collision with the East, and the religions of the East are masculine. It's only a superficial trick of speech which attributes to us a machine civilization; this is too hard on the machine. The civilization which we shall oppose to the Orient will rest, like their civilization, upon a philosophy. We used to think the East rather passive, the West creative. This contrast might still hold if we were setting Europe against Asia, but Europe is in danger of destroying itself, and the inheritance may be in our hands. Too bad if we change it beyond recognition before we ship it across the Pacific Ocean! The Oriental learns to contemplate the universe, he measures himself against an enormous past, an inexhaustible future, his dignity is modest and patient, he accepts life as an opportunity not for comfort but for excellence, even though his virtue may be without applause. The feminized religion of America encourages us to contemplate not the universe but ourselves. Our doctrine is that the universe, properly grasped in a course of lectures, will make us cheerful even when the cook leaves or the husband can't buy us a new car.

NOTE

1. Erskine probably alludes to Father Charles E. Coughlin (1891–1979), a Catholic priest who achieved a wide following with the radio program *The Golden Hour of the Little Flower*, begun in 1926 and chiefly devoted to economic and social issues. Coughlin later revealed himself an anti-Semite and supporter of Adolf Hitler, but in his heyday he attracted as many as forty million listeners.

32.

THE DECLINE OF FEMININITY

(1945)

Joseph H. Fichter, SJ

Joseph H. Fichter (1908–1994) became a Jesuit in 1930 and was ordained in 1942. He was for many years a professor of sociology at Loyola University (1947–1962, 1972–1994); from 1965 to 1970 he held the Chauncey Stillman Chair of Catholic Studies at Harvard University. Fichter is the author of many treatises on sociology and religion, including *Religion as an Occupation* (1961) and *A Sociologist Looks at Religion* (1988). He helped to desegregate Roman Catholic parishes in the South; late in life he advocated marriage for priests and became a member of the National Organization for Women. Early in his career, however, he wrote "The Decline of Femininity" (*Catholic World*, April 1945), asserting that women should not do men's work and that many women (except for Catholics) are being led by

Source: Joseph H. Fichter, SJ, "The Decline of Femininity," *Catholic World* 161, no. 1 (April 1945): 60–63.

contemporary societal influences into a licentious lifestyle.

*T*he war has emphasized a number of social abnormalities in our modern civilization, and it seems to me that the most significant of these is the present status of women. For a long time there has been a more or less accepted trend away from the quality of femininity in women, but the trend has grown to such proportions that to accept it without warning or protest would be disastrous. I do not wish to cause alarm, nor do I think I am old-fashioned, by saying that women have allowed themselves "to get out of hand." Social life is not what it used to be (and we don't want it to be) but it is certainly not changing *progressively*.

I am trying to point out here a *general* attitude, not the attitude of any particular group of American women. From such general statements I would except the large portion of Catholic women who are keeping steadfastly to the principles of modesty and decency and femininity. By and large Catholic women manifest a wonderful goodness; they are faithful to the sacraments; they are devoted and devotional; they are interested in maintaining a clean and wholesome home life. They deserve even more praise for being fine representative Catholics because they are operating under great external difficulties.

But these Catholics are distinctly a numerical minority among the women of our country. They have noticed that American womanhood is drifting (or is it plunging?) away from the ideal that Catholic women try to uphold. Since the start of the war I have traveled this country from Boston to El Paso, from Milwaukee to Miami, and have heard the problem come up in many random conversations and in some serious discussions. I can only conclude that American women are on the downgrade, and that they cannot be pulled up unless they are willing to accept Catholic principles of conduct.

How did such a situation come into existence? You cannot put your finger on one isolated activity and call it the sole cause. People blame the war; but the war has merely served to etch the problem more clearly. All the symptoms of the present phenomenon were present in our society long before the war began. You might say that it all began with the hue and cry for the "emancipation" of women that were heard everywhere toward the end of the last century. Women yelled loudly for the equality of the sexes, for abolition of the so-called "double" standard of morality. "It's a man's world," they said, "and we want to get in on it!"

Well, they "got in on it" with a subtle shifting of values that brought them *down* to popular masculine standards. That is the ludicrous fact in the feminine battle for "equality." Instead of choosing the manly virtues they have aped those actions of men that have always been deemed something less than virtuous.

Of course, that was not the feminine intent at the beginning of the crusade. The determination to vote at the polls, to have at least that *political equality*, was fair enough, for there is no reason why women cannot vote as intelligently as men. But that was not satisfying. Women had to show that they could hold office; and they did it too, in Texas, New Jersey, Connecticut and other states. There was probably no direct danger in all this political activity but it constituted a kind of opening wedge for conditions that are definitely dangerous.

Then there was the fight for *economic equality* with men. Women demanded the right to work, whether they needed the work or not, and they got it. They wanted equal pay for equal work, and in some places they are getting that. For the most part the patriotic motive for women at work in wartime industries has been a colossal farce. Before the war they lost their self-respect in offices and stores; since the war "they've gone about as far as they could go" in factories and shipyards.

Newspapers and newsreels have dramatized, even glamorized, the fact that women are doing the roughest, toughest kind of work: stoking factory furnaces, swinging a sledgehammer on railroad crews, driving busses and streetcars. Women are even delivering ice, the job that husky football players take to keep in condition, and believe it or not, they are driving garbage trucks and collecting garbage! Is all of this bad? Certainly there is nothing immoral in the act of work itself, though frequently enough in modern industry it is an occasion of sin. Aside from its morality, it is a coarsening process which civilized women should not have to undergo, much less desire.

Women doing men's work is physically and psychologically harmful, and in some cases it is also morally bad in its consequences. Everybody knows about juvenile delinquency, which Walter Lippmann has rightly styled "parental" delinquency. A short time ago a Judge in Boston scolded a woman shipyard welder for trying to be "half a mother and half a worker." She had asked for a divorce from her husband and custody of her seven-year-old daughter, and she was denied both. This incident could be multiplied by hundreds of others written up in the daily papers, and undoubtedly by thousands more that you never hear about.

The successful crusades for political and economic equality on the part of women can in some cases be justified, but there is another that is much worse and unjustifiable. I call it the feminine desire for *convivial equality*. This is nothing but the old fight over the double standard of social morality: women ought to be allowed the same social freedom (license) that men enjoy. They express it this way: "What's right for a man is right for a woman." That is perfectly true, but women do not mean it in its true sense. To conform their words to their actions they should really say, "What's wrong for a man is also wrong for a woman."

This convivial equality says that it is a woman's privilege to sit at a bar and toss off whisky, drink for drink, with a man; the privilege to come back with a dirty story or joke after a man has told one, and to use the same filthy language and gutter remarks that some men use. Women who did these things not so long ago were given an uncomplimentary label, and that label was not "sophisticate."

Anyone with his eyes open to the signs of the time must admit that these remarks only scratch the surface, that I am not painting a picture more gaudy than reality. You can agree or disagree on the numerical extent of this condition according to what you have seen and heard in your own experience with such women, perhaps some of them Catholic, too. Whatever the details of the picture, they constitute a fearful kind of ingratitude to Christ, Who established the only kind of equality that can exist between men and women—the equality of the children of God.

In spite of what Christianity has done for them women seem intent upon plunging back into the deadening servility of paganism. At the time Christ came on earth the Pharisees used to say an official daily prayer of thanksgiving to God for not having made them *Gentiles, slaves* or *women.* They considered these three categories a kind of secondary class of human beings, who were, at best, to be pitied. The pagans of Greece and Rome had an even lower theory and a worse practice in their treatment of women because they did not enjoy the civilizing knowledge of the true God.

Christ deliberately set the world straight on the relationship between men and women, even though it took centuries of Christianity to effect a large scale change. He put women on exactly the same moral footing with men, not subordinate but co-ordinate with them. St. Paul brought this out clearly when he wrote to the Galatians: "You are all the children of God by faith in Christ Jesus. For as many of you as have been baptized in Christ have put on Christ. There is neither Jew nor Greek: there is neither bond nor free: there is neither male nor female. For you are all one in Christ Jesus."[1]

Like all the other teachings of Christ, this particular truth has been maintained and preserved intact by the Catholic Church. Of course, there are many Christian women outside the Church who are trying to uphold a high ideal of moral femininity, who deprecate the pseudo-modernity of many of their sex. But Catholic women *as a group* are the only ones who can perceive the full significance of feminine decline, and who have the intellectual and sacramental means at their command to reverse the trend. Unfortunately, they are inundated with the opposite views, in the movies, in the schools, on the radio, everywhere.

Is the blame to be placed on these agencies of propaganda, advertisement and "education"? Is the fault to be found in that triple demand for political, economic and convivial equality on the part of women? Some women are willing to admit that part of the fault lies in the foolish and weak-kneed moral compromise of women themselves. But many of them immediately and belligerently make the excuse: "We women try to be the way men want us to be." Even if that were true, it would be an irrational explanation, the stupid desire to come down to the lower standard that men supposedly follow.

Is the diminishing charm of womanhood therefore the fault of the masculine population? Individual cases can undoubtedly be cited in which men have helped to lower the ideals. Many men admit, and even contribute to the popularity of loose-thinking and vulgar-talking women. But the almost universal male attitude can be seen in their reluctance to marry that type of woman. Men may be shy about saying so, but they do cherish an imaginative ideal of all the womanly qualities, and they claim that the lack of those qualities in the modern woman is the fault of women themselves.

It seems to me that both sexes are wrong in one sense and right in another. The moral and social status of the world is what it is because human beings, both men and women, have made it that way. It is erroneous to say that one sex has been worse than the other; it is correct to say that human beings as such have been at fault. A still deeper question must be asked: Why do people act the way they do? And the answer to that is the quaint and ancient statement: modern civilization has lost its sense of sin and moved away from God.

The return to God is, of course, the only dependable remedy and the only definite solution. I must bring this article to a close and I could not do that soon if I tried to show the application of the religious solution. I am content for the moment if people admit the existence of the problem of declining womanhood. Too many brush it off as a passing phase in our social life. "There's nothing to be alarmed about. Everything's going to be all right." Please God it will.

NOTE

1. Gal. 3:26–28.

Part 10
WOMEN AND SUFFRAGE

33.

THE WOMAN QUESTION

(1869)

Orestes Augustus Brownson

Orestes Augustus Brownson (1803–1876) was raised in a Calvinist Congregationalist home and was ordained as a Universalist preacher in 1826, then as a Unitarian in 1832. At this time he spoke against organized religion and slavery and endorsed women's rights and education. In 1844, however, he converted to Roman Catholicism and violently repudiated his earlier Protestantism, chiefly on the grounds that it vaunted individualism and was opposed to the organic unity of society that Brownson sought. He founded *Brownson's Quarterly Review* to expound his views, frequently launching polemics against his religious and political enemies. His political philosophy is summed up in *The American Republic: Its Constitution, Tendencies, and Destiny* (1865). In the following article, published

Source: [Orestes Augustus Brownson], "The Woman Question," *Catholic World* 9, no. 2 (May 1869): 145–46, 147–53, 155.

anonymously in *Catholic World* (May 1869) and purporting to be a review of several feminist tracts, Brownson claims that suffrage is not a natural right and that granting women the suffrage will not be of any use in solving the problems of society; in fact, woman suffrage would "weaken and finally break up and destroy the Christian family."

We say frankly in the outset that we are decidedly opposed to female suffrage and eligibility. The woman's rights women demand them both as a right, and complain that men, in refusing to concede them, withhold a natural right, and violate the equal rights on which the American republic professes to be based. We deny that women have a natural right to suffrage and eligibility; for neither is a natural right at all, for neither men or women. Either is a trust from civil society, not a natural and indefeasible right; and civil society confers either on whom it judges trustworthy, and on such conditions as it deems it expedient to annex. As the trust has never been conferred by civil society with us on women, they are deprived of no right by not being enfranchised. [. . .]

Suffrage and eligibility are not natural, indefeasible rights, but franchises or trusts conferred by civil society; and it is for civil society to determine in its wisdom whom it will or will not enfranchise; on whom it will or will not confer the trust. Both are social or political rights, derived from political society, and subject to its will, which may extend or abridge them as it judges best for the common good. Ask you who constitute political society? They, be they more or fewer, who, by the actual constitution of the state, are the sovereign people. These, and these alone, have the right to determine who may or may not vote or be voted for. In the United States, the sovereign people has hitherto been, save in a few localities, adult males of the white race, and these have the right to say whether they will or will not extend suffrage to the black and colored races, and to women and children. Women, then, have not, for men have not, any natural right to admission into the ranks of the sovereign people. This disposes of the question of right, and shows that no injustice or wrong is done to women by their exclusion, and that no violence is done to the equal rights on which the American republic is founded. It may or it may not be wise and expedient to admit women into political, as they are not admitted into civil, society; but they cannot claim admission as a right. They can claim it only on the ground of expediency, or that it is necessary for the common good. For our part, we have all our life listened to the arguments and declamations of the woman's rights party on the subject; have read Mary Wollstonecraft, heard Fanny Wright, and looked into *The Revolution*,[1] conducted by some of our old friends and acquaintances, and of whom we think better than many of their countrymen do; but we remain decidedly of the opinion that harm instead of good, to both men and women, would result from the admission. We say not this because we think lightly of the intellectual or moral capacity of women. We ask not if women are equal, inferior, or superior to men; for the two sexes are different, and between things different in kind there is no relation of equality or of inequality. Of course, we hold that the woman was made for the man, not the man for the woman, and that the husband is the head of the wife, even as Christ is the head of the church, not the wife of the husband; but it suffices here to say that we do not object to the political enfranchisement of women on the ground of their feebleness, either of intellect or of body, or of any real incompetency to vote or to hold office. We are Catholics, and the church has always held in high honor chaste, modest, and worthy women as matrons, widows, or virgins. Her calendar has a full proportion of female saints, whose names she proposes to the honor and veneration of all the faithful. She bids the wife obey her husband in the Lord; but asserts her moral independence of him, leaves her conscience free, and holds her accountable for her own deeds.

Women have shown great executive or administrative ability. Few men have shown more ability on a throne than Isabella, the Catholic, of Spain; or, in the affairs of government, though otherwise faulty enough, than Elizabeth of England, and Catharine II of Russia.[2] The present queen of the British Isles[3] has had a most successful reign; but she owes it less to her own abilities than to the wise counsels of her husband, Prince Albert, and her domestic virtues as a wife and a mother, by which she has won the affections of the English people. Others have shown rare administrative capacity in governing religious houses, often no less difficult than to govern a kingdom or an empire. Women have a keener insight into the characters of men than have men themselves, and the success of female sovereigns has, in great measure, been due to their ability to discover and call around them the best men in the state, and to put them in the places they are best fitted for.

What women would be as legislators remains to be seen; they have had little experience in that line; but it would go hard, but they would prove themselves not much inferior to the average of the men we send to our State legislatures or to our national Congress.

Women have also distinguished themselves in the arts as painters and sculptors, though none of them have ever risen to the front rank. St. Catharine of Egypt cultivated philosophy with success.[4] Several holy women have shown great proficiency in mystic theology, and have written works of great value. In lighter literature, especially in the present age, women have taken a leading part. They almost monopolize the modern novel or romance, and give to contemporary popular literature its tone and character; yet it must be conceded that no woman has written a first-class romance. The influence of her writings, speaking generally, has not tended to purify or exalt the age, but rather to enfeeble and abase it. The tendency is to substitute sentiment for thought, morbid passion for strength, and to produce a weak and unhealthy moral tone. For ourselves, we own, though there are some women whose works we read, and even re-read with pleasure, we do not, in general, admire the popular female literature of the day; and we do not think that literature is that in which woman is best fitted to excel, or through which she exerts her most purifying and elevating influences. Her writings do not do much to awaken in man's heart the long dormant chivalric love so rife in the romantic ages, or to render the age healthy, natural, and manly. We say *awaken*; for chivalry, in its true and disinterested sense, is not dead in the coldest man's heart; it only sleepeth. It is woman's own fault, more than man's, that it sleeps, and wakes not to life and energy.

Nor do we object to the political enfranchisement of women in the special interest of the male sex. Men and women have no separate interests. What elevates the one elevates the other; what degrades the one degrades the other. Men cannot depress women, place them in a false position, make them toys or drudges, without doing an equal injury to themselves; and one ground of our dislike to the so-called woman's rights movement is, that it proceeds on the supposition that there is no interdependence between men and women, and seeks to render them mutually independent of each other, with entirely distinct and separate interests. There is a truth in the old Greek fable, related by Plato in the *Banquet*, that Jupiter united originally both sexes in one and the same person, and afterward separated them, and that now they are but two halves of one whole.[5] "God made man after his own image and likeness; male and female made he *them*."[6] Each, in this world, is the complement of the other, and the more closely identified are their interests, the better is it for both. We, in opposing the political enfranchisement of women, seek the interest of men no more than we do the interest of women themselves.

Women, no doubt, undergo many wrongs, and are obliged to suffer many hardships, but seldom they alone. It is a world of trial, a world in which there are wrongs of all sorts, and sufferings of all kinds. We have lost paradise, and cannot regain it in this world. We must go through the valley of the shadow of death before re-entering it. You cannot make earth heaven, and there is no use in trying; and least of all can you do it by political means. It is hard for the poor wife to have to maintain a lazy, idle, drunken vagabond of a husband, and three or four children into the bargain; it is hard for the wife delicately reared, accomplished, fitted to adorn the most intellectual, graceful, and polished society, accustomed to every luxury that wealth can procure, to find herself a widow reduced to poverty, and a family of young children to support, and unable to obtain any employment for which she is fitted as the means of supporting them. But men suffer too. It is no less hard for the poor, industrious, hard-working man to find what he earns wasted by an idle, extravagant, incompetent, and heedless wife, who prefers gadding and gossiping to taking care of her household. And how much easier is it for the man who is reduced from affluence to poverty, a widower with three or four motherless children to provide for? The reduction from affluence to poverty is sometimes the fault of the wife as well as of the husband. It is usually their joint fault. Women have wrongs, so have men; but a woman has as much power to make a man miserable as a man has to make a woman miserable; and she tyrannizes over him as often as he does over her. If he has more power of attack, nature has given her more power of defence. Her tongue is as formidable a weapon as his fists, and she knows well how, by her seeming meekness, gentleness, and apparent martyrdom, to work on his feelings, to enlist the sympathy of the neighborhood on her side and against him. Women are neither so wronged nor so helpless as *The Revolution* pretends. Men can be brutal, and women can tease and provoke.

But let the evils be as great as they may, and women as greatly wronged as is pretended, what can female suffrage and eligibility do by way of relieving them? All modern methods of reform are very much like dram-drinking. The dram needs to be constantly increased in frequency and quantity, while the prostration grows greater and greater, till the drinker gets the *delirium tremens*, becomes comatose, and dies. The extension of suffrage in modern times has cured or lessened no social or moral evil; and under it, as under any other political system, the rich grow richer and the poor poorer. Double the dram, enfranchise the women, give them the political right to vote and be voted for; what single moral or social evil will it prevent or cure? Will it make the drunken husband temperate, the lazy and idle industrious and diligent? Will it prevent the ups and downs of life, the fall from affluence to poverty, keep death out of the house, and prevent widowhood and orphanage? These things are beyond the reach of politics.

You cannot legislate men or women into virtue, into sobriety, industry, prudence. The doubled dram would only introduce a double poison into the system, a new element of discord into the family, and through the family into society, and hasten the moment of dissolution. When a false principle of reform is adopted, the evil sought to be cured is only aggravated. The reformers start wrong. They would reform the church by placing her under human control. Their successors have in each generation found they did not go far enough, and have, each in its turn, struggled to push it farther and farther, till they find themselves without any church life, without faith, without religion, and beginning to doubt if there be even a God. So, in politics, we have pushed the false principle that all individual, domestic, and social evils are due to bad government, and are to be cured by political reforms and changes, till we have nearly reformed away all government, at least, in theory; have well-nigh abolished the family, which is the social unit; and find that the evils we sought to cure, and the wrongs we sought to redress, continue undiminished. We cry out in our delirium for another and a larger dram. When you proceed on a true principle, the more logically and completely you carry it out the better; but when you start with a false principle, the more logical you are, and the farther you push it, the worse. Your consistency increases instead of diminishing the evils yon would cure.

The conclusive objection to the political enfranchisement of women is, that it would weaken and finally break up and destroy the Christian family. The social unit is the family, not the individual; and the greatest danger to American society is, that we are rapidly becoming a nation of isolated individuals, without family ties or affections. The family has already been much weakened, and is fast disappearing. We have broken away from the old homestead, have lost the restraining and purifying associations that gathered round it, and live away from home in hotels and boarding-houses. We are daily losing the faith, the virtues, the habits, and the manners without which the family cannot be sustained; and when the family goes, the nation goes too, or ceases to be worth preserving. God made the family the type and basis of society; "male and female made he them." A large and influential class of women not only neglect but disdain the retired and simple domestic virtues, and scorn to be tied down to the modest but essential duties—the drudgery, they call it—of wives and mothers. This, coupled with the separate pecuniary interests of husband and wife secured, and the facility of divorce *a vinculo matrimonii* allowed by the laws of most of the States of the Union, make the family, to a fearful extent, the mere shadow of what it was and of what it should be.

Extend now to women suffrage and eligibility; give them the political right to vote and to be voted for; render it feasible for them to enter the arena of political strife, to become canvassers in elections and candidates for office, and what remains of family union will soon be dissolved. The wife may espouse one political party, and the husband another, and it may well happen that the husband and wife may be rival candidates for the same office, and one or the other doomed to the mortification of defeat. Will the husband like to see his wife enter the lists against him, and triumph over him? Will the wife, fired with political ambition for place or power, be pleased to see her own husband enter the lists against her, and succeed at her expense? Will political rivalry and the passions it never fails to engender increase the mutual affection of husband and wife for each other, and promote domestic union and peace, or will it not carry into the bosom of the family all the strife, discord, anger, and division of the political canvass?

Then, when the wife and mother is engrossed in the political canvass, or in discharging her duties as a representative or senator in Congress, a member of the cabinet, or a major-general in the field, what is to become of the children? The mother will have little leisure, perhaps less inclination, to attend to them. A stranger, or even the father, cannot supply her place. Children need a mother's care; her tender nursing, her sleepless vigilance, and her mild and loving but unfailing discipline. This she cannot devolve on the father, or turn over to strangers. Nobody can supply the place of a mother. Children, then, must be neglected; nay, they will be in the way, and be looked upon as an encumbrance. Mothers will repress their maternal instincts; and the horrible crime of infanticide before birth, now becoming so fearfully prevalent, and actually causing a decrease in the native population of several of the States of the Union as well as in more than one European country, will become more prevalent still, and the human race be threatened with extinction. Women in easy circumstances, and placing pleasure before duty, grow weary of the cares of maternity, and they would only become more weary still if the political arena were opened to their ambition.

Woman was created to be a wife and a mother; that is her destiny. To that destiny all her instincts point, and for it nature has specially qualified her. Her proper sphere is home, and her proper function is the care of the household, to manage a family, to take care of children, and attend to their early training. For this she is endowed with patience, endurance, passive courage, quick sensibilities, a sympathetic nature, and great executive and administrative ability. She was born to be a queen in her own household, and to make home cheerful, bright, and happy. Surely those women who are wives and mothers should stay at home and discharge its duties; and the woman's rights party, by seeking to draw her away from the domestic sphere, where she is really great, noble, almost divine, and to throw her into the turmoil of political life, would rob her of her true dignity and worth, and place her in a position where all her special qualifications and peculiar excellences would count for nothing. She cannot be spared from home for that.

It is pretended that woman's generous sympathies, her nice sense of justice, and her indomitable perseverance in what she conceives to be right are needed to elevate our politics above the low, grovelling and sordid tastes of men; but while we admit that women will make almost any sacrifice to obtain their own will, and make less than men do of obstacles or consequences, we are not aware that they have a nicer or a truer sense of justice, or are more disinterested in their aims than men. All history proves that the corruptest epochs in a nation's life are precisely those in which women have mingled most in political affairs, and have had the most influence in their management. If they go into the political world, they will, if the distinction of sex is

lost sight of, have no special advantage over men, nor be more influential for good or for evil. If they go as women, using all the blandishments, seductions, arts, and intrigues of their sex, their influence
will tend more to corrupt and debase than to purify and elevate.
Women usually will stick at nothing to carry their points; and when
unable to carry them by appeals to the strength of the other sex, they
will appeal to his weakness. When once they have thrown off their
native modesty, and entered a public arena with men, they will go to
lengths that men will not. Lady Macbeth looks with steady nerves and
unblanched cheek on a crime from which her husband shrinks with
horror, and upbraids him with his cowardice for letting "I dare not wait
upon I would."[7] It was not she who saw Banquo's ghost.

We have heard it argued that, if women were to take part in our elections, they would be quietly and decorously conducted; that her presence
would do more than a whole army of police officials to maintain order,
to banish all fighting, drinking, profane swearing, venality, and corrup-
tion. This would undoubtedly be, to some extent, the case, if, under the
new *régime*, men should retain the same chivalric respect for women that
they now have. Men now regard women as placed in some sort under
their protection, or the safeguard of their honor. But when she insists that
the distinction of sex shall be disregarded, and tells us that she asks no
favors, regards all offers of protection to her as a woman as an insult, and
that she holds herself competent to take care of herself, and to compete
with men on their own ground, and in what has hitherto been held to be
their own work, she may be sure that she will be taken at her word, that
she will miss that deference now shown her, and which she has been
accustomed to claim as her right, and be treated with all the indifference
men show to one another. She cannot have the advantages of both sexes
at once. When she forgets that she is a woman, and insists on being
treated as a man, men will forget that she is a woman, and allow her no
advantage on account of her sex. When she seeks to make herself a man,
she will lose her influence as a woman, and be treated as a man.

Women are not needed as men; they are needed as women, to do,
not what men can do as well as they, but what men cannot do. There

is nothing which more grieves the wise and good, or makes them tremble for the future of the country, than the growing neglect or laxity of family discipline; than the insubordination, lawlessness, and precocious depravity of Young America. There is, with the children of this generation, almost a total lack of filial reverence and obedience. And whose fault is it? It is chiefly the fault of the mothers, who fail to govern their households, and to bring up their children in a Christian manner. Exceptions there happily are; but the number of children that grow up without any proper training or discipline at home is fearfully large, and their evil example corrupts not a few of those who are well brought up. The country is no better than the town. Wives forget what they owe to their husbands, are capricious and vain; often light and frivolous, extravagant and foolish, bent on having their own way, though ruinous to the family, and generally contriving, by coaxings, blandishments, or poutings, to get it. They set an ill example to their children, who soon lose all respect for the authority of the mother, who, as a wife, forgets to honor and obey her husband, and who, seeing her have her own way with him, insist on having their own way with her, and usually succeed. As a rule, children are no longer subjected to a steady and firm, but mild and judicious discipline, or trained to habits of filial obedience. Hence, our daughters, when they become wives and mothers, have none of the habits or character necessary to govern their household and to train their children. Those habits and that character are acquired only in a school of obedience, made pleasant and cheerful by a mother's playful smile and a mother's love. We know we have not in this the sympathy of the women whose organ is *The Revolution*. They hold obedience in horror, and seek only to govern, not their own husbands only, not children, but men, but the state, but the nation, and to be relieved of household cares, especially of child-bearing, and of the duty of bringing up children. We should be sorry to do or say anything which these, in their present mood, could sympathize with. It is that which is a woman's special duty in the order of providence, and which constitutes her peculiar glory, that they regard as their great wrong. [. . .]

We know men often wrong women and cause them great suffering by their selfishness, tyranny, and brutality; whether more than women, by their follies and caprices, cause men, we shall not undertake to determine. Man, except in fiction, is not always a devil, nor woman an angel. Since the woman's rights people claim that in intellect woman is man's equal, and in firmness of will far his superior, it ill becomes them to charge to him alone what is wrong or painful in her condition, and they must recognize her as equally responsible with him for whatever is wrong in the common lot of men and women. There is much wrong on both sides; much suffering, and much needless suffering, in life. Both men and women might be, and ought to be, better than they are. But it is sheer folly or madness to suppose that either can be made better or happier by political suffrage and eligibility; for the evil to be cured is one that cannot be reached by any possible political or legislative action.

That the remedy, to a great extent, must be supplied by woman's action and influence we concede, but not by her action and influence in politics. It can only be by her action and influence as woman, as wife, and mother; in sustaining with her affection the resolutions and just aspirations of her husband or her sons; and forming her children to early habits of filial love and reverence, of obedience to law, and respect for authority. That she may do this, she needs not her political enfranchisement or her entire independence of the other sex, but a better and more thorough system of education for daughters—an education that specially adapts them to the destiny of their sex, and prepares them to find their happiness in their homes, and the satisfaction of their highest ambition in discharging its manifold duties, so much higher, nobler, and more essential to the virtue and well-being of the community, the nation, society, and to the life and progress of the human race, than any which devolve on king or kaiser, magistrate or legislator. We would not have their generous instincts repressed, their quick sensibilities blunted, or their warm, sympathetic nature chilled, nor even the lighter graces and accomplishments neglected; but we would have them all directed and harmonized by solid intellectual instruction, and moral and religious culture. We would have them, whether rich or poor, trained to find the centre of their affections in their home; their chief ambition in making it cheerful, bright, radiant, and happy. Whether destined to grace a magnificent palace, or to adorn the humble cottage of poverty, this should be the ideal aimed at in their education. They should be trained to love home and to find their pleasure in sharing its cares and performing its duties, however arduous or painful.

NOTES

1. Fanny Wright (1795–1852), Scottish-born heiress who emigrated to the United States in 1818 and advocated abolition of slavery, socialism, and woman suffrage. *The Revolution* (1868–1972) was a weekly feminist newspaper edited by Elizabeth Cady Stanton and others.

2. Isabella I, queen of Castile (1474–1504); Elizabeth I, queen of England (1558–1603); Catherine II ("the Great"), empress of Russia (1762–1796).

3. Victoria, queen of England (1837–1901).

4. Catherine of Alexandria was a legendary martyr who purportedly displayed her learning to her persecutors during the reign of the Roman emperor Maxentius (306–317).

5. The myth (placed in the mouth of Aristophanes) is found in Plato *Symposium* 189C–193E.

6. Gen. 1:27.

7. Shakespeare, *Macbeth*, 1.7.44.

34.

WOMAN SUFFRAGE: THE REFORM AGAINST NATURE

(1869)

Horace Bushnell

Horace Bushnell (1802–1876) graduated from Yale University (1827) and Yale Law School (1831), but abandoned work at Yale Divinity School to become a Congregational minister in Hartford, Connecticut. He was a prolific writer and lecturer. An early work—*Views of Christian Nature* (1847; revised as *Christian Nurture*)—recommends the indoctrination of infants into religion and also reveals significant elements of race prejudice.[1] Violently anti-Catholic, Bushnell joined the Christian Alliance to oppose the papacy and promote Protestantism. His opposition to woman suffrage emerged as early as the 1840s, and is most exhaustively embodied in the treatise *Woman Suffrage: The Reform against Nature* (1869), in which he maintains that women's

Source: Horace Bushnell, *Woman Suffrage: The Reform against Nature* (New York: Charles Scribner, 1869), pp. 49–57, 61–64.

physical weakness unfits them positions of authority in social and political life.

*I*t is not to be denied that women are made in the image of God as truly as men, having faculties and categories of mind that are equal in number, and so far similar in kind, as to pass under the same general names. What is right and true to one sex, is right and true also to the other. They think by the same laws, they perceive, and judge, and remember, and will, and love, and hate, in the exercise of functions that compose personalities psychologically similar, however different in degree, and however differently tempered, fibered, tensified, and toned for action. In a word, they are equally human, and compared with orders of being above and below them are of the same kind. And yet in their relationship of sex, within their own human order, they are so widely different, nevertheless, that the distinction never misses observation. Their very personality, which even seemed identical in the inventory, taking on sexhood, becomes broadly differential in that fact, and submits to a deep-set, dual classification.

A mere glance at the two sexes, externally related, suggests some very wide distinction of mold whatever it be. The man is taller and more muscular, has a larger brain, and a longer stride in his walk. The woman is lighter and shorter, and moves more gracefully. In physical strength the man is greatly superior, and the base in his voice and the shag on his face, and the swing and sway of his shoulders, represent a personality in him that has some attributes of thunder. But there is no look of thunder in the woman. Her skin is too finely woven, too wonderfully delicate to be the rugged housing of thunder. Her soft, upper octave voice, her small hands, her features played as in quality and not for quantity, her complexion played as if there were a principle of beauty living under it—there is abundance of expression here, as many great, proud souls of heroes have been finding in all ages, but it is unOlympic as possible in kind. Glancing thus upon man, his look says, Force, Authority, Decision, Self-asserting Counsel, Victory. And the woman as evidently says, "I will trust, and be cherished, and give sympathy and take ownership in the victor, and double his honors by the honors I contribute myself." They are yet one species, but if they were two, they would be scarcely more unlike. So very wide is the unlikeness, that they are a great deal more like two species, than like two varieties. Their distinction of sex puts them in different classes of being, only they are classes so nearly unified by their unlikeness, that they compose a whole, so to speak, of humanity, by their common relationship. One is the force principle, the other is the beauty principle. One is the forward, pioneering mastery, the out-door battle-ax of public war and family providence; the other is the indoor faculty, *covert*, as the law would say,[2] and complementary, mistress and dispenser of the enjoyabilities. Enterprise and high counsel belong to one, also to batter the severities of fortune, conquer the raw material of supply; ornamentation, order, comfortable use, all flavors, and garnishes, and charms to the other. The man, as in fatherhood, carries the name and flag; the woman, as in motherhood, takes the name on herself and puts it on her children, passing out of sight legally, to be a covert nature included henceforth in her husband. They are positivity and receptivity, they are providence and use, they are strength and beauty, they are mass and color, they are store-house and table, they are substance and relish, and nothing goes to its mark or becomes a real value till it passes both.

But we are dealing, so far, in this outward delineator of the sexual distinctions, in matters general, and have not taken up, as yet, the more particular matter at issue in our question of suffrage. The precise point here to be observed, is that masculinity carries, in the distribution of sex, the governmental function. The forwarding force, the brave-and-dare element, whether toward nature or against human opposers, the responsible engineering of place and work and calling, all determinations outward, whether toward enemies, or among causes, or in ventures of commerce, or in diplomatic treaties and warlike relations of peoples, belong to man and to what may be called his manly prerogative. That is, man is to govern; all government belongs to man. Not that women are never set in kingly positions to represent, or personate the kingly power; of that I shall speak hereafter in another place. For the present, I simply remark, that the authority they wield in such cases is only what the masculine traditions put upon them, or into them, when they are used to fill the gaps of kinghood, by maintaining the court pageantries and the royal signature; they do not reign as kings do by an authority that is largely personal in themselves. Were they obliged to maintain themselves in that way, it would very soon be discovered how little authority there is in women. We take pleasure not seldom in allowing women to rule us by the volunteering deference we pay to their womanhood; we often talk of our loyalty to the sex; but we never see the woman who can hold a particle of authority in us by her own positive rule or the emphasis of her own personality.

To prevent misunderstanding it may be proper to say that I am not asserting a right here in men to bolt upon women, wives for example, in the peremptory way of command; I am only asserting the natural leadership, the decision-power, the determinating will of the house and the state, as belonging to men. Certain engineering questions, for example, must be settled, the question of expenditure as related to income, the question of residence, occupation, emigration; where of course every endeavor should be made to compose differences of feeling and judgment, and settle points by agreement. But if a case arises, where agreement is impossible, one of the two, clearly, must decide, and it must be the man. The woman's law of allegiance, sometimes a hard one, requires it of her to adhere to the man, submit herself to his fortunes, and go down with him bravely, when his day of disaster comes. The sway, the determinating mastership, must so far be with him, and it can not be anywhere else, without some very deplorable consequences to his manhood. If he has no sway-force in him equal to this, no authority of will and council that enables him to hold the reins, he is no longer what nature means when she makes a man. And the refractory woman who has so far balked his manhood will have honored herself quite as little as him.

Happily, it is just as natural to woman to maintain this beautiful allegiance to the masterhood and governing sway-force of men, both in the family and the state, as we could wish it to be. Nothing, in fact, is more touching than to see how far they will go, how much they will bear, how absurdly persist in dressing up the masculine idol they have undertaken to crown, or exalt. They do no such thing toward other women, and can not even think it possible for women to preside in their assemblies. They do not ask, it may be, how, or why it is that they insist on having a man preside? but if they could see the reason, as it lies in the inner feeling, they would discover in it a most complete refutation of their claim to suffrage itself. Looking on their chairman —a man, and why a man?—they would confess that, by that sign, their very cause is convicted of incongruity. Or if it occurs to them to urge, in excuse, that women have no experience in the ordering of assemblies, they can be more easily qualified, than they can to make a speech. They are, some of them, quick enough to learn Jefferson's Manual[3] quite through, in half a day. Probably enough, too, the man they have chosen, never before presided over an assembly in his life.

Now the right of suffrage as demanded for women, is itself a function of government. Besides, it contemplates, also, as an integral part of the proposed reform, that women should be eligible for office. For if this were not conceded, we know perfectly beforehand, that the women voters would so wield their balance of power as to conquer the right of office in a very short time. All office must, of course, be open to them, as certainly as the polls are open. Indeed they sometimes take the jubilant mood even now, in their anticipation of the day, when they will have their seat in Congress, on the bench of justice, in the President's cabinet, and why not in the chair of the Presidency itself? when the missions abroad, the collectorships, the marshal and police functions, will be theirs, and finally, the heroic capabilities of women so far discovered, as to allow them a place in the command of fleets and armies, and full chance given their ambition, to win, as for solid history, what many call the mythic honors of a Semiramis or a Deborah.[4]

The claim put forward then is, and will be commonly allowed to be, a claim of authority; a claim by women to govern, or be forward in the government of men; wherein they deny, in fact, a first distinction of their sex. The claim of a beard would not be a more radical revolt against nature. It says: "give us force, give us the forward right, give us authority, let us take our turn also at the thunder." Just contrary to this, I feel obliged to assert the natural subordination of women. They are put under authority by their nature itself, and if they will not take it as their privilege to be, they call it insult and oppression, they set a character on their position which no man could; they put contempt themselves on their womanhood. Indeed, their very claim of suffrage on the ground of their equality with men, ignores just what is most distinctive in their kind, and is neither more nor less than a challenge of the rights of masculinity. And the harshest thing that can be said of their reform would be, that they mean it as it is.

Asserting in this very decisive manner the natural submission of women, and their very certain lack, whether as respects the right or the fact, of authority, it will seem to many, as I very much fear, to be a harsh, or even a rude and coarse attack upon their sex. If it is so taken, it certainly need not be. We Americans take up some very crude notions of subordination, as if it implied inferior quality, character, power. No such thing is true, or less than plainly false. Subordination is one thing, inferiority an immensely different thing. Subordinate as they are, in their naturally sheltered relation, I seriously doubt whether we should not also assert their superiority. They do quite as much, and I strongly suspect, more for the world. Their moral nature is more delicately perceptive. Their religious inspirations, or inspirabilities, put them closer to God, as having a more celestial property and affinities more superlative. It may be that men have larger quantity in the scale of talent, while yet they are enough coarser in the grain of their quality to more than balance the score. [. . .]

There can not, in this view, be a greater mistake, or one that indicates a coarser apprehension, than when our women, agitating for the right of suffrage, take it as an offense against their natural equality, that they are not allowed to help govern the world. It is as if the gentle mignonnette and violet were raised in protest against the regal dahlia, when they are in truth a great deal more potentially regnant themselves. What do these women ask, in fact, but to be weighed in the gross weight-scales of force, making nothing of that higher, finer nature, by which God expects it of them to flavor the world. They must govern, they must go into the fight, they must bruise and batter themselves—what are they equal to, if they are not equal to men? As if it were nothing, a little way back, after all the coarse things of the world are done, to govern, by graces, the man that govern by forces, and go through family and country, and the times, with a ministry more powerful, finer in the motive, less mixed with selfishness and will, and just as much closer to the really celestial type of good. God save us from the loss of this better, almost divinely superior ministry; for lost it will assuredly be, when our women have come down to be litigators with us in the candidacies, contests, and campaigns of political warfare. Still life is then no more, and the man who goes home at night from his caucus fight, or campaign speech, goes in, not to cease and rest, but to be dinned with the echo, or perhaps bold counter-echo of his own harsh battle. The kitchen dins the parlor, and one end of the table dins the other. Up-stairs, down-stairs, in the lady's chamber—every where the same harsh gong ringing, from year to year. Oh! if we could get away! how many will then say it, and pray it—into some bright corner where yet there are true women left—women with soft voices, shrilled by no brassiness or dinging sound of party war!

Why, if our women could but see what they are doing now, what superior grades of beauty and power they fill, and how far above equality with men they rise, when they keep their own pure atmosphere of silence, and their field of peace, how they make a realm into which the poor bruised fighters, with their passions galled, and their minds scarred with wrong—their hates, disappointments, grudges, and hard-worn ambitions—may come in, to be quieted, and civilized, and get some touch of the angelic, I think they would be very little apt to disrespect their womanly subordination. It will signify any thing but their inferiority. If they are already taken with the foolish ambition of place, or of winning a public name, they may not be satisfied. But in that case they barter for this honor a great deal more than they can rightly spare. God's highest honors never go with noise, but they wait on silent worth, on the consciousness of good, on secret charities, and ministries untainted by ambition. Could they but say to the noisy nothings of the bribery, "Get thee hence, Satan,"[5] as Christ did to the same coarse nonsense of flattery, they would keep their subject way of life as he kept his, and would think it honor enough that they also came not to be ministered unto, but to minister. And if it be the question for them, whether it is better to be classed in privilege with Jesus the subject, or with Cæsar the sovereign, it should not be difficult to decide.

Thus far we go in the principle that women are made to be subordinate, and men to be the forward operators and dominating authorities of the world. They have another field, where their really finer qualities and more inspirable gifts may get full room and scope for the most effective and divinest offices of life. Indeed we do not evenly set the balance of the question, if we do not say that woman has her government as truly as man, only it is not political, not among powers, and laws, and public causes. He governs from without downward, and she from within upward, and though there be a great difference in kind between our two words master and mistress, using this latter in its true, good sense, there is not a whit more of control signified, when we say that the man is the mastering power of the woman, than that she is the mistressing power of the man. He is at a point of sway more coarse, direct, and absolute—more nearly akin to force. She is at a point where she captivates the force, by a beautiful and right enjoyment of it, takes possession of the man, property, and soul, and will, and calling, and makes him joyfully her own. If the cases were inverted, he would make a coarse, awkward figure doubtless in the mistressing kind of government; but if we are to agitate for equality, why should he not have the beautiful chance given him of being a mistress-power in life—on the score of equality, even as she obtains a mastering power in life, when she obtains the suffrage.

NOTES

1. See the extracts from *Christian Nurture* reprinted in my *Documents of American Prejudice* (New York: Basic Books, 1999), pp. 208–11.

2. See William Blackstone, *Commentaries on the Laws of England* (pp. 247–51 in this book).

3. Thomas Jefferson's *Manual of Parliamentary Practice* (1801), written when Jefferson was vice president and presiding over the US Senate, and long regarded as a seminal work on parliamentary procedure.

4. Semiramis, wife of the Assyrian king Shamshi-Adad V (r. 824–811 BCE), mother of Adadnirari III (r. 810–783), and queen regent from 810 to 806. Deborah, wife of Lappidoth, a Jewish prophetess and judge (see Judg. 4:4–22).

5. Matt. 4:10.

35.

THE BLANK-CARTRIDGE BALLOT

(1896)

Rossiter Johnson

Rossiter Johnson (1840–1931) was a prolific American journalist, historian, and editor. He wrote numerous treatises on the various wars in which the United States has been involved, including *A Short History of the War of Secession* (1888; 5th ed. 1910) and *The Clash of Nations* (1914), on the outbreak of World War I. He gained greatest celebrity as the editor of several multivolume compilations, including *Little Classics* (1874–1881, 18 vols.), a collection of short stories; *The World's Great Books* (1898–1901, 40 vols.); and *Authors Digest* (1908, 20 vols.). His pamphlet *The Blank-Cartridge Ballot* (1896) is a blunt statement of the view that suffrage should not be extended to women because they would be unable to enforce it by physical force. Rossiter's wife, Helen (Kendrick) Johnson (1844–1917), also

Source: Rossiter Johnson, *The Blank-Cartridge Ballot* (New York: New York Association Opposed to the Extension of the Suffrage to Women, 1896), pp. 7–15, 16–18.

> wrote pamphlets against woman suffrage,
> including a full-length treatise, *Woman and
> the Republic* (1897).

A ballot put into the box by a woman would be simply a blank cartridge; and already we have more than a million blank-cartridge ballots, all of which are solemnly warranted by law, but all of which count for nothing, and will continue to count for nothing until each is backed by a pellet of lead and a pinch of powder, ready to enforce its decree. Our greatest peril arises from the even division of parties. When we elect a president by a popular majority of less than one per cent of all the votes, there must always be a temptation to the defeated party to try the experiment of not submitting, and we have seen what this led to in one notable instance. Nor is that the only instance. When a newly elected legislative body shows an almost even division of parties, there is pretty certain to be an attempt on the part of the minority to seize the place and power of the majority. Then we see a city hall besieged, or the doors of an assembly-chamber battered down with axes. To make any party victorious at the polls by means of blank-cartridge ballots would only present an increased temptation to the numerical minority to assert itself as the military majority. Under ordinary circumstances the law might be allowed to have its way; but sooner or later we should arrive at an extraordinary election, and then —revolution. Doubtless it would be a righteous spectacle to see a million women and half a million men outvoting eight hundred thousand men on some great moral question; but when the eight hundred thousand men decline to submit, who is going to make them? "You are to bid any man stand, in the prince's name. *How if he will not stand?* Why, then, take no note of him, but let him go; and presently call the rest of the watch together and thank God you are rid of a knave. You are to call at all the ale-houses, and bid those that are drunk get them to bed. *How if they will not?* Why, then, let them alone till they are sober; if they make you not then the better answer, you may say they are not the men you took them for."

"But," says a woman who seeks to be a voter, "I own property, and I pay taxes on it, and I cannot think that taxation without representation is just." This plea has been repeated so often that it is time to point out its fallacy. There are two kinds of taxes—a money tax, and a service tax. The money tax is levied on property, men's and women's alike, *pro rata*. The service tax is levied on men alone. It calls for jury service, police service, military service, and every man takes his chances on it. Sometimes one goes through his seventy years without suffering from it at all; again he spends weary hours in the jury room, or he is sworn in as a special constable to quell a riot and fight a mob, or he is called to camp and battlefield, where he may lose a limb, or an eye, or his life. Representation goes with this kind of taxation, and not with the other. Property is protected by the Government, as women are; but property, whether man's or woman's, has no representation. If it had, it must necessarily be in some degree proportional. Mr. Astor[1] would have hundreds of times as many votes as I, and I perhaps would have twice as many as the man that sweeps out my office. Instead of that, Mr. Astor has one vote, the sweeper has one vote, and I have one vote. And the reason is plain and unanswerable; it is because Mr. Astor can carry one musket, the sweeper can carry one musket, I can carry one musket. We are all equal on the ballot, because we are all equal on what the ballot represents. Mr. Astor enjoys his great property because the sweeper and I are ready to shoulder our muskets and protect him in it; the sweeper is secure in his little earnings because Mr. Astor and I are ready to stand by him with our muskets; I find it worth while to be industrious because Mr. Astor and the sweeper make it dangerous for anybody to molest me. Without this protection, our possessions would be of no value; this protection we contribute in equal measure, man for man; and this same protection we extend to our sisters, our cousins, and our aunts. Frequently an election is for the purpose of determining under what and in what manner this protection shall be exercised; and those who furnish the protection rightfully claim the privilege of dictating its form. The woman-suffragists, so far from suffering taxation without representation, are asking to be represented where they are not taxed.

Properly speaking, no woman is taxed, and no property is represented. The woman's property is taxed; and for that money it and she get exactly what the man and his property get—police protection, fire service, lighting and cleaning of streets, maintenance of courts, etc. Every man is taxed, even if he owns no property—a tax that is laid upon his time, his strength, and often upon his life; he bears this tax for the protection of all the lives in the community, no matter whose; and all the property, no matter whose; and to this tax the women contribute nothing and are not asked to contribute.

The Suffragists appear to think they dispose of this consideration when they speak of men who are "exempt" from military service and still vote. The immediate answer is, that there is no real exemption. All the men are liable; but when it happens that the Government, in an emergency, does not need all at once, it takes its pick, and speaks of the others as "exempt." It may at first call only for the men under twenty-five; but when more are wanted it does not hesitate to call for men as old as thirty-five, and so on. Many now living remember an emergency in which ten States called out every man, of whatever age, who could shoulder a musket at all.

But even this is not the root of the question. For regular service in a long campaign, the Government would not take a man forty-five years of age, with weak lungs, if it could get as many as it wanted who were but twenty-five and had strong lungs. But suppose the weak-lunged man of forty-five is "agin the Government," and disposed to unite in an attempt to overthrow it, will he "exempt" himself? Will he refrain from joining an insurgent force, on the ground that he is over age and not in robust health? Youth or age, lungs or no lungs, that man is a power to be reckoned with; and this is why he is allowed to vote, in order that when the ballots are counted he may see that he and his kind are in the minority, and it would be hopeless for them to attempt an overthrow of the Government.

Some advocates of woman suffrage profess to answer all this by pointing to the State of Wyoming, where women *have* voted for several years, or have had the privilege of doing so.[2] As a matter of fact, the women of that State have not voted to any alarming extent. One farmer being asked how he managed them on election day, answered: "If I find that the women of my family are not going to vote as I want them to, I don't hitch up the team that day. And the polls are held fifteen miles from our house." It will be logical to point to Wyoming only after its women have carried an election, on an important issue, against the men.

It is not to be wondered at that an educated and patriotic woman frets a little when she sees an ignorant or vicious man going to the polls while she stays at home, nor that she should sometimes assert herself by asking if she is not intellectually and morally superior to him. So is a man intellectually superior to a sledge-hammer; but when he wishes to rend a granite rock he does not pry at it with his fingers; he persuades the sledge-hammer to do his bidding. Similarly, it would be futile for her to go to the ballot-box and with her own fair hand throw in a blank-cartridge ballot; but if through argument or entreaty she can persuade a musket-bearer to throw a right ballot instead of a wrong one, she can accomplish something worthy. And the means of enlightening and convincing voters, through print and oratory, are all quite as free to women as to men.

It should be remembered that every popular election has two phases—the phase of discussion, and the phase of determination. In the canvass (the phase of discussion), men exchange facts and arguments and express their opinions. When that is over, they go to the polls, where each one expresses his determination that the conduct of the government shall be thus and so—provided enough men are found to be on his side. A woman who is familiar with our politics and knows how to address an audience might take a very forcible part in the phase of discussion, and she would be listened to as eagerly and respectfully as any orator we have. Facts and logic are quite as powerful from a woman's mouth as from a man's. And it seems a little singular that none of the Suffragist speakers ever use their eloquence to turn (as presumably they might) hundreds of votes and make an election go right instead of wrong. If they really want to benefit the community, there could be no better way. Instead, they appear to be only anxious to get their single forceless ballots into the box,—reminding one of the Irishman who thought he could produce cooler weather by rubbing the thermometer with ice. They find it impossible to realize that the ballot is not a power, but only a means of reckoning power.

This subject of the suffrage is not a question of courtesy and chivalry toward women—those are abundantly shown in the statutes of nearly every State, which are more favorable to women than to men. It is a question of the stability of our government, and the success of democratic institutions. Universal peace has not yet arrived; the great struggle that has wrenched mankind through the ages is still going on, and one may see it in various phases in our own country as well as in the bristling armies of Europe. Men, whether savage or civilized, never have been accustomed, in fighting their battles, to put the non-combatants in the forefront, whose station in the rear may be quite as honorable and far more useful. Wherever we place the ballot, manhood must necessarily be the power behind it to give it effect; and manhood suffrage is therefore the logical suffrage and the only safe experiment.

[. . .] Boast as we may of our inventions, our arts, and our learning, our fair gardens, our romantic palaces, and our courts of equity, we have yet but a thin crust of civilization spread over a heated mass of savagery; and organized force is all that saves us from anarchy. Of all the women who are asking for an irresponsible ballot, there is not one who would dare to walk through our metropolis in broad daylight, past its churches, its art-galleries, and its court-houses, if it were not for the policeman at the corner and the great armory whose shadow crosses the avenue and falls upon the steps of the sanctuary; and of the unthinking men who wish to give it to them from a vague sense of fairness, there is not one who could have gone alone into the coal-regions and proclaimed his opinion that the great strike was unjust.

Such is the brutal truth about the suffrage and its basis; and a brutal truth, when it exists, must be admitted and reckoned with like any other truth. In our elections as now held, there is no security for the verdict unless the majority is sufficient to assure those who are in the minority that if they refuse to submit they will be coerced. With the proposed extension of the suffrage, if the votes of the women were so divided as not to affect the result, then the women might as well not have voted, and their presence at the polls would be a useless and costly addition to the electoral machinery. If women voted in the State of New York, the additional cost of the annual elections, to the tax-payers, would be equal to that of building and endowing a college like Vassar every five years. On the other hand, if an election is carried by a preponderance of votes cast by women, who is to enforce the ver-dict? When a few such verdicts have been overturned, we shall find ourselves in a state of anarchy.

We may admit all that those excellent women say about the purity of their politics, their determination to educate themselves on public questions, and the probability that they would vote in the interests of civilization and good morals. The difficulty is, that the ignorant are not ignorant enough. When the virtuous woman, the well-bred woman, the enlightened woman, goes to the polls, she will meet there no man so ignorant as not to know perfectly well that his ballot has a metallic basis and must be respected, while hers is nothing but paper, and he may respect it or not, as he pleases.

NOTES

1. John Jacob Astor (1864–1912), great-grandson of the capitalist John Jacob Astor (1763–1848), who established a fortune in New York City from fur trading and other ventures.

2. Wyoming, as a territory, became the first region in the United States to grant women the suffrage, in 1869.

36.

THE WRONG AND PERIL OF WOMAN SUFFRAGE

(1909)

James Monroe Buckley

James Monroe Buckley (1836–1920) entered the ministry in 1858, becoming a Methodist elder in 1859. Over the next twenty years he served in various churches in New Hampshire; Detroit, Michigan; Brooklyn, New York; and Stamford, Connecticut. In 1880 he became editor of the *Christian Advocate*, the oldest and largest Methodist paper in the nation. For the next thirty-two years he used this publication as a forum for his views on religion, society, and politics. In the following excerpt from *The Wrong and Peril of Woman Suffrage* (1909), Buckley maintains that granting the vote to women will make men and women the same, thereby destroying the family unit. This excerpt is from the chapter "The Nature of Womanhood in Relation to Society."

Source: James Monroe Buckley, *The Wrong and Peril of Woman Suffrage* (New York: Fleming H. Revell, 1909), pp. 41–49.

$\mathcal{T}$he relation of the sexes is the most fundamental problem of society. The domestic life of its individual members turns upon it, and the increase, and consequently the very existence of population on the earth. Were the race separated into units,—universal prostitution, with little or no care or training of children, would be the result. In the civilization represented by Europe and the civilized parts of America, the foundation of society is the family, consisting of one husband and one wife; the contract between them being for life, never to be broken except for extraordinary causes and by due processes of law.

As marriage is the general law for the race, and is a life partnership "for better or for worse," how is it made to cohere? A vital question, for wedlock is a partnership indeed imposing mutual rights, and equal, though not identical, responsibilities.

Upon these principles and facts I assume that the family is the foundation of the social organization; that it could not cohere without certain intellectual and moral differences between husband and wife; that nature, in the constitution of woman, has made the permanency of the marriage relation possible and actual; and that a training different from that of man, and in harmony with the different tendencies, realm of action, and mode of influence which distinguish woman is essential to her highest usefulness and happiness in the family and the state. This training in large part is provided in the family from childhood.

While the individuals who form the state are constantly being removed by death, the state endures, being replenished by the offspring of the families into which society is divided. Their parents are their rulers, responsible for their support, and exercising the prerogative of government, issuing mandates, requiring submission; permitted to chastise and to direct their actions in numberless ways. It depends upon the parents to train them in such a manner as to qualify them for the duties of citizenship, according to the statutes and laws of the land. Only when parents are incapable or unwilling to discharge the responsibilities does the state take cognizance of the situation. As children increase in age and reach a degree of self-control and self-protection, the state provides schools, but leaves to the parents the prerogative of choosing whether the required education shall be procured in the public or private schools, or under individual tutors. In proportion as the family, practically a state within a state, is maintained in its integrity is the nation strong, happy and prosperous. The family also is the fountain of private, and the source of public, morality.

Whatever may be said of a few minds of a peculiar structure, life-long partnerships for better or worse could not be maintained by two natures of the same kind, debating all questions in the same plane, with no natural predominating tendency. There is abundant evidence that, except in very rare cases, it would be impossible. The socialistic experiments of men alone have failed, as have the very few attempts of women to live together permanently, except where powerful religious organizations control the experiment.

The permanence of the marriage tie depends upon the difference in the mental and emotional constitutions of men and women. The family is a union of two different manifestations of a common human nature;—moulding, governing and guiding the children, each after its own manner, and diffusing through society the blended influence of wife, mother, daughter, sister, and husband, father, son and brother. Such an institution involving two distinct personalities of the same kind, requiring lifelong living together, day and night, would break down under the strain if there were no natural and spontaneous predominating tendency. When the warmth of passion had subsided, the novelty of the relation disappeared, the imperfections of each had become apparent, and the struggles and disappointments of life accumulate, discord would soon arise and each will refusing the bend, the breach would widen and secret aversion or open rupture ensue.

But the marriage relation does hold together, and by what means? Tennyson answers thus:

Woman is not undeveloped man,
But diverse. *Could we make her as the man*
Sweet love were slain, whose dearest bond is this:
Not like to thee, but like in difference.[1]

Man reasons, debates, decides, and the tendency is to his headship. Woman, if she approves, conforms; but if she does not approve, endeavours to modify,—not in an authoritative, imperative spirit, but gently, tenderly, persuasively.

In the perfect family, the husband would never be actively conscious of his headship, or the wife of her natural tendency to regard it; and since no one proposes to reform the masculine characteristics, the feminine must be maintained. This creates the necessity for a development from childhood of the woman, peculiar to her in distinction from man, even as his training is peculiar to him as distinguished from her. This she early manifests in the capacity of daughter and sister, and later as wife. Her sons, self-reliant, soon assert their independence. The daughter clings to her father and brothers, and if poverty does not compel a different course, receives support and protection from them, which, if a true woman, she returns in her own way. The sons meanwhile are learning what each needs to know, to enable him to assume the position which awaits him in the family to be set up in its season. Thus the influence of husband and wife in the family is equal but not identical. On this the institution of marriage rests. The woman may be more intellectual than her husband, or she may be less so. She may have quicker perception and more tact; but she takes his name, and her sons and daughters after her.

The bearing of these principles upon the relations of wives and mothers to the suffrage is that to govern in the state would unfit woman for her position in the family.

It is mere sophism to say that the simple dropping of a piece of paper into a ballot-box could not produce such a result.

Unless women are to be treated like children, and furnished with the ballot by men, it is not the mere dropping of a piece of paper, for it implies a whole mode of thinking, feeling, and acting, of which a vote is the concentrated expression. "The vote is the expression of government; voting is governing." To vote intelligently is to think and act in the imperative mood; and to be qualified as voters, girls must be trained to think, feel, and act in the spirit of men. To avoid the force of this statement it would be necessary to show that women will not be affected by this training, or that, should they be, no harm will result. Mill admits that it will produce this very effect and asserts that women are held "in subjection" in the family, and should be emancipated. Wendell Phillips said, "No one can foresee the effect; therefore the only way is to plunge in."[2] On an important issue "plunging in," without a high probability almost equal to a certainty, is another way of spelling recklessness.

Others affirm that "under all circumstances feminine instincts will preserve woman."

To assume that either men or women will remain unchanged in their intellectual, moral, and emotional susceptibilities, whatever their situation, is contrary to the facts of evolution, environment, and culture. In countless individual cases, and even in nations, woman has shown a capacity to rise or fall, a susceptibility to moral and intellectual modifications not surpassed, if equalled, by men.

Not only would the governing spirit become a part of her character, greatly obstructing the discharge of the duties of home, but it would make her position there an insupportable restraint. Man is naturally self-reliant; woman may, in an emergency, develop self-reliance and complete independence; but is naturally disposed either to coalesce in the determining tendency of her husband, or to control it by persuasion. Imbued with the governing spirit, she will become as restive in her position as would he if similarly placed. This is avowed by many advocates of Woman Suffrage, and held up as a result to be desired. The more consistent go fearlessly to the end, and define marriage as a civil contract to be terminated at the will of either party, and society as a collection of independent units instead of an assemblage of families.

That there are exceptions to the ideal family, here assumed as the nucleus of society, is true. Some women rule their husbands; a larger number through the misfortune, weakness, or wickedness of the husband are obliged to support the family, and there are many single women and widows. These exceptions to the general law often have much to bear; but not so much as to justify the overthrow of the whole structure with a view to rebuild upon exceptions. Every female child must be presumed eligible to wifehood and motherhood; therefore the whole sex should be left to the exercise of that kind of influence for which their nature and relation to the family qualify them, and which is required in the interest of society.

An argument drawn from exceptions may be very plausibly affirmed.

Ancient philosophers thought that children should be brought up by the state.[3] Suppose, then, a movement to enact a law requiring the training of all children in public institutions. In its support it might be maintained that there are numerous orphans, that many children have lost one parent, and that many parents are cruel, intemperate, incompetent, or unfaithful; that relatively few feel, and conscientiously and intelligently discharge, their responsibilities. These propositions are indisputable: how then shall the scheme to require all children to be educated by the state be shown to be untenable? Only by affirming that the general law of nature is that parents must be responsible for their offspring. To remove the children of those willing and able to train them, because of these exceptions, would be cruel and unjust; and such a wholesale destruction of home life is not necessary, because the general rule is that parents, with all their imperfections, do train their children in a manner better adapted to promote the public weal than is any institutional training. Individual exceptions must be cared for by private philanthropy, or by special statutes which are compatible with the effectual working of the general law.

The same reasoning vindicates the conclusion that the general law necessary for the preservation of the family should not be overthrown in order that unmarried women and widows might be introduced into political life.

Nor would a specific statute admitting single women to the suffrage, and excluding married women therefrom, be expedient or right; for then another evil of stupendous proportions would result, namely: the *putting of a premium upon the unmarried or childless condition*, since such women would have much more time and strength for the political arena than wives and mothers, and could gain many more personal, pecuniary, and political advantages.

NOTES

1. Alfred, Lord Tennyson, *The Princess: A Medley* (1847), 7.259–62.

2. Wendell Phillips (1811–1884), American advocate of abolition, woman suffrage, and other reforms. The quotation appears to be a loose paraphrase of a remark found in his speech, "Woman's Rights" (1851): "The broadest and most far-sighted individual is utterly unable to foresee the ultimate consequences of any great social change." See Phillips's *Speeches on Rights of Women* (Philadelphia: Alfred J. Ferris, 1898), p. 10.

3. The reference is specifically to Plato, who advocated the communal raising of children; see *Republic* 541A.

37.

WOMAN ADRIFT: THE MENACE OF SUFFRAGISM

(1912)

Harold Owen

Harold Owen (1872–1930) was a British journalist and playwright who wrote several polemical treatises on politics and society, including *Disloyalty: The Blight of Pacifism* (1918) and *Unpopular Opinions* (1922). In one of the most hostile attacks on woman suffrage ever written, *Woman Adrift* (1912; reprinted in the United States by E. P. Dutton), Owen maintains that women are in no way essential to the state except in their capacity as mothers, so that there is no need to grant them the vote. The following chapter from this work is titled "Superfluous Woman."

*I*n the previous chapter it was parenthetically stated that the function of bringing children into the world was the only function which made woman *essential* to the State.

That may seem a very surprising statement to those who have not

Source: Harold Owen, *Woman Adrift: The Menace of Suffragism* (London: Stanley Paul, 1912), pp. 69–78.

thought the matter out beyond the "logical" or "democratic" basis of women's claim to vote. But it is strictly true. A modified form of that statement would be, however, of wider truth, and if we say that woman is not essential to the State except in so far as she is essential to the Home we have said all that can be said for woman's essentially necessary place in the social organism.

If we first consider the State as a centralised government, and examine woman's relation to it; and if we then consider the State as limited not only to a centralised executive government, but including also those material and moral activities which make up a modern community of human beings, not touching the family life, we shall see that it is equally true, whether the first limited or the second wider view is taken of what constitutes the State, that woman is wholly superfluous to the State except as a bearer of children and a nursing mother.

THE STATE INDEPENDENT OF WOMAN

It is obvious that the State, considered merely as a government, has no need of woman at all, and that is the State into which she wishes to penetrate by the legal key of a vote that will afterwards unlock all other doors. The State does not need woman, first, as soldiers or as sailors, that is for its defence. I need not linger on that proposition, as it expresses a self-evident fact. Nor does the State, considered as government, need women as statesmen, ambassadors, civil servants or police. That statement also is self-evident, for it is the statement of existing fact. And the whole machinery of government could still go on working if the direst calamity that ever could afflict man fell upon him, and woman ceased to be. To give no opportunity for a debating point—or rather to close it right away—I admit it is clear to the lowest intelligence that the State, in such a case, would not need to provide for any remote contingencies, but that is because the function reserved to woman, making her by that alone indispensable to the State, is that she should bear children (although, as we shall later see, maternity serves the family rather than the State just as paternity does). But for the time being, and for the purposes of its current existence, woman could be dispensed with entirely, so far as the State is concerned. That proposition also requires no proof. For as things actually are—save for a few women officials in the central administration—the whole machinery of the State into which some women wish that all women may enter at the present moment goes on absolutely unimpeded and unassisted by women. There are also women outside the central administration—in the Post Office, for instance, and as workhouse and infirmary officials, and as school teachers. But they are there not because they are *sexually* necessary, and they could be replaced by men to-morrow (with those few exceptions where women are preferable because of the domestic nature of their occupations) without materially affecting the efficient working of the machinery of government—central, subordinate, and local. So that almost at the outset of considering this whole question, we are confronted by the fact that the sphere into which woman wishes to enter is a sphere that has no need of her whatever.

INDUSTRIALISM WITHOUT WOMAN

And now we have to consider the relation of women to the State in its less restricted aspect—viz., the general community, into which women may penetrate, if they wish, without the vote at all. We are now considering the State as the general community, outside the Home altogether, and therefore as regards its non-domestic activities; and we are supposing that women are not immured in their homes, but are left to their own devices, but that they have nothing whatever to do with any trade, profession, or occupation outside the four walls of their homes.

Well, the transport services of the country, to begin with, would still go on exactly in the same way, for the simple reason that the transport services of the country by rail, tram, 'bus, or boat, as things are, receive no assistance whatever from women—except a few wives of a few bargees, who are not indispensable to working the canal-boats,

however, though they occasionally take a little exercise along with the
horse on the towing-path, but who use the canal-boats as dwellings, so
that they are still at home. And the iron and coal industries of the
country would continue in the same unhindered way, for just the same
reason. For though there are, in the case of the coal industry, a few pit-
brow women (concerning whom Suffragists are not quite sure whether
man ought to be ashamed of himself for allowing them to work at such
an unwomanly occupation, or ashamed of himself for contemplating
such an interference with woman's freedom as to stop them working
at it)—though a few pit-brow women are to be found in Lancashire,
no one will contend that if they all went to the Isle of Man to-morrow
their places could not be filled, I will merely say adequately, by masculine muscles. Nor would the building trades, the shipping, the
docks, and the engineering trades be affected in the slightest degree if
women remained at home and only emerged to do their shopping, for
the simple reason that as far as those trades are concerned the women
already stay at home. And all those trades are the most wealth producing and the most essential industries of the country.

In the next group of trades, such as the textile, dressmaking, and
pottery trades, there would be for the time being an absolute stoppage
if women remained at home; and the trades would be entirely dislo-
cated. But the stoppage would only be temporary, and the dislocation
would last only as long as was necessary to adjust the trades to the
fresh economic conditions involved by the increase of the cost of production due to the higher rates of payment to men, but if the purely
economic condition is ignored, these trades also would be entirely
unaffected by woman's withdrawal from them. If women clerks were
withdrawn from the Post Office counters, the male substitutes that
would be found for them would, in the opinion of some people—not
necessarily a right opinion, but it is not very far wrong—improve the
service. In the whole banking and brokering world the withdrawal of
women would disturb merely the clerical machinery, and restore to
something like "economic independence" the poor male clerk who
now goes to the wall mainly because girls who live at home, and hope

some day to marry, are willing and able to do his work, more or less efficiently, for a less reward. Take the whole body of industry from end to end, and there is not one of the chief wealth producing industries that depends upon women for its existence, if we delete the economic advantages of female labour to the employers in certain industries. The fact that in these industries women are employed—always in a subordinate capacity—must not confuse the fact that they are there for capitalistic economic advantage, and not because as a sex they are necessary for the work to be done; and if their places were supplied by men and boys to-morrow the industries could go on just the same as before—temporary economic disturbance apart.

WOMAN AND THE ARTS

Leaving trades, and coming to professions, the same rule holds. No woman is needed in the legal profession whatever—a fact which is proved by its own self. No woman is needed in the medical profession—a fact which is not affected by the fact that the medical profession includes women. If every woman doctor retired to-morrow, the practice of surgery and medicine would continue unimpaired—and unassisted by any contribution to medical or surgical science that women have ever made. To say that no woman is needed in art and literature would be too sweeping a statement, so crudely put, but we can nevertheless bring it without any difficulty within the scope of the hypothesis that no woman need leave her home, and yet the State, in all its activities, could go on. But when I say that no woman is needed in art and literature, I have my mind on this fact: That the whole body of literature and art left after subtracting from it the best that women have contributed to either branch, would be just what would be left if the same number of second-rate male artists and literary men had never been born. There would be a gap, but the body of art and literature left after woman's contributions had been taken away would be quite enough to go on with—no gap would be made by the withdrawal of any work of the first rank. But somebody will say that, in talking about art, I have forgotten the dramatic art and actresses. Well, even the word "actresses" has no terrors for me; for the English stage flourished in Shakespeare's day when women were forbidden by law to take part in stage plays, and boys took the female parts. But I concede the wholly immaterial point so far as the dramatic art is concerned, that though no woman has yet written a play that the world will ever want to resurrect, it is desirable that actresses should still charm us on the stage and bore us (as I am afraid we must say they sometimes do) in the illustrated papers.

But no single work of art of supreme genius has been produced by a woman since the world began, though the whole realm of art has been open to her since Sappho sang, and though neither her domestic subjection nor her political inequality can have restrained her if she had the impulse within her. But perhaps I had better here take Mill's own words on the point. They were included in that chapter of his book, "The Subjection of Women," in which he was, broadly speaking, trying to prove the contrary of what is being maintained in this chapter. For he was endeavouring to prove the fitness of women to share in the work of the State, and not what I am endeavouring to show, that so alien is the State to woman that, apart from her maternal functions in the home, the State does not *need* her at all. And Mill admitted: "But they have not yet produced any of those great and luminous new ideas which form an era of thought, nor those fundamentally new conceptions in art which open a vista of possible effects not before thought of, and found a new school." And though woman's activities in literature and art since Mill's day have enormously and amazingly increased, that admission still holds good: even the highest and best of them only attains a place in the second rank.

WOMAN IN LITERATURE AND SCIENCE

In literature she could be deleted with more loss and regrets than in art, and in contemporary fiction especially she would be missed; but neither art nor literature would be sensibly affected. We should be sorry to have to miss "Jane Eyre," or "Aurora Leigh," or "Adam Bede," or "Robert Elsmere,"[1] but though a few women writers have attained a very high rank, even the best of them lack that quality which *transfigures*. And if we have to compare what would be missed by woman's withdrawal from art and literature, as compared with man's, we may say that, in the case of woman's accomplishment, it would be like missing five hundred pounds out of a very big fortune indeed, but that in the case of what man has accomplished it would be like missing an arm or a leg, or even a head, from a body. And art and letters do not depend on voting power or even economic independence—they are the media of self expression. Amongst the arts, music is that which owes least to culture and most to the possession of original powers. And as far as creative music is concerned, woman would not be missed in the slightest degree, for she has created no music whatever that comes anywhere near the first rank. In executive music she is outdistanced by the great male performers; and we have to come to vocal music and to the contralto and soprano voices of women before we stumble on a single instance in which woman is *indispensable* in the State (considered, moreover, in its widest possible aspect as the general community)—and even so we have the choir of St Peter's and our own memories of the angelic voices of boys in our own cathedrals to show us that still woman would not be indispensable even in that class of work and achievement which it becomes a mere fanciful exercise to exclude her from.

To science—mechanical, electrical and physical—woman has contributed nothing of essential importance. I dodge two stock brickbats thrown at me—one, Madame Curie, who shared with her husband a glorious discovery, and the other, Mrs. Ayrton,[2] who has made some researches into the behaviour of the electric arc which are no doubt important, though I am scientifically incompetent to say how important. But for these two solitary examples of any original achievement performed by woman in the realm of science to be made to disprove my point so far even as science is concerned, it will be necessary to prove that the *collaborated* discovery made by Madame Curie, and the original researches of Mrs. Ayrton, would not have been made by a man, if not thereabout, then very shortly after.

And even if we include domestic occupations outside the domestic sphere—cooking and sewing for instance—the best journeymen in these occupations are still men and not women, and as for what it is a pleasure to call *la haute école de la cuisine*, the name of M. Soyer just now is quite enough.[3] But the significance of M. Soyer deserves, I think, a chapter all to himself. In short there is not a single relation that woman holds either to the State or the general community, outside her maternal functions, in which she is indispensable.

TWO HYPOTHESES

That surely is not merely a very significant but a stupendous fact. For it means, if we care to conceive the horrid possibility, that if women were limited merely to the purposes of reproduction, the State and the nation could still continue. Nay, deprive her even of her duties as a mother, once a mother, take her own offspring off her hands, and delete all that is meant by a mother's care, and still she is not indispensable to the material needs of the State. Deprive her, in fact, of the priceless part of her—her place in the Home itself—deprive her of all relation with the outside world and the world would still go on. It would not be the same world if the priceless part of woman were suppressed. For it is impossible to estimate what the race of man owes to the work of woman in the home as wife or mother—even as that marred soul, the housekeeper. But nobody but the Suffragist wishes to cheapen or weaken the priceless part of her. But what we could deprive her of without loss to the State or the nation in any single material particular is all that work which lies outside the home.

And if we want really to find out what woman's place in the world is, let us imagine two things. Let us first imagine that the woman's movement had taken her away from the home altogether, leaving it just the sort of thing it would be like if every man were a bachelor looking after himself. The picture will hardly bear being looked upon. And now let us suppose that the woman's movement had been not what we know it to be but its very opposite—and there is indeed such a movement, only the other and more strident movement drowns the voices of those who are going more quietly about their work. But let us suppose that the woman's movement as we know it had taken quite another turn, and that "Back to the Home!" was the modern woman's cry, and that women threatened that they would withdraw themselves entirely from the outside world if man did not do something or other, and would henceforth do nothing but mind their own homes and babies. If that threat were held over our heads—if we were told that we should have to carry on the State and the industry and all the professions of the country without woman's assistance—with what composure should we receive the announcement, nay, with what relief! And that will help us to realise how far woman is unnecessary in the State—not only the governmental State into which she wishes to penetrate, and in which she is, at any rate, no more necessary than a man in a nunnery, but that wider aspect of the State which means the whole community outside the home.

Now reverse the case. Consider, if you can, an outside world in which man took no part, and in which its work was left entirely to woman. You must not conceive a race of women so changed in nature as to be able to perform man's work in some fashion or other. You must conceive of woman, as we know her to-day; doing man's work as we know it to-day in such a world as that in which we live. The difficulty of that conception, and its contrast with the ease with which we can conceive an outside world in which woman takes no part (a conception *actually realised* so far as the State into which she wishes to enter is concerned, and sufficiently realised in regard even to the State considered as a community) that contrast, I say, is the result of our enquiry into the question stated in the last chapter, viz.: How far woman's physical inferiority to man has carried her. It has carried her to the point that she has no necessary relation whatsoever to the work of the State and the community—except in so far as she contributes to the only kind of state and community we can pleasantly imagine, by her duties as a wife and mother in that little kingdom of her own, the family home.

The rest of this book is really unnecessary. That truth is the unanswerable answer to the "demand" of woman to share in the control of the State. She is utterly unnecessary to the control of the State.

NOTES

1. *Jane Eyre* (1847) by Charlotte Brontë, *Aurora Leigh* (1857) by Elizabeth Barrett Browning, *Adam Bede* (1859) by George Eliot, and *Robert Elsmere* (1888) by Mrs. Humphry Ward.

2. Hertha Ayrton (1854–1923), British physicist and author of *The Electric Arc* (1902) and other works. She advocated woman suffrage.

3. Alexis Soyer (1809–1858), celebrated French chef who spent most of his career in England.

38.

SOCIALISM, FEMINISM, AND SUFFRAGISM: THE TERRIBLE TRIPLETS

(1915)

Benjamin Vestal Hubbard

Benjamin Vestal Hubbard (1854–1934) was admitted to the bar in 1878 and practiced law in Indianapolis, Indiana. In 1905 he established the B. V. Hubbard Fund to promote the teaching of art and political science in high schools. He wrote several treatises on insurance as well as *Making America Safe for Democracy* (1926), in which he advocated the use of the referendum in American politics. In *Socialism, Feminism, and Suffragism: The Terrible Triplets* (1915), Hubbard maintains that granting women the suffrage will lead inevitably to rampant feminism and socialism. The following chapter is titled "The Complaint of Feminism."

Source: Benjamin Vestal Hubbard, *Socialism, Feminism, and Suffragism: The Terrible Triplets* (Chicago: American, 1915), pp. 207–12.

$\mathcal{F}$eminists as a class are man haters. The first prominent Feminist was Delilah, who was so jealous of Samson that she used every possible way to ascertain what his great strength consisted of, and not being able to ascertain his strength, after taking advantage of him when he was unconscious through sleep, had him bound with strong cords and delivered him to the Philistines on several occasions intending his destruction. Finally she persuaded Samson by her blandishments to reveal the secret of his strength, which consisted in his long hair, after which, when he slept she cut off his hair and delivered him to the Philistines. This is about the spirit of the Feminist mind, who frame all sorts of laws and restrictions against the rights and liberties of men, but do not have judicial minds to compel themselves to go under the same restrictions. For example, they introduce laws compelling every man to submit to a medical test before marriage. Another favored law of theirs is to make the age of consent as high as possible, so that designing females of mature age can inveigle young men into situations where they compel them to give up money or some other valuable consideration as victims. This class of women want to be made in law and in fact equal or superior to men. In fact, to obtain advantages over men by legal enactments.

The equality of man, except that all men are equal in the law view in all having the same duties, rights and protection under the law, is an obvious untruth. It is a fallacy which should be denied on all occasions. The law can not make men equal any more than a statute can declare that all persons shall have blue eyes or wear No. 6 shoes. The Feminists who claim that women in all respects, physical and mental, are equal to men, utter a falsehood which is patent. The facts are that the Feminist is painfully aware of her physical and mental inequality with man, and this is the cause of her envy of the opposite sex. If her inferiority was not the cause of her envy, her outcry would not be made. If she was equal or could attain equality, her hysteria would cease.

This is not to be taken to the discredit of women because a woman with a faculty to create, nurture and nurse a human being, gives up in such maternity so much of her physical and mental strength, which vigor goes into her offspring, and that therefore she cannot retain for herself as much strength as a man who does not perform these maternal functions. The weakness due to motherhood is the crowning glory of woman, and it is this weakness which true gentlemen venerate by means of chivalric attentions.

Even if Feminists should obtain the franchise and elect the legislature and judges, no law that they could pass or decree that they could render would make men and women equal, or make two plus two equal five. The Feminists would do well to repress their envy and cease attempting the impossible. There are a few Feminists who are equal to men. They are those who have no maternal impulses and no mother-love, or have a masculine form of mind or body, or have passed the child-bearing period; but these persons cannot be termed women and compared to man, as they are a third sex and are incapable of classification. Such a third sex creature is not honored as the plain womanly woman who acknowledges her weakness compared to man because she has generously divided her strength with others and exhibited her motherliness, and in reward for this sacrifice, "her children shall rise up and call her blessed,"[1] and when the hates and envies of the Feminists have inflicted their temporary hurts, the real woman's love will spring up perennially in hearts and outlive the things of earth with an eternal fruitage.

THE DEGRADATION AND PERIL OF FEMINISM

Women will be very much what men want them to be. If women become "manly women," it will be because men cease to fill their places as providers, defenders and protectors of the wife, of the family, and of the nation. It will be because men become weak and futile and inefficient, and because there will be a necessity for the woman to take his place and to fulfil his mission and to do his work as well as she may be able to do while trying to do her own work also. If the men are willing to give up their knighthood, their chivalry, and their strength, and subordinate themselves to the places of the weaker sex, then the woman, in a half, makeshift, inefficient way, must take the man's place. If the man gives up his place at the throttle of the engine, at the lever of the car, or at the ballot box, the woman will take his former position and will assume the direction of affairs.

With her nervous condition and her half logic, the safety valve of society will be lifted and she will drive swiftly to the wreck of both man and woman. The industrial welfare of both will be imperilled. The former higher wage of men will be reduced to the level of the woman's wage from the fact that commercialism desires women, not for women's work, but for cheapness and for cheapness only. Then there can be no hope for either men or women accumulating a competency; pride of personal achievement will vanish; black despair will pall the world, and capitalists will accumulate enormous fortunes from the lower wages brought about by entering commercial and industrial life and wages being paid both sexes upon the women's level. There being no such institution left as a home protected by the stronger sex with ample, efficient bulwarks, public and private morals will become a negligible quantity and hope will disappear.

It seems to be the fashion of some labor organizations to favor Suffragism. The theory advanced by them is that woman's wages will be increased and her general interests safeguarded; but on the contrary, the very opposite will occur. The man and woman in the next generation under woman suffrage will work for the same relative wages that the man himself has received during the preceding generation. There will not be earned between the two enough money to support the child, so that this political economy of Suffragism and Feminism is in the direct trend of Socialism, and if there is to be a child, the state will be compelled to provide him a nursing bottle the hour after he is born, and drag him away from his mother's breast, from the motherhood loaded with ineffable love, to the blue whey of the state nursery, because the mother must go to earn the half wages that she through Suffragism has brought upon herself, upon her husband, upon society, and upon her first-born. Through misdirected pride and the turning of the love of motherhood to the love of self. Under Feminism and Suffragism the next generation of our children will be both fatherless and motherless, and this is too high a price to pay for the pride of Feminism and the folly of Suffragism.

GRIEVANCES OF FEMINISTS
SHOULD NOT BE MADE PUBLIC

The Feminist is not to be classed with Women, and it is fortunate for humanity that among women there is perhaps not two Feminists to the thousand. To avoid duty, Feminists would repeal the Mosaic law and amend the moral code. The Feminist, instead of having the affections of a normal woman, and a regard for duty, has no affection for either man, child, church, state or God. She is a moral anarchist, obsessed by her personal importance and vanity.

She hates the home; she abhors it because she feels that it is a mere baby rearing establishment. She would wish the death of a baby at its birth if she felt the child would take an hour of her time from displaying herself in public.

She decries the "home" as having corrupting influences on women, and sees in the birth of babies nothing but shackles and shame for their mother.

She would take precautionary measures against motherhood wherever possible.

The Feminists and Suffragets bring forward complaints that man-made laws are unjust to women, and by iteration and reiteration and shouting their complaints on all occasions and echoing and re-echoing these charges, many people take them as true, when they are only noisy lies based on confused ideas of the women and men who utter them.

Anyone has a legitimate right to infer that these disturbances of the peace of society are living unhappily with their husbands, or that they did not get a husband, or that they did not succeed in getting as much alimony as they demanded, or that they failed in blackmailing some mere man in a breach of promise suit, or that they are avoiding some duty, the care and nursing of a baby, or allowing their homes to become untidy and disorderly.

Whatever this private grouch or personal failure of duty may be, it would be a mercy to the general public if the Feminist and Suffraget should keep it concealed and not expose it to the general public, and thus set the whole world in turmoil, and bring discontent and unhappiness to thousands who heretofore have been dutiful to their obligations and happy and contented.

A few cats in an alley yowling their sex troubles often disturb the virtuous rest of scores of people.

NOTE

1. Prov. 31:28.

39.

THE FUNDAMENTAL ERROR
OF WOMAN SUFFRAGE

(1915)

William Parker

Little is known about William Parker (1865–?),
author of several eccentric religious and political polemics, including *The United States the
Antitype of Joseph* (1917) and *The Judgment of
Nations* (1920). Parker also wrote *The Fundamental Error of Woman Suffrage* (1915), in
which he maintains that woman suffrage is
anti-Christian and therefore "in opposition to
the fundamental and divine order of life." The
following chapter is titled "Woman Suffrage
Antichristian."

One of the principal effects of this error of woman suffrage is a
materialistic idealism, which embraces economic determinism
and innumerable conceptions of life that are materialistic and
directly opposed to the principles of Christianity. These beliefs are in
many respects a close counterfeit of the true Christian belief, and for
this reason tremendously deceptive. The substance of this error exists

Source: William Parker, *The Fundamental Error of Woman Suffrage* (New York: Fleming H. Revell,
1915), pp. 106–15.

in the fact that it proposes quick returns with large temporal and material benefits. It excludes the Christian conception of humility or sacrifice. There is no atonement, no cross, or Calvary, in its philosophy of life, but rather a worldly kingdom, created by temporal and material forces, founded upon man-made laws. By a militant attitude, both physical and mental, they would force their economic and social reforms upon the people, peaceably if possible, but by violence and bloodshed if not. By these means do they hope to cure the ills of humanity and thereby establish a permanent and lasting government.

You can readily see the fallacy of this antichristian spirit. It is the supreme temptation with which the prince of this world deceives and seduces mankind. Fall down and worship me and I will give you the kingdoms of the world.

It is a notable fact that women are more easily deceived than men. It largely accounts for the eagerness with which they embrace these false and antichristian teachings. A strategic move was made when this antichristian spirit enlisted so many women in its cause. It accomplishes this by promising them freedom from the bondage and servitude imposed by man, a release from the restraints of that institution called home. No longer hampered by the necessity of motherhood, she can take her place beside man and vie with him in those things that will stultify her God-given nature, debase her womanhood, cause her to deny her Creator, and, in the end, to repudiate her own soul. You can readily see that such doctrines are directly antagonistic to true Christianity. When you consider the indisputable fact, Christianity is the only religion that re-establishes the home, sanctifies motherhood, and glorifies womanhood.

However, the time is rapidly approaching when all of these antichristian forces will be compelled to come out into the open and show their colours. To unmask and reveal these errors should be the duty of all who love the truth. In times past might was right; the world was governed by material forces. But by the spread of knowledge and the coming of truth in the form of Christianity, we have created a deadly conflict between these material forces on the one hand, and spiritual forces on the other. The principal effect of this conflict is a social evolution and one of the products of this evolution is the economic and social freedom of women. When brute force was the rule, women in an economic sense were unequal to men, but by the evolution of knowledge and invention women are in competition with men. With this social freedom of women comes a corresponding moral responsibility; for you can readily see that there would be a tendency to merge and confuse her proper sphere of work and usefulness with that of men. The great spread of knowledge as a result of Christianity is necessitating the readjustment of social conditions in their relation to women. In this respect women, like men, are extending the scope of their influence, which necessitates the elimination of many non-essentials, those things which are detrimental to woman's higher growth and spiritual development. But in this process of elimination ungodly women are taking occasion to pervert and destroy the essentials and fundamentals, those spiritual elements so essential through women to the perpetuation of the social order.

By usurping the prerogative which rightly belongs to men, women are lusting after temporal power and thereby surrendering spiritual power. We find a good comparison in the case of a man who suddenly acquires great material wealth and influence; it should not necessarily interfere with his spiritual life, but the facts are in most cases it does. The same is true of woman's economic liberties in its relation to her spiritual liberty in the same sense that woman's economic freedom is subjecting her to a severe moral test, "Tried as by fire,"[1] and many of our women are failing.

The same spirit so prominent in our women and in the Church is also animating the nations—an insatiate and avaricious greed for power. We observe this especially among the smaller nations who by changing conditions have lately come into prominence and influence. Intoxicated by their success, they disregard all precedent or sense of decency in their mad scramble for territory and power. This also applies to the larger nations who although more diplomatic and dignified in their demands are none the less guilty.

While we can in some degree, at least, excuse men and the State, who represent the temporal elements, for exhibiting a spirit of this kind, it ill becomes women and the Church, who represent the spiritual elements, to manifest this spirit. The Church also is dominated by this spirit to a degree equalling that of women. By the increase of knowledge it becomes necessary to readjust the existing conditions within the Church. To eliminate many non-essentials of doctrine, creed and dogma, ungodly men by this readjusting process are taking occasion to disrupt and destroy the essentials and fundamentals of the Church. This is due to the fact that people in general fail to distinguish between the essentials and non-essentials. For in becoming a powerful social and economic factor, and because of her great popularity with the world, the Church, like women, has been seduced from the divine object and purpose for which she was created. By lusting after temporal power the Church is losing spiritual power.

By analysis and comparison you can readily discern this spirit in the woman suffrage movement. Intoxicated by her new-born freedom, women are not only appropriating those things which rightly and justly belong to her, but they are literally grabbing everything in sight. They fail to make any distinction between the temporal and spiritual, or the sacred and secular. In the same sense that the spirit of greed for temporal power is detrimental to the peace and stability of nations, disastrous to the spiritual growth and prosperity of the Church, it is likewise a calamity to our women and all that this implies. On every hand it has become a mad rush for power, a survival of the fittest. Every man's hand is against his neighbour. And the saddest part of it all is the fact that our women have been drawn into the vortex. For when women become imbued with this spirit, her desires become insatiable and know no bounds or limitations. This is the final conclusion of woman suffrage, to disregard all authority, precedent, or the established order of things. When told that it is contrary to the Scriptures and the teachings of Christ, she will repudiate Christianity. In this respect woman suffrage will become one of the chief elements in the modern antichristian movement. When we consider how much women owe to Christian influences, it is certainly the dregs of ingratitude that any part of them should oppose Christianity or the Church. From this face we get some idea as to the severity of the condemnation and punishment that will be visited upon such women as commit this transgression.

Without regard to what Socialism or women suffrage may claim, there can be no disputing the fact that their adherents are opposed to the real spirit and teachings of Christianity. We would class woman suffrage as one of the leading forces in the antichristian movement and any claims of fidelity or belief in Christianity that their apostles may make are but deceptive subterfuges to hide their real intent and purposes until such time as they become strong and powerful enough to come out in open opposition to the Church and Christianity. They must first deceive the people before they can consummate their purpose.

One of the chief forms of this deception to appropriate to themselves many of the characteristics of true Christianity; as Paul says: "Having the form of Godliness but denying the power thereof."[2] They would create a social unity founded upon economic determinism, which is directly opposed to the real principle of Christianity; therefore it is a false unity, and opposed to the true unity in the same sense that the antichrist is opposed to the Christ.

It is a significant fact that all of these liberalistic, optimistic, atheistic classes of religious beliefs or social movements favour woman suffrage, such as Socialism, Mormonism, Christian Science, Spiritualism, or New Thought.[3] Every radical unorthodox or atheistic belief in the country favours this movement. In fact, the growth and development of woman suffrage have been contemporaneous with these liberalistic beliefs. You will observe that many of these beliefs originate with, and are promulgated by, women. As we have said elsewhere, beware of any religious belief that originates with a woman. It is false. The same is true of government or economic reforms that are fostered by women.

As the social order is but a reflex of the individual, we find that the source of these liberalistic elements exists in the individual. Consequently, you can scarcely find a Socialist, an Atheist or Anarchist in the country but what advocates woman suffrage. In this respect woman suffrage like Socialism is destructive and not constructive. In its final analysis, woman suffrage is opposed to all law, precedent or established order of things. Due to this fact, there is very little danger of women actually running or controlling governments as some fear; the greatest danger lies in the destructive character of the movement. In this militant suffrage movement we can discern the end from the beginning. The more rights and privileges women are granted, the more intolerant and unreasonable they will become, creating a hysterical condition of society, which is due to the involuntary nature of woman, and the fact that she has become perverted from her true sphere of action.

As action and reaction are equal, the sure result of the increase of these liberalistic elements in society will be a corresponding reaction. When the people in general once realize that the present great increase of crime is largely due to these optimistic, atheistic beliefs, that have promised the people much, but have not made good, the public conscience will suddenly swing its influence from the liberal to the conservative force of society in a vain endeavour to suppress the liberals. We can already see the lines of the conflict being drawn especially in the Church. The Roman Catholic Church, already bitterly opposed to Socialism and all liberal beliefs, is lining up in opposition to woman suffrage.

There is also a conservative orthodox element in Protestantism that will oppose these liberals, which means that the temporal Church in general will suffer a severe reaction in a fruitless endeavour to put down and suppress by law and force this atheism and unbelief. You can readily see that both of these extremes are wrong; for the greatest enemies of the temporal Church, and in fact all government, is constituted in infidelity and unbelief on the one side and religious intolerance on the other. The compact and conflict between these dynamic forces of evil will be terrific. We may also add that woman's activities will be very much in evidence on both sides of the question; for it is a woman's nature to act and react with startling rapidity. Therefore, we can come to no other conclusion. The logical and inevitable result of the dominant influence of women and the Church in matters of State means the end and destruction of temporal government. It means a universal condition similar to the French Revolution in which women and unbelief were the ruling factors. As to the final outcome of this conflict, it is not within the range of this little book on woman suffrage to define. We would only seek to emphasize this fact, that the decision that women make upon this question will have much to do with her eternal destiny, for the woman who subscribes to woman suffrage must eventually repudiate Jesus Christ.

We must therefore conclude that the woman suffrage movement is antichristian for many reasons and from many points of view. In the first place, woman suffrage is founded upon the error of economic determinism, which affirms that the moral regeneration of the individual and the home depends upon the economic and social conditions, which is contrary to the teachings of Christianity.

We also conclude that woman suffrage is antichristian because of the fact that it is opposed to both the letter and the spirit of the Scriptures, which are divinely inspired, and reveal the fundamental and essential principles of life, applicable to all times, states or conditions of life.

Woman suffrage is opposed to Christianity for the reason that it is a perversion and prostitution of woman's nature and the divine order of her creation, consequently, having a tendency to make woman less modest, less kind, less Godlike, less fitted for motherhood, which is the supreme purpose of womanhood; for it is very evident that woman, like the Church, is the more sacred vessel, set apart to preserve and conserve the more spiritual elements of man; and the very desire on the part of woman to vote and to participate in such things as pertain to men constitutes a moral error on the part of woman.

The motive which actuates woman suffrage is the opposite from a true spiritual motive. It is not a question as to what its advocates can do or suffer for the redemption of society, but rather a demand upon society for what they claim to be their economic rights. It is not a question of what they can give, but rather what they can get. That is unchristian, unwomanly and unchristlike. Therefore, woman suffrage being in opposition to the true principles of Christianity, it is antibiblical, antichristian, and in opposition to the fundamental and divine order of life.

NOTES

1. A misquotation either of 1 Pet. 1:7 ("That the trial of your faith, . . . though it be tried with fire") or Rev. 3:18 ("I counsel thee to buy of me gold tried in the fire").

2. 2 Tim. 3:5.

3. New Thought was a mystical mind-healing movement in late nineteenth-century America popularized by Phineas P. Quimby (1802–1866) and others.

Part 11
WOMEN HATING WOMEN

40.

DISCONTENTED WOMEN

(1896)

Mrs. Amelia E. Barr

Amelia Edith Huddleston Barr (1831–1919) was born in England and began attendance at the Normal School in Glasgow, Scotland, but predictably abandoned her teacher training when she married the Scottish wool merchant Robert Barr in 1850. Facing bankruptcy, the Barrs came to New York in 1853, eventually settling in Austin, Texas. Amelia gave birth to twelve children; seven of them died before their first birthday, and her husband and two more children died in the yellow fever epidemic of 1867. Returning to New York, Barr began writing for magazines on a wide array of subjects, then began producing novels in rapid succession. Over her career she wrote more than eighty novels, most of them romances with historical settings. Her autobiography appeared as *All the Days of My Life*

Source: Amelia E. Barr, "Discontented Women," *North American Review* 162, no. 2 (February 1896): 201–209.

(1913). In the following essay, published in the *North American Review* (February 1896), Barr accuses women of discontent with their "duties" as housekeepers, wives, and workers; she concludes that most of these discontents must be "dull women."

*D*iscontent is a vice six thousand years old, and it will be eternal; because it is in the race. Every human being has a complaining side, but discontent is bound up in the heart of woman; it is her original sin. For if the first woman had been satisfied with her conditions, if she had not aspired to be "as gods,"[1] and hankered after unlawful knowledge, Satan would hardly have thought it worth his while to discuss her rights and wrongs with her. That unhappy controversy has never ceased; and, with or without reason, woman has been perpetually subject to discontent with her conditions and, according to her nature, has been moved by its influence. Some, it has made peevish, some plaintive, some ambitious, some reckless, while a noble majority have found in its very control that serene composure and cheerfulness which is granted to those who conquer, rather than to those who inherit.

But with all its variations of influence and activity there has never been a time in the world's history, when female discontent has assumed so much, and demanded so much, as at the present day; and both the satisfied and the dissatisfied woman may well pause to consider, whether the fierce fever of unrest which has possessed so large a number of the sex is not rather a delirium than a conviction; whether indeed they are not just as foolishly impatient to get out of their Eden, as was the woman Eve six thousand years ago.[2]

We may premise, in order to clear the way, that there is a noble discontent which has a great work to do in the world; a discontent which is the antidote to conceit and self-satisfaction, and which urges the worker of every kind continually to realize a higher ideal. Springing from Regret and Desire, between these two sighs, all horizons lift; and the very passion of its longing gives to those who feel this divine discontent the power to overleap whatever separates them from their hope and their aspiration.

Having acknowledged so much in favor of discontent, we may now consider some of the most objectionable forms in which it has attacked certain women of our own generation. In the van of these malcontents are the women dissatisfied with their home duties. One of the saddest domestic features of the day is the disrepute into which housekeeping has fallen; for that is a woman's first natural duty and answers to the needs of her best nature. It is by no means necessary that she should be a Cinderella among the ashes, or a Nausicaa washing linen, or a Penelope for ever at her needle,[3] but all women of intelligence now understand that good cooking is a liberal science, and that there is a most intimate connection between food and virtue, and food and health, and food and thought. Indeed, many things are called crimes that are not as bad as the savagery of an Irish cook or the messes of a fourth-rate confectioner.

It must be noted that this revolt of certain women against housekeeping is not a revolt against their husbands; it is simply a revolt against their duties. They consider house-work hard and monotonous and inferior, and confess with a cynical frankness that they prefer to engross paper, or dabble in art, or embroider pillow-shams, or sell goods, or in some way make money to pay servants who will cook their husband's dinner and nurse their babies for them. And they believe that in this way they show themselves to have superior minds, and ask credit for a deed which ought to cover them with shame. For actions speak louder than words, and what does such action say? In the first place, it asserts that any stranger—even a young uneducated peasant girl hired for a few dollars a month—is able to perform the duties of the housemistress and the mother. In the second place, it substitutes a poor ambition for love, and hand service for heart service. In the third place, it is a visible abasement of the loftiest duties of womanhood to the capacity of the lowest paid service. A wife and mother can not thus absolve her own soul; she simply disgraces and traduces her holiest work.

Suppose even that housekeeping is hard and monotonous, it is not more so than men's work in the city. The first lesson a business man has to learn is to do pleasantly what he does not like to do. All regular useful work must be monotonous, but love ought to make it easy; and at any rate, the tedium of housework is not any greater than the tedium of office work. As for housekeeping being degrading, that is the veriest nonsense. Home is a little royalty; and if the housewife and mother be of elements finely mixed, and loftily educated, all the more she will regard the cold mutton question of importance, and consider the quality of the soup, and the quantity of chutnee in the curry, as requiring her best attention. It is only the weakest, silliest women who cannot lift their work to the level of their thoughts, and so ennoble both.

There are other types of the discontented wife, with whom we are all too familiar: for instance, the wife who is stunned and miserable because she discovers that marriage is not a lasting picnic; who cannot realize that the husband must be different from the lover; and spends her days in impotent whining. She is always being neglected, and always taking offence; she has an insatiable craving for attentions, and needs continual assurances of affection, wasting her time and feelings in getting up pathetic scenes of accusation, which finally weary, and shall alienate her husband. Her own fault! There is nothing a man hates more, than a woman going sobbing and complaining about the house with red eyes; unless it be a woman with whom he must live in a perpetual fool's paradise of perfection.

There are also discontented wives, who goad their husbands into extravagant expenditure, and urge them to projects from which they would naturally recoil. There are others, whose social ambitions slay their domestic ones, and who strain every nerve, in season and out of season, and lose all their self-respect, for a few crumbs of contemptuous patronage from some person of greater wealth than their own. Some wives fret if they have no children, others just as much if children come. In the first case, they are disappointed; in the second, inconvenienced, and in both, discontented. Some lead themselves and others wretched lives because they have not three times as many servants as are necessary; a still greater number because they cannot compass a life of constant amusement and excitement.

A very disagreeable kind of discontented woman is the wife who instead of having a God to love and worship, makes a god of her religion, alienates love for an ecclesiastical idea, or neglects her own flesh and blood, to carry the religious needs of the world; forgetting that the good wife keeps her sentiments very close to her own heart and hearth. But perhaps the majority of discontented wives have no special thing to complain of, they fret because they are "so dull." If they took the trouble to look for the cause of this "dullness," they would find it in the want of some definite plan of life, and some vigorous aim or object. Of course any aim implies limitation, but limitation implies both virtue and pleasure. Without rule and law, not even the games of children could exist, and the stricter the rules of a game are obeyed, the greater the satisfaction. A wife's duty is subject to the same conditions. If aimless plaintive women would make strict laws for their households, and lay out some possible vigorous plan for their own lives, they would find that those who love and work, have no leisure for complaining.

But from whatever cause domestic discontent springs, it makes the home full of idleness, ennui, and vagrant imaginations; or of fierce extravagance, and passionate love of amusement. And as a wife holds the happiness of many in her hands, discontent with her destiny is peculiarly wicked. If it is resented, she gets what she deserves; if it is quietly endured, her shame is the greater. For nothing does so much honor to a wife as her patience; and nothing does her so little honor as the patience of her husband. And however great his patience may be, she will not escape personal injury; since none are to be held innocent, who do harm even to their own soul and body. Besides, it is the inflexible order of things, that voluntary faults are followed by inevitable pain.

Married women, however, are by no means the only complainers. There is a great army of discontents who, having no men to care for them, are clamoring, and with justice, for their share of the world's work and wages. Such women have a perfect right to make a way for themselves, in whatever direction they best can. Brains are of no sex or condition, and at any rate, there is no use arguing either their ability or their right, for necessity has taken the matter beyond the reach of controversy. Thousands of women have now to choose between work, charity, or starvation, for the young man of to-day is not a marrying man. He has but puny passions, and his love is such a very languid preference that he cannot think of making any sacrifice for it. So women do not marry, they work; and as the world will take good work from whoever will give it, the world's custom is flowing to them by a natural law.

Now, earnest practical women-workers are blessed, and a blessing; but the discontented among them, by much talking and little doing, continually put back the cause they say they wish to advance. No women are in the main so discontented as women-workers. They go into the arena and, fettered by old ideas belonging to a different condition, they are not willing to be subject to the laws of the arena. They want, at the same time, the courtesy claimed by weakness and the honor due to prowess. They complain of the higher wages given to men, forgetting that the first article of equal payment is equal worth and work. They know nothing about what Carlyle calls "the silences"; and the babble of their small beginnings is, to the busy world, irritating and contemptible. It never seems to occur to discontented working-women that the best way to get what they want is to act, and not to talk. One silent woman who quietly calculates her chances and achieves success does more for her sex than any amount of pamphleteering and lecturing. For nothing is more certain than that good work, either from man or woman, will find a market; and that bad work, will be refused by all but those disposed to give charity and pay for it.

The discontent of working women is understandable, but it is a wide jump from the woman discontented about her work or wages to the woman discontented about her political position. Of all the shrill complainers that vex the ears of mortals there are none so foolish as the women who have discovered that the Founders of our Republic left their work half finished, and that the better half remains for them to do.

While more practical and sensible women are trying to put their kitchens, nurseries and drawing-rooms in order, and to clothe themselves rationally, this class of Discontents are dabbling in the gravest national and economic questions. Possessed by a restless discontent with their appointed sphere and its duties, and forcing themselves to the front in order to ventilate their theories and show the quality of their brains, they demand the right of suffrage as the symbol and guarantee of all other rights.

This is their cardinal point, though it naturally follows that the right to elect contains the right to be elected. If this result be gained, even women whose minds are not taken up with the things of the state, but who are simply housewives and mothers, may easily predicate a few of such results as are particularly plain to the feminine intellect and observation. The first of these would be an entirely new set of agitators, who would use means quite foreign to male intelligence. For instance, every favorite priest and preacher would gain enormously in influence and power; for the ecclesiastical zeal which now expends itself in fairs and testimonials would then expend itself in the securing of votes in whatever direction they were instructed to secure them. It might even end in the introduction of the clerical element into our great political Council Chambers—the Bishops in the House of Lords would be a sufficient precedent—and a great many women would really believe that the charming rhetoric of the pulpit would infuse a higher tone in legislative assemblies.

Again, most women would be in favor of helping any picturesque nationality, without regard to the Monroe doctrine, or the state of finances, or the needs of the market. Most women would think it a good action to sacrifice their party for a friend. Most women would change their politics, if they saw it to be their interest to do so, without a moment's hesitation. Most women would refuse the primary obligation on which all franchises rest—that is, to defend their country by force of arms, if necessary. And if a majority of women passed a law which the majority of men felt themselves justified in resisting by physical force, what would women do? Such a position in sequence of female suffrage is not beyond probability, and yet if it happened, not only one law, but *all* law would be in danger. No one denies that women have suffered, and do yet suffer, from grave political and social disabilities, but during the last fifty years much has been continually done for their relief, and there is no question but that the future will give all that can be reasonably desired. Time and Justice are friends, though there are many moments that are opposed to Justice. But all such innovations should imitate Time, which does not wrench and tear, but detaches and wears slowly away. Development, growth, completion, is the natural and best advancement. We do not progress by going over precipices, nor re-model and improve our houses by digging under the foundations.

Finally, women cannot get behind or beyond their nature, and their nature is to substitute sentiment for reason—a sweet and not unlovely characteristic in womanly ways and places; yet reason, on the whole, is considered a desirable necessity in politics. At the Chicago Fair,[4] and at other convocations, it has been proven that the strongest-minded women, though familiar with platforms, and deep in the "dismal science" of political economy, when it came to disputing, were no more philosophical than the simplest housewife. Tears and hysteria came just as naturally to them, as if the whole world wagged by impulse only; yet a public meeting in which feeling and tears superseded reason and argument, would in no event inspire either confidence or respect. Women may cease to be women, but they can never learn to be men, and feminine softness and grace can never do the work of the virile virtues of men. Very fortunately this class of discontented women have not yet been able to endanger existing conditions by combinations analogous to trades-unions; nor is it likely they ever will; because it is doubtful if women, under any circumstances, could combine at all. Certain qualities are necessary for combination, and these qualities are represented in women by their opposites.

Considering discontented women of all kinds individually, it is evident that they must be dull women. They see only the dull side of things, and naturally fall into a monotonous way of expressing themselves. They have also the habit of complaining, a habit which quickens only the lower intellect. Where is there a more discontented creature than a good watch dog? He is forever looking for some infringement of his rights; and an approaching step, or a distant bark, drives him into a fury of protest. Discontented women are always egotists; they view everything in regard to themselves, and have therefore the defective sympathies that belong to low organizations. They never win confidence, for their discontent breeds distrust and doubt, and however clever they may naturally be, an obtrusive self, with its train of likings and dislikings, obscures their judgment, and they take false views of people and things. For this reason, it is almost a hopeless effort to show them how little people generally care about their grievances; for they have thought about themselves so long, and so much that they cannot conceive of any other subject interesting the rest of the world. We may even admit, that the women discontented on public subjects are often women of great intelligence, clever women with plenty of brains. Is that the best? Who does not love far more than mere cleverness, that sweetness of temper, that sunny contented disposition, which goes through the world with a smile and a kind word for every one? It is one of the richest gifts of heaven; it is, according to Bishop Wilson, "nine-tenths of Christianity."[5]

Fortunately, the vast majority of women have been loyal to their sex and their vocation. In every community the makers and keepers of homes are the dominant power; and these strictures can apply only to two classes—first, the married women who neglect husband, children and homes, for the foolish *éclat* of the club and the platform, or for any assumed obligation, social, intellectual or political, which conflicts with their domestic duties: secondly, the unmarried women who, having comfortable homes and loving protectors, are discontented with their happy secluded security and rush into weak art or feeble literature, or dubious singing and acting, because their vanity and restless immorality lead them into the market place, or on to the stage. Not one of such women has been driven afield by indisputable genius. Any work they have done would have been better done by some unprotected experienced woman already in the fields they have invaded. And the indifference of this class to the money value of their labor has made it difficult for the women working because they must work or starve, to get a fair price for their work. It is the baldest effrontery for this class of rich discontents to affect sympathy with Woman's Progress. Nothing can excuse their intrusion into the labor market but unquestioned genius and super-excellence of work; and this has not yet been shown in any single case.

The one unanswerable excuse for woman's entrance into active public life of any kind, is *need*, and alas! need is growing daily, as marriage becomes continually rarer, and more women are left adrift in the world without helpers and protectors. But this is a subject too large to enter on here, though in the beginning it sprung from discontented women, preferring the work and duties of men to their own work and duties. Have they found the battle of life any more ennobling in masculine professions, than in their old feminine household ways? Is work done in the world for strangers, any less tiresome and monotonous, than work done in house for father and mother, husband and children? If they answer truly, they will reply "the home duties were the easiest, the safest, and the happiest."

Of course all discontented women will be indignant at any criticism of their conduct. They expect every one to consider their feelings without examining their motives. Paddling in the turbid maelstrom of life, and dabbling in politics and the most unsavory social questions, they still think men, at least, ought to regard them as the Sacred Sex. But women are not sacred by grace of sex, if they voluntarily abdicate its limitations and its modesties, and make a public display of unsexed sensibilities, and unabashed familiarity with subjects they have nothing to do with. If men criticize such women with asperity it is not to be wondered at; they have so long idealized women, that they find it hard to speak moderately. They excuse them too much, or else they are too indignant at their follies, and unjust and angry in their denunciation. Women must be criticized by women; then they will hear the bare uncompromising truth, and be the better for it.

In conclusion, it must be conceded that some of the modern discontent of women must be laid to unconscious influence. In every age there is a kind of atmosphere which we call "the spirit of the times," and which, while it lasts, deceives as to the importance and truth of its dominant opinions. Many women have doubtless thus caught the fever of discontent by mere contact, but such have only to reflect a little, and discover that, on the whole, they have done quite as well in life as they have any right to expect. Then those who are married will find marriage and the care of it, and the love of it, quite able to satisfy all their desires; and such as really need to work will perceive that the great secret of Content abides in the unconscious acceptance of life and the fulfillment of its duties—a happiness serious and universal, but full of comfort and help. Thus, they will cease to vary from the kindly race of women, and through the doors of Love, Hope and Labor, join that happy multitude who have never discovered that Life is a thing to be discontented with.

NOTES

1. Cf. Gen. 3:5: "ye shall be as gods, knowing good and evil" (spoken by the serpent to Eve).

2. The date reflects the Christian fundamentalist belief (first propounded by Archbishop James Ussher, 1581–1656) that the Bible, by implication, establishes the beginning of the world at c. 4000 BCE.

3. In Homer's *Odyssey*, Nausicaa (daughter of Alcinous) is first seen by Odysseus washing clothes in a river (6.48f.). Penelope, wife of Odysseus, spends much of her time weaving (and secretly unweaving) a burial robe for Laertes, her father-in-law, as a means of fending off her importunate suitors.

4. The reference is to the World's Fair, held in Chicago in 1893.

5. Daniel Wilson (1778–1858), bishop of Calcutta.

41.

THE ABDICATION OF MAN

(1898)

Elizabeth Bisland

Elizabeth (Bisland) Wetmore (1861–1929) was born in Louisiana and married Charles W. Wetmore in 1891. She wrote for the *New Orleans Times-Democrat* and the *Washington Post* and was for a time an editor at *Cosmopolitan* (not then a "women's" magazine). In addition to several novels and travel books, she wrote *The Truth about Men and Other Matters* (1927). In the following essay, first published in the *North American Review* (August 1898), Bisland sees in the Spanish-American War of 1898 a reassertion of the "feudal relation" between men and women, but maintains that men have themselves relinquished their role of supremacy over women and thereby engendered the movement for the extension of women's rights.

Source: Elizabeth Bisland, "The Abdication of Man," *North American Review* 167, no. 2 (August 1898): 191–99.

$\mathcal{I}$n the midst of the excursions and alarums of war and preparation for war a sudden and great silence has fallen upon the everlasting discussion of the relations of the sexes. Before the stern realities of that final and bloody argument of Republics as well as Kings further dissection of the Woman Question has been deferred. The most vociferous of the "unquiet sex" have been regarding respectfully the sudden transformation of the plain, unromantic man who went patiently to business every morning in a cable car, and sat on a stool at a desk, or weighed tea, or measured ribbon, into a hero ready to face violent annihilations before which even her imagination recoils. The grim realisms of life and death have made the realism of such erstwhile burning dramas as The Doll House[1] shrink into the triviality of a drama fit only for wooden puppets. Sudden and violent readjustments of ideas are apt to be brought about when human relations are jarred into their true place by the thunder of cannon. War legitimatizes man's claim to superiority. When the sword is drawn he is forced to again mount that ancient seat of rule from which he has only recently been evicted: or rather from which he has himself stepped down. The democracy of sex at once becomes ridiculous—the old feudal relation reasserts itself.

It is interesting to note that there has not been one feminine voice raised to protest against the situation. The entire sex, as represented in this country, has, as one woman, fallen simply and gladly into the old place of nurse, of binder of wounds, of soother and helpmeet. Not one has claimed the woman's equal right to face villainous saltpetre, or risk dismemberment by harbor mines.

I believe this to be because woman prefers this old relation. I believe that if man were willing she would always maintain it; that it depends upon him whether she returns to it permanently or not. I believe that her modern attitude is not of her own choosing—that man has thrust that attitude upon her. For the oldest of all empires is that of man; no royal house is so ancient as his. The Emperors of Japan are parvenus of the vulgarest modernity in comparison, and the claims of long descent of every sovereign in Europe shrivel into absurdity beside the magnificent antiquity of this potentate. Since the very beginning of things, when our hairy progenitors fought for mastery with the megatherium, and scratched pictorial epics upon his victim's bones, the House of Man has reigned and ruled, descending in an unbroken line from father to son in direct male descent. His legitimacy was always beyond dispute; his divine right to rule was not even questioned, and was buttressed against possible criticism not only by the universal concurrence of all religious and philosophic opinion, but by the joyful loyalty of the whole body of his female subjects. Moses and Zoroaster, St. Paul and Plato all bore witness to his supremacy, and the jury of women brought in a unanimous verdict in his favor without calling for testimony.

Women yet living can recall a day when they forgot their pain for joy that a man-child—heir to that famous line of Kings—was born into the world. They can remember a time when their own greatest claim to consideration rested upon the fact that they were capable of perpetuating the royal race. They recollect a period when even from his cradle the boy was set apart to be served with that special reverence reserved for those whose brows are bound with the sacred circlet of sovereignty—when a particular divinity did hedge even the meanest male; a tenfold essence being shed about all those who were of the tribe of Levi.

Why then—since all this is of so recent existence, since man's rule was founded so deep on woman's loyalty—has he been swelling the melancholy ranks of Kings in Exile? For that he has ceased to reign over woman does not require even to be asserted. It is self-evident.

When was this amazing revolution effected? Who led the emeute that thrust man from his throne? It is a revolt without a history; without the record of a single battle. Not even a barricade can be set up to its credit, and yet no more important revolution can be found in the pages of the oldest chronicles. So venerable, so deep-rooted in the eternal verities seemed the authority of man over woman that the female mind, until the present day, never doubted its inevitableness. Indeed, as is the case with all loyal natures, she was jealous for the absolutism of her master, and was quick to repair any such small omissions as he himself might have made in the completeness of his domination. All of her sex were trained from their earliest infancy to strive for but one end—to make themselves pleasing to their rulers. Success in the court of man was the end and aim of their existence, the only path for their ambition, and no other courtiers ever rivaled these in the subtle completeness of their flattery. Man's despotism, of course, like all other tyrannies, was tempered by his weaknesses, but while woman wheedled and flattered and secretly bent him to her projects she did not question his real right to govern.

Here and there through the past there arose a few scattered pioneers in recalcitrance. One of the first to deny the innate supremacy of the male was a woman who herself wore a crown. Elizabeth Tudor had a fashion of laying heavy hands upon her rightful lords whenever they displeased her, and she appears to have rejected the whole theory of feminine subordination. John Knox—strong in the power of the priest, whose sublimated prerogatives man had skillfully retained in his own hands—could and did dominate Mary Stuart even upon the throne, but when he blew from Geneva his "First Blast of the Trumpet Against the Monstrous Regiment of Woman," and called all the ages to witness that the rule of a female was an affront to nature, that trenchant lady who held the English sceptre forbade him ever to set foot in her domains.[2]

Elizabeth, however, was a unique personality and had few imitators. The literature of her day abounds with expressions of supreme humility and loyalty from the one sex to the other. Elizabethan poets deigned to play at captivity and subjection to the overwhelming charms of Saccharissa and her sisters, and turned pretty phrases about her cruelty, but this was merely poetic license of expression. All serious, unaffected expression of conviction, such as was to be found in the religious writings of the time, and in the voluminous private correspondence which gives us the most accurate description obtainable of the real actions and opinions of our ancestors, never suggested a doubt of man's natural and inalienable superiority, mental, moral, and physical. So undisturbed was this conviction down almost to our own day, that the heresy of Mary Wollstonecraft gave the severest of shocks to her own generation. So heinous seemed her offense of *lèse-majesté* in questioning man's divine right that one of the most famous of her contemporaries did not hesitate to stigmatize her as "a hyena in petticoats."[3]

History gives us but one record of a general outbreak. In the 13th Century the Crusades had so drained Europe of its able-bodied men that the women were forced to apply themselves to the abandoned trades and neglected professions. They shortly became so intoxicated by the sense of their own competency and power that when the weary wearers of the cross returned from the East they were at first delighted to discover that their affairs were prospering almost as well as ever, and then amazed and disgusted to find the women reluctant to yield up to the natural rulers these usurped privileges. Stern measures were necessary to oust them: Severe laws were enacted against the admission of women into the Guilds—the labor organizations which at that period governed all the avenues of industrial advancement; and the doors of the professions were peremptorily slammed in the women's faces. Such episodes as these, however, were detached and accidental. Female treason never dared unrebuked to lift its horrid head until within the present generation.

The emancipated new woman has various methods of accounting for the humbling of this hoary sovereignty. Some find it only a natural concomitant of the general wreck of thrones and monarchical privilege—in other words, that it is but one phase of advancing democracy. By some it is supposed that in this Age of Interrogation man's supremacy, along with all other institutions, has been called upon to produce an adequate reason for being, and having no answer that seems satisfactory, he has been summarily forced to abandon pretensions which rested merely upon use and wont. It is said by some that woman has been examining with coldly unprejudiced eye the claim of man to rule, has been measuring his powers against her own and has not been daunted by the comparison. The more noisy declare that she has stripped him of his royal robe and that, like Louis XIV minus his high heels and towering peruke, she finds him only of medium stature after all; that she has turned the rays of a cynical democracy upon the mystery encompassing his Kingship and refuses to be awed by what she sees there; that it is because of this she begins to usurp his privileges, thrust herself into his professions, shoulder him even from the altar, and brazenly seating herself on the throne beside him she lifts the circlet from his brows to try if it be not a fit for her own head.

The weakness of all such explanations is that they do not take into account the fact that woman is not by nature democratic. Whatever political principles the occasional or exceptional woman may profess, the average woman is in all her predilections intensely aristocratic; is by nature loyal, idealistic, an idolator and a hero worshiper. Strong as the spirit of democracy may be, it could not by itself alone in one generation change the nature of woman. The explanation must lie elsewhere.

In the language of a now famous arraignment—"*J'accuse*" man himself.[4]

No ruler is ever really dethroned by his subjects. No hand but his own ever takes the crown from his head. No agency but his can wash the chrism from his brow. It is his own abdication that drives him from power—abdication of his duties, his obligations, his opportunities. Ceasing to rule, he ceases to reign. When he ceases to lead he wants for followers, and the revolt which casts him from power is only the outward manifestation of his previous abdication of the inward or spiritual grace of kingship. When man ceased to govern, woman was not long in throwing off the sham of subjection that remained.

Like other subjects, woman required of her master two things—*panem et circenses*, bread and circuses.[5] When the industrial changes brought about by the introduction of machinery put an end to the old patriarchal system of home manufactures, man found it less easy to provide for his woman-kind—more especially his collateral woman-kind—and without any very manifest reluctance he turned her out into the world to shift for herself. Here was a shock to her faith and loyalty! The all-powerful male admitted his inability to provide for these sisters, cousins, aunts, and more distant kin who had looked up to him as the fount of existence, and had toiled and fed contentedly under his roof, yielding to him obedience as the natural provider and master. Woman went away sorrowful and—very thoughtful.

This alone was not enough to quite alienate her faith, however. Woman was still, as always, a creature of imagination—dazzled by color, by pomp, by fanfaronade. A creature of romance, adoring the picturesque, yielding her heart to courage, to power, to daring and endurance—all the sterner virtues which she herself lacked. The man of the past was often brutal to her—overbearing always, cruel at times, but he fascinated her by his masterfulness and his splendor. She might go fine, but he would still be the finer bird. When she thought of him she was hypnotized by a memory of gold, a waving of purple, a glitter of steel, a flutter of scarlet. He knew that this admiration of hers for beauty and color was as old as the world. From primordial periods the male has recognized this need of the female. The fish in the sea, the reptile in the dust, the bird in the forest, the wild beast in the jungle are all aware of their mates' passion for gleaming scales, for glowing plumes, for dappled hides and orgulous crests of hair. They know, they have always known, that no king can reign without splendor. Only man, bent solely upon his own comfort and, it would seem, upon the abandonment of his power, deliberately sets himself against this need of the female, which has become imbedded in her nature through every successive step up in the scale of evolution. He alone fatuously prides himself on the dark, bifurcated simplicity of his attire; intended only for warmth and ease and constructed with a calculated avoidance of adornment. To avoid criticism he has set up a theory that a superior sort of masculinity is demonstrated by the dark tint and unbeautiful shape of garments; (as if the fighting man, the soldier—who is nothing if not masculine—were not always a colorful creature;) and chooses to ignore or resent woman's weakness for this same gold-laced combatant, and the silken, picturesque actor.

"*J'accuse*" the man of abandoning his mastership and becoming a bourgeois in appearance and manner through a slothful desire for ease. There can hardly be a question that Louis le Grand's red heels and majestic peruke were uncomfortable and a bore, but his sense of humor and knowledge of men were such that his bed curtains were never untucked until his lion's mane had been passed in to him on the end of a walking stick, and was safely in its place. He could imagine how imposing the King of Beasts might be in *negligé*. He knew that to be reverenced one must be imposing. Louis the unfortunate found it far less tedious to abandon stateliness and work wigless and leather-aproned at his locksmith's forge, while his feather-headed queen played at being a dairy-maid at Trianon, forgetting that the populace, which had submitted humbly to the bitter exactions of the man who dazzled them, seeing the bald head and leathern apron would get abruptly up from its knees and say: "What, submit to the pretensions of a locksmith and a dairy-maid—common folk like ourselves—certainly not!" and proceed to carry their sovereign's suggestion of equality to the distressingly logical conclusion to be found at the mouth of the guillotine.

"*J'accuse*" man of carrying further this democracy of sex by adding rigid plainness of behavior to ugliness of appearance, forgetting that a woman, like the child and the savage, loves pomp of manner as well as of garment, and that what she does not see she finds it hard to believe. Every wise lover soon learns that it is necessary to reinforce the tenderness of his manner by definite assurances of affection several times in every twenty-four hours. Then, and then only is a woman sure she is loved.

How can she believe man heroic unless he use the appearance and manner of the hero?

Sir Hilary of Agincourt, returning from France, found his lady from home, and he and all his weary men-at-arms sat there—mailed cap-a-pie—throughout the entire night until she returned to welcome them home and receive their homage. What if at other times Sir Hilary may have been something of a brute?—Lady Hilary, flattered by this fine piece of steel clad swagger, would, remembering it, forgive a thousand failures of temper or courtesy.

When El Ahmed held the pass all through the darkness while his women fled across the desert, and his foes feared to come to hand grips with him, not knowing he stood there dead, propped against the spear he had thrust into his mortal wound to hold himself erect—there was no female revolt against the domination of men who were capable of deeds that so fired women's imaginations.

These may, after all, seem to be frivolous accusations—that men do not dress well; do not behave dramatically; but the signification of these seemingly capricious charges lies deeper than may appear. Man has been seized with a democratic ideal, and after applying it to political institutions has attempted to carry it into domestic application. He is relentlessly forcing a democracy of sex upon women; industrially, mentally, and sentimentally. He refuses to gratify her imagination; he insists upon her development of that logical selfishness which underlies all democracy, and which is foreign to her nature. Now, nature has inexorably laid upon woman a certain share of the work that must be done in the world. In the course of ages humanity adjusted itself to its shared labors by developing the relation of master and defender, of dependent and loyal vassal. Sentiment had adorned it with a thousand graces and robbed the feudal relation of most of its hardships. Mutual responsibilities and mutual duties were cheerfully accepted.

Woman was obliged to perform certain duties, and these could only be made easy and agreeable by sentiment, by unselfishness. Man needed her ministrations as much as she needed his. He realized that sentiment was necessary to her happiness and he accepted the duty of preserving that sentiment of loyalty and admiration for himself which made her hard tasks seem easy when performed for a beloved master. He took upon himself that difficult task of being a hero to a person even more intimate than his valet. He took the trouble to please woman's imagination.

The hard democracy of to-day will take no note of the relation of master and dependent. Each individual has all the rights which do not come violently in contact with other's rights, and has no duties which are not regulated by the law. Unselfishness is not contemplated in its scheme. Every individual has a right to all the goods of life he can get.

Women are beginning to accept these stern theories; beginning to apply the cruel logic of individualism. So far from the power to win his favor being her one hope of advancement or success she does not hesitate to say on occasion that to yield to his affections is likely to hamper her in the race for fame or achievement. So far from giving an heir to his greatness being the highest possibility of her existence, she sometimes complains that such duties are an unfair demand upon her energies, which she wishes to devote exclusively to her own ends.

The universal unpopularity of domestic service proves that the duties of a woman are in themselves neither agreeable nor interesting. Where is the man in all the world who would exchange even the most laborious of his occupations for his wife's daily existence? The only considerations that can permanently reconcile human beings to unattractive labors is first the sentiment of loyalty—that such labors are performed for one who is loved and admired—and second the fine, noble old habit of submission. These incentives to duty, these helps to happiness, man has taken from woman by weakly shuffling off his mastership.

I accuse man of having willfully cast from him the noblest crown in the world—of having wrongfully abdicated. War has at least this merit that it forces him to drop the vulgar careless ease of the bourgeois and resume for the time at least those bold and vigorous virtues which made him woman's hero and cheerfully accepted master.

NOTES

1. The reference is to Henrik Ibsen's *Et Dukkehjem* (1879; translated as *A Doll's House*), about a wife who leaves her husband and child to realize her ambitions.

2. John Knox (c. 1513–1572), Scottish clergyman, published the violently antifeminist tract *The First Blast of the Trumpet against the Monstrous Regiment of Women*, in 1558, while in Geneva. Chiefly directed against Mary of Guise and Mary Tudor, it asserted the unnaturalness and impiety of a government run by a woman. Queen Elizabeth I, who had just acceded to the English throne, thereupon prohibited Knox from passing through England on his way back to Scotland in 1559.

3. The comment is by British man of letters Horace Walpole (1717–1791), in a letter to Hannah More (January 24, 1795).

4. The expression "*J'accuse*" ("I accuse") was used by French novelist Émile Zola (1840–1902) in the article "J'Accuse" (*L'Aurore*, January 13, 1898), condemning the actions of the French judicial system in the Dreyfus affair.

5. Juvenal *Satires* 10.81.

42.

THE BUSINESS OF BEING A WOMAN

(1912)

Ida M. Tarbell

Ida Minerva Tarbell (1857–1944) was one of the most remarkable women of her generation. She was the only female in her freshman class at Allegheny College (Meadville, Pennsylvania), where she graduated with a degree in biology in 1880. She soon joined the staff of the *Chautauquan*, a magazine run by the Chautauqua Institute, devoted to adult education; at this time she lived with three other women who, like her, preferred a career to marriage, and she rejected several men who courted her. She spent the years 1891 to 1894 in Paris researching a biography of Madame Roland,[1] published in 1895. She was then hired by the magazine publisher S. S. McClure, and wrote biographies of Napoleon Bonaparte and Abraham Lincoln that proved hugely popular. Both were serialized in

Source: Ida M. Tarbell, *The Business of Being a Woman* (New York: Macmillan, 1912), pp. 218–22, 228–33, 238–42.

McClure's Magazine, whose associate editor she became in 1897. With other investigative reporters on McClure's staff, including Lincoln Steffens and Ray Stannard Baker, Tarbell became a leading "muckraker" (a term coined by Theodore Roosevelt). She devoted years to pursuing the shady business practices of John D. Rockefeller and other officials of the Standard Oil Company, publishing the landmark treatise *The History of the Standard Oil Company* (1904). Her work led the United States to apply the Sherman Antitrust Act to the corporation, dissolving it into separate state oil companies. Subsequently she criticized the practice of imposing protective tariffs on foreign imports, claiming that they merely aided big business in securing illegitimate profits for domestic products. Her findings were published in *The Tariff in Our Times* (1911). By this time, however, she had adopted a conservative stance on women's rights, maintaining that women are obligated to marry and stay in the home in order to preserve the family life that she felt was being eroded by modern conditions. Her views found expression in two treatises, *The Business of Being a Woman* (1912) and *The Ways of Women* (1915). Although she served on the staffs of several government agencies during and after World War I, she never regained the celebrity or dynamism she achieved as a muckraker. Her autobiography appeared as *All in the Day's Work* (1939). This excerpt is from the chapter titled "On the Ennobling of the Woman's Business."

$\mathcal{T}$he movement for a fuller life for American women has always suffered from the disregard of some of its noblest followers, both for things as they are and for things as they have been. The persistent belittling for campaign purposes of the Business of Being a Woman I have repeatedly referred to in this little series of essays; indeed, it has been founded on the proposition that the Uneasy Woman of to-day is to a large degree the result of the belittlement of her natural task and that her chief need is to dignify, make scientific, professionalize, that task.

I doubt if there is to-day a more disintegrating influence at work—one more fatal to sound social development—than that which belittles the home and the position of the woman in it. As a social institution nothing so far devised by man approaches the home in its opportunity, nor equals it in its successes.

The woman's position at its head is hard. The result of her pains and struggles are rarely what she hopes, either for herself or for any one connected with her, but this is true of all human achievement. There is nothing done that does not mean self-denial, routine, disillusionment, and half realization. Even the superman goes the same road, coming out at the same halfway-up house! It is the meaning of the effort, not the half result, that counts.

The pain and struggle of an enterprise are not what takes the heart out of a soldier; it is telling him his cause is mean, his fight in vain. Show him a reason, and he dies exultant. The woman is the world's one permanent soldier. After all war ceases she must go daily to her fight with death. To tell her this giving of her life for life is merely a "female function," not a human part, is to talk nonsense and sacrilege. It is the clear conviction of even the most thoughtless girl that this way lies meaning and fulfillment of life, that gives her courage to go to her battle as a man-in-line to his, and like him she comes out with a new understanding. The endless details of her life, its routine and its restraints, have a reason now, as routine and discipline have for a soldier. She sees as he does that they are the only means of securing the victory bought so dearly—of winning others.

From this high conviction the great mass of women never have and never can be turned. What does happen constantly, however, is loss of joy and courage in their undertaking. When these go, the vision goes. The woman feels only her burdens, not the big meaning in them. She remembers her daily grind, not the possibilities of her position. She falls an easy victim now to that underestimation of her business which is so popular. If she is of gentle nature, she becomes apologetic, she has "never done anything." If she is aggressive, she becomes a militant. In either case, she charges her dissatisfaction to the nature of her business. What has come to her is a common human experience, the discovery that nothing is quite what you expected it to be, that if hope is to be even halfway realized, it will be by courage and persistency. It is not the woman's business that is at fault; it is the faulty handling of it and the human difficulty in keeping heart when things grow hard. What she needs is a strengthening of her wavering faith in her natural place in the world, to see her business as a profession, its problems formulated and its relations to the work of society, as a whole, clearly stated. [. . .]

Moreover, all things considered, she has been no greater sufferer from injustice than man. I do not mean in saying this that she has not had grave and unjust handicaps, legal and social; I mean that when you come to study the comparative situations of men and women as a mass at any time and in any country you will find them more nearly equal than unequal, all things considered. Women have suffered injustice, but parallel have been the injustices men were enduring. It was not the fact that she was a woman that put her at a disadvantage so much as the fact that might made right, and the physically weaker everywhere bore the burden of the day. Go back no further than the beginnings of this Republic and admit all that can be said of the wrong in the laws which prevented a woman controlling the property she had inherited or accumulated by her own efforts, which took from her a proper share in the control of her child,—we must admit, too, the equal enormity of the laws which permitted man to exploit labor in the outrageous way he has. It was not because he was a man that the labor was exploited—it was because he was the weaker in the prevailing system. Woman's case was parallel—she was the weaker in the system. It had always been the case with men and women in the world that he who could took and the devil got the hindermost. The way the laborer's cause has gone hand in hand in this country the last hundred years with the woman's cause is a proof of the point. In the 30's of the nineteenth century, for illustration, the country was torn by a workingman's party which carried on a fierce agitation against banks and monopolies. Many of its leaders were equally ardent in their support of Women's Rights as they were then understood. The slavery agitation was coupled from the start with the question of Women's Rights. It was injustice that was being challenged—the right of the stronger to put the weaker at a disadvantage for any reason—because he was poor, not rich; black, not white; female, not male,—that is, there has been nothing special to women in the injustice she has suffered except its particular form. Moreover, it was not man alone who was responsible for this injustice. Stronger women have often imposed upon the weak—men and women—as strong men have done. In its essence, it is a human, not a sex, question—this of injustice.

The hesitation of this country in the earlier part of the nineteenth century to accord to women the same educational facilities as to men is often cited as a proof of a deliberate effort to disparage women. But it should not be forgotten that the wisdom of universal male education was hotly in debate. One of the ideals of radical reformers for centuries had been to give to all the illumination of knowledge. But to teach those who did the labor of the world, its peasants and its serfs, was regarded by both Church and State as a folly and a menace. It was the establishment of a pure democracy that forced the experiment of universal free instruction in this country. It has met with opposition at every stage, and there is to-day a Mr. Worldly Wiseman at every corner bewailing the evils it has wrought. He must, too, be a hopeless Candide who can look on our experiment, wonderful and inspiring as it is, and say its results have been the best possible.

It was entirely logical, things beings as they were, that there should have been strong opposition to giving girls the same training in schools as boys. That objection holds good to-day in many reflective minds. He again must be a hopeless optimist who believes that we have worked out the best possible system of education for women. But that there was opposition to giving women the same educational facilities as men was not saying that there was or ever had been a conspiracy on foot to keep her in intellectual limbo because she was a woman. The history of learning shows clearly enough that women have always shared in its rise. In the great revival of the sixteenth century they took an honorable part. "I see the robbers, hangmen, adventurers, hostlers of to-day more learned than the doctors and preacher of my youth," wrote Rabelais, and he added, "why, women and girls have aspired to the heavenly manna of good learning."[2] Whenever aspiration has been in the air, women have responded to it as men have, and have found, as men have found, a way to satisfy their thirst. [. . .]

It is not alone that justice is wounded by denying women a part in the making of the civilized world—a more immediate wrong is the way the movement for a fuller, freer life for all human beings is hampered. A woman with a masculine chip on her shoulder gives a divided attention to the cause she serves. She complicates her human fight with a sex fight. However good tactics this may have been in the past, and I am far from denying that there were periods it may have been good politics, however poor morals, surely in this country to-day there is no sound reason for introducing such complications into our struggles. The American woman's life is the fullest in its opportunity, all things considered, that any human beings harnessed into a complicated society have ever enjoyed. To keep up the fight against man as the chief hindrance to the realization of her aspiration is merely to perpetuate in the intellectual world that instinct of the female animal to be ever on guard against the male, save in those periods when she is in pursuit of him!

But complicating her problem is not the only injury she does her cause by this ignoring or belittling of woman's part in civilization. She strips herself of suggestion and inspiration—a loss that cannot be reckoned. The past is a wise teacher. There is none that can stir the heart more deeply or give to human affairs such dignity and significance. The meaning of woman's natural business in the world—the part it has played in civilizing humanity—in forcing good morals and good manners, in giving a reason and so a desire for peaceful arts and industries, the place it has had in persuading men and women that only self-restraint, courage, good cheer, and reverence produce the highest types of manhood and womanhood,—this is written on every page of history.

Women need the ennobling influence of the past. They need to understand their integral part in human progress. To slur this over, ignore, or deny it, cripples their powers. It sets them at the foolish effort of enlarging their lives by doing the things man does—not because they are certain that as human beings with a definite task they need—or society needs—these particular services or operations from them, but because they conceive that this alone will prove them equal. The efforts of woman to prove herself equal to man is a work of supererogation. There is nothing he has ever done that she has not proved herself able to do equally well. But rarely is society well served by her undertaking his activities. Moreover, if man is to remain a civilized being, he must be held to his business of producer and protector. She cannot overlook her obligation to keep him up to his part in the partnership, and she cannot wisely interfere too much with that part. The fate of the meddler is common knowledge!

A few women in every country have always and probably always will find work and usefulness and happiness in exceptional tasks. They are sometimes women who are born with what we call "bachelor's souls"—an interesting and sometimes even charming, though always an incomplete, possession! More often they are women who by the bungling machinery of society have been cast aside. There is no reason why these women should be idle, miserable, selfish, or antisocial. There are rich lives for them to work out and endless needs for them to meet. But they are not the women upon whom society depends; they are not the ones who build the nation. The women who count are those who outnumber them a hundred to one—the women who are at the great business of founding and filling those natural social centers which we call homes. Humanity will rise or fall as that center is strong or weak. It is the human core.

NOTES

1. Marie-Jeanne Phlipon Roland (1754–1793) and her husband, Jean-Marie Roland (1734–1793), were significant figures in revolutionary France.

2. The quotation is from bk. 2, chap. 8 of *Gargantua et Pantagruel* (1532–1552) by François Rabelais (1490–1553).

Part 12

BACKLASH—
MEN FIGHT BACK

43.

FOR MAIDS AND MOTHERS: THE WOMAN OF TO-DAY, AND OF TO-MORROW

(1899)

Harry Thurston Peck

The life of Harry Thurston Peck (1856–1914) ran the gamut of triumph and tragedy. Graduating from Columbia University in 1881, Peck studied abroad for a year before returning to Columbia, where he became a popular and highly regarded professor of classics. He wrote numerous treatises on classical literature, edited *Harper's Dictionary of Classical Literature and Antiquities* (1897), was a cofounder of Columbia University Press, edited the leading literary magazine in the nation, *The Bookman* (1897–1902), and wrote the popular treatise *Twenty Years of the Republic* (1906), a history of the United States from 1882 to 1901. One of the most highly respected critics of his day, Peck suffered a collapse in his reputation when his second wife left him in 1910 after a secretary in Boston sued him for breach of promise and

Source: Harry Thurston Peck, "For Maids and Mothers: The Woman of To-day, and of Tomorrow," *Cosmopolitan* 27, no. 2 (June 1899): 154–55, 156, 160–61.

subsequently published his love letters (some dating back as early as 1889, during his first marriage) in the newspaper. Peck was immediately dismissed from Columbia, and magazine and book publishers refused to publish his work. Forced to declare bankruptcy in 1913, he suffered a nervous breakdown shortly thereafter. His first wife had him released from the hospital and attempted to cure him by Christian Science methods, but he failed to respond and committed suicide. In "For Maids and Mothers," published in *Cosmopolitan* (June 1899), Peck lashes out at feminists who dare to question man's superiority; such women should be put in their place by "a short, sharp word" and "that will be the end of it."

We hear so much about the rights of woman, that just for the sake of variety it ought not to be displeasing to hear a little something said about the rights of man. When one comes down to the plain facts of human life on its serious side, it is man who is the finest and the noblest and the most godlike figure in the world wherein we live. The earth, indeed, has been given to him. It is his own. He is its master, and in him there are found implanted all those qualities and attributes that have made his mastery unquestioned in the past and that will keep it indestructible in the future. He has the physical power to work his will, and this alone is a lasting badge of his superiority; while he has also the moral traits that are fitted to direct and exercise this physical power in the best and most efficient way for the welfare of the world. It is he, and not woman, who throughout the centuries has battled with the forces of nature and has subdued them to his will; it is he who has swept away the jungle and the forest, who has made the desert blossom like a rose, who has reared great cities and created states and founded empires, who has called commerce into being, and flecked the ocean with his fleets, who has girdled the earth with the cincture of civilization, who has united humanity into one great brotherhood, and who has established law and evolved the sciences that enshrine the True, and the arts that glorify the Beautiful. It is man and not woman in whom are born the instinct of even-handed justice, the love of unsullied truth, the capacity for large-minded generosity and for civic self-devotion. The world to-day, in fact, is just what man has made it, and the world as it shall be a thousand years from now must be what man shall then elect to make it. On every side defects and imperfections and makeshifts and incongruities are visible, and these must be rectified and changed or gradually eliminated; but the foundations of society have been so securely laid and the great framework of it all has been built so strong and with so perfect an adaptation of means to ends that we can think of both of them only as destined to endure forever.

The place of woman in this world of ours has also been marked out for her by man, and he has so marked it out for her with a perfect knowledge, in the first place, of his own necessities, and in the second place, of her nature, her endowments and her limitations. In that place she is bound to stay because for him and, it may be added, because for her as well, it is wholly best that she should do so. To say this is to speak quite frankly, and there is no reason why the painful frankness of the philosophical woman should not be met with equal frankness by the man who answers her. Plain speech and the assertion of a fundamental truth may serve at least one most important purpose. They free the mind at once from speculative theory, from quibbling and from casuistry, and they go with swiftness and directness to the heart of the whole issue. They may be brutal, but they are wholesome none the less—an admirable antidote to the neurotic caterwaulings of feminine hysteria.

Consider for a single moment the real meaning of the social order as it now exists. If woman has it in herself to do the work of man, to rival him in the great task which now for unnumbered centuries he has been fearlessly performing, why has she never shown the evidence of that capacity? She started even in the race of life in the days when man and woman were alike unfettered and unhindered, since both alike were savages in a thinly peopled world. What made the woman, from the very earliest times, not so much the fellow-worker and the competitor of the man, as his companion, his encouragement, his consolation, the sharer of his home, the mother of his children? Why from the outset did she not live her life apart from him and treat with him on equal terms, giving him only what she chose, and keeping from him all that would preserve her from the need of blending her existence into his? Why has she always not merely endured, but even chosen, to be his mate and not his rival, to glory in her self-effacement, to love the happiness that he has given her and because he gave it to her, to lean upon him, and to find her deepest joy, her most perfect rest and her supreme contentment by his side and not apart from him? If, as the reformers seem to think, there is no fundamental difference in the needs and the capacities of men and women, and if, as must have been the case, both men and women began the evolution of their history with equal opportunities save in so far as nature herself endowed them differently, why, after a thousand centuries, do men and women still hold the same relation to each other which they held in the days when the world itself was young? Is it not because this one relation is the only one that satisfies the real needs of both and that is, therefore, by its continuous existence the demonstration of an imperishable truth?

[. . .] There are all sorts of men and women in this world and they construct all sorts of marriages; but in a general way, when a normal woman makes up her mind to marry any man, what is it to be supposed that she has in her thoughts? Is she speculating as to whether his protection and support of her are scientifically an equivalent for the service which she is to render him in a domestic way, and whether her economic reward is accurately adjusted to the conditions under which she is going to live? Does she go over several tables of statistics to see what ought to be the proper ratio between the average approximate expenses of the wife of a bricklayer and the wife of a clergyman, with a glance at other tables to discover the scientific relation of her husband's probable income to their domestic expenses on the one hand

and to her pin-money on the other? A woman who would be capable of doing this would not very readily find a man who was capable of proposing for her hand. No; but when a woman marries a man, the presumption is that she does so because she loves him and trusts him and because her whole happiness lies in being with him and because she thinks that his happiness also lies in her; and just because she loves and trusts him, she is willing with him to face the uncertainties of life, to share them by his side, to make his joys hers and his sorrows also hers, and to find, perhaps, the most exquisite delight of all in the thought of her very dependence upon him, and in her pride at looking to his strength as a shelter for her weakness, and because in return she can give him not what Mrs. Stetson[1] calls "domestic service," or "the lowest grade of unskilled labor," but infinite sympathy, and the tenderest affection. This may not be very scientific, from the point of view of the person who reduces all the facts of life to figures and to formulas; but it is the way that things go in this delightfully illogical world of ours. It is true enough that woman is often disappointed, and that her life after a little while may prove to be a life of care and toil and perpetual anxiety. But so is man, too, often disappointed, and so is his life often one filled full of disillusions. These women writers have a deal to say about the brutal man and the unloving man, the slothful man and the man who is dissolute and heartless; but why not say a little about the peevish woman, the extravagant woman, the selfish woman, the domestic slut, and the woman who is faithless and forgetful of her duty? And when the element of disappointment has been eliminated from some other spheres of human life, perhaps we may concede that there is some way also of getting rid of it in marriage. [. . .]

Economic freedom, the elimination of sex, the subordination of love in the scheme of things, can never be secured. Even could it be assumed that women were unanimous in wishing it, they would still find this to be impossible without the aid of man. Woman might change her nature could she isolate herself from man, but that is just the one thing that she cannot do. She can decry the theory of marriage; she can make herself, on the one hand, arrogant, unpleasant and dogmatic, or she can become, on the other hand, neurotic, capricious, unstable and insincere, so that man himself will shrink from linking his own life with hers; but, do what she will, she cannot leave the other sex out of her reckoning. She can make a husband quite impossible; yet if so this will only give her over far more surely to a lover. She may destroy the home, but she cannot blot out sex.

And these considerations make it obvious why man should set his face like flint against this new crusade for woman's economic independence. Its theories have already borne some fruit in the marked distaste for marriage that is growing among men. If [. . .] "club-life is charming and *sub rosa* mistresses are numerous"[2] to-day, the cause is not to be discovered in man's profligacy, but in the fanaticism and unwisdom of the modern woman. To every man who is deserving of the name, a true home is of all things in this world the most desirable and beautiful. But if he sees about him only women who regard maternity with loathing, who shrink from the responsibilities of sex, who believe that they have "missions" in this world far greater than the noble ones of wifehood and of motherhood—or women who crave continual excitement and who say that their own natures are so complex that no one man can ever fully satisfy their needs, then what is left for men but club-life and *sub rosa* mistresses?

The agitation of this subject is, in one way, quite unfortunate, but in the end it must do good; for the time is not far distant when the terrible significance of these strange theories will come home with startling force to all men and will rouse them from the half-amused and half-contemptuous tolerance which they show to-day. When marriage, as an institution, really seems to be in danger, when the growth of the population of our country, like the growth of the population of the French republic, shows a marked decline, when the influx of women into all the occupations now controlled by men has so overcrowded them as to cut down the reward of labor to starvation rates, then men will be roused out of their complacency and will take some serious thought of what is striking at the base of society. And in the end, and after the real gravity of the danger has been realized, the remedy will be applied with swiftness and with certainty. Man works his will when once to his own mind his purpose has been clearly outlined. The instinct of self-preservation will compel him to cut short a movement that can only be disastrous to the race. The remedy may be brutal, but it will be quite effective when it comes, and it will be ultimately put in force with something of the primitive severity of primeval days. In the last resort it is physical strength that rules the world, and it is in man and not in woman that this court of last appeal resides. Few seem to recognize this very fundamental truth, and yet unconsciously it gives the explanation of some difficult questions. Why is it, for example, that the suffrage has not been bestowed with perfect freedom upon women? The formal logic of their claim to it is sound. Yes, but the higher logic shows it to be utterly preposterous; for laws imposed by suffrage are not really binding unless there lies directly back of them the power to give them real effectiveness. Take such a state as Massachusetts, where the women are more numerous than the men, and suppose them to possess the franchise unrestrictedly; and suppose that some grave issue should arise which ranged the women on one side and the men upon the other. Suppose the women, being in a large majority, should pass a set of laws imposing various restrictions which the common sense of men rejected. What may it be assumed, then, that the men would do? They would doubtless smile with most exasperating blandness and quietly ignore the laws and go about their business precisely as though such laws did not exist. And what again, in that case, may we suppose that the ladies would on their side do? It is rather difficult to see, except, perhaps, that they would resort to the last refuge of all womankind and go off somewhere by themselves and have a real good cry. When the time comes, therefore, this grasping after economic independence in the Stetsonian sense will sooner or later be very sharply and effectively suppressed, for it is the same with women as a class as it is with individuals. It sometimes happens that a particular woman, who has been spoiled and pampered, becomes utterly unreasonable and impossible to satisfy. The man she loves will study all her whims and seek to anticipate her slightest wish and bear with all her humors, only to find that she is growing more and more impossible and peevish; and then at last, perhaps, he loses patience and turns on her with a touch of masculine roughness and becomes peremptory, and plainly shows that he will stand no further nonsense. And this is just the very thing she wants. The shock acts as a tonic to her nerves; the note of mastery, of domination, thrills her through and through, and she becomes again at once serene and soothed and wholly charming. And this, in a large way, is what will happen if the woman essayists and the lady lecturers and the female sociologists shall ever bring about a state of things where man collectively begins to be uncomfortable. He will speak the word—a short, sharp word— and that will be the end of it.

NOTES

1. Charlotte Perkins (Stetson) Gilman (1860–1935), leading American feminist and reformer; author of such works as *Women and Economics* (1898) and *Man-Made World* (1911).

2. The quotation is from a letter by "a West Virginian lady" quoted earlier in Peck's article (not printed here).

44.

EQUAL RIGHTS FOR MEN

(1937)

Harry Hibschman

Harry Jacob Hibschman (1879–?) wrote numerous tracts on law and religion for the radical publisher Emanuel Haldeman-Julius, including *Why I Am a Heretic* (1927), *Everyman's Legal Manual* (1938), and a pamphlet supporting the legal recognition of Ben B. Lindsey's "companionate marriage."[1] In "Equal Rights for Men," published in the *Forum and Century* (December 1937), Hibschman maintains that the law is now stacked in favor of both single and married women. He concludes the article with a variety of what he fancies are radical proposals for the equalization of legal and social relations between men and women, most of which would now be accepted without challenge.

Source: Harry Hibschman, "Equal Rights for Men," *Forum and Century* 98, no. 6 (December 1937): 305–306, 307–309.

J'm a gallant rogue. For almost a century a lot of our women, most of them past the menopause, have been crying for Equal Rights for Women, and many members of my trousered sex have been deriding and belittling their demands. But not I, because to me their slogan sounds alluring. It titillates the ear, it intrigues the mind, and it captivates the heart. It makes a susceptible male revert to the inclinations of an older era and tempts him to buckle on armor and ride forth to break a lance for fair femininity. So I, for one, am in favor of giving the dear ladies what they profess to want; and that, I realize perfectly, is the meanest thing that we can do to them.

What the women seem to overlook is the fact that, as we learned in school, if *a* equals *b*, *b* must also equal *a*. According to their interpretation, equal rights mean getting without giving. They expect to obtain all the rights that men now have and at the same time to retain all the privileges that now adhere in the mere fact of being a female. They ask for identical rights with men on the ground of woman's natural equality but consider themselves entitled to retain all their special advantages on the ground of woman's natural weakness. They ask for equality, but what they really want is equality plus all their traditional feminine prerogatives.

I recently asked a woman long prominent in the movement for women's rights this question: "Since, to use the words of the National Women's Party, 'the women demand the same rights, in law and in custom, as men,' are we to understand that you favor equality so far as the accepted social customs are concerned—that, for example, you no longer expect us males to practice good manners, to step aside and let you precede us into a room or into an elevator or to stand with our hats off while we talk to you on a street corner?"

"Oh, no," she replied, "those things have nothing to do with equal rights. In social matters women will, of course, continue to be women, and gentlemen will continue to observe the social amenities."

Now, I leave it to you—isn't that just like a woman? One moment she claims equal rights with men "in custom" and the next she naively reserves for herself all the privileges now possessed by her sex as a matter of social usage. She asserts the right to stand among men with her feet on the brass rail; but, when it comes to "buying one," she folds herself in the tattered cloak of outworn tradition or hides behind the skirts of Emily Post. Yet, obviously, until she learns to say, "The next round's on me," her pretensions of hundred proof equality remain a gross and ingenuous fraud.

That the women have not yet learned the beauty of the words quoted is clear, not merely from what any curious and scientifically minded male can learn in any barroom by personal observation but also from the highbrow investigations of several groups of professional pundits. Thus a learned report from dear old Yale tells us that women in general are flatly opposed to "going Dutch" with men for meals, theater tickets, and sodas—stronger beverages being, of course, unmentioned; and another issued in Washington, D. C., last summer announces that, of more than 300 women gravely interrogated on this momentous subject, only 3.5 per cent were willing to subscribe to the Dutch-treat code so far as men were concerned. If that isn't sufficient, there is the evidence of Charley, that master mixologist around the corner, who testifies on oath, "Women at the bar! Faugh! They mooch but they never buy. They're nothing but a new breed of damn bar fly."

In short, all this talk of equal rights in law and in custom, is just hooey and blather. The fair ladies simply do not mean what they say. Their real aim is to do successfully what no one has yet been able to accomplish in all the world's history—to eat one's cake and to keep it, too; only in this case it is the man's cake that they want to eat, and they have already bitten more than one sizable chunk out of it.

As it is, the women have all the best of the men, but they are smart enough to make the poor males think otherwise. As compared with their alleged oppressors, the women are sitting pretty. At this very moment they hold one fourth of the country's jobs and own three fourths of the country's wealth. Because of the operation of our inheritance laws and because of the carefully fostered belief that it is the American male's first and primary duty to provide at all costs for his weak and unprotected females, women are right now the beneficiaries under 80 per cent of the country's life-insurance policies, women have in their names 65 per cent of the country's savings accounts, women hold 44 per cent of the country's public-utility securities, and women own 40 per cent of the country's real estate.

LOADED DICE

It is useless, of course, to talk equality so far as the operation of the law is concerned. For neither the law nor the courts can cope with or curb the intangibles or the imponderables of human nature; and, so long as the Lord's creatures remain male and female, as he is reputed to have made them, the pull of sex will play its part to mislead and befool the poor male, whether on the bench or in the jury box. Mr. Dooley said long ago, "The wimmen haven't th' right iv a fair thrile be a jury iv their peers; but they have th' priv'lege iv an unfair thrile be a jury iv their admirin' infeeryors."[2] The dice of justice are, therefore, *ipso facto* loaded in favor of the female litigant or supplicant. But that is all the more reason why the man should stand before the bar on an equality with the woman according to the letter of the law. He is completely justified in demanding that at least as written—in its codes, its statutes, and its judicial formulations—the law shall not discriminate against him. The women profess to want no more than that, and the men cannot be blamed for refusing to be satisfied with less. [. . .]

THE POOR HUSBAND

Glaring, however, as are the law's discriminations in favor of single women, they are infinitely more so as between married women and their humble spouses. The wives of today claim the same right to "live their own lives" as their husbands, meaning by that expression the right to have whatever interests they wish outside the home—a position, a business, or a profession—and not to be tied down to the dull and commonplace job of making and keeping a home or of bearing and rearing children. They want to be "emancipated"—emancipated from their homes and their husbands—but they blissfully ignore the fact that the husband, too, may have a claim to emancipation—emancipation from the drudgery of making a living, emancipation from the ceaseless demands of his own household, and emancipation from the chains that the State has forged on his limbs by virtue of his entry into the marriage bond. If the ancient conjugal rights of the husband and the traditional obligations of the wife are to be consigned to the scrap pile, then logically so must the traditional obligations of the husband and the ancient rights of the wife.

Not content to proceed, as in Wisconsin, by obtaining the enactment of favorable State legislation, a strong feminist element in this country is now working for the adoption of an amendment to the federal constitution which is to read as follows: "Men and women shall have equal rights throughout the United States and all places subject to its jurisdiction." And at least one congressional committee has given its approval to the proposal.

While the suggested amendment is manifestly ambiguous, leaving wholly unanswered the question whether, where rights are unequal, they shall be equalized according to the standards in effect for males or according to those applying to females, we men, realizing in how many instances the leveling for us would necessarily be upward, may, nevertheless, give our endorsement to its professed purpose, provided that liabilities be equalized coincidently with rights. As to that, however, the women are strikingly silent; and, if we of the male sex hope to avoid further discrimination and to escape from the feminine subjection under which the law now in many instances places us, it behooves us to bestir ourselves and to do a little agitating and propagandizing of our own.

PLATFORM OF THE TURNING WORM

Venturing, then, by the grace of the editors of this unbiased periodical and my own audacity, to speak for the members of my sex, I propose the following planks in a program for a crusade for Equal Rights for Men. Resolved:

1. That all extralegal advantages and privileges now appertaining to women by the mere fortuity of their sex be forthwith abolished.
2. That all rights and precedents and all duty and deference based on differences of sex be henceforth renounced.
3. That the canons of the social code, evolved in the dead age of chivalry and founded on an obsolete concept of woman as a glorified and superior vessel, be revised so as to put men and women on an equal footing in their private and public relations.
4. That the employment by any female of the allure of sex as a means of attaining business or professional preferment be made a penal offense.
5. That, accepting the dictum of Mr. Justice Sutherland,[3] of the United States Supreme Court, that "it cannot be shown that well paid women safeguard their morals more carefully than those poorly paid," all laws fixing minimum wages for female workers be annulled or repealed or that they be made to apply to men as well as to women.
6. That, since the affirmation of Mr. Justice Holmes,[4] "It will need more than the Nineteenth Amendment to convince me that there are no differences between men and women," is to be rejected and the doctrine that the sexes are equal physically, mentally, and otherwise is to be adopted, all social legislation applicable to women alone, including the maternity and mothers' pension acts, be abrogated or its benefits and protection be extended to both sexes alike, with special compensation to Dad for his fatherhood.

7. That all laws fixing an age of consent, an age of majority, or an age point for any other purpose whatever be applied without discrimination to males as well as to females and that the age set be the same in all cases for both sexes.

8. That women be compelled to answer, both civilly and criminally, for sex offenses, when the elements of the crime are established, precisely to the same extent and in the same manner as men.

9. That actions for breach of promise to marry be abolished entirely or recovery limited to actual expenditures made in preparation for the marriage or, in the alternative, that the man be given exactly the same relief in case of the breach of such a contract as the woman under similar circumstances and that he be entitled particularly to a return of all presents made to the woman, including the engagement ring, and be reimbursed for all money expended on the woman in the course of the courtship.

10. That all the conditions imposed on the man seeking a marriage license be made to apply with equal force to the woman, discrimination in this respect being both an indignity and an injustice.

11. That the correlative rights and liabilities of husband and wife be made equal.

12. That, where the wife has separate property or a separate income or follows some remunerative pursuit outside the home, the husband be released from the primary and exclusive duty of providing for her support and that she be made jointly liable under the law for the maintenance of the family in proportion to her financial ability.

13. That, where the parties prior to their marriage enter into an agreement fixing the family domicile, settling their respective property rights, and naming the amount of financial support the husband is to give the wife or releasing him from all liability in that respect, such agreement be made legally binding

and enforceable and not subject to arbitrary repudiation or revocation, as, for instance, on the ground that the wife is entitled to a "home of her own."

14. That, if a wife exercises the right, claimed for her by the feminists, of selecting a residence other than that of her husband, the burden of maintaining it fall exclusively on herself.

15. That the husband shall not be subject to suit for any unlawful act of the wife, except where under the law he would be responsible were she some other person, and that she alone be made answerable for her own torts.

16. That all legal presumptions that the wife in committing a criminal offense acts under coercion from her husband be definitely discarded and that a married woman be held responsible under the penal code exactly as if she were single.

17. That within the home—with reference to the family policies, the family standard of living, and the upbringing of the children—the husband have an equal voice and equal authority with the wife.

18. That, where the wife does not contribute to the maintenance of the family, she be compelled faithfully and efficiently to perform her duties as the keeper of the home and that, since the law has taken away from the husband his ancient right to enforce such performance with a stick no thicker than a thumb, it now furnish him some other legal means of compelling it.

19. That, in proceedings involving the custody of children, the old dictum, "The child needs its mother," be permanently disavowed and the husband given equal consideration with the wife in reaching a determination.

20. That in case of separation or divorce the husband be relieved of all financial obligation to the wife where she has independent means or an independent income and that, where he is required to contribute to her support, the amount be fixed not according to the standard of living established by him but

according to that to which the wife was accustomed before her marriage to him or by a just averaging of the two but that, in any event, imprisonment for nonpayment of alimony in any guise be absolutely abolished.

21. That, unless the wife is ill or physically or mentally incompetent, all payments for separate maintenance or alimony, except such as are to be made for the benefit of minor children, cease within a limited, stated time—say two years—after the entry of the decree and in all cases come to an end if the wife remarries, regardless of the financial status of her new spouse.

22. That the wife be held liable for separate maintenance and alimony, according to the circumstances, precisely the same as the husband.

23. That, since husband and wife are no longer one, each be made answerable, both civilly and criminally, for any wrongful act against the other, just like two strangers, so that, for example, it will be a criminal offense, as it is not now, for a wife to raid her husband's pockets.

24. That women be made liable for jury duty on the same conditions as men and excusable only for the same reasons.

25. That the law in general quit making a pet of the female and begin to mete out even-handed justice between the sexes, holding fair women offenders, especially husband killers, liable exactly the same as men offenders and imposing on them the same penalty.

HEAVEN FORFEND!

"America," recently boasted a national woman's organization in a full-page advertisement in the *New York Times*, "is not a Democracy. It is a Matriarchy."

While exaggerated, that assertion in its implications forecasts the fate that awaits the masculine portion of our population, unless it awakes from its lethargy. Already its subjugation is well under way, and, given time, our women, like those of ancient Egypt, will require the men to agree in the marriage contract to obey their wives and will rule the house and the family with despotic power. The program outlined above may be sufficient to save us, if we act boldly and unitedly before it is too late. But, if we don't, our destiny seems certain—to live in a woman-made, a woman-owned, a woman-ruled, and a woman-ruined world.

NOTES

1. See note 6 in Hugh L. McMenamin's "Evils of Woman's Revolt against the Old Standards" (chap. 2 of this book, p. 47).

2. "Mr. Dooley" is an Irish character created by American journalist Finley Peter Dunne (1867–1936) for a newspaper column, first appearing in the *Chicago Post*. The column was subsequently syndicated in numerous newspapers and collected in several volumes, beginning with *Mr. Dooley in Peace and War* (1898).

3. George Sutherland (1862–1942), US senator from Utah and member of the US Supreme Court (1922–1938).

4. Oliver Wendell Holmes Jr. (1841–1935), renowned jurist and member of the US Supreme Court (1902–1932).

45.

SO WHY DO RAPES OCCUR?

(1979)

Roy U. Schenk

Roy Urban Schenk (b. 1929) received his PhD in chemistry in 1954 and has taught at several universities, including the University of Kentucky and the University of Wisconsin. Since 1973 he has been president of Bioenergetics, Inc., and he is also director of the Madison Men's Organization in Madison, Wisconsin. Schenk was a pioneer in the "men's movement," believing that men's interests and perspectives have been given short shrift in the wake of feminism. Among his books are *The Other Side of the Coin: Causes and Consequences of Men's Oppression* (1982) and *Thoughts of Dr. Schenk on Sex and Gender* (1991). See his Web sites, www.worldpeaceseeker.org and www.shametojoy.com. In the following essay, published in the *Humanist* (March–April 1979), Schenk claims that rapes are generally a result of women teasing men

Source: Roy U. Schenk, "So Why Do Rapes Occur?" *Humanist* 39, no. 2 (March–April 1979): 47–50.

sexually and of a general cultural perception that men are morally inferior to women. The essay was followed by a rebuttal by Gina Allen, chairwoman of the American Humanist Association Women's Caucus.

*R*ape and the threat of rape cause serious and quite legitimate concern among women. And any suggestions that women, by their dress or actions, in any way contribute to the occurrence of rape is met with intense, even violent, reactions from women, particularly, it seems, from feminists. An illusion [*sic*] of this is the recent recall election in Madison (Dane County), Wisconsin, of Judge A. Simonson who dared to suggest that this is so.

It does seem important to try to understand what the basic causes of this violent treatment of women are, rather than merely to expend enormous effort in trying to prevent rapes. We have to understand the nature of the problem before we can remove the causes. Otherwise it is like treating a cancer-caused headache without trying to understand and treat the basic disease that caused the headache.

It appears to be rather well accepted by persons who have studied the occurrence of rape that given the right circumstances any woman is at the risk of being raped and that given the right circumstances any man is apt to assault a woman. Yet as feminist Freda Salzman insists in a recent article, probably correctly, there are no clear genetic differences that make men more aggressive than women. This leads me to believe that there is something in the male-female relationship that sets up the dynamic which causes rape to occur; just as Dr. Paul Kaunitz recently pointed out: there is a dynamic in sado-masochistic marriages that causes the battering of wives (or occasionally of husbands).

In a search for the causes of rape, it seems appropriate to start by stating what I believe are well-known and accepted facts, and then to develop further from these statements. Fact 1: Men rape women. Seldom do women even attempt to rape men. Fact 2: Women can sell sex (prostitution). Seldom do men even try to sell sex, except to other men. Fact 3: Women are neither more good nor more evil than men are. Fact 4: Men tend to take out their anger in more physically violent ways than women do.

From these facts, I believe we can deduce other facts. For example, if women can sell sex and men can't, then sex must be less readily available, on the average, to men than to women. Of course, this is well known because women are socially conditioned to believe they don't need sex, while men are conditioned to actively pursue sex. As a result of this, women seeking sex at any one time can usually secure a sexual partner whenever they want one, so they really don't have any need to pursue sex. The argument that sex usually involves one man and one woman and so must be equally available, which I often hear, is fallacious simply because at any one time there are far more men seeking sex than there are women. So, on the average, sex is far more readily available to women than to men.

A psychiatric study of men who have raped women, which I read about several years ago but have not been able to locate, reported that in about 70 percent of rapes the primary motivating emotion was rage. One must necessarily understand the causes of this rage, then, to understand why rapes happen. Many, if not most, feminists apparently believe that rage occurs because men perceive women as sexual objects that men have a right to have sex with, and that the rage occurs when women reject them. Here we see an expression of what I refer to as the Innocent Victim Syndrome—the perception of women as innocent victims of evil men—which seems to be prevalent among women, feminists and nonfeminists alike. But I think the facts contradict the idea that women are so blameless, so morally superior to men.

So what *does* cause this rage? If we can return to our earlier gathered facts, we established that, on the average, sex is far more readily available to women than to men; indeed it can be said that women have a surplus of sexually available partners and men have a deficit of sexually available partners; that is, women can usually get all the sex they want and have even more offered and pushed on them, whereas men do not.

Developing this idea further, some time ago, on the same day, a fellow said to me: "I don't see why women think jobs are so important," and a women said to me: "I don't know why men think sex is so important." Here we see serious insensitivity; each one failing to recognize that relative unavailability increases importance, just as water becomes far more important in a desert.

It's time that women recognize that sex, because of this unavailability, is far more important to men than it is to women. So sexual teasing and manipulation is a far more serious provocation, more serious violence, than most women seem to recognize. The best analogy I can think of is when men dangle job promises and manipulate women with threats to their jobs—behavior which certainly enrages women.

As we are surely all aware, the results of sexual inequality are that women are socially conditioned in practice to use sex and the direct or indirect promise of sex (flirting, teasing, and so on) to control and manipulate men. Unfortunately this manipulative behavior is accepted as normal behavior in our society. But in my opinion, if this manipulative kind of treatment of men by women were directed against any other creature, it would be labeled for what it is—namely, cruel and sadistic. For example, a person who dangled a beefsteak in front of a hungry dog time after time, and then yanked it away when the dog reached out for it, would certainly be called cruel and sadistic. His actions would be considered violent and the dog would ultimately become enraged. But dangling sex in front of sex-hungry men and yanking it away are practiced routinely by women. And rage by men is a most natural response to this cruelty, this violence.

I think it would not be surprising if a dog, enraged at the violence of humans who have teased and tantalized it, given the opportunity, would respond in a violent manner by attacking a human, and the behavior, dress, and so on of that particular person would probably be largely irrelevant. I think it is not surprising that an occasional man, enraged at the violence of women who have teased and tantalized him, might, if the opportunity occurred, attack a woman, and the behavior, dress, and so on of that particular person might be largely irrelevant. Since the rage was generated by sexual manipulation, it would frequently be directed toward the sexuality of the woman.

It is a common human experience that violence begets violence. If a person hits another person, there is a strong likelihood that the second person will strike back. Or, if he cannot, he will likely react violently to someone or something else. What also needs to be recognized is that not all violence is physical. An insulting put-down can be as violent as, or even more violent than, a physical blow.

I think it is important to recognize that rape is a violent response to violence. But I do not believe that sexual teasing and tantalizing by women is the only or perhaps even the primary violence that causes the violent response of rape. I believe there is an even more serious form of violence that women do to men.

Returning now to another fact, the relative moral goodness or evil of men and women. This is probably the most-likely-to-be-challenged issue of this essay, because, just as we have been socially conditioned to perceive men as superior in leadership ability, job skills, and so on, so have we also been socially conditioned to perceive women as morally and spiritually superior to men. For example, women are perceived as the peace lovers and men as the aggressors and warmakers; women are also perceived as maintaining higher sexual moral standards than men do.

My feminist associates define chauvinism as an attitude of superiority of one group over another, so it seems only reasonable to conclude that all of these perceptions of superiority are chauvinistic. And if male-chauvinist attitudes are sexist, it certainly seems appropriate that we recognize that these female-chauvinist attitudes are also sexist behavior.

This attitude of moral superiority is probably the cause for the harpylike response by some feminists that I have regularly experienced and observed when I or anyone else even hints that women's behavior may in any way contribute to the occurrence of rape (for example, the Simonson affair). It appears that these women want to retain at all costs the image that women are innocent victims of evil men. I suggest that this attitude of moral superiority and of women as innocent victims is obviously sexist and should be labeled as such.

A recent radio advertisement encouraged people to be sure to buy enough photographic film so that they could get plenty of pictures of their little angels—and also their little devils. It doesn't take a degree in psychology to perceive that the angels are girls and the devils are boys.

This perception of girls as sugar and spice and everything nice, and boys as dirty, vulgar, evil, and unnice, pervades our whole culture and the upbringing of our children. But somehow it has escaped the consciousness of almost everyone that the perception of boys through their upbringing as morally inferior, by their nature, to girls must have a psychologically devastating effect on boys and ultimately on the men they become, when they continue to carry the same negative perceptions of themselves. Just as women's negative attitudes toward themselves in other areas have had psychologically devastating effects on women, these social attitudes about moral inferiority hurt men.

Actually, the devastating effects on men are quite evident in the ease with which women can use shame and guilt-feelings to manipulate men. They are further manifest in the quoted remarks of men when they rape women, remarks about bringing women down, of the woman not being able to be so high and mighty anymore; and also the remarks of raped women themselves, remarks of feeling degraded, unclean, and lowered parallel the attitude.

The damage to men's egos resulting from their social conditioning as morally inferior persons needs to be recognized as a destructive form of violence. Indeed, if one can seriously hear what Fredric Storaska, executive director of the National Organization for the Prevention of Rape and Assault says, this is evidently the major violence to men that is countered by men through the violence of rape.

Storaska, in his book *How to Say No to a Rapist—and Survive*,[1] reports that a sure way to prevent rape is to treat the man as a human being. What Storaska, in his guilt-laden male state, fails to perceive is the obvious fact that if this is so, then women must not normally treat men as human beings, that is, as morally equal to women. Rather, many women treat men as dirt, as morally inferior, as beings to be used and manipulated and walked over, as economic objects—violence of a severity so great that only men laden with intense moral guilt-feelings, would tolerate.

But violence begets violence; and men's response to the violence they experience from women is on occasion expressed by turning the violence that women train men to use to protect women back against the women themselves.

So, finally, I think we can add another fact: Women, as a class, by their socially conditioned manipulative sexual behavior and their attitude of moral superiority, create the conditions that cause rape; but it is an individual woman, often no more responsible than any other woman, who gets raped.

Of course, women welcome the power that sexual manipulation and tantalizing of men gives them. As one woman put it: "You've got to use your body. It's the only asset you've got . . ." But obviously women do not normally welcome the undesirable consequences of their behavior, the violence of rape and assault. So we can add another fact: Most, if not all, women do not want to be raped.

Another consequence of the sexist perception that women are morally superior to men is the reality that we men are assaulted from birth (primarily by women, for example, mothers, teachers, and so on) with the perception that we should be morally ashamed of ourselves because we are men. The result of this is that men seem unable to look at their exploited situation and cannot demand an end to this exploitation and oppression. Instead, ironically, men have been socially conditioned to protect and defend their oppressors—"morally superior" women. But I am no longer willing to accept this sexist attitude of moral inferiority for men. In fact, I confess to being rather proud that we men control our rage at women so well that so few of us express it violently.

It shouldn't be necessary for me to say this, but this does not mean I think rape is acceptable behavior. I do not approve of rape, and I do not consider it or other forms of violence as acceptable behavior. But

I also do not think the manipulative, teasing behavior and the attitude of moral superiority held by many women to be acceptable behavior either; they are merely other forms of violence. It needs to be recognized that as long as women persist in these latter forms of violent behavior, rapes and other violence will also continue. Women who demand that men change their behavior, while refusing to examine and change their own violent behavior toward men, are just plain sexists.

So what of the future? Is there a possibility to eliminate sexual assaults? If there is, it will surely come, not by legislating greater penalties and attempting to generate even greater guilt-feelings in men, but by removing the basic causes of rape—the manipulation, the teasing, and the dangling of sex by women, the unavailability of sex for men, and the chauvinist attitude that women are morally superior to men.

This is a challenge for mothers, and for the increasing numbers of fathers who are succeeding in the struggle to have more involvement with their children. And this will not be an easy struggle, because quite a lot of women appear to like the advantages of their current roles. The control over men and the feelings of self-righteous indignation and moral superiority may simply be too much to give up for mere equality. A great many women may choose to maintain their female chauvinistic attitudes and other sexist behavior; in which case men will continue to respond to this violence by violence of their own, and rape and assault will continue to be an ongoing threat to all women.

Since we men stand to benefit greatly by the elimination of both male and female chauvinism, through a better self-image, greater availability of sex, prolonged lifespan, and the elimination of other special privileges of women, I hope the choice will be to eliminate the violence by both sexes—though whether this is possible in a highly competitive society such as ours remains to be seen.

NOTE

1. Frederic Storaska (b. 1942), *How to Say No to a Rapist and Survive* (1975).

FURTHER READING

1. GENERAL STUDIES

Beauvoir, Simone de. *The Second Sex.* Translated by H. M. Parshley. New York: Alfred A. Knopf, 1953.

Boulding, Elise. *The Underside of History: A View of Women through Time.* Boulder, CO: Westview Press, 1976. Rev. ed., Newbury Park, CA: Sage, 1992.

French, Marilyn. *From Eve to Dawn: A History of Women.* 3 vols. Toronto: McArthur, 2002–2003.

Friedan, Betty. *The Feminine Mystique.* New York: W. W. Norton, 1963.

———. *The Second Stage.* New York: Summit Books, 1981.

Greer, Germaine. *The Female Eunuch.* London: MacGibbon & Kee, 1970.

———. *The Whole Woman.* New York: Alfred A. Knopf, 1999.

Hughes, Sarah Shaver, and Brady Hughes. *Women in World History.* 2 vols. Armonk, NY: M. E. Sharpe, 1995.

LeGates, Marlene. *In Their Time: A History of Feminism in Western Society.* New York: Routledge, 2001.

Lerner, Gerda. *The Creation of Patriarchy.* New York: Oxford University Press, 1986.

Osborne, Martha Lee, ed. *Woman in Western Thought.* New York: Random House, 1979.

Rowbotham, Sheila. *A Century of Woman: The History of Women in Britain and the United States.* London: Viking, 1997.

Scott, Joan Wallach, ed. *Feminism and History.* New York: Oxford University Press, 1996.

2. GENERAL STUDIES (UNITED STATES)

Collins, Gail. *America's Women: Four Hundred Years of Dolls, Drudges, Helpmates, and Heroines.* New York: William Morrow, 1993.

Cott, Nancy F. *The Grounding of Modern Feminism.* New Haven, CT: Yale University Press, 1987.

Encyclopedia of Women in American History. 3 vols. Armonk, NY: M. E. Sharpe, 2002.

Evans, Sara M. *Born for Liberty: A History of Women in America.* New York: Free Press, 1989.

————. *Tidal Wave: How Women Changed America at Century's End.* New York: Free Press, 2003.

Flexner, Eleanor. *Century of Struggle: The Women's Rights Movement in the United States.* Cambridge, MA: Harvard University Press, 1959.

Gillmore, Inez Haynes. *Angels and Amazons: A Hundred Years of American Women.* Garden City, NY: Doubleday, Doran, 1933.

Henry, Sherrye. *The Deep Divide: Why American Women Resist Equality.* New York: Macmillan, 1994.

Hewitt, Nancy A., ed. *A Companion to American Women's History.* Oxford: Blackwell, 2002.

Kinnard, Cynthia D. *Antifeminism in American Thought: An Annotated Bibliography.* Boston: G. K. Hall, 1986.

Kleinberg, S. J. *Women in the United States, 1830–1945.* New Brunswick, NJ: Rutgers University Press, 1999.

Margolis, Maxine L. *Mothers and Such: Views of American Women and Why They Changed.* Berkeley and Los Angeles: University of California Press, 1984.

Roberts, Cokie. *We Are Our Mothers' Daughters.* New York: William Morrow, 1998.

3. WOMEN AND INTELLECT

Bleier, Ruth. *Science and Gender: A Critique of Biology and Its Theories on Women.* New York: Pergamon, 1984.

Fausto-Sterling, Anne. *Myths of Gender: Biological Theories about Men and Women.* New York: Basic Books, 1985. Rev. ed., 1992.

Harvey, Elizabeth D., and Kathleen Okruhlik, eds. *Women and Reason.* Ann Arbor: University of Michigan Press, 1992.

Kimura, Doreen. *Sex and Cognition.* Cambridge, MA: MIT Press, 1999.

Moir, Ann, and David Jessel. *Brain Sex: The Real Difference between Men and Women.* Secaucus, NJ: Carol, 1991.

Rogers, Lesley. *Sexing the Brain.* New York: Columbia University Press, 2001.

Tooley, James. *The Miseducation of Women.* London: Continuum, 2002.

4. WOMEN IN THE ARTS

Millett, Kate. *Sexual Politics.* Garden City, NY: Doubleday, 1970.

Reckitt, Helena, ed. *Art and Feminism.* London: Phaidon, 2001.

Woolf, Virginia. *A Room of One's Own.* New York: Harcourt, Brace, 1929.

5. WOMEN AND WORK

Baxandall, Rosalyn, Linda Gordon, and Susan Reverby, eds. *America's Working Women: A Documentary History, 1600 to the Present.* New York: W. W. Norton, 1995.

Bergmann, Barbara R. *The Economic Emergence of Women.* New York: Basic Books, 1986.

Fuchs, Victor R. *Women's Quest for Economic Equality.* Cambridge, MA: Harvard University Press, 1988.

Goldin, Claudia. *Understanding the Gender Gap: An Economic History of American Women.* New York: Oxford University Press, 1990.

Harris, Barbara J. *Beyond Her Sphere: Women and the Professions in American History.* Westport, CT: Greenwood Press, 1978.

Kessler-Harris, Alice. *Out to Work: A History of Wage-Earning Women in the United States.* New York: Oxford University Press, 1982. Rev. ed., 2003.

Konek, Carol Wolfe, and Sally L. Kitch, eds. *Women and Careers: Issues and Challenges.* Thousand Oaks, CA: Sage, 1994.

6. WOMEN AND SEX

Ferguson, Ann. *Blood at the Root: Motherhood, Sexuality and Male Dominance.* London: Pandora, 1989.

Hite, Shere. *The Hite Report: A Nationwide Study of Female Sexuality.* New York: Dell, 1976.

Jackson, Stevi, and Sue Scott, eds. *Feminism and Sexuality: A Reader.* New York: Columbia University Press, 1996.

Jeffreys, Sheila. *Anticlimax: A Feminist Perspective on the Sexual Revolution.* London: Women's Press, 1990.

7. WOMEN AND MARRIAGE

De Marneffe, Daphne. *Maternal Desire: On Children, Love, and the Inner Life.* Boston: Little, Brown, 2004.

Hartog, Hendrik. *Man and Wife in America: A History.* Cambridge, MA: Harvard University Press, 2000.

Lasch, Christopher. *Women and the Common Life: Love, Marriage, and Feminism.* New York: W. W. Norton, 1997.

Ogden, Annagret S. *The Great American Housewife: From Helpmate to Wage Earner, 1776–1986.* Westport, CT: Greenwood, 1986.

Yalom, Marilyn. *A History of the Wife.* New York: HarperCollins, 2001.

8. WOMEN AND RELIGION

Anderson, Leona M., and Pamela Dickey Young, eds. *Women and Religious Traditions.* New York: Oxford University Press, 2004.

Daly, Mary. *Beyond God the Father: Toward a Philosophy of Women's Liberation.* Boston: Beacon, 1973.

Goldenberg, Naomi R. *Changing of the Gods: Feminism and the End of Traditional Religions.* Boston: Beacon, 1979.

Gross, Rita M. *Feminism and Religion: An Introduction.* Boston: Beacon, 1996.

King, Ursula, ed. *Women in the World's Religions, Past and Present.* New York: Paragon House, 1987.

Lindley, Susan Hill. *You Have Stept out of Your Place: A History of Women and Religion in America.* Louisville, KY: Westminster John Knox Press, 1996.

Porterfield, Amanda. *Feminine Spirituality in America: From Sarah Edwards to Martha Graham.* Philadelphia: Temple University Press, 1980.

Young, Serenity, ed. *Encyclopedia of Women and World Religion.* 2 vols. New York: Macmillan, 1999.

9. WOMEN AND SUFFRAGE

Baker, Jean H., ed. *Votes for Women: The Struggle for Suffrage Revisited.* New York: Oxford University Press, 2002.

Benjamin, Anne M. *A History of the Anti-Suffrage Movement in the United States from 1895 to 1920: Women against Equality.* Lewiston, ME: Edwin Mellen, 1991.

Daley, Caroline, and Melanie Nolan, eds. *Suffrage and Beyond: International Feminist Perspectives.* New York: New York University Press, 1994.

DuBois, Ellen Carol. *Feminism and Suffrage: The Emergence of an Independent Women's Movement in America, 1848–1869.* Ithaca, NY: Cornell University Press, 1999.

Lumsden, Linda J. *Rampant Women: Suffragists and the Right of Assembly.* Knoxville: University of Tennessee Press, 1997.

Marilley, Suzanne M. *Woman Suffrage and the Origins of Liberal Feminism in the United States, 1820–1920.* Cambridge, MA: Harvard University Press, 1996.

Marshall, Susan E. *Splintered Sisterhood: Gender and Class in the Campaign against Woman Suffrage.* Madison: University of Wisconsin Press, 1997.

INDEX

Abbott, Lyman, 69–73
"Abdication of Man, The" (Bis-
	land), 396–406
Adam Bede (Eliot), 140, 365
Adams, Clifford R., 242
Addams, Jane, 198, 202
African Americans, 15, 16, 19, 21
Ahmed, El, 403–404
Albert, Prince, 326
Alcott, Amos Bronson, 252
Alcott, Louisa May, 252
Alcott, William A., 252–57
Allen, Gina, 436
American Annals of Education, 252
American Civil Liberties Union,
	198–99
American Woman Suffrage Associa-
	tion, 19
Anthony, Katharine, 228n4
"Anti-metaphysical Remarks"
	(Mach), 106

Astor, John Jacob, 347
Athenaeum, 142
Atlantic Monthly, 149, 184, 224
Augustine (saint), 310
Aurora Leigh (Browning), 365
Austen, Jane, 141–42, 143
Ayrton, Hertha, 365–66

Baker, Ray Stannard, 408
Balch, Emily Green, 22, 198–206
Barr, Amelia E., 385–95
*Beauty: Illustrated by an Analysis
	and Classification of Beauty in
	Woman* (Walker), 83
Beecher, Catherine E., 16, 293–301
Beecher, Henry Ward, 69, 293
Beecher, Lyman, 293
Beethoven, Ludwig van, 216
Bell, Andrew, 60
Bernard, Jesse, 284n4
Bernays, Martha, 229